CompTIA Project+ PK0-005 Cert Guide

Companion Website and Pearson Test Prep Access Code

Access interactive study tools on this book's companion website, including practice test software, review exercises, Key Term flash card application, a study planner, and more!

To access the companion website, simply follow these steps:

1. Go to **www.pearsonitcertification.com/register** by December 31, 2027.
2. Enter the **print book ISBN: 9780138074425**
3. Answer the security question to validate your purchase.
4. Go to your account page.
5. Click on the **Registered Products** tab.
6. Under the book listing, click on the **Access Bonus Content** link.

When you register your book, your Pearson Test Prep practice test access code will automatically be populated with the book listing under the Registered Products tab. You will need this code to access the practice test that comes with this book. You can redeem the code at **PearsonTestPrep.com**. Simply choose Pearson IT Certification as your product group and log in to the site with the same credentials you used to register your book. Click the **Activate New Product** button and enter the access code. More detailed instructions on how to redeem your access code for both the online and desktop versions can be found on the companion website.

If you have any issues accessing the companion website or obtaining your Pearson Test Prep practice test access code, you can contact our support team by going to **pearsonitp.echelp.org**.

CompTIA® Project+ PK0-005 Cert Guide

Robin M. Abernathy

Ann Lang

Pearson

CompTIA® Project+ PK0-005 Cert Guide

ISBN-13: 978-0-13-807442-5

ISBN-10: 0-13-807442-9

Library of Congress Cataloging-in-Publication Data: 2023910066

2 2024

Trademarks

All terms mentioned in this book that are known to be trademarks or service marks have been appropriately capitalized. Pearson IT Certification cannot attest to the accuracy of this information. Use of a term in this book should not be regarded as affecting the validity of any trademark or service mark.

Warning and Disclaimer

Every effort has been made to make this book as complete and as accurate as possible, but no warranty or fitness is implied. The information provided is on an "as is" basis. The authors and the publisher shall have neither liability nor responsibility to any person or entity with respect to any loss or damages arising from the information contained in this book.

Special Sales

For information about buying this title in bulk quantities, or for special sales opportunities (which may include electronic versions; custom cover designs; and content particular to your business, training goals, marketing focus, or branding interests), please contact our corporate sales department at corpsales@pearsoned.com or (800) 382-3419.

For government sales inquiries, please contact governmentsales@pearsoned.com.

For questions about sales outside the U.S., please contact intlcs@pearson.com.

Cover: Deemerwha studio/Shutterstock

Chapter Opener: Charlie Edwards/Getty Images

Vice President, IT Professional
Mark Taub

Director, ITP Product Management
Brett Bartow

Executive Editor
Nancy Davis

Development Editor
Eleanor C. Bru

Managing Editor
Sandra Schroeder

Senior Project Editor
Mandie Frank

Copy Editor
Bart Reed

Indexer
Erika Millen

Proofreaders
Debbie Williams
Barbara Mack

Technical Editor
Chris Crayton

Publishing Coordinator
Cindy Teeters

Designer
Chuti Prasertsith

Compositor
codeMantra

Graphics
Vived Graphics

Pearson's Commitment to Diversity, Equity, and Inclusion

Pearson is dedicated to creating bias-free content that reflects the diversity of all learners. We embrace the many dimensions of diversity, including but not limited to race, ethnicity, gender, socioeconomic status, ability, age, sexual orientation, and religious or political beliefs.

Education is a powerful force for equity and change in our world. It has the potential to deliver opportunities that improve lives and enable economic mobility. As we work with authors to create content for every product and service, we acknowledge our responsibility to demonstrate inclusivity and incorporate diverse scholarship so that everyone can achieve their potential through learning. As the world's leading learning company, we have a duty to help drive change and live up to our purpose to help more people create a better life for themselves and to create a better world.

Our ambition is to purposefully contribute to a world where

- Everyone has an equitable and lifelong opportunity to succeed through learning
- Our educational products and services are inclusive and represent the rich diversity of learners
- Our educational content accurately reflects the histories and experiences of the learners we serve
- Our educational content prompts deeper discussions with learners and motivates them to expand their own learning (and worldview)

While we work hard to present unbiased content, we want to hear from you about any concerns or needs with this Pearson product so that we can investigate and address them.

Please contact us with concerns about any potential bias at https://www.pearson.com/report-bias.html.

Contents at a Glance

Table of Contents

Online Elements

About the Authors

Robin M. Abernathy has been working in the IT certification preparation industry for more than 20 years. She is currently the Content Development Manager and an edutainer at ACI Learning. She has written and edited certification preparation materials for many (ISC)2, Microsoft, CompTIA, PMI, Cisco, EC-Council, and ITIL certifications and holds multiple IT certifications from these vendors.

Robin provides training on computer hardware and software, networking, security, and project management. She has served as technical editor for several publications and coauthored Pearson's *CISSP Cert Guide, Fourth Edition*. She also gives presentations at technical conferences and hosts webinars on IT certification topics.

Ann Lang has been a technical writer for 20 years and a project manager for 5 years. As the managing editor at CyberVista (an N2K Networks brand), she writes and edits practice exam content and helps produce learning modules for online training. She has worked continually in IT education since 2005 and holds multiple CompTIA and Microsoft certifications, including A+, Security+, and Project+. So far, technical communication and project management have been the best possible use for her English Lit degree (she's still hunting for a use for that German minor).

Dedications

Thanks Mom and Dad for encouraging all my intellectual pursuits! This one's dedicated to you!—Robin Abernathy

I dedicate this book to the memory of my father, Marlon. A lifelong electrical engineer, he thought the logical way for me to learn to drive was to diagram all parts of a combustion engine, hand-gap a spark plug, change the engine oil, and identify an engine's RPM by sound—all before I ever sat behind a wheel. He gave me both the ability to overcomplicate the simplest process and the skill to find a solution to any problem by breaking it down to its component parts.

And to the readers, may this book serve you well in your certification journey!—Ann Lang

Acknowledgments

First, I once again thank my Heavenly Father for knowing what I was meant to do, even when in my early adult years I said, "I will never work on computers or write for a living." God always has a plan. And I know He has a sense of humor!

My life would not have been complete without my surrogate brothers. While you entered my world through tragic circumstances, you have come to be my real brothers. Doug Carey and John Carey, thanks for introducing me to all things Cincinnati Reds, Batman, Star Trek, and Elvis. Thanks for adopting two little sisters, which I know as teenagers must have been trying at times. Love you both! Lynne and Lorrie, we love having you in our family as well! Will Carey, Bobby Carey, Christian Carey, and Jacob Carey, you have fine fathers, and I love watching as you become so much like them!

I would like to acknowledge all my nieces and nephews, who were my surrogate children before God blessed me with my own child. Jordyn Abernathy, Chase Abernathy, Chad Abernathy, Cassie Bonds, Caitie Bonds, Zack Stadler, Noah Stadler, and Gabe Stadler, you were my first children, even though your parents think otherwise. Tyler Loggins, thanks for stepping in as an older brother to the Stadler boys. And finally, Luke and Jordyn McDaniel, our family and your parents waited a long time for you. It is our joy to watch you grow and become a central part of our family stories!

I must thank my husband, Michael, and son, Jonas, for once again being willing to do "guy things" while I was locked away in the world of project management.

Thanks to all at Pearson for once again assembling a wonderful team to help Ann and me get through this Project+ journey.

To you, the reader, I wish you success in your IT certification goals!

—Robin Abernathy

I credit all success in this endeavor to the unwavering support of my family and friends—most especially my mother, Carolyn, and my mom-away-from-mom, Lindy. I also wish to thank my co-author, Robin Abernathy, for the opportunity to join her in this book, as well as the dynamic editorial team of Nancy Davis and Eleanor Bru at Pearson.

—Ann Lang

About the Technical Editor

Chris Crayton is a technical consultant, trainer, author, and industry-leading technical editor. He has worked as a computer technology and networking instructor, information security director, network administrator, network engineer, and PC specialist. Chris has authored several print and online books on PC repair, CompTIA A+, CompTIA Security+, and Microsoft Windows. He has also served as technical editor and content contributor on numerous technical titles for several of the leading publishing companies. He holds numerous industry certifications, has been recognized with many professional and teaching awards, and has served as a state-level SkillsUSA final competition judge. Chris tech edited and contributed to this book to make it better for students and those wishing to better their lives.

We Want to Hear from You!

As the reader of this book, *you* are our most important critic and commentator. We value your opinion and want to know what we're doing right, what we could do better, what areas you'd like to see us publish in, and any other words of wisdom you're willing to pass our way.

We welcome your comments. You can email or write to let us know what you did or didn't like about this book—as well as what we can do to make our books better.

Please note that we cannot help you with technical problems related to the topic of this book.

When you write, please be sure to include this book's title and authors as well as your name and email address. We will carefully review your comments and share them with the authors and editors who worked on the book.

Email: community@informit.com

Reader Services

Register your copy of *CompTIA Project+ PK0-005 Cert Guide* for convenient access to downloads, updates, and corrections as they become available. To start the registration process, go to www.pearsonitcertification.com/register and log in or create an account.* Enter the product ISBN 9780138074425 and click Submit. When the process is complete, you will find any available bonus content under Registered Products.

*Be sure to check the box that you would like to hear from us to receive exclusive discounts on future editions of this product.

Introduction

The CompTIA Project+ certification is an excellent entry-level project management certification. As a globally recognized credential, the Project+ certification demonstrates that the holder has knowledge and skills across a broad range of project management topics.

Every day, in every industry, organizations large and small launch new projects. Many of these organizations realize that personnel with skills and knowledge in project management are vital to successful projects. Project+ certified professionals have more than just basic project management knowledge; to pass the Project+ exam, certification candidates must understand all aspects of project management.

Project management knowledge and skills apply to all types of projects—from construction to software development, to manufacturing and all other fields. However, the Project+ exam itself focuses on IT and software development projects. Earning Project+ certification demonstrates the project management professional's ability to initiate, plan, execute, monitor and control, complete, and close projects.

Goals of the Project+ Certification

The Project+ certification is created and managed by the Computing Technology Industry Association (CompTIA), a well-known certification body. CompTIA Project+ certification has a number of stated goals. Although not crucial for passing the exam, having knowledge of the CompTIA organization and its goals for the Project+ certification can be helpful in understanding the motivation behind the creation and contents of the exam.

Sponsoring Body

CompTIA is a nonprofit trade association that provides a vendor-neutral certification process and works with partners to create educational materials. The Project+ certification is one of a number of certifications offered by CompTIA:

- A+
- Network+
- Security+
- Linux+
- Cloud+
- Server+
- Data+

CompTIA also offers three master-level security certifications:

- CASP+
- CySA+
- PenTest+

Stated Goals

The goal of CompTIA in its administration of the Project+ certification is to provide a reliable instrument to measure an individual's knowledge and skills for managing the project life cycle, coordinating small-to-medium-sized projects, establishing a communication plan, managing resources and stakeholders, maintaining project documentation and artifacts, and supporting the completion of larger projects within an information technology (IT) environment. The topics covered in the exam are technically more shallow than those tested by some other project management certifications.

The topics that comprise the four domains of knowledge covered by the Project+ exam (PK0-005) are discussed later in this Introduction.

Value of the Project+ Certification

The Project+ certification holds value for both the exam candidate and the organization. Project management is a job skill that is increasing in popularity on job sites. Project+ is often seen as a great entry-level certification for people who are new to the project management field.

To the Project Professional

Many reasons exist for a project management professional to spend the time and effort required to achieve Project+ certification:

- To meet growing demand for project management professionals
- To become more marketable in an increasingly competitive job market
- To enhance skills in a current job
- To qualify for or compete more successfully for a promotion
- To increase earnings

In short, this credential demonstrates that the holder not only has the knowledge and skills tested on the exam but also the wherewithal to plan and implement a course of study that addresses a broad range of project management topics.

To the Organization

For an organization, the Project+ certification offers a reliable benchmark against which job candidates can be measured by validating both knowledge and experience. Individuals holding this certification stand out, making the hiring process easier and adding a level of confidence in the final selection.

Project+ Objectives

The material contained in the Project+ exam (PK0-005) is divided into four domains, with several objectives in each:

- Project management concepts domain
- Project life cycle phases domain
- Tools and documentation domain
- Basics of IT and governance domain

For the most part, this book devotes a chapter to each of these objectives. A few objectives have been combined logically into one chapter. Some overlap is inevitable between the domains and objectives, leading to some overlap between topics covered in the chapters. This section describes the domains and topics covered.

Project Management Concepts Domain

The *project management concepts domain* covers a broad spectrum of general project management topics:

- Characteristics of a project
- Project methodologies and frameworks
- Project change control process
- Project risk management
- Project issue management
- Project schedule development and management
- Project quality and performance management
- Project communication management
- Project meeting management
- Project team and resource management
- Project procurement and vendor selection

Project Life Cycle Phases Domain

The *project life cycle phases domain* covers the phases of a project:

- Project discovery/concept preparation phase
- Project initiation phase
- Project planning phase
- Project execution phase
- Project closing phase

Tools and Documentation Domain

The *tools and documentation domain* covers all the tools and documents that are used to manage a project successfully:

- Project life-cycle management tools
- Project management productivity documents
- Quality and performance charts

Basics of IT and Governance Domain

The *basics of IT and governance domain* covers understanding the impacts of IT and governance on projects:

- Environmental, social, and governance (ESG) factors
- Information security concepts
- Compliance and privacy considerations
- Basic IT concepts
- Operational change control processes

Steps to Becoming CompTIA Project+ Certified

To become CompTIA Project+ certified, the candidate must meet certain prerequisites and follow certain procedures. This section covers those topics.

About the Project+ Exam

The Project+ exam is a computer-based test that the candidate can spend up to 90 minutes completing. There are no formal breaks, but you are allowed to take short breaks. You must bring a government-issued identification card. No other forms of ID are accepted.

The test will have up to 90 multiple-choice questions and drag-and-drop questions. The passing grade is 710 on a scale of 100 to 900. Candidates will receive the results at the test center from the test administrator.

Qualifying for the Exam

While there are no experience requirements for taking the exam, CompTIA recommends at least 12 months of cumulative project management experience. Because this is not a requirement, candidates can sign up for the exam without this experience but should spend adequate study time to ensure they have the knowledge needed for this exam.

Signing Up for the Exam

CompTIA exams are offered at Pearson VUE testing centers around the world. Certain qualified students or other individuals in the U.S. and Canada may be eligible to take the Project+ exam remotely through ProctorU instead of visiting a testing center. If you want to take the exam online, review the requirements and follow the instructions at https://www.proctoru.com/portal/comptia.

The steps to sign up for the Project+ exam at your local Pearson VUE testing center are as follows:

1. Create a Pearson VUE account (https://www.pearsonvue.com/comptia).
2. Schedule your exam at your nearest Pearson VUE facility.
3. Save your exam appointment confirmation.

After you complete the exam, you will be given a score report. Save this score report until you confirm that you have been awarded the credential by logging into https://www.certmetrics.com/comptia/login.aspx.

How to Use This Book

The goal of this book is simple: to help you to pass the CompTIA Project+ certification exam (PK0-005).

The Project+ exam stresses a complete understanding of the knowledge areas and experience of project management. Whether you have an extensive background as a project manager in multiple industries or are entering the project management field for the first time, this book is designed to help you understand and master the required objectives for the exam.

This book uses several methodologies to help you 1) discover the exam topics on which you need more review, 2) fully understand and remember details about those topics, and 3) prove to yourself that you have retained your knowledge of those topics. To pass the exam, memorizing terminology is not sufficient; you must understand the concepts covered in the exam and this book.

Each chapter is structured in the following way:

- **Objectives:** The chapter opens with a list of Project+ exam topics covered in the chapter, a brief introduction to those topics, and a list of the corresponding CompTIA Project+ objectives.
- **"Do I Know This Already?" Quiz:** This quiz tests your knowledge and understanding of the main topics covered in the chapter. Detailed answers are in Appendix A, "Answers to the 'Do I Know This Already?' Quizzes and Review Questions." The quiz helps you to assess whether you should read the entire chapter, read only the sections on unfamiliar topics, or jump immediately to the "Exam Preparation Tasks" section.
- **Foundation Topics:** This section holds the core content of the chapter. It explores the chapter topics with both theory and examples. In-depth descriptions, lists, tables, and figures are geared toward building your knowledge so that you can pass the Project+ exam.
- **Examples:** This book presents true-to-life examples that demonstrate how project management actually *works* in the phases, tasks, documents, processes, and so on that are part of the project manager's job. These examples are designed to give you real-world insight that is particularly useful in scenario-based questions on the live Project+ exam.
- **Key Topics:** The Key Topic icon in the margin indicates important information that you should know for the exam. Although the contents of the entire chapter could be on the exam, you should definitely know the information listed in each key topic. All of the key topics for the chapter are gathered in a Key Topics table at the end of the chapter for quick reference to the material covering each key topic.
- **Exam Preparation Tasks:** This section of the chapter moves from active learning to active exam preparation. Now that you have grasped the chapter contents, use the activities in this section to test your understanding of the information in the chapter:

- **Review All Key Topics:** The Key Topics table in this section provides a brief summary of each chapter element marked with the Key Topic symbol described earlier. Review the contents of this table carefully to check your understanding of each topic. In case you need to refresh your memory or learn more, the table lists the corresponding page number where each topic begins, so you can jump instantly to that point in the chapter.
- **Define Key Terms:** This section lists all the important terms discussed in the chapter. You are expected to be familiar with these key terms for the Project+ exam. Provide your own definitions for the terms in the list and then compare your definitions against those in the glossary at the end of the book. The glossary combines all the key terms from all the chapters, listed alphabetically to make each term easy to find.
- **Review Questions:** Each chapter ends with multiple-choice questions, designed to test your knowledge of the chapter content. Check your selections against the answers and descriptions in Appendix A.

Who Should Read This Book?

The CompTIA Project+ examination is designed for project management in any field. The exam certifies that the successful candidate has the requisite knowledge and skills to manage projects for any type of organization.

As mentioned earlier, no project management experience is required for taking the exam. However, CompTIA recommends at least 6-12 months of cumulative project management experience.

This book is intended for the wide range of Project+ certification candidates—from people who seek entry-level project management know-how, all the way up to experienced project managers who want to keep skills sharp, increase income, improve organizational ranking or title, or meet their organization's policies mandating certification.

Strategies for Exam Preparation

How you use this book to prepare for the exam will vary depending on your existing skills and knowledge. The ideal exam preparation would consist of years of active project management experience, followed by rigorous study of the exam objectives, but that may not be practical in your case. The best way to determine your readiness for the Project+ exam is to work through the "Do I Know This Already?" quiz at the beginning of each chapter and review the foundation topics and key topics presented in each chapter. If possible, work your way through the entire book until you can complete each subject without having to do any research or look up any answers.

If you need to study particular areas in the PK0-005 certification exam outline, find those sections in the book and review them carefully. Table I-1 lists the objectives in the Project+ exam and where those objectives are covered in this book.

Table I-1 CompTIA Project+ PK0-005 Exam Topics Mapped to Chapters

Project+ Objective	Description	Chapter
1.1	Explain the basic characteristics of a project and various methodologies and frameworks used in IT projects.	1
1.2	Compare and contrast Agile vs. Waterfall concepts.	1
1.3	Given a scenario, apply the change control process throughout the project life cycle.	3
1.4	Given a scenario, perform risk management activities.	4
1.5	Given a scenario, perform issue management activities.	4
1.6	Given a scenario, apply schedule development and management activities and techniques.	5
1.7	Compare and contrast quality management concepts and performance management concepts.	6
1.8	Compare and contrast communication management concepts.	7
1.9	Given a scenario, apply effective meeting management techniques.	7
1.10	Given a scenario, perform basic activities related to team and resource management.	2
1.11	Explain important project procurement and vendor selection concepts.	8
2.1	Explain the value of artifacts in the discovery/concept preparation phase for a project.	9
2.2	Given a scenario, perform activities during the project initiation phase.	9
2.3	Given a scenario, perform activities during the project planning phase.	10
2.4	Given a scenario, perform activities during the project execution phase.	11
2.5	Explain the importance of activities performed during the closing phase.	12
3.1	Given a scenario, use the appropriate tools throughout the project life cycle.	13
3.2	Compare and contrast various project management productivity tools.	13

Project+ Objective	Description	Chapter
3.3	Given a scenario, analyze quality and performance charts to inform project decisions.	14
4.1	Summarize basic environmental, social, and governance (ESG) factors related to project management activities.	15
4.2	Explain relevant information security concepts impacting project management concepts.	15
4.3	Explain relevant compliance and privacy considerations impacting project management.	15
4.4	Summarize basic IT concepts relevant to IT project management.	16
4.5	Explain operational change-control processes during an IT project.	16

When you feel confident in your skills, work through the "Exam Preparation Tasks" section of each chapter and then attempt the practice exams in the Pearson Test Prep practice test software online. As you work through a practice exam, note the areas where you lack knowledge or confidence and then review those concepts in the book. After you have reviewed those areas, work through the practice exam a second time and rate your skills. Keep in mind that the more you work through a practice exam, the more familiar the questions will be.

After you have worked through the practice exams successfully, schedule your CompTIA Project+ PK0-005 exam as described earlier. Typically, candidates should take the exam within a week of when they feel ready for the exam.

Companion Website

Register this book to get access to the Pearson Test Prep practice test software and other study materials, plus additional bonus content. Check the site regularly for new and updated postings written by the authors that provide further insight into the more troublesome topics on the exam. Be sure to check the box that you would like to hear from us to receive updates and exclusive discounts on future editions of this product or related products.

To access this book's companion website, follow these steps:

1. Go to www.pearsonITcertification.com/register and log in or create a new account by December 31, 2027.
2. On your Account page, tap or click the **Registered Products** tab and then tap or click the **Register Another Product** link.

3. Enter this book's ISBN: 9780138074425.
4. Answer the challenge question as proof of book ownership.
5. Tap or click the **Access Bonus Content** link for this book to go to the page where your downloadable content is available.

NOTE Keep in mind that companion content files can be very large, especially image and video files.

If you are unable to locate the files for this title by following these steps, please visit www.pearsonitcertification.com/about/contact_us, select the **Site Problems/Comments** option, enter the requested information, and tap or click **Submit**. Pearson's customer service representatives will assist you.

Pearson Test Prep Practice Test Software

In addition to the bonus content on the book's companion website, this book comes complete with the Pearson Test Prep practice test software. The practice tests are available to you either online or as an offline Windows application. To access the practice exams that were developed with this book, please see the instructions below.

How to Access the Pearson Test Prep (PTP) App

You have two options for installing and using the Pearson Test Prep application: a web app and a desktop app. To use the Pearson Test Prep application, start by finding the registration code that comes with the book. You can find the code in these ways:

- You can get your access code by registering the print ISBN (9780138074425) on pearsonitcertification.com/register. Make sure to use the print book ISBN, regardless of whether you purchased an eBook or the print book. After you register the book, your access code will be populated on your account page under the Registered Products tab. Instructions for how to redeem the code are available on the book's companion website by clicking the Access Bonus Content link.
- Premium Edition: If you purchase the Premium Edition eBook and Practice Test directly from the Pearson IT Certification website, the code will be populated on your account page after purchase. Just log in at pearsonitcertification.com, click Account to see details of your account, and click the digital purchases tab.

NOTE After you register your book, your code can always be found in your account under the Registered Products tab.

Once you have the access code, to find instructions about both the PTP web app and the desktop app, follow these steps:

Step 1. Open this book's companion website as shown earlier in this Introduction under the heading, "Companion Website."

Step 2. Click the Practice Exams button.

Step 3. Follow the instructions listed there for both installing the desktop app and using the web app.

Note that if you want to use the web app only at this point, just navigate to pearsontestprep.com, log in using the same credentials used to register your book or purchase the Premium Edition, and register this book's practice tests using the registration code you just found. The process should take only a couple of minutes.

Premium Edition

In addition to the free practice exams provided with your purchase, you can purchase expanded exam functionality from Pearson IT Certification. The digital-only *CompTIA Project+ Cert Guide Premium Edition eBook and Practice Test* contains additional practice exams as well as the eBook (in PDF and ePub formats). In addition, the *Premium Edition* title links each question to the specific part of the eBook related to that question.

This chapter covers the following topics:

- **Characteristics of a Project:** Covers project characteristics, including start and finish, unique, reason/purpose, project as part of a program, and project as part of a portfolio.
- **Methodologies and Frameworks Used in IT Projects:** Covers methodologies and frameworks, including Software Development Life Cycle (SDLC), Waterfall, PRojects IN Controlled Environments (PRINCE2), DevOps, DevSecOps, Agile, Kanban, scrum, Scaled Agile Framework (SAFe), and Extreme Programming (XP). Also compares Agile to Waterfall, including the criteria for selecting a method and composing a team.

Project Characteristics, Methodologies, and Frameworks

Every industry has projects. Contractors build buildings. IT companies launch new services. Hospitals revise processes to conform with new standards or regulations. Retail businesses launch new mobile apps for their customers. All of these activities are projects, even if the organization does not expressly call them "projects" or complete the formal project management phases.

A project is temporary in that it has a defined beginning and end, scope, budget, and resources. If all of these parameters are not defined at the beginning of the project, you have no way of measuring the success or failure of the project. For this reason, all types of organizations should employ professionals with project management knowledge.

Project management knowledge involves understanding the properties of all projects and understanding projects as part of an organization's overall program and portfolio.

Projects are completed based on project management methodologies and frameworks. Project managers must understand the types of development approaches and the specific IT project methodologies and frameworks that are available. This allows project managers to guide organizations in developing an approach that works both for the organization and for the type of project being undertaken.

This chapter covers the following objectives for the CompTIA Project+ exam:

- **1.1** Explain the basic characteristics of a project and various methodologies and frameworks used in IT projects.
- **1.2** Compare and contrast Agile vs. Waterfall concepts.

"Do I Know This Already?" Quiz

The "Do I Know This Already?" quiz allows you to assess whether you should read this entire chapter thoroughly or jump to the "Exam Preparation Tasks" section. If you are in doubt about your answers to these questions or your own assessment of your knowledge of the topics, read the entire chapter. Table 1-1 lists the major headings in this chapter and their corresponding "Do I Know This Already?" quiz questions. You can find the answers in Appendix A, "Answers to the 'Do I Know This Already?' Questions and Review Quizzes."

Table 1-1 "Do I Know This Already?" Section-to-Question Mapping

Foundation Topics Section	Questions
Characteristics of a Project	1, 2
Methodologies and Frameworks Used in IT Projects	3–10

CAUTION The goal of self-assessment is to gauge your mastery of the topics in this chapter. If you do not know the answer to a question or are only partially sure of the answer, you should mark that question as wrong for purposes of the self-assessment. Giving yourself credit for an answer you correctly guess skews your self-assessment results and might provide you with a false sense of security.

1. Which of the following is *not* a quality of a project?
   a. Start and finish
   b. Permanent
   c. Unique
   d. Reason

2. Which of the following statements regarding programs and portfolios is true?
   a. All projects are part of the portfolio.
   b. Only certain programs are part of the portfolio.
   c. Each project must be part of a program.
   d. Each program within a project is managed in a coordinated method.

3. Which quality of Agile projects allows a project to meet changing conditions?
   a. Incremental
   b. Predictive
   c. Iterative
   d. Adaptive

4. Which of the following statements describes the iterative quality of an Agile project?
   a. It breaks the project into smaller components.
   b. It provides a linear development plan that is structured around the desired result.
   c. Each incomplete area is refined until the result is satisfactory.
   d. Completed work is delivered throughout the project life cycle.

5. What tool is used in Agile planning to help with requirements gathering?
   a. Burndown charts
   b. User stories
   c. Scrum retrospectives
   d. Questionnaires

6. What key component is required for an Agile project to succeed?
   a. Burndown charts
   b. Continuous feedback
   c. Scrum master
   d. Scrum retrospective

7. Which of the following is *not* one of the questions answered in the daily scrum meeting?
   a. What did the team member do yesterday?
   b. What will the team member do today?
   c. Are any obstacles in the way?
   d. What went wrong during this sprint?

8. Which description best fits Agile teams?
   a. Centrally organized and directed
   b. Self-organized and self-directed
   c. Centrally organized but self-directed
   d. Self-organized but centrally directed

9. Which of the following is a predictive model?
   a. SDLC
   b. XP
   c. Scrum
   d. Kanban

10. Which four steps of the DevOps model are the responsibility of the operations team?
    a. Plan, Code, Build, and Test
    b. Release, Deploy, Operate, and Monitor
    c. Plan, Code, Operate, and Monitor
    d. Build, Test, Release, and Deploy

Foundation Topics

Characteristics of a Project

The Project Management Institute (PMI) defines a ***project*** as "a temporary endeavor undertaken to create a unique product, service, or result." A project is based on the needs of the project sponsor or customer and may be terminated by the same entity. Every project creates a unique product, service, or result. Once the project is complete, the project's product, service, or result may continue to affect society, the economy, the sponsor, and the environment.

Projects are undertaken at all levels and in all departments of an organization. No matter which levels or departments are involved, the project team will be responsible for completing the project within budget and on schedule.

EXAMPLE: Upper management has a project to analyze the organization for Lean practices. The human resources (HR) department has a project to deploy a new employment application. All departments are involved in a project to redesign the network infrastructure, with the IT department heading the project.

Projects happen all around us every day and involve every industry. To ensure project success, organizations should employ personnel who understand project management and grasp the difference between projects and day-to-day operations. To fully comprehend the distinction, compare the examples in the two columns in Table 1-2.

Table 1-2 Projects Versus Day-to-Day Operations

Project	Day-to-Day Operation
Launching a new web server	Upgrading a web server's operating system
Developing processes for backing up a file server	Backing up the file server according to established processes and procedures
Documenting the help desk process	Performing daily tasks at the help desk
Constructing a new facility	Maintaining a facility
Launching a new jewelry line in a retail chain	Adding new inventory to a current jewelry line
Upgrading a fleet of automobiles to include video recorders	Performing routine maintenance (such as oil changes) on a fleet of automobiles
Designing a training program for teachers' aides	Training teachers' aides on new school system policies

Projects may produce tangible and/or intangible outcomes. ***Tangible outcomes*** are physical assets that can be measured, such as land, vehicles, equipment, machinery, furniture, inventory, and cash. ***Intangible outcomes*** are nonphysical assets such as patents, trademarks, franchises, good will, and copyrights.

All projects are temporary, have a defined start and finish, have a unique outcome, and have a reason or purpose. The following sections describe these project characteristics.

Start and Finish

The temporary nature of projects indicates that a project is undertaken for a set time period and will finish at some point. Being temporary has nothing to do with the length of the project—just that it has initiation and completion dates. The result of the project is not necessarily temporary—only the project itself.

Defined start and finish dates for a project are critical. Without defined start and finish dates, a project is not constrained by time and can become part of the day-to-day operations. Defining start and finish dates helps personnel to ensure that the project is completed. Project management professionals must be able to analyze the scope of the project to determine the amount of time needed to complete the project. To complete a project within a set time limit, you may also need to trim back other aspects of the project, such as its scope or budget. Setting the start and finish dates should be completed during the early phases of the project.

Unique

The result of the project should be unique. Although some projects may contain repetitive elements, each project remains unique, with different design, location, circumstance, stakeholders, or other elements. Most projects result in a lasting outcome. Outcomes from the projects in Table 1-2 include a web server, a backup process and procedure, a help desk process, a new building, a new jewelry line, video recorders in a fleet of automobiles, and a training program.

EXAMPLE: A construction company builds many types of buildings. Most of the buildings have the same elements, such as the foundation, framing, plumbing, electrical, and so on. However, no two buildings are exactly alike. Even if two buildings follow the same building plan, the buildings will not be built in exactly the same location with exactly the same team members and supplies.

Reason/Purpose

The project's reason or purpose should be stated clearly to ensure that the project sponsor and all other stakeholders understand it. Projects should provide business value to the sponsoring organization. Value may be created by a new physical asset or process. It can even be created through effective redesign of ongoing operations. However, the project must have a reason or purpose to ensure that this business value is provided. The outcome of the project is intended to provide value to the project sponsor or customer until the result is no longer needed or no longer meets the sponsor's or customer's needs.

Project as Part of a Program

A ***program*** is a grouping of related projects or activities that are managed in coordination to obtain benefits not available if they were managed individually. The projects within a program are related because they have a common outcome.

EXAMPLE: An organization's program includes several projects that involve the renovation of multiple facilities. Each facility renovation or each facet of renovation (plumbing, electrical, and so on) is a project, with all the projects together comprising the program.

TIP A project does not have to be part of a program, but a program always includes projects.

Because the primary benefit from a program is coordination, a program should be used to ensure that each project's resources, conflicts, goals, objectives, and changes are managed from a program perspective. Projects within a program must focus on the interdependence between the projects.

TIP If projects do not share an outcome but are related through a shared client, seller, technology, or resource, they are part of the same portfolio—not the same program.

Project as Part of a Portfolio

A ***portfolio*** includes all of the projects, programs, and operations managed by an organization to allow it to reach strategic objectives. The projects and programs included in a portfolio do not necessarily depend on each other.

To fully understand the relationship between projects, programs, and the portfolio, keep these points in mind:

- All projects are part of the portfolio.
- All programs are part of the portfolio.

- Each project may be part of a program or be independent.
- Each project within a program is managed in a coordinated method.
- All projects and programs within the portfolio are linked to the organization's strategic plan.

Methodologies and Frameworks Used in IT Projects

Methodologies and frameworks are often used by organizations to guide the way a project is completed. Often these terms are used interchangeably in the real world, but they are actually two different but closely related terms. A project manager should understand the differences between the two terms and why both are important to projects.

> **NOTE** A ***methodology*** is prescriptive and defines steps to be completed. Methodologies explain why the steps are essential and how each step should be accomplished. A framework is much more flexible and is intended to be adapted to fit the problem. ***Frameworks*** are more skeletal in nature and act more as guidelines. In some circles both methodologies and frameworks may be referred to as development approaches. It does not really matter which term you use—it is important that you understand the basic tenets and conditions under which each may be chosen.

No matter which term is used, there are some basic facets of project development methodologies and frameworks that project managers need to understand. Terms used to describe methodologies and frameworks include predictive, adaptive, hybrid, iterative, and incremental.

Predictive approaches provide a linear development plan with a known outcome. A structured process is used for producing a pre-determined result within a specific time frame. Predictive approaches have very little uncertainty and are often used when there is a significant investment being made or a high level of risk. Predictive projects strive to reduce uncertainty.

Predictive planning uses historical data to provide a linear development plan structured around the desired result. For example, the process to build most homes is generally the same: ground preparation, foundation, framing, and so on. Predictive planning works well for these types of projects.

Adaptive approaches break a project into small components over an undetermined timeline, thereby allowing flexibility throughout the project. Adaptive projects produce an end result that is not very clear at product initiation and can have surprising outcomes. Each component that is produced can be referred to as a sprint, iteration, or increment. Adaptive approaches are used when requirements may change over the project life cycle because of uncertainty and volatility. Requirements and project scope are refined or changed as the project progresses. Adaptive approaches use iterative and incremental methods, which are explained later in this chapter.

Adaptive planning allows a project to evolve as needed to face changing conditions. By breaking the project into small components created over an undetermined timeline, adaptive planning gives the project flexibility. Results from one project task can cause the project to be changed to adapt to the changing environment.

A ***hybrid*** approach combines both predictive and adaptive methods within the same project. This approach is often used when certain features or functions can be easily defined during project planning, while other features and functions are not fully understood.

An ***iterative*** method is an adaptive method wherein the product team builds up the features and functions of the product over time. Each feature or function is usually released separately without waiting on other features or functions. These features or functions are referred to as ***iterations***. When each iteration starts, the scope, approach, and requirements of that iteration are defined, with each iteration adding functionality to the previous iterations.

EXAMPLE: To understand an iterative approach, think of a sculpture. The sculptor starts with the raw material and carves it into a general shape. The earliest tasks are roughing out the form and removing excess material from all areas of the piece. During the next stages, the sculptor refines the work, adding details to each area that was previously roughed out. However, the sculpture is not finished until the entire work is complete. The sculptor may need to return to certain areas to refine and revise the work before the final product reflects the sculptor's intended design.

An ***incremental*** method is one wherein the product team divides the product into fully operational features or functions. Like the iterative method, each feature or function is released separately without waiting on others. The features or functions are referred to as ***increments***. Each increment completes the plan/design/build process until the project is complete.

EXAMPLE: To understand an incremental approach, think of a suburban housing development. The developer hires an architect to produce concept drawings of the homes and plan the lot lines, roads, and utilities for the new community. Once the concept is approved, the architect creates blueprints that can be used to estimate costs and construct the buildings. After the blueprints are final, the developer builds a model home that home buyers can tour during the sales process. When the lots are sold to buyers, the developer constructs the final homes.

An incremental approach does not revisit previous steps in the process. In this example, once the utility lines are installed, the developer would not return to the first step to redraw the lot lines or move the home sites.

To be able to better understand the difference between iterative and incremental, consider the following example:

EXAMPLE: You are managing a project that is tasked with producing a new application. This application includes four basic parts. In an iterative method, an early edition of all four parts would be developed and released. Then each part would be refined over time to improve or enhance the capabilities of the part. In an incremental method, each part is built and released. Then each of the other parts are added to the application as they are ready.

With an iterative project, the application may initially have all the parts of the application but not all the functionality of each part. With an incremental project, the application may initially have a single part of the application but not all the parts.

Figure 1-1 is a graphical representation of how an iterative approach versus an incremental approach works.

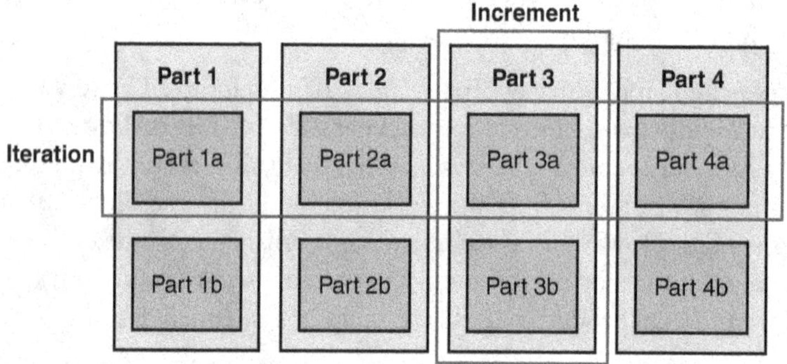

Figure 1-1 Iterative Versus Incremental

All methodologies or frameworks based on Agile are iterative and incremental, while most predictive approaches such as Waterfall are not.

The methodology or framework implemented may vary based on your organization's needs, project type, and even industry. As a project manager, it is important that you understand the different methodologies and frameworks available to help your organization determine the approach the organization will use.

For the Project+ exam, project managers need to understand the following methodologies and frameworks: Software Development Life Cycle (SDLC), PRojects IN Controlled Environments (PRINCE2), Waterfall, Agile, scrum, Kanban, DevOps and DevSecOps, Scaled Agile Framework (SAFe), and Extreme Programming (XP). In addition, project managers will need to be able to compare and contrast Agile versus Waterfall qualities, including criteria for selecting a method and team composition.

Software Development Life Cycle

The ***Software Development Life Cycle (SDLC)*** is more of a process framework than a methodology. The specific methodology chosen to execute the software development process can be an Agile model, a Waterfall model, or a hybrid approach. The goal of the SDLC is to provide predictable procedures to identify all requirements with regard to functionality, cost, reliability, and delivery schedule and ensure that each is met in the final solution. As a result, the SDLC is considered to be a predictive model. However, some companies alter the SDLC process to make it adaptive. The steps in the SDLC can vary based on the provider, and this section covers one popular example.

The steps in the Software Development Life Cycle are as follows:

1. Plan/Initiate Project
2. Gather Requirements
3. Design
4. Develop
5. Test/Validate
6. Release/Maintain
7. Certify/Accredit
8. Change Management and Configuration Management/Replacement

In the Plan/Initiate Project phase of the SDLC, the organization decides to initiate a new software development project and formally plans the project. In the Gather Requirements phase, both the functionality and the security requirements of the solution are identified. These requirements could be derived from a variety of sources, such as evaluating competitor products or surveying the needs of users for an internal solution. In some cases, these requirements could come from a direct request from a current customer.

From a security perspective, an organization must identify potential vulnerabilities and threats. When this assessment is performed, the intended purpose of the software and the expected environment must be considered.

In the Design phase, an organization develops a detailed description of how the software will satisfy all functional and security goals. It attempts to map the internal behavior and operations of the software to specific requirements to identify any requirements that have not been met prior to implementation and testing. During this process, the state of the application is determined in every phase of its activities. The state of the application refers to its functional and security posture during each operation it performs. Therefore, all possible operations must be identified. Identifying the attack surface is also a part of this analysis. The amount of attack surface might change at various states of the application, but at no time should the attack surface provided violate the security needs identified in the Gather Requirements phase.

The Develop phase involves writing the code or instructions that make the software work. The emphasis of this phase is strict adherence to secure coding practices. Many security issues with software are created through insecure coding practices, such as lack of input validation or data type checks. Identifying these issues in a code review that attempts to assume all possible attack scenarios and their impact on the code is needed.

In the Test/Validate phase, several types of testing should occur, including ways to identify both functional errors and security issues. Software is typically developed in pieces or modules of code that are later assembled to yield the final product. Each module should be tested separately. Having development staff carry out this testing is critical, but using a group of engineers different from the ones who wrote the code can ensure that an impartial process occurs. This is a good example of the concept of separation of duties.

NOTE Software testing methods are covered in detail in Chapter 6, "Quality, Cost, and Performance Management."

The Release/Maintain phase includes the implementation of the software into the live environment and the continued monitoring of its operation. Finding additional functional and security problems at this point, as the software begins to interface with other elements of the network, is not unusual.

In the Certify/Accredit phase, the organization needs to evaluate software security and obtain formal acceptance of the software. Certification is the process of evaluating software for its security effectiveness with regard to the customer's needs. Accreditation is the formal acceptance of the adequacy of a system's overall security by the management. Provisional accreditation is given for a specific amount of time and lists required changes to applications, systems, or accreditation documentation. Full accreditation grants accreditation without any required changes. Provisional accreditation becomes full accreditation once all the changes are completed, analyzed, and approved by the certifying body.

After a solution is deployed in a live environment, there will inevitably be additional changes that must be made to the software due to security issues that occur in the Change Management phase. In some cases, the software might be altered to enhance or increase its functionality. In either case, changes must be handled through a formal change and configuration management process. Keep in mind that the change management being discussed at the end of the SDLC occurs *after* the software project is completed and the software is deployed.

NOTE Change control within a project (discussed in Chapter 2, "Team and Resource Management") involves changes to the application that are identified and resolved during the project.

The purpose of this process is to ensure that all changes to the source code itself are approved by the proper personnel and are implemented in a safe and logical manner. This process should always ensure continued functionality in the live environment, and changes should be documented fully, including all changes to hardware and software.

In some cases, it may be necessary to completely replace applications or systems. While some failures may be fixed with enhancements or changes, a failure may occur that can only be solved by completely replacing the application.

PRojects IN Controlled Environments

PRojects IN Controlled Environments (PRINCE2) is a predictive, process-based project management methodology. With a focus on organization and control over the entire project, PRINCE2 ensures that projects are thoroughly planned before kickoff, with all project stages being very structured.

There are seven phases in the PRINCE2 methodology:

1. Start the project.
2. Direct the project.
3. Initiate the project.
4. Control a stage.
5. Manage product delivery.
6. Manage stage boundaries.
7. Close the project.

The Start phase entails a request for a new project, called the project mandate. The project mandate is very brief, covering only why the project is necessary and what it will ideally accomplish. An assessment is performed for the mandate. If the project is approved, the original requestor then submits a detailed project brief covering the actions and resources needed to execute the project.

During the Direct phase, the project board evaluates project briefs based on business justification and viability. The project board then approves or disapproves the project. If the project is approved, the project board decides what is needed to organize and execute the project and what powers will be delegated to the project manager. The Direct phase continues throughout the project.

In the Initiate phase, the project manager creates all initiation documentation, including the project management plans and the time, cost, quality, scope, risk, and benefits baselines. The project board approves the documentation (once the documents are completed to the board's satisfaction) and approves the project.

The project then moves into the Control phase, where the project manager splits the project into work packages, which are then turned over to team managers and teams to complete. The project manager oversees the work package progress during each stage and helps the teams to overcome roadblocks or correct any mistakes. Team managers coordinate the teams' daily work and act as a liaison between the project manager and individual team members.

The Manage Product Delivery stage involves checking project progress against the project brief and ensuring deliverables meet PRINCE2 quality expectations. The project board either approves work packages or requests changes to them.

During the Manage Stage Boundaries phase, the project manager and project board review each stage to make sure the project is progressing according to plan and meeting requirements. Each stage review includes a decision by the project board on whether to continue or abandon the project. Retrospectives led by the project manager are conducted to document lessons learned, which are used to improve the next stage.

The Close phase ensures that the project documentation, outcomes, and reporting are completed according to PRINCE2 procedures.

PRINCE2 does have an Agile version, called PRINCE2 Agile. It follows the same phases in PRINCE2 and includes stages, releases, and iterations. Each stage contains one or more releases, and each release contains one or more iterations. Iterations are usually called timeboxes in PRINCE2 Agile.

NOTE Agile is discussed later in this chapter.

Waterfall

The original ***Waterfall*** model breaks the development process into distinct phases.

This model is predictive, with the basic process being a sequential series of steps that are followed without going back to earlier steps. Figure 1-2 is a representation of the Waterfall process.

Key Topic

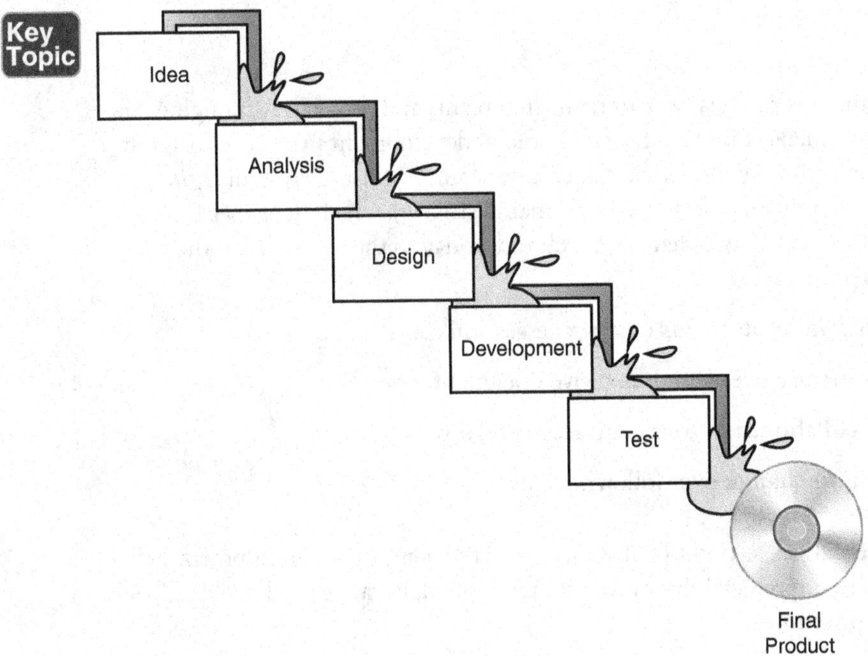

Figure 1-2 Waterfall Model

In the modified Waterfall model, each phase in the development process is considered its own milestone in the project management process. Unlimited backward iteration (returning to earlier stages to address problems) is not allowed in this model. However, product verification and validation are performed in this model. Problems that are discovered during the project do not initiate a return to earlier stages but rather are dealt with after the project is complete.

During the Idea stage, developers document the requirements. The requirements document defines what the software should do but not necessarily how it will work. The requirements document acts as the basis for all future project work.

In the Analysis stage, developers use the requirements document to determine system design. The project progresses into the Design stage, where developers alter the design of the system to ensure it works with the available hardware and software.

Once the design is finalized, the project enters the Development (or Coding) stage. In this stage, developers write the actual code needed for the system to operate. After the system has been coded, the Testing stage occurs, where testers provide bug reports and developers patch the most urgent issues.

In the final stage, Deployment, developers release the system to users, provide support, perform system maintenance, and deploy system upgrades as needed.

Agile

Agile development is a special way of managing teams and projects. Although Agile is used mostly to manage information technology development projects, this methodology is suitable for any project in which uncertainties exist. The term ***Agile*** is derived from the Agile manifesto (see agilemanifesto.org), which describes four important value comparisons that are as relevant today as they were when the manifesto was published in 2001:

Individuals and interactions over processes and tools

Working software over comprehensive documentation

Customer collaboration over contract negotiation

Responding to change over following a plan

By seeking alternatives to traditional project management, Agile development helps teams respond to unpredictability through incremental, iterative work and feedback. Agile is an adaptive model.

Agile development is both iterative and incremental, changing in response to feedback while it is still in process:

- **Iterative:** Agile development is iterative in that the project team plans to improve on the work of one iteration during subsequent iterations.
- **Incremental:** Agile development is incremental in that completed work is delivered throughout the project's life cycle. Constant feedback from stakeholders, users, and the sponsor allows the project team to change the project requirements over time.

As one of the most popular approaches to IT projects, Agile has spawned numerous variants. Scrum, Kanban, Scaled Agile Framework (SAFe), and Extreme Programming (XP) all fall within the Agile family. Agile principles can be incorporated into other frameworks to add flexibility in key areas. DevOps and DevSecOps, while not strictly Agile, incorporate Agile principles.

DevOps and DevSecOps

Two modern application development approaches, ***DevOps*** and ***DevSecOps***, have three main areas where they are similar: collaboration, automation, and active monitoring. But there are differences in the two approaches.

Collaboration helps the team achieve development goals without jeopardizing application safety and security. With collaboration, teams that were separated in other approaches now converge together.

Automation is shared by them in that both approaches can utilize artificial intelligence (AI) to automate steps in the application development process. For DevOps, developers use auto-completed code and anomaly detection. Developers in DevSecOps perform automated and continuous security checks and anomaly detection to proactively identify vulnerabilities and threats.

Active monitoring plays an important role in both DevOps and DevSecOps. Developers capture and analyze application data to provide improvements. Using real-time data allows the developers to optimize the application's performance, minimize the application's attack surface, and improve the organization's security posture overall.

DevOps increases the frequency of deployments and ensures the predictability and efficiency of the application, but because the focus is more on speed, DevOps teams do not prioritize security threat prevention, leading to vulnerabilities that can jeopardize the application, data, and company assets.

On the other hand, DevSecOps integrates security management earlier throughout the development process. Application security is a focus from the beginning of the build process, rather than at the end of the development pipeline. With DevSecOps, developers create code with security in mind, thereby solving the issues with security that DevOps doesn't address.

DevOps has two teams: development and operations. The development team plans, codes, builds, and tests the application. Then the operations team releases, deploys, operates, and monitors the application. The processes flow in this manner:

1. Plan
2. Code
3. Build
4. Test
5. Release
6. Deploy
7. Operate
8. Monitor

Those are the eight processes of the DevOps approach. The 6 Cs of DevOps processes are shown in Figure 1-3.

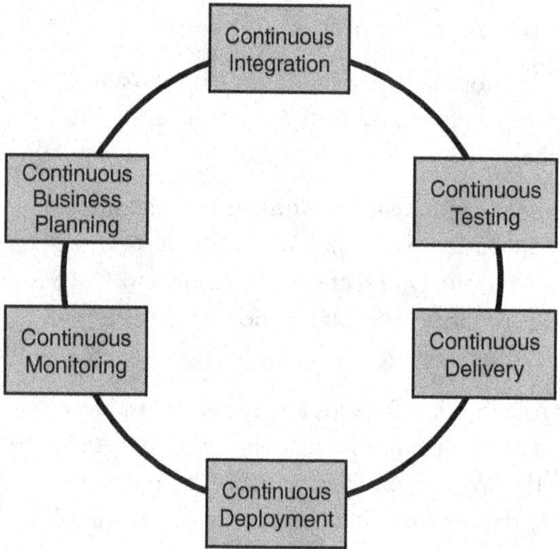

Figure 1-3 The 6 Cs of DevOps

DevSecOps takes the same eight processes as DevOps and weaves security into every one. By including security in every process, the team produces a product with fewer security vulnerabilities and threats.

Kanban

Kanban is an Agile method that visually manages the project workflow. It places all work into three categories: To Do (Requested), Doing (In Progress), and Done. The ***Kanban board*** lists these three categories in the columns at the top. Individual activities or tasks are written on ***Kanban cards*** and start off in the far-left column (To Do). Kanban cards just list the particular task that is being completed. When the task is started, its Kanban card moves from To Do to Doing. When it is completed, the Kanban card moves to Done.

Kanban fundamentals can be broken down into two types of principles and six practices. The two principles are Change Management and Service Delivery. The six practices are evenly distributed between the two principles in the following manner:

- Change Management Principle
  - Start with what you do know.
  - Agree to pursue incremental, evolutionary change.
  - Encourage acts of leadership at all levels.

- Service Delivery Principle
  - Focus on customer's needs and expectations.
  - Manage the work, not the workers.
  - Regularly review the network of services.

Kanban includes six core practices that ensure successful projects:

- Visualize the workflow.
- Limit work in progress.
- Manage flow.
- Make process policies explicit.
- Implement feedback loops.
- Improve collaboratively.

Kanban uses many terms that other framework and methodologies do not use. Some of the terms a project manager might use include the following:

- **Swimlanes**: The horizontal lines that split a Kanban board into sections. These lanes are used by teams to visually separate different work types and organize homogenous tasks together.
- **Cycle time**: The time from when a new task enters the Doing stage of the workflow until the task is complete.
- **Lead time**: The time from when a new task is requested until its final departure from the system.
- **Throughput**: The number of work items passing through a system or process into the Done stage over a certain period. This key indicator shows how productive the team is over time.
- **Work in progress (WIP)**: The amount of work currently in progress and not completed.
- **WIP limits**: The limit to the number of tasks that can be in progress simultaneously to avoid overburdening and context switching.
- **Classes of service**: The policies that help Agile teams prioritize work items and projects.
- **Kanban cadences**: Cyclical meetings that drive evolutionary change and fit-for-purpose service delivery.
- **Kanban software**: A digital system that allows Kanban practices and principles to be used by various teams and organizations of all sizes.

Kanban is relatively simple, but never think of it as just a board with some sticky notes. Those are just the visual elements used to keep a project team on track.

Scrum

Scrum is a project management framework that emphasizes teamwork, accountability, and iterative progress toward a well-defined goal. The most popular Agile methodology, scrum is both simple and flexible. The scrum method centers around a repeated, iterative work cycle called a ***sprint***. The goal of a sprint is to complete one of the product's requirements in a usable form. Sprints typically start with a sprint planning meeting, cycle through daily scrum meetings, and end with a retrospective meeting.

In the scrum methodology, the ***scrum master*** handles any outside distractions or internal complications that could prevent the team from making progress on the project. The scrum master helps translate stakeholder needs into requirements and enforces scrum policies while maintaining the team's focus on project design. The scrum master's goal is to keep the team actively moving forward and on track. Unlike a traditional project manager, a scrum master does not assign work to team members or direct the project's strategy. The ***product owner*** role handles many of the traditional project management tasks, such as prioritizing the order of work, managing the budget, accepting deliverables, and setting release dates. The product owner is the Agile product's key stakeholder, who provides the overall vision for the product.

While ***user stories*** are most often written at the beginning of a sprint, team members may actually create user stories at any time in the cycle. Requirements are then created from the user stories. Agile development teams maintain a ***backlog*** as the project progresses. This backlog contains any requirements that are not being addressed in the current sprint. With Agile, the sprint backlog is fed into the project as the development team completes work.

Scrum meetings are typically held in the same location and at the same time each day, usually first thing in the morning. These meetings are strictly timed at 15 minutes. All team members must attend the meetings. The scrum master and product owner should also attend the meetings to show support and note any issues. If other people are allowed to attend the meeting, they should only expect to listen.

Each team member is given time to speak, answering the following questions:

1. What did the team member do yesterday?
2. What will the team member do today?
3. Are any obstacles in the way? If so, what are they?

By answering these three questions, each team member commits to accomplishing certain tasks to help the team reach its sprint goal. Any obstacles raised become the responsibility of the scrum master, although the scrum master may enlist someone else's help in removing the obstacle.

Properly held daily scrum meetings help the team share responsibility for the backlog and the burndown chart. They also help team members hold each other accountable for achieving their daily obligations.

Extreme Programming

Extreme Programming (XP) is the most specific of the Agile frameworks. Its five values are communication, simplicity, feedback, courage, and respect. XP encourages a cross-functional team that sits together in the same space without barriers to communication. It uses pair programming and user stories. A weekly cycle is an iteration, and a quarterly cycle is a release. It adheres to the Ten-Minute Build, which automatically builds the entire system and runs all tests in ten minutes, and Test-First Programming, which reduces the developer feedback cycle to identify and resolve issues, thereby decreasing the number of bugs that get introduced into production.

As Kanban, scrum, and XP are all types of Agile, it can often be hard to differentiate between them. Table 1-3 provides a comparison of these three Agile types to make selecting the correct one a bit easier.

Table 1-3 Kanban, Scrum, and XP Comparison

Quality	Kanban	Scrum	XP
Team size	Unlimited (whatever is used by organization)	Small team	Small team
Iteration	1 week	30 days	1–2 weeks
Roles	Undefined (whatever is used by organization)	Defined	Defined
Process- vs. people-centric	Process	People (Process is important, but secondary.)	People
Virtual team support	Somewhat (via virtual boards)	Somewhat	Not supported
Customer interaction	Low	Medium	High

Quality	Kanban	Scrum	XP
Pros	■ Allows visualization ■ Eliminates bottlenecks ■ Can lead to improvements in operational efficiency and quality	■ Maximizes communication and knowledge sharing ■ Breaks project into manageable pieces ■ Progress made even if unstable requirements	■ Simple and iterative ■ Values communication ■ Emphasis on design
Cons	■ JIT delivery issues lead to delays ■ Dependent tasks aren't captured well ■ Overall project status hard to see	■ Weak measurement practices ■ Weak business system, technical, and concept development practices	■ Lacks design documentation ■ Lacks measurement practices ■ Does not address deployment

Scaled Agile Framework

Scaled Agile Framework (SAFe) is a way to implement Agile at the enterprise level and consists of three metaphorical pillars: team, program, and portfolio. With SAFe, an organization can leverage existing Agile frameworks, such as Kanban, scrum, and XP, and apply them at the team, program, and portfolio pillars.

At the team level, the team has specific goals and responsibilities. The program level relies on each team's output so that each team's components can be combined with everyone else's into something complementary, cohesive, and consistent. The program level includes roles, activities, and artifacts to deliver solutions through the Agile Release Train (ART), which is a long-lived collection of Agile teams that incrementally develops and delivers. Portfolios include multiple programs and have a longer-term vision that spans multiple quarters or even an entire year. At the portfolio level, budgeting and milestones are defined and set, and strategic planning includes project planning. There is an optional level called the value stream level that targets large solutions and requires multiple ARTs.

Agile Versus Waterfall

Predictive projects produce outputs that are expected, whereas adaptive projects can yield surprises. Because adaptive projects are incremental, the end results may differ greatly from the original plan.

Because Agile projects use adaptive planning, project teams must remain flexible and open to change. As a project is completed in stages with a series of deliverables, Agile allows the project's direction to be modified based on the organization's needs. Agile methods tend to lead to improved quality and productivity.

With Waterfall projects and their predictive planning, team flexibility is not as important. The project is documented completely up front, with the project's direction known at that time.

Project managers have great influence over the method that an organization chooses. For this reason, understanding the situations wherein the different methods should be used is vital. The criteria for selecting between an Agile or Waterfall method include the tolerance for change/flexibility, environmental factors, team composition, and differences in communication methods, all of which will be covered in the next sections.

Tolerance for Change/Flexibility

One of the factors that affects the project management method chosen is tolerance for change or flexibility. This flexibility must be gauged based on the environment within which the organization operates and the risks that the organization is willing to take. A high tolerance for change means greater risks. Each project must be analyzed separately to determine the project requirements, budget, and schedule flexibility so that the best method is chosen.

Requirements

In an Agile project, constant feedback from the stakeholders is used to refine the project requirements, which may mean that the requirements at the end of the project differ from the requirements at the beginning. Requirements are frequently rewritten as the project's needs change or as new design considerations are revealed.

Project stakeholders in an Agile project are actively engaged in generating *user stories* for new features and requirements. A user story captures software feature descriptions based on a particular user. A user story has three basic parts:

- Who are we building it for?
- What are we building?
- Why are we building it?

To better understand user stories, examine the following user story examples:

Editor: I want to see all of my active publications on the main screen.

Student: I want to see all of my old grades on the board.

Researcher: I want to see the last five searches I have done.

The project team documents requirements based on the user stories:

Editor: Show active publications on the main screen.

Student: Show old grades on the board.

Researcher: Show the last five searches.

By continuing to gather design requirements while project work is underway, the project team can shape the product to meet the customer's needs. Project results are released intermittently to the customer, allowing testers, engineers, and the customer to fully study the design.

Agile teams often use the ***story mapping*** technique to discover requirements and generate a full map of the project. With this technique, the team maps out user stories to discover the features that the customer needs. As they write user stories, the team gathers requirements. These active discussions help the team to determine the full feature design. Story mapping is effective because it produces active discussion, step visualization, and requirements gathering based on the user stories. However, scope changes occur regularly in an Agile project.

With Waterfall projects, the project manager and project team establish project requirements at the start, making project execution less complex and with fewer moving targets. The project team identifies the stakeholders and gathers the requirements from them during project planning. They document the requirements, turn those requirements into the project scope, and break the scope down into individual activities in the work breakdown structure (WBS). Once that is done, any scope change requests can only be included if approved.

In summary, Agile projects have high flexibility when it comes to requirements changes, while Waterfall projects have very little flexibility regarding requirements.

Budget and Schedule

Because changes are welcome in an Agile project, the final project result often differs greatly from what was first envisioned. As with the project requirements, the budget in an Agile project is flexible. With Waterfall projects, the project budget and resources are known from the start, making expectations and risks easier to manage. Agile projects tend to be cheaper and faster, while Waterfall projects tend to be more expensive and slower.

As with requirements and budget, Agile projects allow greater schedule flexibility. With the start of each sprint or iteration, the project team sets the schedule. This means that as the project progresses, the schedule is refined. But with Waterfall projects, the schedule planning occurs early and includes all activities and their estimated durations.

Budget and schedule can be summarized similarly to requirements: Agile projects have high flexibility when it comes to budget and schedule changes, while Waterfall projects have very little budget and schedule flexibility.

Environmental Factors

Along with project flexibility, environmental factors affect the project management method chosen. Agile and Waterfall projects operate very differently. Project managers must understand the cultural, developmental, and industry standards that affect a project to guide the organization or project management office so that the correct method is selected.

Cultural

Agile is more collaborative than Waterfall. The Agile focus is working together as a team and improving as the project progresses. In Waterfall, the focus is more on following the plan and reaching the documented end result.

Agile teams react much quicker to changes and tend to let those changes minimally affect their progress. Waterfall teams, on the other hand, tend to experience more issues with changes as the method is rigid and follows strict rules.

Agile projects require much more interaction with project stakeholders than Waterfall projects. Agile teams actively engage with the stakeholders to refine the project requirements each time a new sprint or iteration begins. Waterfall teams commonly interact more with stakeholders early in the project to define the requirements. During the collaboration process with internal and external stakeholders, trust, transparency, and cultural backgrounds should be considered and appreciated.

Developmental

The developmental differences have been covered several times in this chapter. Waterfall follows a strict, linear development life cycle, with scope, schedule, and budget being fully documented at the project start. In contrast, Agile projects perform in a cyclical manner, with each sprint or iteration returning to planning to more fully document the project scope.

While Waterfall is very structured, Agile is geared toward change and innovation. Waterfall is best used when projects are very predictable, and Agile is best used when the final result is hard to define early in the project life cycle.

Industry Standards

Industry standards as well as governmental regulations affect projects. Standards and regulations often require a project manager to closely monitor a project's compliance with said standards and regulations. As a result, the project development needs to be more rigid and defined.

If industry standards and regulations will affect the project's result, the Waterfall method is a better choice than Agile. Because the requirements, scope, budget, and schedule are defined during project planning, Waterfall project results are predictable and much easier to monitor and control. The Agile approach leaves the project results too open and susceptible to change. For these reasons, project managers should use the Waterfall method if the project is affected by industry standards and regulations.

Team Composition

Unlike other project management methodologies that rely heavily on the project manager to guide the team, the project team in an Agile project is expected to be self-organized and self-directed, with each team member responsible to the other team members for his or her obligations. Each team member completes the current obligation and then moves on to another one. In most cases, team members select the tasks they want to achieve, which often allows for completing tasks more efficiently.

A disciplined Agile team is much easier to administer than traditional project teams. In many cases, the scrum master acts more as a facilitator than as a project manager. For this reason, a scrum master still needs the interpersonal skills required by a traditional project manager, in order to help team members respond to feedback and reach consensus on tasks.

In the following sections, the Agile and Waterfall methods will be compared in regards to product ownership. Roles and responsibilities, team size, and resource allocation and commitment are also discussed.

Product Ownership

To understand product ownership, project managers need to understand two roles: product manager and product owner. In Waterfall environments, the product manager is the person who owns the product scope, advocates for the product, and represents the customer. The product manager is usually a job title. The product owner role does not exist.

In Agile environments, the role of product owner is used. While the product manager can serve as the product owner as well, the product owner role could be filled by any individual with the desire to be the product advocate. The product owner maximizes product value and is accountable for the end product. This person works with the project manager and team to manage scope expectations, budget implications, and team availability. The product owner meets with stakeholders and prioritizes the backlog.

In smaller projects, the product manager and product owner can be the same person. But in medium to larger projects, it is best to have separate individuals in these two roles.

The product owner is actively engaged in the project throughout its life cycle and proactively engages with both the stakeholders and the project team.

Roles and Responsibilities

Roles and responsibilities in Waterfall versus Agile projects have both similarities and differences. In addition to the product manager role, Waterfall teams typically have five other roles: developer, tester, business analyst, stakeholder, and project manager. However, organizations may include other roles per the project needs.

One of the most important roles in Waterfall teams is the developer, who creates the code and needs to avoid coding bugs. A single defect can negatively affect the entire project from the very beginning.

The tester in a Waterfall project is also extremely important. Tests are usually conducted at the end. Testers need to find all the bugs in final products and notate the issues so developers can fix the defects.

A business analyst is a person responsible for making the software product popular in the digital market. This person's main task is to write business strategies.

Stakeholders work with the project manager and project team to define the requirements early in the Waterfall project. While stakeholders may receive reports on project progress and may even make the occasional new request, stakeholders in Waterfall projects are not as active in the day-to-day work as stakeholders in Agile projects.

As the main person in every Waterfall project, the project manager is responsible for the application's quality. This person's main task is to manage the project and to subdivide tasks among other team members.

Agile teams have a slightly different structure that includes product owner (discussed earlier), team lead or scrum master, developers, and stakeholders. Other roles can be included in large Agile projects.

The team lead or scrum master coordinates the team's work. This role works closely with the product owner, taking the instructions and ensuring that activities are completed. Facilitating daily scrum and sprint initiatives and encouraging team communication are also team lead duties. This role acts as the liaison between the product owner and the project team.

The development team in Agile projects is very similar to that in Waterfall projects. This team takes the project requirements and turns them into a tangible product. Within the development team, the members may provide different services, including product design, code writing, code testing, and user interface specialist. They perform work sprints as per the requirements and attend the daily scrum meeting.

Stakeholders include end users, business executives, production support staff, and any other personnel that have a stake in the project. Stakeholders in Agile products are routinely engaged by the product owner.

Some large Agile projects can include other roles:

- Technical and domain experts have specialized knowledge of technology or stakeholder requirements.
- Independent testers and auditors may ensure that the product works as expected.
- An integrator may help ensure that work is coordinated with organizational operations or subsystems.
- An architect may be required for architectural planning and decision making.

Keep in mind that, no matter the method used to manage the project, any team can be customized to include the roles identified by the organization and project manager. However, responsibilities should be clearly delineated to prevent confusion and wasted effort.

Team Size

While both Agile and Waterfall can be adapted to fit any project or team size, Waterfall projects tend to have larger teams but can easily work for a small team. Agile projects are more efficient with small- to medium-sized teams. If Agile projects require a larger team, multiple teams may be working in tandem, each with a separate team lead. The team leads work together with the teams to logically divide the sprints or iterations.

However, with the COVID-19 pandemic and the need to work remotely, organizations had to stray from the preconception that Agile teams needed to be in a controlled, local office setting. With the tools that we have in today's world, teams can be highly productive working remotely, and team size may be affected by this. This affects all roles within the team, as remote team collaboration is not as hard as it once was.

Resource Allocation and Commitment

With Waterfall, requirements are developed and the scope is thoroughly documented during planning. Resource and time estimates are generated based on the fixed scope and are tracked and managed throughout the project. Resources and time are adjusted easily. A single team member being unavailable is not much of an issue in that it will not impact the project much.

Agile places emphasis on resources and time over scope. Agile projects commit to delivering project outcomes within a fixed time frame with fixed resources. The project team is vital to the success of the project. Because the team members work so closely together, a single team member being unavailable can negatively affect the sprint or iteration. Team member commitment to the project is much more important in Agile projects than in Waterfall projects.

Differences in Communication Methods

Agile development requires continuous feedback to ensure project success. Each team member plays an important role in the project and must adapt to new processes. Without continuous feedback, a team member may repeat mistakes. With daily scrum meetings, Agile teams can provide feedback to ensure quick improvement and adaptation. Constructive feedback for a team member should be based on past instances; the giver provides examples of past behavior and suggestions on how the receiver could have better handled the situation. Equally important to the team is feedback about process improvements. Techniques that can be used for exchanging feedback include one-on-one feedback, group feedback, written feedback, and feedback coaching.

In any Agile project, team members should work to cultivate a culture of continuous feedback. Project managers or scrum masters may need to implement exercises that help develop this continuous feedback culture within the team and the organization. As the project progresses, continuous feedback will become a habit among the team members and stakeholders.

In Waterfall projects, communication is not as vital in day-to-day progress. The communication plan, including the preferred method of communication, is documented during project planning. Daily meetings and stakeholder input are not part of Waterfall projects.

Exam Preparation Tasks

As mentioned in the section "How to Use This Book" in the Introduction, you have a few choices for exam preparation: the exercises here, Chapter 17, "Final Preparation," and the exam simulation questions in the Pearson Test Prep Software Online.

Review All Key Topics

Review the most important topics in this chapter, noted with the Key Topics icon in the outer margin of the page. Table 1-4 lists each reference of these key topics and the page number on which each is found.

Table 1-4 Key Topics for Chapter 1

Key Topic Element	Description	Page Number
Paragraph	Definition and overview of project	7
Paragraph	Relationship between project and program	9
Paragraph	Relationships between project, program, and portfolio	9
Paragraph	Predictive approach versus adaptive approach	10
Paragraph	Hybrid approach	11
Paragraph	Iterative method versus incremental method	11
List	Software Development Life Cycle (SDLC) steps	13
List	PRINCE2 methodology phases	15
Figure 1-2	Waterfall model	17
Paragraph	DevOps explanation	19
List	DevOps process	19
Paragraph	Overview of Kanban	20
Paragraph	Overview of scrum development, sprints, scrum master and product owner, and backlog	22
Paragraph	Overview of XP	23
Table 1-3	Kanban, scrum, and XP comparison	23
Paragraph	Agile versus Waterfall	24

Complete Tables and Lists from Memory

Print a copy of Appendix C, "Memory Tables" (found on the companion website), or at least the section for this chapter, and complete the tables and lists from memory. Appendix D, "Memory Tables Answers," also on the companion website, includes completed tables and lists to check your work.

Define Key Terms

Define the following key terms from this chapter and check your answers in the glossary:

project, tangible outcomes, intangible outcomes, program, portfolio, methodology, framework, predictive, adaptive, hybrid, iterative, iteration, incremental, increment, Software Development Life Cycle (SDLC), PRojects IN Controlled Environments (PRINCE2), Waterfall, Agile, DevOps, DevSecOps, Kanban, Kanban board, Kanban cards, scrum, sprint, scrum master, product owner, user story, backlog, Extreme Programming (XP), Scaled Agile Framework (SAFe), and story mapping

Review Questions

The answers to these questions appear in Appendix A. For more practice with sample exam questions, use the Pearson Test Prep practice test software online.

1. Which of the following is *not* a project?
   a. Deploying a new web server
   b. Building a new customer app
   c. Installing the latest operating system and application updates
   d. Designing a new electric engine

2. Your company currently has the following projects in progress:
   - Deploying a new file server for a single department
   - Documenting the IT change management process
   - Installing the flooring as part of the first floor remodeling
   - Painting the walls as part of the first floor remodeling
   - Purchasing new accessories and office furniture as part of the first floor remodeling
   - Updating the antivirus and antimalware signatures on all client and server computers.

   Which of the following statements is *not* true for these projects?
   a. The three remodeling projects are part of a program.
   b. The three remodeling projects are part of the project portfolio.
   c. Updating the antivirus and antimalware signatures is not a project.
   d. All of the projects listed are part of the project portfolio.

3. Which of the following is a valid reason for using Agile versus other project management methods?
   a. Agile uses extensive requirements gathering that includes user stories and questionnaires.
   b. Agile allows the project direction to be modified easily based on the organization's needs.

c. Agile requires the scrum master to maintain tight control over the project tasks.

d. Agile specializes in smaller projects that need small teams to complete.

4. Which statement *best* describes what happens with each iteration in an Agile project?

a. The product is improved.

b. The schedule is shortened.

c. The budget is made more accurate.

d. The schedule is made more accurate.

5. You are the scrum master for an Agile project. You hold a meeting with the project team during which the user stories are written. Which process are you completing?

a. Holding daily scrum meetings

b. Creating burndown charts

c. Gathering requirements

d. Holding a scrum retrospective

6. During a daily scrum meeting, who should give updates regarding sprint tasks?

a. The scrum master

b. A designated team member

c. All team members

d. The product owner

7. In the SDLC, what step is completed after initiating a project?

a. Design

b. Gather Requirements

c. Develop

d. Test/Validate

8. What is the second phase of PRINCE2?

a. Direct the project.

b. Initiate the project.

c. Control a stage.

d. Manage product delivery.

9. What is the final phase of DevOps?
   a. Test
   b. Release
   c. Deploy
   d. Monitor

10. Which approach is likely to work best with a project that is heavily influenced by regulations and industry standards?
    a. Scrum
    b. Kanban
    c. Waterfall
    d. Agile

This chapter covers the following topics:

- **Team Performance Considerations:** Team building, trust building, team selection, remote versus in-house personnel resources, momentum building and team leadership, personnel removal/replacement, and performance feedback
- **Roles and Responsibilities:** Functional/extended versus operational/core team members, sponsor, stakeholders, senior management, product owner, scrum master, project manager (PM), project scheduler/coordinator, program manager, product manager, tester/quality assurance (QA) specialist, business analyst, subject matter expert (SME), architect, developer/engineer, project management office (PMO), and end user

CHAPTER 2

Team and Resource Management

Resource management ensures that all project personnel and other physical resource needs required to complete a project are identified and managed appropriately. Personnel needed for the project include the core team members, extended team members, and stakeholders. Team members may be removed or added as the project progresses, and they may need to obtain training prior to joining the team. The project manager must clearly define each team member's responsibilities and keep them motivated to achieve the best possible work. The project manager may also have to negotiate with functional managers, other project management teams, and/or other organizations to obtain the appropriate team members.

Other project resources include equipment, supplies, and items to be purchased (procurements). If even one of its resources is not available at the correct time, an entire project could be delayed. Resources must be managed for the duration of their life cycle, from acquisition to decommissioning (of physical resources) or successors (for human resources). To ensure resource needs are identified during the Planning phase and then acquired where necessary, the project manager will perform a needs assessment during the early stage of the resource life cycle, followed by a gap analysis that seeks to address missing functionalities, skills, and materials or equipment before project work begins.

This chapter covers the following objective for the CompTIA Project+ exam:

1.10 Given a scenario, perform basic activities related to team and resource management.

NOTE Depending on the organization and project, personnel may or may not be considered a project resource. CompTIA regards personnel as a resource for the purposes of the Project+ exam. However, even if the people working on a project are counted among the project's resources for planning purposes, they are managed as team members, not as physical resources.

NOTE CompTIA might use slight variations of industry-standard terminology on the Project+ exam. Many project management standards refer to "human resource management" instead of "team management."

"Do I Know This Already?" Quiz

The "Do I Know This Already?" quiz allows you to assess whether you should read this entire chapter thoroughly or jump to the "Exam Preparation Tasks" section. If you are in doubt about your answers to these questions or your own assessment of your knowledge of the topics, read the entire chapter. Table 2-1 lists the major headings in this chapter and their corresponding "Do I Know This Already?" quiz questions. You can find the answers in Appendix A, "Answers to the 'Do I Know This Already?' Questions and Review Quizzes."

Table 2-1 "Do I Know This Already?" Section-to-Question Mapping

Foundation Topics Section	Questions
Organizational Structures	1–2
Resource Life Cycle	3
Resource Types and Criticality	4
Gap Analysis	5
Team Performance Considerations	6
Roles and Responsibilities	7–11

CAUTION The goal of self-assessment is to gauge your mastery of the topics in this chapter. If you do not know the answer to a question or are only partially sure of the answer, you should mark that question as wrong for the purposes of the self-assessment. Giving yourself credit for an answer you correctly guess skews your self-assessment results and might provide you with a false sense of security.

1. Which of the following is *not* a project team structure?
   a. Matrix
   b. Hybrid
   c. Functional
   d. Projectized

2. Which of the following statements is true for a projectized team structure?
   a. Resources report to the project manager.
   b. Authority is shared between the project manager and the functional manager.
   c. Authority belongs to the functional manager.
   d. It ranges from weak to strong.

3. While performing project planning, how should a project manager document the chance that a team member may retire during the project?
   a. As a risk
   b. As a change
   c. As a resource contention
   d. As an issue

4. Which of the following resources could be considered critical?
   a. A team member with a unique skill set who is not currently assigned to any project
   b. A team member with a unique skill set who is assigned to a high-priority project
   c. A company-owned tool that is required to complete a high-priority project task
   d. A resource being used by multiple projects with overlapping schedules

5. Which documents or tools would help a project manager perform a resource gap analysis? (Choose all that apply.)
   a. Team member skills assessments
   b. Resource calendar
   c. List of project roles
   d. Updated inventory of computer hardware

6. Which of the following statements describes storming?
   a. The team meets and learns about how they will work together in the project.
   b. The team learns to resolve interpersonal conflict.
   c. The team starts making decisions about the project.
   d. Team communication breaks down.

7. Which role is accountable for managing and prioritizing the product backlog in an Agile project?
   a. Sponsor
   b. Product owner
   c. Program manager
   d. Scrum master

8. Which individual or organization gives final approval for a project?
   a. Sponsor
   b. Project manager
   c. Stakeholder
   d. PMO

9. Which of the following is *not* a responsibility of the project manager?
   a. Managing the team
   b. Creating the project deliverables
   c. Creating the budget
   d. Creating the schedule

10. Which of the following is a responsibility of the project stakeholders?
    a. Creating the business case
    b. Creating the budget
    c. Providing project requirements
    d. Creating project deliverables

11. Which of the following is *not* a responsibility of the PMO?
    a. Setting project management standards
    b. Providing templates
    c. Estimating costs
    d. Providing tools

Foundation Topics

Organizational Structures

Project team structures are controlled by the organization's structure, which in turn affects the availability of resources. The project team's structure affects the project manager's role and authority, resource availability, budget management, and the availability of project management administrative staff.

Project team structures are broadly categorized as functional, matrix, and projectized. Table 2-2 summarizes how project team structures affect these project characteristics.

Table 2-2 Influence of Project Team Structures on Projects

Project Characteristic	Functional	Weak Matrix	Balanced Matrix	Strong Matrix	Projectized
Project manager authority	Little or none	Low	Low to moderate	Moderate to high	High to almost total
Resource availability	Little or none	Low	Low to moderate	Moderate to high	High to almost total
Project budget management	Functional manager	Functional manager	Mixed	Project manager	Project manager
Project manager's role	Part time	Part time	Full time	Full time	Full time
Administrative staff	Part time	Part time	Part time	Full time	Full time

Functional

In an organization that uses a ***functional team structure***, each employee reports to a single ***functional manager*** or supervisor rather than to a project manager. Employees are grouped by job role and specialty, such as marketing, sales, or accounting.

The project manager has little to no authority in a functional team structure and is usually not dedicated full time to managing the project. Because of the reporting structure, project managers need to approach the functional manager to request scheduling of the resources, or multiple functional managers if the team members come from multiple functional areas. In most cases, a functional manager also manages the budget. Projects may suffer if issues or emergencies arise and the needs of the functional unit are perceived to take precedence over the needs of the project.

Figure 2-1 demonstrates project management within a functional organization. In this example, the project team members are taken from multiple functional areas, with each functional manager having authority over their respective staff members.

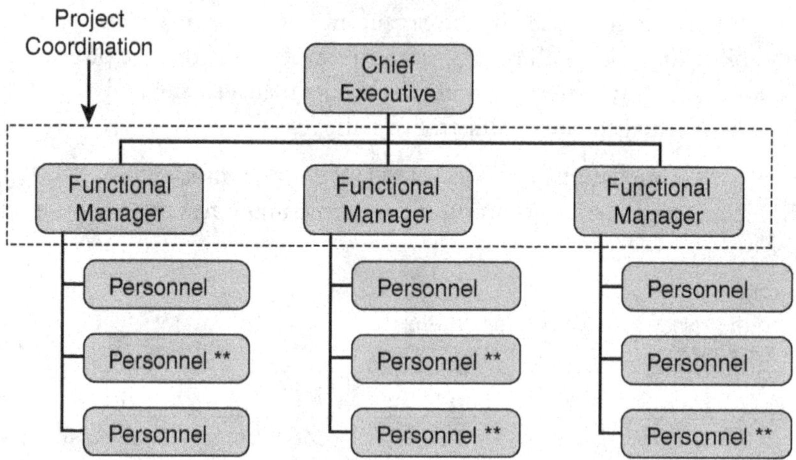

Figure 2-1 Functional Team Structure

Projectized

In an organization that uses a ***projectized team structure***, each employee reports to a project manager. The project manager oversees the budget and has full authority to assign tasks to all resources. Resources are allocated on an ad hoc basis, moving between projects as needed. This arrangement is the opposite of a functional team structure.

Projects benefit from a projectized structure because resources are led by a single manager and develop a cohesive identity with their team members. One possible downside is that the organization may pay for staff with duplicate skill sets, such as employing one graphic designer for each of four projects rather than a single three-person graphic design department that serves all projects.

Figure 2-2 demonstrates project management within a projectized structure. All personnel within the organization are under the authority of a project manager. Project managers work together to ensure that the appropriate resources are available to each of the organization's projects.

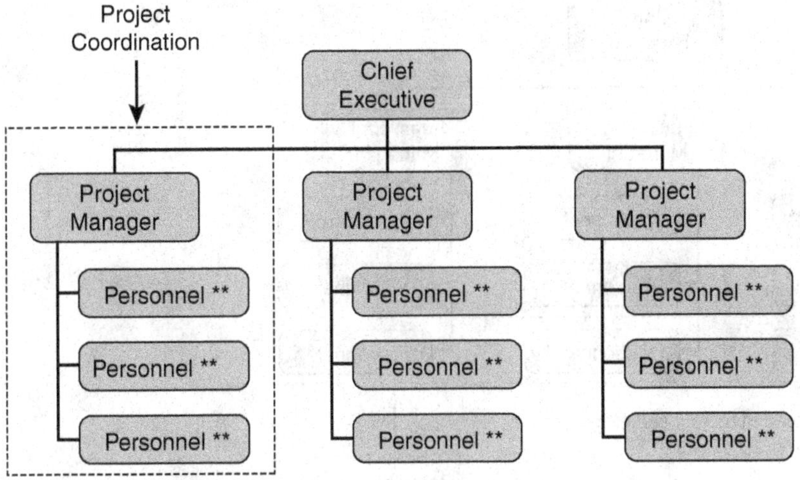

Figure 2-2 Projectized Team Structure

Matrix

In an organization that uses a ***matrix team structure***, each employee usually reports to a functional manager. However, authority is shared between the functional manager and the project manager. Matrix team structures are termed *weak*, *balanced*, or *strong*, depending on the level of power and influence between the functional managers and project managers.

Resources are assigned from the functional area to the project in most cases, but the functional manager usually has the ultimate authority for scheduling. The project manager functions more as a coordinator or expediter.

Figure 2-3 demonstrates project management within a weak matrix organization. Some personnel are allocated to the project for project coordination. Other personnel who are part of the project mainly work in their functional departments but are also engaged in project activities.

Figure 2-4 demonstrates project management within a balanced matrix organization. In this structure, some personnel are allocated to the project for project coordination. Other personnel who are part of the project mainly work in their functional departments but are also engaged in project activities. In this type of matrix, the project manager is usually a staff member from within one of the functional areas.

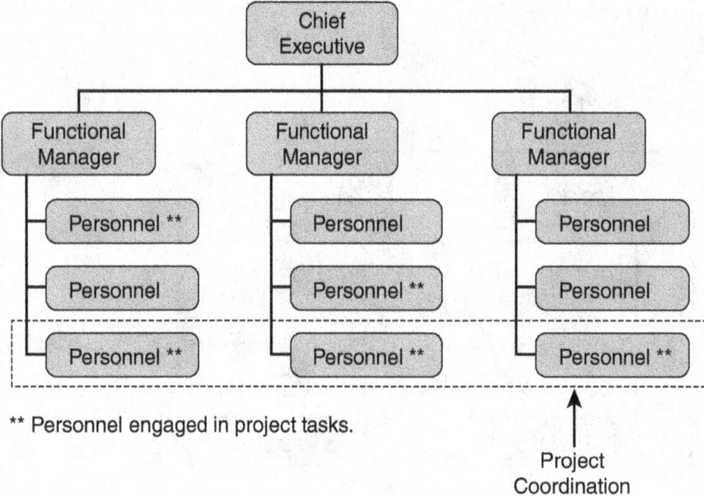

Figure 2-3 Weak Matrix Team Structure

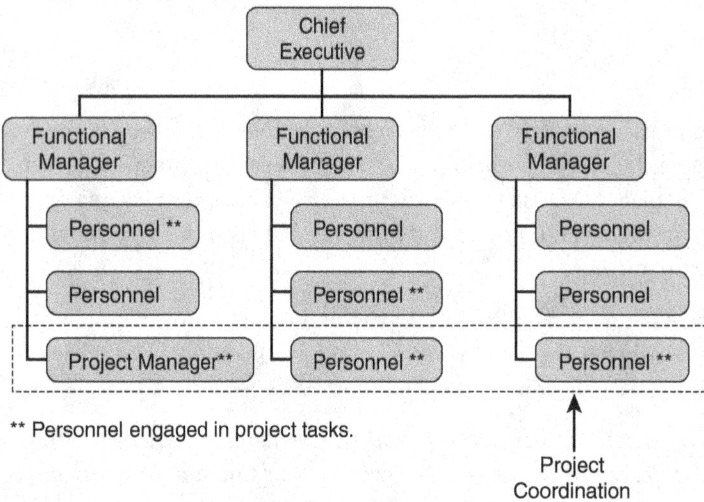

Figure 2-4 Balanced Matrix Team Structure

Figure 2-5 demonstrates project management within a strong matrix organization. As in the previous examples, some personnel are allocated to the project for project coordination, and other personnel perform project activities while still mainly working in their functional departments. In this type of matrix, the project manager reports to the manager of project managers within a project management office (PMO). (PMOs are covered in more detail later in this chapter.)

As it moves from a weak matrix to a strong matrix, an organization's team structure comes closer to being projectized. The primary advantage of a matrix organization is the flexibility to support both project goals and each department's functional goals. Its disadvantage, as with functional organizations, is that team members may have conflicting priorities set by different projects or different managers.

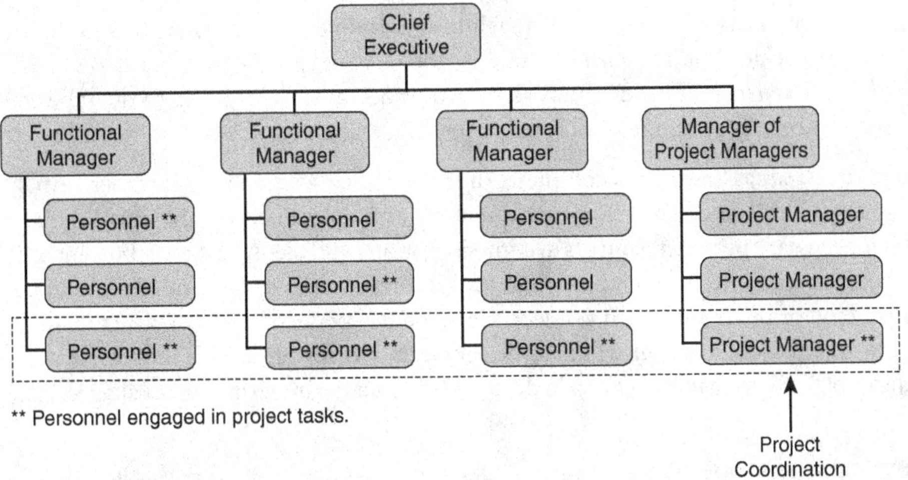

Figure 2-5 Strong Matrix Team Structure

Resource Life Cycle

A ***resource life cycle*** describes the stages that a physical or human resource goes through while employed for project work by an organization. For a human resource, this would include processes like hiring, training, assignment, performance reviews, and succession or termination. The life cycle for a physical resource, such as a computer, application, or device, includes the stages of acquisition, maintenance, and decommissioning for both software- and hardware-based resources.

Acquisition

During the Planning phase of a project, the project manager must identify all the required resources. If the organization does not own all the necessary resources, missing resources must be purchased or arranged as part of procurement management. New team members may be hired, or existing team members trained to fill new roles. Resources owned by the organization must be scheduled at the appropriate times for use as project resources. A resource calendar should be developed to show all resources needed by the project and when they will be used. Procurements must be managed, from the planning, conducting, and controlling of the procurements through to the closing of the procurements when the resources are obtained and ready for use. These topics are covered more in Chapter 5, "Schedule Development and Management," as part of project scheduling.

Needs Assessment

A procurement ***needs assessment*** is the process by which the project manager reviews the project's requirements to determine which resources are needed for the individual work tasks. In a predictive project, the project manager would analyze the work breakdown structure (WBS), while an adaptive project manager would review the backlog and the sprint plan. One tool that helps this process is a ***resource breakdown structure***. This chart breaks down project work according to the types of resources needed to complete each task, such as "Drupal developers" or "forklifts."

Once the needs assessment is complete, the project manager will use it to perform a gap analysis (covered later in this chapter). The completed gap analysis will show which necessary project resources are missing or unavailable. A make-or-buy analysis can be used to decide whether work, physical resources, or deliverables should be outsourced or purchased from vendors versus being produced by the project team. Ideally, the project manager will pad the requirements for physical resources by a margin of 10% so that tasks are not delayed by defective materials or breakages.

NOTE Some standards use the term *needs assessment* to refer to the process of outlining a business case to justify a project's charter.

Maintenance

Regular maintenance for physical assets includes regular upgrades, updates, and security patches for operating systems and firmware, as well as normal operations such as network security. The project manager should coordinate with functional managers or operations managers to ensure that all project equipment is maintained to support project work and provide the anticipated degree of usage.

Project managers should also monitor end user licenses for any software required for project work and ensure that there are enough licensed seats to support team members. If software licenses will expire during project execution, there should be enough budget allocated to renew the licenses.

Hardware Decommissioning

Hardware reaches the end of its life cycle when it is no longer supported or regularly patched by the vendor, when it can no longer meet the performance needs of the organization, when it becomes more expensive to maintain than to replace, or when it breaks down. There should be a documented process in place to decommission hardware that includes the following tasks:

- Acquiring replacements and establishing a milestone plan for transferring operations to the new equipment

- Ensuring the data is backed up and then securely wiped from the old hardware
- Ensuring that servers removed from production do not leave holes in network security
- Maintaining a log of decommissioned equipment that includes identification, the decommissioned date, and the chosen method of destruction (shredding, zeroization, and so on)

End-of-Life Software

Once software is no longer supported by the vendor, project managers must ensure that the software is removed from production systems. Out-of-date or unpatched software is a common security vulnerability that hackers may use to breach internal networks. If your organization has business-critical applications running on ***end-of-life software***, it should at a minimum be transferred to a virtual machine in a sandboxed environment until a replacement application can be found.

Successor Planning

While it is not always possible to anticipate the loss of a team member, project planning should anticipate any gap in project work left by team member resignations, removals, or retirements. This is one reason why the project manager must fully understand the skill set and work rate of every team member. If a team member is simply removed or replaced, their work will need to be allocated to another resource, and the project manager will have to adjust the project schedule and budget for this change.

EXAMPLE: A team member who is working on two projects resigns. Replacing that person's skill sets requires two separate resources. Hiring those resources will likely result in higher costs to both projects. However, because two resources are now available, the work rate may actually increase, meaning that the project tasks allocated to these resources will be completed more quickly. So while the budgets for the two projects may increase, the project manager may see an improvement in the project schedules.

If you know that a certain team member may retire during a project, you should make plans in advance to ensure the role does not go unfilled—whether by reallocating other team members from other projects, shifting tasks to another team member, hiring a temporary contract worker, or making a new permanent hire. Because an upcoming retirement is a predictable event, it should be listed as a project risk.

To minimize the impact of losing a key team member to retirement, you can prepare by doing the following:

- Documenting the skills and institutional knowledge held by the outgoing team member
- Gaining ownership of the outgoing team member's files, digital resources, user accounts, and passwords
- Identifying internal resources who could be trained or quickly reskilled to fill the gap
- Arranging for the outgoing team member to mentor a replacement, if possible
- Preparing more than one individual to take over the outgoing team member's tasks

The project manager should communicate team member changes to all project stakeholders. The project manager should also distribute applicable high-level documents to the appropriate stakeholders after a team member change that will require adjustments to the project budget and schedule.

Resource Types and Criticality

A critical resource is one that is limited in supply and crucial for project work to go forward and achieve its stated goals, whether it is a team member or a specialized tool. Team members with skills not replicated in the team can be particularly critical resources, especially for a project that relies on that skill set.

Critical resources should be identified during project planning. Any resource that is critical should be denoted as such in the project schedule to ensure its availability for project work, especially if it is shared with other projects or departments. If it is being acquired for the project as a procurement, it should be scheduled to arrive in time for project work to begin. For example, a project to install a network in a newly purchased building requires both routers and cabling. It would be impossible to install routers if the wiring were not installed first. A delay in wiring would affect every activity that occurs after the wiring installation, making the wiring a critical component of the project.

When documenting team member criticality, project managers may need to list the specific skills that the member has and an estimated cost to replace that team member. Each team member will need a calendar so that the team member's project availability can be charted to correspond with activities on the project schedule.

The types of resources needed for a project are as follows:

- **Physical resources**: The physical assets that are needed to produce the project results, such as computers, applications, devices, wiring, and operating systems
- **Human resources**: The team members that produce the project results
- **Capital resources**: Resources that support the project environment

Human Resources

Human resources are the team members that produce the project results. Team members have a big impact on project success. In adaptive projects, this is the case because of fast sprints and the need for the team to work so closely together.

The project team may be selected by preassignment, negotiation, or acquisition:

- **Preassigned resources:** Personnel assigned to the project from the start, based on position in the organization and/or knowledge and skill sets
- ***Negotiated resources***: Personnel the project manager wants on the project team and must negotiate with other managers to obtain
- **Acquired resources:** Personnel from outside sources, such as consultants and subcontractors

No matter how the resources are obtained, the project manager must understand the skill set and work rate of each team member. Depending on the skill set, the team member will be assigned to certain activities or tasks within the project. The work rate is important because, for example, knowing how many square feet of brick a bricklayer can lay per hour would help estimate how long a wall would take to build.

Although not all activities or tasks can be broken down by work rate, team members often can provide the project manager with an estimate of how long a certain task will take to complete. Such estimates are important for making best-guess determinations for the *resource calendar*, which lists all resources and the dates and times when they are available to the project. Because work rates can differ, one person may be able to complete certain work much faster than another person can. The project manager must understand and document these details along with the skill set information to determine the best use of personnel resources.

For all personnel resources, the project manager will need to document the following information to record in the resource calendar and stakeholder register:

- **Availability:** Indicates when each resource can actually perform work
- **Cost:** Specifies the rate at which the resource will be paid

- **Experience:** Documents the resource's work background
- **Ability:** Records the resource's competencies
- **Knowledge:** Describes the resource's understanding of customers, similar projects, and the project environment
- **Attitude:** Documents how the resource feels about the project and team, focusing on whether the person will be able to work well in the team environment
- **International factors:** Lists the resource's location, time zone, communications capabilities, and any customs/norms that may not be understood by the other members of the project team

Documenting all of this information helps the project manager acquire a project team that will be able to work well together toward the project's completion. Once the project team is acquired, the project manager should ensure that the appropriate training is provided to the team members (if needed) and that project team members are assigned to the appropriate activities or tasks.

Physical Resources

Physical resources are the non-living assets that are required to complete project work and that will be consumed by the process of creating project deliverables. Resources vary by project. To compile a comprehensive list of needed resources, the project manager may need to consult with subject matter experts. The goal of physical ***resource allocation*** is to acquire enough material by the start of project work that tasks can begin on time, while not spending the budget on unneeded materials.

EXAMPLE: For a project that adds a new subnet to a network, the physical resources could include network devices, cabling, peripherals, and software licenses. Ordering two extra routers would ensure that installation can go forward if one device does not work when unboxed.

Physical resources can also be virtual. In the context of an IT project, physical resources could include virtual machines or a dedicated percentage of the compute resources available from the organization's cloud provider. Even if the compute resources (such as CPUs or instances) are released at the end of the project, and therefore not permanently "consumed," they are consumed for the duration of project work.

Capital Resources

Capital resources are infrastructure resources that are not consumed by one specific project but are required to produce the project's deliverables and are necessary to the project's success. Capital resources can be office equipment, functional employees such as accountants, computer equipment used by the product team, tools, or company vehicles. Project managers must work with the project team to identify these resources and ensure they are available when needed.

In the example of installing a network inside a newly constructed building, the physical resources would be the cabling, peripherals, licenses, and routers. The capital resources would be the tools used to cut and splice the wires, ladders used to access ceiling panels, and vans used to transport project materials, as well as the warehouse staff who accepted delivery of the raw materials and drove them to the job site on behalf of the project team.

Internal vs. External

The project manager may need to consider both ***external*** (remote) and ***internal resources*** when acquiring project team members. Managing a project team that works from the same location is much easier than managing a remote or virtual project team. In either case, however, the project manager must rely on their interpersonal skills and productivity tools to help the team work together efficiently.

In a virtual team, all or part of the team works remotely. Virtual teams work together to meet the project's goals while collaborating via email, conferencing technologies, and instant messaging. The disadvantages of virtual teams include issues with communication, feelings of isolation, collaboration difficulties, and technology costs. The project manager should be aware of these disadvantages and work to help facilitate team communications. Coming up with ways to deal with conflict is also important. Finally, cultural differences may need to be explored if team members are global.

Shared vs. Dedicated

When allocating resources to a project, the project manager must understand the difference between shared and dedicated resources:

- ***Shared resource***: Used jointly between multiple projects. When using shared resources, the project manager will need to negotiate with department managers or other project managers for resource availability. This negotiation may also involve the PMO if one exists. Keep in mind that the type of organization and project team structure (projectized, matrix, or functional) affect resource negotiation.
- ***Dedicated resource***: Allocated to a single project. When using dedicated resources, the project manager has full access to the resource for the project. Core team members are dedicated resources.

EXAMPLE: An IT project requires access to a lab environment that is shared with another department. It may be possible to grant both the project team and the department personnel concurrent access to the lab environment without causing resource contention. However, if a conflict arises, the project manager will need to work with the department supervisor to adjust schedules to give both the project team and the department personnel time in the lab.

Because resource availability may affect project schedules, it is important to identify these resources and document the resource calendar prior to creating the baseline project schedule.

If multiple projects need to share personnel and other resources, each project must rely on the other projects to release resources on time for all projects to succeed. When multiple projects require a particular resource at the same time, it causes ***resource contention***. The organization should have a method for determining project priority when resource contention occurs, including each project's priority, schedule, budget, or other constraint. Some organizations define resource contention guidelines to ensure that all projects follow the same rules when making resource contention decisions.

Gap Analysis

A ***gap analysis*** is a method of comparing actual results or performance (current state) with desired results or performance (end state). The distance between the two states is the gap. Businesses often perform a gap analysis to study operational issues, such as missed sales, or to map growth strategies. In the context of resource management, project managers would use a gap analysis to analyze the project resource's capacity and size to make decisions about budgeting, procurements, features, and staffing. Resources can mean team members, tools/equipment, software, and processes. The results of the gap analysis (the difference between actual vs. desired) are often referred to as the delta.

Gap analysis identifies three main issues with resource deployment: gaps that affect the viability of product features or functionalities, gaps in team member knowledge and/or skills, and gaps in utilization that could lead to over- or under-allocation of both personnel and physical resources. Identifying gaps in knowledge and skills should always be accompanied by strategies to address those gaps through training, mentoring, or coaching.

Because gap analyses can be applied to nearly any aspect of a project, there is no set format. The typical elements of a gap analysis spreadsheet would include the following:

- A description of the focus area (with an optional ID or reference number)
- A description of the current state (such as number of existing resources or existing skill level)

- A description of the desired future state (such as required number of resources or target skill)
- A gap estimate or description
- Proposed remediation (action) to bridge the gap
- A priority assignment (high, medium, or low)
- A start and end date for the action
- An owner for the action
- Resources required to implement the action and close the gap
- A status column
- A column for comments

Figure 2-6 shows a sample feature gap analysis for various project aspects.

Project Name	Abernathy Campus LAN Installation	Project ID	PK0-00501
Project Manager	Shah, M	Date	7/1/2023

Requirement	Available Qty	Required Qty	Gap Δ	Implications/Impact	Priority	Action to Bridge Gap	Owner	Status	Target Date
Firewall/security appliances	10 units	30 units	75%	Project start date delayed ~2 weeks at estimated cost of $10,000/week	High / Medium / Low	Purchase additional units @ $300 ea ($6,000); reduce budget for training (delay rollout)	Winter, E	Not started	12/1/2023
Software licenses									

Skill Description	Current Level	Required Level	Action Plan	Priority	Risk/Reward	Owner	Status	Target Date
Ruby on Rails dev	Basic	Expert	* Release Cody from project work for month of August to attend training * Assign Julie as ROR mentor for 2 weeks	Medium	4-week delay in backlog + cost of training vs. recovering budget allocated to contractor	Lee, C	In progress	9/1/2023

Figure 2-6 Sample Gap Analysis

Feature/Functionality

After performing a gap analysis, a project manager might discover that developing the next feature in the backlog will cause a delay in the release date due to resource contention. The project manager may decide to omit or delay the product feature or functionality from the current sprint until sufficient resources can be obtained. Once the resources are obtained, the team can address that feature or functionality in a future release.

Gap analysis may also reveal a mismatch between an existing feature and actual user demand for the feature, or between a target customer profile and the actual consumers. Plans to address these gaps could be addressed in future sprints. Finally, it can reveal gaps in inventory when actual equipment on hand is surveyed and compared with manifests and inventory registers.

Skills

A gap analysis allows a project manager to make decisions about hiring, outsourcing, and any skills gap within their current project team. The skills gap should begin with a current-state assessment of skills available within the project team or the organization, and it should end with a list of skills required to implement the project, including the project roles. Depending on the schedule and budget, the project manager may decide to hire a temporary team member or an extended team member or to train a current team member to provide the skills needed, each of which will have different costs and risks.

Utilization

A gap analysis will help identify problems with resource utilization. Most projects strive to limit the number of idle resources. A resource that is being used at lower rates than the minimum project usage estimates may be shifted to other project activities, or even to other projects.

A resource shortage occurs when a project does not have enough of a particular resource to complete an activity or task, and a resource overallocation occurs when the project has too much of a particular resource, resulting in leftover inventory or idle team members. A resource shortage usually affects the project schedule because project activities or tasks cannot proceed until more of the missing resources are available. It also affects the project budget because the resources will have a cost. For example, even if missing parts can be scheduled for a same-day delivery, thereby preserving the schedule, the project budget will have to stretch to include any rush delivery costs. A resource overallocation means that more resources were purchased or allocated than needed, usually resulting in wasted budget.

Failing to reallocate an idle resource, or underutilizing a resource, can result in benched resources. This term most often refers to personnel, but it can also refer to any available unused resource. While some reasons for benching a resource may be beyond the control of the project manager, benching should be avoided where possible. If a team member does not have the skills to complete a certain activity or task, another activity or task could be split to include that person, or the team member could be sent to acquire training. Benched personnel may experience low morale, while benched physical resources may occupy space needed by active resources or require ongoing maintenance.

Team Performance Considerations

A goal of effective project leadership is to ensure that the team has a shared ownership, meaning the teams feel invested in and responsible for the outcomes of the project. The team members' skill sets affect team selection and performance, and team members' locations (remote and/or in-house) affect how the team is managed. The project manager also handles personnel removal or replacement on the team and must be able to resolve communication issues and conflicts.

Leadership motivates a team to do the best work possible. There are two types of motivation that can be applied to improve a team's performance: intrinsic and extrinsic. Extrinsic motivation is rewards that can be earned or punishments that can be avoided by displaying a certain act. These are usually tangible benefits like a salary raise, extra vacation days, a bonus, or being called out for honors on the company intranet.

Intrinsic motivation is intangible and often associated with an internal sense of achievement without expecting something in return. Examples are a mastery of new skills, a sense of autonomy and trust, a boost in confidence, and encouraging camaraderie.

Assessing the Team Life Cycle

Team building is a never-ending process. Even after a team matures, team-building efforts should be regularly renewed or continued. The project manager should work with team members to ensure that the team moves through the team-building stages identified in what is known as the Tuckman ladder: forming, storming, norming, performing, and adjourning.

The project manager will need to help the team develop trust in each other to raise morale, lower conflict, and increase the team's efficiency. For that reason, the project manager must have the appropriate skills to manage personnel, including team building and trust building.

In some cases, a team may skip one of these stages. Alternatively, the team may need to return to a previous stage if certain events happen, such as a new team member being added to the team.

- ***Forming***: The team meets and learns about how they will work together in the project. During this stage, team members may not yet be open to trusting each other. The team members focus more on their assigned tasks than communication in this stage.
- ***Storming***: The team starts making decisions about the direction of project work. Because this stage requires collaboration and conflict resolution, team members should be open to differing ideas and perspectives.
- ***Norming***: The team starts working together, and team members adjust their work to support the team as a whole. During this phase, team members start to trust each other.

- ***Performing***: The team starts working as a unit. Team members depend on each other and work through issues easily. This is the most productive stage of the team life cycle.
- ***Adjourning***: The team completes the project. Team members are released to other projects once the project closes.

Maintaining Project Momentum

Project managers are responsible for maintaining project momentum through leadership. A variety of leadership styles can be used, including autocratic, democratic, directive, participative, and supportive. Leaders should keep an eye on the team and its progress. In moments of chaos, project managers should adopt a directive style rather than a collaborative style to maintain momentum. If team momentum lags over a particularly difficult activity, the project manager may identify quick and easy wins to build momentum. For example, if team members complete a particularly grueling sprint in an Agile project and are approaching burnout, the project manager might choose a much easier activity to complete in the next sprint to turn momentum back in the right direction.

Providing Project Team Performance Feedback

Project managers must be leaders and should adopt a servant leadership style that focuses on understanding and addressing team members' needs and development. In addition, project managers should encourage and guide team members. Team member successes should be recognized and celebrated throughout the duration of project work, especially when team members demonstrate dedication, innovation, problem-solving, adaptation, service to others, and learning. Recognizing these achievements on an ongoing basis, rather than just at the end of the project, is also a key factor in team motivation.

Roles and Responsibilities

Project roles describe the skills required to perform project work and the responsibilities of the team members. Each project includes project roles that are responsible for certain project tasks or performance areas and have predetermined levels of authority and project involvement. Every project will have a project sponsor, a project manager (who might be the product owner in Agile environments), stakeholders, and a project team. Some organizations have a central project management office to provide guidance and resources.

Some roles are specific to IT projects, such as developers and architects. Some roles are specific to Agile-style projects but not present in Waterfall projects, or they have differently defined responsibilities depending on whether the project framework is Agile-based or process-based. Not all projects will include each of these roles. However, you will need to be familiar with the primary responsibilities of all of these roles for the Project+ exam. This section discusses all of the roles and the responsibilities that can be involved in a project.

> **NOTE** Several of the roles explained in the upcoming sections were previously introduced in Chapter 1, "Project Characteristics, Methodologies, and Frameworks," in the context of Agile environments. They are redefined here as a study aid and so that the student can more clearly compare roles across different project frameworks.

Functional/Extended vs. Operational/Core Team Members

This chapter introduced functional, projectized, and matrix organizations. These organizational structures affect how team members are allocated to a project. In projectized organizations, team members work only on project activities and do not have functional job duties. ***Core team members*** share equal ownership of the project roadmap. For IT projects, they are typically a company's in-house developers. Some standards refer to core team members as ***operational team members***, meaning they are part of the project's core operations.

An ***extended team member*** is acquired from another organization or department to augment the core team for the duration of the project's needs. They may also be called ***functional team members***. Extended team members are usually acquired to provide specific skills or subject matter expertise that the core team lacks. They take ownership at the project task level and may be added to address the product backlog.

While extended team members are sourced from other countries, they differ from outsourced labor in that project managers do not direct an outsourced team's work; instead, they acquire the end result of that work through a procurement. An extended team member is a temporary or long-term remote team member who interacts daily with the core team. In functional organizations, they may be team members allocated to the project's work for a specified number of hours.

Extended team members benefit a project by bringing unique skills or supplying manpower that core team members cannot provide. However, they leave the project team after completing their work or reaching a project milestone. Core team members may move from project to project while remaining on the same team, forming a stronger working relationship and reaching higher levels of performance.

Sponsor

The ***project sponsor***, also referred to as the project champion, is the individual or organization that authorizes the project. The sponsor is responsible for providing funding for the project and establishing the project charter, project baseline, and high-level requirements. Ultimate control of the project lies with the project sponsor, who is also responsible for marketing the project across the organization to ensure stakeholder buy-in. The sponsor must document all project roadblocks and work with the project manager to alleviate them. The sponsor completes the business case/justification for the project and selects or approves the project manager. The sponsor may or may not be a member of senior management.

In most cases, the project sponsor must be consulted for any potential project changes. The sponsor authorizes or provides all resources and is responsible for canceling or formally closing the project.

The project sponsor is a mandatory role.

Stakeholders

Every project has stakeholders. A project ***stakeholder*** is any individual, group, or organization with a vested interest in the success or outcome of a project. Stakeholders provide input and project requirements to the project manager and have the largest effect on the scope of the project. They also provide project steering and expertise. In Agile, project stakeholders generate user stories to capture new requirements or features and provide continuous feedback on project work.

The stakeholder role can and frequently does overlap with other project roles. Some stakeholders are external, such as vendors, suppliers, and customers, while internal stakeholders could be the project's sponsor, team members, and the product owner. Stakeholders will be documented in the stakeholder register, along with their roles, level of knowledge, and project expectations.

Obviously, not every stakeholder is equally involved in the project or has the same power over its outcome. The process of identifying stakeholders and assessing their levels of interest, power, and authority over the project is done during project initiation, which is covered in Chapter 9, "Project Life Cycles, Discovery/Concept Preparation Phase, and Initiating Phase Activities."

The project manager should determine the best communication method to use with each stakeholder. Managing stakeholder expectations is a key task for the project manager because not every expectation will be achievable. In fact, one stakeholder's expectation may be directly opposite to another's. For this reason, the project manager will need interpersonal skills to negotiate with stakeholders to determine which expectations are attainable and ensure the project's success.

Senior Management

Senior management consists of the higher-level executives of the organization sponsoring the project, if it is outsourced, or performing the project, if it is in-house. They may or may not be identified stakeholders. Senior management is primarily concerned with managing risk for the organization and ensuring that projects achieve value in line with business objectives, so project managers may be required to seek their approval for high-cost procurements and high-risk activities. They may sit on the change control board (CCB) to weigh in on changes that affect the project's schedule, budget, or scope. Senior management sets the organization's risk appetite, which determines how much loss or uncertainty the organization can bear in the pursuit of value.

Program Manager

The ***program manager*** oversees groups of projects, called a program, that are linked through a common organizational goal. The program manager works to make sure the program is aligned with the organization's larger strategy. The program manager handles major program scope changes, optimizes the use of shared resources across all projects, and manages risks and interdependencies among projects.

The program manager role may sometimes be handled by a PMO, discussed in the next section.

Project Management Office

The ***project management office (PMO)*** provides project management governance (including standards and practices) and ensures that resources, methods, tools, and techniques are shared or coordinated across all projects. The PMO sets deliverables, key performance indicators, and other project parameters. It also outlines the consequences of non-performance and provides standard documentation and templates. This is an optional project role that appears more in large organizations.

PMOs support, control, or direct projects. Supportive PMOs supply projects with access to the project knowledge base and exercise low-level project control. Controlling PMOs provide the same access but also require compliance with established PMO standards and processes, exercising moderate project control. Directive PMOs directly manage all projects and exercise high-level project control.

The PMO supports project managers by identifying and developing project management standards, managing shared resources, monitoring compliance, and coordinating communication.

Project Manager

The ***project manager (PM)*** is the individual selected by the sponsor to lead the project team. Project managers do not oversee functional departments or manage daily operations. Their responsibility is to lead the team performing the project work. The project manager is the project linchpin, anchoring all project processes and acting as a liaison between the project team members, other managers, the PMO, governing bodies, the project sponsors, senior management, and stakeholders.

The project manager is responsible for ensuring that the project is a success. Project managers should assess project needs, task needs, and team needs, using these assessments strategically to guide the project toward its goal. A project manager must have project management knowledge and experience and must know how to accomplish the project goals. Finally, the project manager must have personality characteristics, interpersonal skills, and leadership skills to lead the project team effectively.

The project manager must manage the team, communication, scope, risks, budget, time, and quality assurance for the project. All project documentation and artifacts are the responsibility of the project manager.

The project manager must communicate appropriately with all project stakeholders but is ultimately accountable to the project's sponsor. Project managers may report to a functional manager, depending on the structure of the organization.

The project manager is a mandatory role.

Project Coordinator

The ***project coordinator*** is an optional role that supports the project manager by coordinating activities, resources, equipment, and information. They may schedule resources, help check the quality of deliverables, and help with project documentation and administrative support. Their primary focus is project implementation and cross-functional coordination of all project tasks. If the project coordinator cannot resolve an issue, the coordinator will escalate the issue to the project manager.

Some organizations use project coordinators when multiple projects must share resources. This type of project coordinator helps resolve issues regarding shared resources.

The project coordinator role is not mandatory, meaning that projects can succeed without filling this role.

Project Scheduler

A ***project scheduler*** develops and maintains the project schedule and works to ensure that resources are available when needed. This individual determines schedule, cost, and resource deviations through trend analysis and earned value management, thereby reporting on schedule performance. The scheduler gathers a real-time task status from resources, monitors project milestones, communicates any schedule changes, and takes an active role in all project meetings.

Depending on the project and organization size, this role may or may not be separate from the roles of project manager or project coordinator. In some projects the project scheduler is not a separate role, and the project manager completes these tasks.

Project Team

Project team members contribute project expertise and deliverables according to the project schedule. They can estimate task durations and dependencies and help resolve issues. It is the project manager's responsibility to ensure all team members have the right expertise and can work well together.

Some of the criteria used by the project manager to select project team members may include availability, cost, experience, ability, knowledge, skills, attitude, and location factors.

> **NOTE** While the next three roles—product manager, product owner, and scrum master—were introduced in the prior chapter, they are covered here to illustrate how they differ from other, more traditional project roles.

Product Manager

Product managers, introduced in Chapter 1, keep the product roadmap accurate and aligned with current project work. In Waterfall environments, the product manager is the person who owns the product scope, advocates for the product, and represents the customer to the internal stakeholders and the project team. The product manager is usually a job title.

Product Owner

The product owner, introduced in Chapter 1, is a role found in Agile environments. The product owner is the Agile product's key stakeholder and provides the overall vision for the product. This role is responsible for prioritizing the order of work, managing the budget, accepting deliverables, and setting release dates. Waterfall environments do not use a product owner role. The product owner role functions in many ways like a traditional project manager does in process-driven environments.

Scrum Master

The scrum master, introduced in Chapter 1, is a scrum-specific role that enforces scrum policies while maintaining the team's focus on project design. Unlike a traditional project manager or a product owner, the scrum master does not assign work to team members or direct the project's strategy. Instead, the scrum master blocks outside distractions or removes internal complications that impede project work. The scrum master also helps translate stakeholder needs into project requirements. The scrum master's goal is to keep the team actively moving forward and on track.

Testers/Quality Assurance Specialists

In IT projects, ***testers*** conduct both manual and automated tests of software products and deliverables. Testers need to find all the bugs in final products and document the issues so that the developers can fix the defects before the product or project is released. In Waterfall environments, testing is performed as part of monitoring and controlling as the project work approaches closing; in Agile, testing is an iterative process performed after every sprint. ***Quality assurance (QA) specialists*** verify that the quality system is implemented correctly and conduct quality assurance audits on project deliverables.

Business Analyst

The ***business analyst*** role is concerned with producing the most business value from the project. The analyst helps the Agile product owner determine which elements of the backlog need to be revised, deleted, or produced to create the most marketable product. This role is strategic and concerned with finding the best way to present the project's end result to the marketplace.

Subject Matter Expert

A ***subject matter expert (SME)*** can be a stakeholder, a team member, or an outside consultant with the necessary background and experience to give feedback on aspects of the project that are outside of the project manager's wheelhouse. SMEs can help resolve a project issue or identify and gauge the best response to a project's risk. During project planning, they can help estimate necessary costs or task durations as well as identify resources that will need to be acquired or modified. Finally, they provide expert judgment and analysis during change control.

Architect

The Agile role of ***architect*** is responsible for defining the technical environment, such as the operating system or software architecture, that will best support the product being built for an IT project. This process is referred to as solution design. The architect sources or designs the architecture based on user requirements and stakeholder input, verifies its implementation, and supports the developers who use it in project work. The architect may fill the role of enterprise architect, systems analyst, data architect, or strategist.

Developers/Engineers

One of the most important roles in IT projects, the ***developer*** or ***engineer***, takes the requirements and creates the code that becomes the work product. The development teams in Agile projects are very similar to those in Waterfall projects. Development team skills may include product design, code writing, code testing, and user interface specialist. In Agile projects, they perform work sprints, as per the requirements, and attend the daily scrum meeting. The developer role works closely with testers, as a single defect can negatively affect the entire project from the very beginning.

End Users

End users are the intended recipient of the finished product or project outcome. For IT projects, these would be the app, website, or software users, whether for internal customers (such as help desk staff) or retail customers. End users are typically the stakeholders with the least amount of influence over the project's outcome.

Exam Preparation Tasks

As mentioned in the section "How to Use This Book" in the Introduction, you have a few choices for exam preparation: the exercises here, Chapter 17, "Final Preparation," and the exam simulation questions included in the Pearson Test Prep Software Online.

Review All Key Topics

Review the most important topics in this chapter, noted with the Key Topics icon in the outer margin of the page. Table 2-3 lists each reference of these key topics and the page number on which each is found.

Table 2-3 Key Topics for Chapter 2

Key Topic Element	Description	Page Number
Table 2-2	Influence of Project Team Structures on Projects	41
Paragraph	Functional organizational structure	41
Paragraph	Projectized organizational structure	42
Paragraph	Matrix organizational structure	43
Paragraph	The resource life cycle	45
Paragraph	Successor planning	47
List	Types of resources needed for a project	48
Paragraph	Human resources	49
Paragraph	Physical resources	50
Paragraph	Capital resources	50
Paragraph	Internal resources versus external resources	51
Paragraph	Shared resources versus dedicated resources	51
Paragraph	Gap analysis	52
List	Features of a typical gap analysis	52
Figure 2-6	Sample Gap Analysis	53
Paragraph	Team performance considerations	54
Paragraph	Stages of the team life cycle	55
Paragraph	Maintaining project momentum	56
Paragraph	Providing project team performance feedback	56
Paragraph	Functional/Extended vs. operational/core team members	57
Paragraph	Project sponsor	58
Paragraph	Stakeholders	58
Paragraph	Senior management	59
Paragraph	Program manager	59
Paragraph	Project management office (PMO)	59
Paragraph	Project manager (PM)	60
Paragraph	Product manager	61
Paragraph	Product owner	61
Paragraph	Scrum master	62

Key Topic Element	Description	Page Number
Paragraph	Testers/Quality assurance (QA) specialists	62
Paragraph	Business Analyst	62
Paragraph	Subject matter expert (SME)	62
Paragraph	Architect	62
Paragraph	Developers/Engineers	63
Paragraph	End users	63

Define Key Terms

Define the following key terms from this chapter and check your answers in the glossary:

resource management, functional team structure, functional manager, projectized team structure, matrix team structure, resource life cycle, needs assessment, resource breakdown structure, end-of-life software, successor planning, human resources, negotiated resources, physical resources, resource allocation, capital resources, external resources, internal resources, shared resource, dedicated resource, resource contention, gap analysis, forming, storming, project roles, core team members, operational team members, extended team member, functional team members, project sponsor, stakeholder, senior management, program manager, project management office (PMO), project manager (PM), project coordinator, project scheduler, project team, product managers, testers, quality assurance (QA) specialists, business analyst, subject matter expert (SME), architect, developer, engineer, end users

Review Questions

The answers to these questions appear in Appendix A. For more practice with sample exam questions, use the Pearson Test Prep practice test software online.

1. What is the correct order for the trust-building stages of a project team?
   a. Storming, forming, norming, performing, adjourning
   b. Storming, forming, performing, norming, adjourning
   c. Forming, storming, norming, performing, adjourning
   d. Forming, storming, performing, norming, adjourning

2. Which of the following are disadvantages of using virtual teams? (Choose all that apply.)

    a. Communication issues

    b. Feeling isolated

    c. Collaboration difficulties

    d. Technology costs

3. Your organization has completed a formal project charter and preliminary budget for a new retail app. You need to obtain formal approval of the budget. From whom should you obtain approval?

    a. Stakeholders

    b. Business analyst

    c. Sponsor

    d. Senior management

4. Which project team structure gives project managers the least authority over resources?

    a. Projectized

    b. Strong matrix

    c. Functional

    d. Weak matrix

5. You have been asked to create the project documents for an upcoming project to remodel one of your company's buildings. You will also be responsible for project success and overseeing the project scope, schedule, budget, project team, stakeholders, and quality of the project. Which project role will you fill?

    a. Stakeholder

    b. Product manager

    c. Sponsor

    d. Project manager

6. You are the project manager for a project to set up a new web server and decommission the old server. You are responsible for selecting the appropriate personnel for the project team. Which of the following would *not* be a responsibility for these team members?

    a. Creating the project schedule

b. Contributing expertise to the project

c. Estimating task duration

d. Estimating task costs

7. Which of the following individuals could be identified as a stakeholder for a project? (Choose all that apply.)

    a. The project's sponsor

    b. The customer who commissioned the project's outcome

    c. The vendor who will supply materials for the project

    d. The end user for whom the project is being developed

8. Which Agile project role is responsible for generating user stories to capture new requirements?

    a. Product manager

    b. Product owner

    c. Scrum master

    d. Stakeholder

9. Which of the following is *not* a resource type that would concern a project manager?

    a. Human resource

    b. Capital resource

    c. Tangible resource

    d. Physical resource

10. A key team member who has been with the company for 18 years announces their retirement. You immediately allocate two resources from another department to fill their job role in the short term. What has occurred?

    a. Resource overallocation

    b. Resource shortage

    c. Resource contention

    d. Succession plan

This chapter covers the following topics:

- **Project-Specific Change Control:** Create/receive change requests, document requests in the change control log, conduct preliminary reviews, conduct impact assessments, document change recommendations, determine decision-makers, escalate to the change control board (CCB) if applicable, document the status of approval in the change control log, communicate the change status, update project plan, implement the change, validate the change implementation, and communicate the change deployment
- **Project Change Management:** Manage product change vs. project change, manage scope creep/scope change, and understand the impact of constraints, influences, and common sources of project change

CHAPTER 3

Change Control Process Throughout the Project Life Cycle

Changes to a project occur for a variety of reasons—some desirable, some not—but even a beneficial change can impede a project if it is not correctly managed. Any request to change the project's parameters can make it more challenging to keep the rest of project work within its previously planned constraints. If a change is approved, but not properly documented and communicated—or, worse, implemented without approval—it can force other, unplanned changes by stealing the time, resources, or funds that were allocated to other deliverables. For this reason, it is important for the project team and stakeholders to follow a formal change control process coordinated by the project manager. Change control is ongoing and takes place throughout project execution.

The changes that must be controlled are those requested by a team member, stakeholder, or sponsor and that modify a critical facet of the project, such as its scope, schedule, or budget. Uncontrolled change can result in scope creep. By contrast, scope change is a planned feature of each sprint, iteration, or increment in Agile projects, or an artifact of the change control process in Waterfall projects.

While formal change control is mostly associated with predictive environments, incremental and Agile-based projects require change management as well. This chapter explains the steps in the change control process and the difference between managing *product* changes versus managing *project* changes. It also covers the concepts of project constraints and influences, which affect all aspects of a project from initiation until close, and common categories of project change.

NOTE This chapter refers to activities that occur in specific phases of the project life cycle, such as the Planning phase and the Executing phase. Project life-cycle phases are covered in Chapter 9, "Project Life Cycles, Discovery/Concept Preparation Phase, and Initiating Phase Activities."

This chapter covers the following objective for the CompTIA Project+ exam:

1.3 Given a scenario, apply the change control process throughout the project life cycle.

"Do I Know This Already?" Quiz

The "Do I Know This Already?" quiz allows you to assess whether you should read this entire chapter thoroughly or jump to the "Exam Preparation Tasks" section. If you are in doubt about your answers to these questions or your own assessment of your knowledge of the topics, read the entire chapter. Table 3-1 lists the major headings in this chapter and their corresponding "Do I Know This Already?" quiz questions. You can find the answers in Appendix A, "Answers to the 'Do I Know This Already?' Questions and Review Quizzes."

Table 3-1 "Do I Know This Already?" Section-to-Question Mapping

Foundation Topics Section	Questions
Project-Specific Change Control	1–6
Project Change Management	7–10

CAUTION The goal of self-assessment is to gauge your mastery of the topics in this chapter. If you do not know the answer to a question or are only partially sure of the answer, you should mark that question as wrong for the purposes of the self-assessment. Giving yourself credit for an answer you correctly guess skews your self-assessment results and might provide you with a false sense of security.

1. Three months into a project, a stakeholder wants to add a new feature to the application being developed. The project sponsor approves the scope change and expands the project budget. The project manager extends the schedule to accommodate the extra work. What is this an example of?
   a. Triple constraint
   b. Constraint reprioritization
   c. Scope creep
   d. Change request
2. During which phase(s) of the project life cycle does formal change control occur?
   a. Planning phase
   b. Initiating phase

c. Executing phase

d. All of these phases

3. When should a project manager formally communicate with stakeholders during the change control process? (Choose all that apply.)

    a. When the change request is received

    b. When the initial impact assessment is complete

    c. When the change has been approved or denied

    d. When the change has been implemented

    e. After the change has been deployed and validated

4. What should you do *first* after receiving a change request?

    a. Notify the change approval authority of the upcoming request.

    b. Develop a regression plan.

    c. Evaluate the impact of the change and provide justification.

    d. Identify the change and document the change request.

5. Which entity is most likely to be the approval authority for a change request?

    a. Project sponsor

    b. Senior management

    c. Change control board

    d. Project manager

6. What is the purpose of a regression plan?

    a. To ensure the project sponsor understands the impact of the change

    b. To ensure the project can be rolled back to a prior state

    c. To rebaseline the project schedule after a change is approved

    d. To ensure that all steps required for the change are documented

7. Which of the following is an example of scope creep?

    a. A data center project is $100,000 over budget and 6 months behind schedule because the project sponsor requested 10 additional server racks.

    b. A company has recently experienced financial troubles and requested project budget cuts that result in a lengthened schedule. When originally started, the project needed to be completed as quickly as possible.

c. During project planning, the project sponsor for a new construction project requests that fiber-optic cabling be installed instead of CAT 6 cabling.

d. A project stakeholder requests that a module be added to an application to allow filtered views. This request is approved.

8. What would be the most likely cause of scope creep for an Agile project?

   a. Business requirements for the product are changed after the sprint begins.

   b. New features are added to the backlog during a sprint.

   c. The customer reprioritizes product features after the sprint begins.

   d. The customer requests rework of a deliverable during a sprint.

9. In response to market events, the product owner wants to shorten the development timeline so that the minimally viable product (MVP) is produced 2 weeks earlier than was planned. What is this an example of?

   a. Scope creep

   b. Product change

   c. Project change

   d. Scope change

10. Which factors are referred to as the *triple constraint*?

    a. Scope, time, cost

    b. Resources, time, scope

    c. Time, requirements, quality

    d. Cost, resources, quality

Foundation Topics

Project-Specific Change Control

A ***change request*** is a formal proposal to modify any part of a project's critical success factors, including the *project scope* (requirements), the schedule, the budget (such as the cost baseline), the available resources, the quality of the deliverables, or the acceptance criteria. Any project team member or stakeholder may request a change.

The ***change control*** process is a defined procedure for reviewing change requests, estimating their impact, approving changes, managing the changes, and communicating them throughout the process. These steps should be recorded in the ***change management plan***, along with the responsible roles and templates for the required forms. All stakeholders should be made aware that a change management process is in place and should know the correct method of filing a change request. The change management plan is developed during project planning and is a part of the overall project management plan. It is also referred to as the change control plan.

Managing change is ultimately the responsibility of the project manager, although other project roles may hold approval authority. Remember, a change remains a request until it is approved.

No matter how an organization tailors its process, all formal change control should include these steps:

1. Receive or create the change request.
2. Document the requested change in the change control log.
3. Conduct a preliminary review.
4. Conduct impact assessments.
5. Document change recommendations from experts.
6. Determine the decision-makers.
7. Escalate the request to the change control board (CCB), if applicable.
8. Document the status of the approval in the change control log.
9. Communicate the change status.
10. Update the project plan.
11. Implement the changes.
12. Validate the change implementation.
13. Communicate the change deployment to relevant project stakeholders.

NOTE The only type of change that could circumvent the change control process would be an emergency change. However, an emergency change should still be documented in the change log after the fact and communicated to the change control board and stakeholders. The change management plan should include a procedure for rapid approval of emergency changes.

Create/Receive Change Requests

All change requests should be submitted in writing. If they are communicated verbally to the project manager, they should be transcribed. The change request template (see an example in Figure 3-1) is part of the change management plan. Although the details may vary based on the project and the organization's structure, a change request form should contain at minimum the following components:

- Project name and project manager
- Change request date
- Change control identifier (ID)
- Name of person requesting the change
- Details of the proposed change, such as a description of the change, business justification, priority level, and assumptions surrounding the change
- Results and estimates of change analysis from the project manager, including any effects to scope, schedule, and/or budget
- Sign-off from project manager after analysis
- Sign-off from CCB or relevant decision-maker after approval/denial

Document Requests in the Change Control Log

The ***change control log*** (sometimes called a ***change log***) is a running list of changes requested during the project. It should include the change ID, the date of the request, the category of change and its description, the requestor, the approval status, and comments regarding the approval or implementation (see Figure 3-2 for an example). The project manager, team members, CCB members, and sponsor should all have access to the change control log. All change requests should remain logged, even if they are rejected or deferred.

Change Request Template (Example)

This form is divided into three sections. Section 1 is intended for use by the individual submitting the change request. Section 2 is intended for use by the Project Manager to document/communicate their initial impact analysis of the requested change. Section 3 is intended for use by the Change Control Board (CCB) to document their final decision regarding the requested change.

1) Submitter—General Information				
CR#	*CR001*			
Type of CR	☐ Enhancement	☐ Defect		
Project/Program/Initiative				
Submitter Name	*John Doe*			
Brief Description of Request	*Enter a detailed description of the change being requested.*			
Date Submitted	*mm/dd/yyyy*			
Date Required	*mm/dd/yyyy*			
Priority	☐ Low	☐ Medium	☐ High	☐ Mandatory
Reason for Change	*Enter a detailed description of why the change is being requested.*			
Other Artifacts Impacted	*List other artifacts affected by this change.*			
Assumptions and Notes	*Document assumptions or comments regarding the requested change.*			
Comments	*Enter additional comments.*			
Attachments or References	☐ Yes	☐ No		
	Link:			
Approval Signature	*Approval Signature*		Date Signed	*mm/dd/yyyy*

2) Project Manager—Initial Analysis				
Hour Impact	*#hrs*	*Enter the hour impact of the requested change.*		
Duration Impact	*#days*	*Enter the duration impact of the requested change.*		
Schedule Impact	*WBS*	*Detail the impact this change may have on schedules.*		
Cost Impact	*Cost*	*Detail the impact this change may have on cost.*		
Comments	*Enter additional comments.*			
Recommendations	*Enter recommendations regarding the requested change.*			
Approval Signature	*Approval Signature*		Date Signed	*mm/dd/yyyy*

3) Change Control Board—Decision				
Decision	☐ Approved	☐ Approved with Conditions	☐ Rejected	☐ More Info
Decision Date	*mm/dd/yyyy*			
Decision Explanation	*Document the CCB's decision.*			
Conditions	*Document any conditions imposed by the CCB.*			
Approval Signature	*Approval Signature*		Date Signed	*mm/dd/yyyy*

Figure 3-1 Example of a Change Request Template

Change Control Log							
Project:						**Date:**	
Change No.	**Change Type**	**Description of Change**	**Requestor**	**Date Submitted**	**Date Approved**	**Status**	**Comments**
Each change request is assigned a reference number.	This may be a design, scope, schedule, or other type of change.	The change request should be described in detail.	Who initiated the change request?	When was the request submitted?	When was the request approved?	Is the change request open, closed, or pending? Has it been approved, denied, or deferred?	This section may describe why the change request was rejected or deferred, or provide any other useful information.

Change Control Log							
Project: Network Upgrade Project						**Date:** 04/01/20xx	
Change No.	**Change Type**	**Description of Change**	**Requestor**	**Date Submitted**	**Date Approved**	**Status**	**Comments**
CR001	Design/Scope	The change request calls for replacing existing Asus routers with Cisco routers.	R. Smith	3/25/2023	N/A	Denied	This request was denied by the change control board because adequate funding is not available for the purchase of new routers, and because the request is outside the project's scope.
CR002	Schedule	This change request calls for delaying the existing schedule by one week to ensure that all applications are backed up, which was not considered in the original project plan.	S. Black	3/26/2023	04/10/2023	Approved	This request was approved to ensure the security and continuity of all applications. One week will be added to the project schedule, and the project manager will communicate the impact of this change to all stakeholders.
CR003	Design/Scope	This change request calls for modifying existing network firewalls to add intrusion-detection systems to enhance network security.	M. Reed	3/27/2023	N/A	Deferred	This request was deferred and is pending a determination of the impact to the project's costs, schedule, and scope.

Figure 3-2 Example of a Change Control Log

Conduct a Preliminary Review

During the preliminary review, the project manager identifies all areas of the project that would be affected by the change, such as cost baselines and schedules. The purpose of this initial review is to gather all of the factors needed for the impact analysis so the approver can make the best business decision regarding the change. It may be necessary to meet with the change requestor to request more details or add clarification. If any elements are missing, the impact assessment will be less accurate.

To evaluate the change and identify all project components it would affect, the project manager could solicit feedback from subject matter experts (SMEs) and/or from the team members most familiar with the tasks.

Conduct Impact Assessments

The same tools used to estimate project work should be used for the ***impact assessment***. A change might affect the project's scope, schedule, budget, quality, resources, risks, communication, procurements, and/or stakeholders. First, the project manager should identify any changes to requirements that result directly or indirectly from the change. Next, the project manager should work with the project team to define new work packages and forecast the work hours and resources (including budget, materials, and team members) needed to implement the change. Those forecasts can be used to draft new schedules, scope definitions, and/or budgets, which should be applied to the existing baselines. The changes to the baselines will help provide the most accurate estimate of the requested change's cost and impact.

The impact assessment should include a risk assessment that identifies new project risks or alterations to existing project risks generated from the change. This assessment should also account for changes that reduce existing project risk, such as changing vendors to hire a more stable service provider. Both the project manager and skilled team members who work in the area affected by the change should perform the assessments. The impact assessment should also document the estimated risks and outcome of *not* making the requested change.

Develop a Regression Plan (Optional)

In some cases, even after a change is evaluated and approved, it may be necessary to return to the project state prior to the incorporation of the change. For this reason, the project manager should create a ***regression plan***, which details the process whereby an approved change can be reversed. Regression plans are particularly important for IT projects where existing deliverables (such as the initial release of an application) may be negatively affected by a change.

EXAMPLE: A jewelry company is developing a mobile application that will allow customers to design custom jewelry pieces. The initial release of the application will require customers to visit one of the company's stores to complete their purchase in person. A module that enables in-app purchasing will be added in a later release. In case the shopping cart interferes with the jewelry design module, the software development team should have a regression plan to ensure that changes can be rolled back quickly.

Document Change Recommendations

Once the impact assessment is complete, the project manager should document the outcomes and make a formal change recommendation to implement, delay, or reject the change request. This recommendation is documented in the change request form, not the change control log, and must receive the project manager's sign-off before being forwarded to the decision-maker(s). The recommendation should include the names of any people who contributed their expertise.

Determine Decision-Makers

The decision-maker for a given change will vary based on the project or organization. Some projects or organizations will use a CCB as the decision-maker, while some may use the sponsor or the largest stakeholder as the authority. Others may allocate the decision-making authority based on the aspect of the project that is most affected by the change. For example, the business analyst might approve changes that affect a product's marketability, while the chief financial officer (CFO) might be the final authority for approving changes that increase the project's cost. If approval authority is conditional, the conditions for approval should be recorded in the change management plan. Here are some sample conditions:

- The project manager can approve changes that affect the schedule by less than 2 weeks and/or the budget by less than $10,000 without escalation.
- The change control board must approve changes that affect the budget by more than $10,000 or delay the timeline by more than 2 weeks.
- The project sponsor must approve changes that add or remove a requirement to the project.

If the organization does not have a CCB, the product owner (in Agile projects) or the sponsor (in predictive projects) is usually the designated decision-maker.

Escalate to the Change Control Board (CCB), If Applicable

Larger organizations usually have an established ***change control board (CCB)*** to act as the decision-maker. Ideally, the CCB is a cross-functional group that represents each business process. The CCB makes the decision to accept or reject a change during its monthly meeting. In theory, the only role that can overrule the CCB's decision is the project sponsor. This rarely happens in practice because the CCB usually includes the project sponsor or someone from the sponsoring organization who has expert knowledge regarding the reasons behind approving or denying changes. If the project sponsor is not a member of the CCB, the project manager probably will need to obtain the sponsor's approval as well as the CCB's.

Document the Status of Approval in the Change Control Log

After the change is approved or rejected, the project manager needs to make sure the change log reflects its disposition. Formal sign-offs help to keep expectations aligned and to minimize potential disputes. The change entry in the change control log (refer to Figure 3-2) should be updated with the approval status. The log should also note who was assigned the task of implementing the approved change.

If not approved or denied, a change request can also be deferred for later consideration. If the decision-making authority chooses to defer a change request, the usual response is to give a conditional approval. ("If a certain thing happens, we will approve this change. If not, the change will not be implemented.") All of these conditions should be added to the change control log.

Communicate the Change Status

The project sponsor, the change requestor (if not the sponsor), and affected stakeholders should be informed of the change's status using the method outlined in the change management plan. The change log should always be accessible to project members.

It is important to note that changes should be communicated even when they are not approved. This ensures that the requestor understands the change request resolution and the team members know not to implement the change request, even if requested privately at a later date.

EXAMPLE: A project team works from multiple locations, and team members communicate with each other via weekly video conferences. A project stakeholder requests a feature change in an application that the team is developing. During the formal change control process, the change is denied. The next week, the stakeholder mentions the requested change during a call with one of the application developers. After the call, the developer decides that coding this feature would not affect the schedule, and he implements the code. If the project manager had shared the change log with the entire team, all team members (including the application developer) would have known that the change request was denied.

Update the Project Plan

If a change is approved to become part of the project, the project manager must update the project management documentation, including the baselines, schedules, and subsidiary project plans. Figure 10-4 shows how the change control plan and subsidiary management plans interact. If a baseline must be revised, the revision should show only the changes from the current time going forward. Baseline data prior to the change should be retained. Change logs should also become part of the lessons learned documentation and retained in the project archives.

The project manager should perform a project audit at this point to verify the project is on track. Audit results should be documented and communicated with the project sponsor, stakeholders, and team. If the change is to be performed at a future stage in the project schedule, it might also be necessary to add the change to the risk register in case something occurs to prevent it from being implemented.

Keep in mind that at this point the project probably has multiple versions of some project documents. It is critical to implement version control for all documentation. In most cases, this means using version numbers and providing a chronological listing at the beginning or end of each document that summarizes the changes made. Some organizations take this tracking a step further and retain all historical versions of product documentation. Chapter 9 discusses records management in the project and in the organization.

Implement Changes

Not until all relevant project documents are updated, and the change status is communicated, will it be time for the team members to actually implement the change in the project work. The project manager should ensure that team members understand how the change will be implemented and how it will affect other aspects of their deliverables. The ultimate effects of the change depend on the type of change being implemented. (Change types are discussed later in this chapter.)

Validate the Change Implementation

After going live, the change still needs to be validated against the revised scope and the applicable quality measurements. A team member or SME may be the one to perform validation, such as smoke testing, but it is the project manager's responsibility to ensure the change was implemented correctly and matches the approved parameters. The project manager should also perform quality assurance to ensure that the change did not have a negative effect on project quality. Quality assurance is covered in Chapter 6, "Quality, Cost, and Performance Management."

Validation is particularly important in IT projects where changes may affect code that has already been formally tested, approved, and baselined. It may be necessary to recertify or rebaseline the entire module. If the change created issues in existing deliverables, the regression plan should be used to return the project to its previous state, and the project manager should revisit the change for rework.

Communicate Change Deployment

The change requestor, the CCB, team members, and relevant stakeholders should all be notified once the change is validated using the communication methods in the change management plan and/or the project communication plan. This step may involve demonstrating a new functionality to stakeholders. The change deployment can also be communicated in regular meetings like the weekly project meeting. The announcement should be tailored to the relevancy or urgency of each stakeholder's need to know.

EXAMPLE: The CCB approved a request to add a book ordering functionality to an application being developed for municipal library systems. The change was requested by the project sponsor. According to the change management plan, the project manager should notify the project sponsor by phone when the change is live. The sales team should be notified by email that the application's features have changed and be provided with updated collateral. The CCB can be notified during the next meeting of the board.

Project Change Management

Not all changes that occur in a project are a result of formal change requests. Some arise from risks, issues, or natural project variance, such as differences between estimated and actual effort to complete a task or the projected and actual delivery dates for a procurement.

The project manager needs to control certain changes, including schedule changes, stakeholder changes, resource changes, and budget changes. No matter which type of change occurs, the project manager is responsible for ensuring that the change is properly documented and communicated to the appropriate project entities.

Product Change vs. Project Change

Because the end result for a predictive project is defined before project work even begins and is codified in multiple documents, including the project charter, it is easy to see how a change can knock over a line of dominos if not compensated for by a careful rebalancing of constraints. However, iterative and adaptive projects are flexible by nature and built to incorporate a rapid continual replacement of the goal posts. How, then, does product change management differ from project change management?

Product change refers to the changes to the definition or features of the finished product that are produced through sprints. Each product may include multiple projects over its life cycle—from the initial creation project, to feature-add projects, to revision projects. *Product* changes may or may not create *project* changes. A product change in Agile may not affect current project work but will simply be added to the backlog. Changes may also occur to portions of the product that fall outside the current project's scope.

By contrast, a project change is any change that significantly affects the trajectory of the project currently underway. In traditional project management, any change that will affect a critical success factor or one of the triple constraints (covered later in this chapter) is a project change by default.

EXAMPLE: Your project is creating a multi-city reservation feature for enterprise-level customers of a car rental agency's mobile app. Your project is not affected by a proposed product change to add motorcycle rentals to the agency's consumer rental division.

EXAMPLE: Your project is creating a multi-city reservation feature for all users of a car rental agency's mobile app. The car rental agency wants to add motorcycle rentals in the next 9 months. You must assess the requirements and prioritize the new features in the backlog so that the reservation data fields will accommodate the new vehicle type once the rentals are rolled out to customers. The product change does not affect the release of the current module, which still meets the customer's present requirements.

EXAMPLE: Your project is creating a multi-city reservation feature for all U.S.-based users of a car rental agency's mobile app. The agency acquires locations in Canada and Mexico and requests to change the product so that cross-border rentals will be supported when the feature is released. This is a substantial scope change that redefines the product and affects the project in its current state. If the change request is approved, the product change will trigger project changes.

Manage Scope Creep/Scope Change

Adaptive projects are volatile at the beginning of project work because their requirements will likely change over the project life cycle. Their scope is continually refined in response to stakeholder feedback as the project progresses. In predictive approaches, the project's scope is fixed before project work begins. Regardless of their methodology, *all* projects are prone to scope creep. They need continuous monitoring to verify that the work being performed is actually aligned to the goals of the current increment or sprint, and that all changes to the scope are documented and handled in a uniform process. This is one of the primary responsibilities of the project manager.

Scope Creep

Scope creep begins when new features or requirements are added to a project or product while the project is underway. The change is neither formally signed off on nor communicated to all stakeholders, and the schedule, budget, or resources allocated to the project are not altered to compensate. Scope creep can also result when the original project requirements were too vague or poorly documented when work began and must be revised to produce a workable product. Regardless of how it began, scope creep can threaten the quality of deliverables and lower productivity, especially if team members are rushed to complete additional work or reworks.

Scope creep frequently originates from verbal requests that do not go through the change control process because the customer disregards the effort required by the "simple" change. This is particularly problematic when team members work autonomously from remote locations.

EXAMPLE: ABC Corporation hires XYZ Design, LLC to redesign the ABC Corporation website. XYZ Design, LLC contracts with Jane Smith to code the site and David Jones to design the graphics. Jane and David only interact during project calls. One month into the project, management at ABC Corporation decides that a graphic for one of the new pages is unsatisfactory, even though it meets the contract's quality requirements. ABC Corporation contacts David directly with a request to alter the graphic, which David implements. However, the change is not documented or communicated to the project manager. When David's work is complete, he bills XYZ Design, LLC for his work, including the rework for the graphic. The project manager at XYZ Design, LLC adjusts the budget to cover the extra cost. When the finished graphics are delivered to Jane Smith, she discovers that the graphics change causes a functionality issue with her style sheet. Jane will now need to adjust her coding, resulting in another budget increase. If the higher costs for both workers exceed the budget reserves, XYZ Design, LLC will need to either absorb the budget overage or ask ABC Corporation to increase the budget. This late in the project, a budget increase is unlikely to be approved.

To prevent this kind of scope creep, the project manager should explain to all team members that all changes must go through the formal change control process, even if the change request seems minor and comes directly from the project sponsor or customer.

Agile projects are not immune to scope creep. The Agile process constantly prioritizes which planned feature is being developed during a timebox. When scope creep occurs, it is often because a customer revises a story but (incorrectly) considers the change to involve the same amount of effort as the original story. If a change to that feature is requested after a sprint begins, the change needs to be added to the backlog and prioritized against existing backlog items. However, if the change can be made during ordinary project work without affecting any other aspect, then scope creep did not occur.

Besides documenting the project's initial requirements, the best way to prevent scope creep from affecting the bottom line is to have, *and follow*, the change management plan and communication plan and to educate all stakeholders regarding the change control process.

Scope Change

In Waterfall environments, ***scope changes*** are requests for an addition to or subtraction from the previously agreed-upon scope of work that must follow the change control process. An addition to scope will likely require more budget and additional tasks that lengthen the project schedule. A subtraction from scope will likely reduce costs and remove tasks and time from the project schedule. Either of these changes can affect the resources needed for the project.

EXAMPLE: A project is initiated to replace a company's current twisted-pair network with a fiber-optic network. In the original project, the new network would be implemented in three office buildings. However, halfway through the project, the project sponsor purchases a fourth building and requests that this office also be included in the project. In this case, the project manager will need to determine the cost of supplying the new building with a network and obtain the material and personnel resources to deploy this fourth network. The overall project schedule and project scope will also have to be changed.

Scope change is an artifact of the change control process in Waterfall projects. By contrast, constantly varying scope is an anticipated feature of each sprint, iteration, or increment in Agile projects. In adaptive approaches, the product's scope is refined over and over again with each sprint, iteration, or increment, and changes are documented in the product backlog.

Constraints and Influences

The change control process can affect multiple aspects of a project. It is vital that project managers understand the existing project constraints so that the change control process is effective. They also need to understand the relationships between all the constraints so that they may effectively adjust the project scope, budget, or schedule when other constraints change.

To understand the relationship between project constraints, consider a project with a set delivery date. If project work is taking longer than expected and the schedule (release date) is the priority, then you may have to bring in more resources to complete the work on time, which will mean an increase in budget. Alternatively, you could decrease the scope or quality of the project.

NOTE While the following sections apply more to traditional predictive projects, constraints and influences are present in any project no matter its framework or methodology. In fact, one of the key differences between Waterfall and Agile frameworks is how the relationship between constraints drives project planning:

- **Waterfall:** The priority constraint is the project requirements. The project manager uses them to estimate the resources and schedule required to produce those results.
- **Agile:** The priority constraints are the available resources and the schedule. The requirements are tailored to fit within those limits.

Project Constraints

A ***constraint*** is a factor that limits the scope or execution of a project. Constraints are established during the Initiating phase of the project and documented at a high level in the project charter. During the Planning phase, constraints are further analyzed and documented for the project's scope statement. Common constraints include regulatory and legal requirements, the physical properties of resources (such as weight or durability), the project budget, the availability of skilled resources, the supply chain, and a fixed project end date.

If a change to a constraint is necessary after work begins, the project manager will need to obtain approval from the project sponsor through formal change control. As described in the prior section, the project manager is responsible for evaluating the impact of the change, updating any project documents affected by the change, and communicating the change.

This section covers how to predict the impact of various constraint variables, including cost, scope, time and scheduling, deliverables, quality, environment, resources, and requirements.

Together, cost, scope, and time form the ***triple constraint***. Altering one aspect of the triple constraint automatically affects the other aspects. Each constraint will have advocates. For example, the project sponsor might mainly be concerned with cost (getting the project result as inexpensively as possible), while the project's customer is mainly concerned with time (getting the project result as quickly as possible) and scope (getting all the necessary features in the project).

NOTE Project managers should know the adage of the triple constraint: "Good, fast, cheap—pick any two." Achieving all three goals is rarely possible, as detailed next:

- You can get it fast and cheap, but you will have to sacrifice quality or scope.
- You can get it fast and good (quality and scope), but you will pay more.
- You can get it cheap and good (quality and scope), but it will be slow.

All three aspects of the triple constraint have equal weight when a project starts. As the project is initiated and planned, the constraints must be balanced to ensure that the project result is achieved within the scope, time, and cost constraints defined for the project. In most projects, one or two constraints will have priority. If constraints are reprioritized during the project, a thorough review of the other constraints must be performed.

EXAMPLE: You are managing a project in which the main concern during the Planning phase was the project's cost. To reduce costs, the project schedule is lengthened, the materials are of lower quality, resources are less knowledgeable, and the scope does not include all the features that were originally proposed. Halfway through your project, a rival company starts work on a competing product. If your project's sponsor wants to beat your rival to market, your project's constraints will have to be reprioritized: speeding up the schedule would result in higher costs, achieving an earlier release date might require further reducing the project scope, and so on.

Cost Constraint

Budget is the classic constraint for any project, because no project has unlimited funding. During the Planning phase, the project manager estimates how much money will be required to complete the project. Costs include labor, contractors, risk responses, materials, and so on. The project manager uses these cost details to estimate the project budget. Most projects include reserves, which are monies that are allocated to deal with risks. Even with reserves, however, only a finite amount of money is available for any project.

If a project's cost estimates were inaccurate and more money is ultimately required, either the project budget will need to be increased and approved by the project sponsor, or some other project constraint(s) will need to be adjusted. Both options should follow the change control process.

EXAMPLE: While a project for building a new house is underway, the project manager learns that the lumber costs are significantly higher than projected. The project manager will need to meet with the project sponsor—in this case, the homeowner—to a) obtain additional funds to cover the increased costs, b) decrease costs in other areas, or c) both. Perhaps the homeowner will decide to cut costs in other areas to offset the increase in lumber prices. For example, switching to cheaper light fixtures and omitting crown molding might provide enough money to cover the increased cost of the lumber.

Scope Constraint

Scope is a constraint because it restricts work on the project to only what is required to produce the project's final product, result, or service. Because scope combines with cost and time in the triple constraint, a change in scope alters one or both of the other aspects. If the project scope must change, the project budget will need to be changed and approved by the project sponsor, and/or the project schedule will need to be adjusted.

EXAMPLE: During a project for a new banking application, the project sponsor requests an additional feature. The project manager will need to meet with the project sponsor to a) obtain additional funds to cover the new feature and adjust the schedule to account for development, b) decide which other feature(s) can be sacrificed to offset the budget and schedule changes, or c) both. When the decisions are made, the project will need to be adjusted based on those decisions.

Time and Scheduling Constraints

Time is a project constraint because every project has a limited amount of time available to create the project's deliverables. The available time determines the project schedule, which is the time available to deliver a project. Time affects most other project constraints, including cost, scope, quality, and scheduling.

During the Planning phase, the project manager determines the project schedule, assigning all resources to project tasks or activities. The project schedule is based on the amount of time needed to complete the tasks and the amount of time all resources are available. The minimum amount of time required to complete the project (the critical path) also affects the minimum project budget for paid resource hours. Chapter 5, "Schedule Development and Management," defines the critical path and its calculations.

If the allotted time for a task is overrun, additional costs will be incurred as additional resources become necessary; for example, staff may need to be paid overtime to complete tasks that exceed the allotted hours. Quality and scope may be impacted if additional resource time cannot be obtained.

EXAMPLE: During a project for a new mobile application, the developers realize that tasks will take longer to complete than originally projected. The project manager may need to obtain additional staff to help the project stay on schedule, or she might ask current developers to work overtime to meet the original project release date. Either of these choices will increase project costs. The project manager could also ask for a reduction in the project scope, perhaps by omitting a feature from the application.

Deliverables Constraint

Deliverables are considered project constraints because every project creates some sort of deliverables. These deliverables are considered part of the project scope. Deliverables are also constraints because they must meet specific, measurable benchmarks or key performance indicators (KPIs) to be accepted.

The project manager determines the project deliverables during planning. If the scope of the project changes after planning is complete, the deliverables from the project are usually affected. If the number of deliverables increases, for instance, the project budget and schedule are usually affected.

EXAMPLE: A new book project is underway, and the author decides to add a chapter to the planned outline. The project manager will probably need to adjust the project schedule to include time for writing the new chapter. The project manager might try to work with the author to ensure that the project schedule remains unchanged, but this option may be unlikely with only one author. Hiring another author would result in higher costs.

While deliverables are not part of the triple constraint, changing deliverables in any type of project definitely affects the project scope and may also affect cost and time.

Quality Constraint

Every project has quality parameters that must be met by the finished output. The quality constraint is considered part of the project scope, and it defines the quality of deliverables based on the requirements documented in the requirements management plan. Requirements describe the desired outcome, but quality is how to measure whether that outcome is delivered.

The project manager determines the project quality benchmarks during planning. The project scope affects project quality, and quality in turn affects other project constraints. For instance, if deliverables must be made from an expensive material to meet quality standards, the materials cost will be part of the minimum project budget, making it a priority constraint. If producing a correct deliverable takes a lot of time, sufficient resource hours must be scheduled.

Quality changes in any kind of project affect the project scope and therefore affect the cost (project budget) and time (project schedule).

EXAMPLE: A company is creating a new machine part, and the project sponsor requests changing to a higher-quality metal alloy for the project. The project manager will need to increase the project budget to account for this more expensive material. In addition, the project schedule may be delayed by the time needed to order and receive the new alloy.

Environment Constraint

The environment in which the project takes place can constrain its scope, the quality of its deliverables, the availability of resources, its schedule, or numerous other factors. Environmental constraints include the corporate environment, the global environment outside the organization, and the project environment itself. Changes to the project environment can affect all three triple constraints.

The corporate environment includes the type of organization and the organization's culture. For example, a functional team structure constrains the resources and scheduling available for a project, while a projectized structure does not. The global environment includes the regulatory environment, the physical environment (the natural world), the political environment, and/or the fiscal environment. These issues may vary depending on where the project is being completed. For example, a project to design a new car would be constrained by the regulatory environment (safety tests and emission standards). A solar power project might be constrained by the physical environment (sun availability) and the political environment (located in a market with energy tax incentives). The project environment includes any variables that must be present to complete the project, such as temperatures maintained within a certain range or unlimited bandwidth for Internet connections.

EXAMPLE: A new building project is underway, and the city planning commission reports that the original plans overlap a neighboring property line by six inches. The project manager may need to have the site resurveyed and work with the architect and designers to adjust the building plans. In addition, the project schedule may need to be adjusted to account for construction delays. Alternatively, the project manager could petition the city to obtain the neighboring property if it is available on the market and affordable.

Resources Constraint

Personnel might constrain the project by being available only at certain times, needing a fixed amount of time to perform a task, or lacking the skills to produce the deliverables. For personnel resources, the project manager will need to ensure that the team members have the appropriate skills needed to complete their project tasks. For all other assets, the project manager must ensure that the assets are procured and available in time to be used in the tasks for which they are needed. Project resource changes most likely affect time and cost.

EXAMPLE: After the Planning phase of a new project is complete, the project manager discovers that the limestone required for the project will not be available from the supplier for at least 6 months. Another supplier has enough of the limestone in stock for the project, but at a considerably higher price. The project manager and project sponsor will need to make a choice between three alternatives: 1) Change the schedule to reflect the projected availability of the required limestone at the original cost. 2) Increase the budget to cover the inflated cost of the limestone that is available now. 3) Change the scope of the project to allow for using another building material.

Requirements Constraint

Requirements are conditions that must be present in the project's end product or service. Requirements are also constraints because they directly affect the project scope and determine the criteria by which the final product is graded. As stated earlier, requirements describe the desired outcome, but quality is how you measure whether you have delivered the outcome. Requirements are assessed using key performance indicators and acceptance criteria.

During the Planning phase, the project manager gathers requirements from the project sponsor and stakeholders, documents the requirements, and then negotiates with the project sponsor to determine which requirements will be included in the project. In an Agile framework, this phase includes gathering user stories. The requirements are then used to define the project scope. If the requirements change, the project scope must be changed. In addition, it may be necessary to change the project budget and project schedule. In some cases, requirements are not attainable at all, or they must be delayed until a future revision of the product.

EXAMPLE: A state governmental agency specifies several requirements during an inspection of a construction project. The project manager will need to change the scope of the project to include these requirements, add any necessary tasks to the project to handle the requirements, and allocate resources for those tasks. Finally, the project manager will need to adjust the project budget to include any new costs incurred to meet the requirements.

Project requirement changes usually affect the project's scope, time, and cost.

Project Influences

An ***influence*** is a project event or condition that can affect a project constraint. Project managers must be able to recognize whether an influence is about to occur, taking appropriate actions to either prevent the influence or adjust the project constraints to account for the influence. Two of the major influences are change requests and scope creep, both covered in this chapter. Other recognized categories of influence are constraint reprioritization, the interactions between constraints, other projects, and stakeholders, sponsors, and management.

Constraint Reprioritization

Constraint reprioritization occurs when a project that is limited by a particular constraint must shift priorities to another constraint. When reprioritization occurs, the project manager must fully assess all project constraints to document any effects on them. The project manager will then need to explain to the project sponsor what this reprioritization will do to the project.

If a project's cost estimates were inaccurate and more money is required to produce a deliverable, cost becomes the primary constraint for the project. To meet the original scope, the project budget will need to be increased and approved by the project sponsor. If the budget is not increased, another project constraint will need to be adjusted to reduce the pressure of the cost constraint; the project might need to drop a requirement or change the quality standards.

EXAMPLE: While a publisher is working on a new book project, a competitor announces plans to publish a book on a similar topic with an earlier release date. Because the project's original priority was minimizing costs, only a single author and editor were engaged. However, the publisher now wants to move up the book's schedule to beat its competitor's book to publication. To make the date, the publisher may need to increase the budget to employ additional resources or to give the current resources an incentive to speed up their work. Another option would be to change the scope of the book, perhaps by shortening the content. However, this change probably would also affect quality. No matter which choice is made, the project manager will have to adjust all of the affected project constraints.

Constraint reprioritization affects all three of the triple constraints—scope, time, and cost—and the ultimate effects depend on which constraint is being prioritized.

Interaction Between Constraints

Project constraints directly interact with each other throughout the life cycle of the project. Constraints are analyzed during project planning to create the project documents, budget, schedule, and scope. It is important to realize that other constraints can actually affect one or more of the triple constraints (scope, time, and cost). Resources directly affect project costs. Quality, requirements, and deliverables directly affect project scope. Environment directly affects project time and costs. Results of such changes can be both negative and positive. Suppose two new team members are brought into an engine development project. While this staffing change will likely increase the project budget, it also has a good chance of shortening the project schedule.

EXAMPLE: A key project team member goes on medical leave halfway through a project. The project manager assesses the impact to the project schedule and then presents the sponsor or key stakeholder with possible courses of action. Two suggestions might be securing more funding to hire another team member and extending the project schedule to account for slower progress. These two options affect the project's constraints in different ways:

- If the project will remain understaffed but the schedule can be extended, the project manager will have to reassign the missing team member's work to other resources and adjust the task start/finish dates, dependencies, and critical paths. Project milestones will have to be rescheduled.
- If the original schedule must be followed but more funds will be made available, the project manager should assess the cost to hire new resources, the impact on the schedule if resources must be trained, and the impact on deliverable quality if a sufficiently skilled resource cannot be hired.

Stakeholder, Sponsor, and Management Influences

Stakeholders and sponsors are involved in setting project requirements, which directly affect the project scope. Sponsors establish the project budget and influence the project schedule. Management usually affects the project schedule more than the other constraints, especially if the organization's structure is functional rather than projectized.

EXAMPLE: A key stakeholder asks the project manager to make a significant change in a deliverable. The stakeholder did not consult the project sponsor about this request. The project manager asks the stakeholder to complete a change request that documents the proposed revision and assesses the impact of the change. Only then should the project manager approach the sponsor to seek approval, following the change control procedure detailed in the change management plan.

Influence by Other Projects

Other projects can influence project constraints (for example, by competing for the use of shared resources). During the Planning phase, project managers should document any resources that will be shared with other projects. Inter-project resource conflicts should be negotiated between the project managers. If they are unable to resolve the conflict, upper management or the project management office (PMO), if one is available, should make the decision. In larger corporations, company policies may dictate how such issues will be resolved.

EXAMPLE: Two projects need access to the same laboratory as part of the research portion of each project. During project planning, the project management office (PMO) discovers that the two projects have planned to use the laboratory during the same 2-week period. The PMO works with the project managers of the two projects to come up with three options: 1) finding a way to share the laboratory at the same time; 2) allowing each team half-day access to the laboratory, with one project team having mornings and the other having afternoons; and 3) giving primary laboratory access to the higher-priority project and delaying laboratory access until later for the lower-priority project. The first two choices would require a schedule adjustment for both projects, and the third choice would require a schedule adjustment for only one of the projects. After reaching a decision on how to proceed, the project managers can make the necessary adjustments. In this case, they do not have to follow the change control process because the issue was discovered during the Planning phase, prior to project execution.

Other Common Sources of Project Change

As discussed, constraints and influences are primary drivers of change in projects. Changes may be requested to provide enhancements, preventive actions, and defect repairs. However, project managers should understand how more granular types of project changes should be managed, including changes to the schedule, requirements, procurements, budget, stakeholders, resources, quality, and communication, as well as changes arising from risk events and emergencies. The following sections discuss and provide examples of all of these change types and how they might affect a project.

Schedule Changes

Because schedules are predictive approximations, project schedules are very likely to change. The project manager should regularly evaluate the schedule's accuracy and communicate it to stakeholders. The project sponsor, project stakeholders, and project team members need to be notified each time schedule changes occur.

Schedule changes include any change requests that affect the project schedule, such as task delays, task additions and deletions, task reassignment, revised task duration estimates, and procurement delays. If a task is delayed for any reason, its dependent tasks will also be delayed. When a change such as this occurs, the project manager should meet with the project team members responsible for the dependent tasks to gain their input on the effects of the change. Doing so will often ensure that no relevant detail is forgotten or omitted from consideration.

If the affected tasks are on the critical path, the overall schedule will be affected by the change. However, if an affected task is not on the critical path, the task may have enough float or slack that the change will not affect the overall amount of time needed to complete the project. Normal schedule changes that are accounted for by slack and float do not have to go through formal change control. However, the schedule will need to be updated to ensure that any changes to the float and slack for dependent tasks are adjusted. Float and slack are discussed in Chapter 5.

When schedule changes are requested, the project manager should assess their effect on other aspects of the project. When a schedule change has been approved, the project schedule baseline will need to be updated and milestones may have to be moved. If a task is shortened or deleted, the budget is likely to decrease. If a task is lengthened or added, the budget is likely to increase. If a task assignment changes, the budget may increase or decrease, depending on the cost of the new task resource.

EXAMPLE: A project manager is notified of a delay in the shipment of the cabinetry needed for a new home construction project. Many of the project's tasks can continue without being affected by the cabinetry delay. However, the kitchen and bathrooms cannot be completed until the cabinetry is installed. The project manager will need to adjust dependent tasks (counter installation, sink installation, and appliance installation) for the shipment delay. All of these steps are part of the original schedule change. This type of schedule change could result in a budget increase if the original installers will not be available for the delayed delivery date and the new installers have a higher rate of pay. Similar cost adjustments may be necessary for any other dependent tasks. If the adjusted costs are known at the time of the original schedule change, then those changes should be approved as well, thereby ensuring that the effects on the project constraints are approved.

Resource Changes

Resource changes are any changes to project resources, such as changes in supplies, procurements, and personnel. When a resource change has been approved, the resource calendar, project schedule, schedule baseline, and other documents may need to be updated.

For personnel resource changes, the project manager might attempt to find replacement team members or transfer essential tasks to existing team members. Personnel resource changes might affect the project schedule and budget, depending on the level of expertise or production and the rate of pay, respectively. Personnel resource changes can also affect project scope if a replacement resource cannot produce the same quality expected of the original resource.

EXAMPLE: A project team member must take a leave of absence, and a replacement team member has been allocated to the project. The original team member's tasks are reassigned to the new resource. If the new team member can complete work at the same speed as the original team member, the only project update would be the resource assigned to the task. However, if the new team member completes work at a different speed, the project manager will have to adjust the task durations for the tasks assigned to the new team member, which also affects any dependent tasks. The project sponsor, project stakeholders, and project team members need to be notified that schedule changes have occurred.

Material resource changes may be forced on a project if an identified resource becomes unavailable. Material resource changes usually affect the project schedule and budget.

EXAMPLE: A road paving project allocated a piece of equipment owned by the project sponsor to complete the road. Just before that equipment is needed, it is allocated to a higher-priority project. The project manager has a couple of options on how to resolve this issue. One option is to find a substitute resource, such as renting the necessary equipment from a rental company, but such a resource change would result in higher costs. The other option is to wait until the original equipment is available, which would result in a schedule delay.

The project manager should notify the project team and stakeholders of all personnel changes. For supply or procurement changes, the project manager only needs to notify the team members who are affected by the resource, and then only if the change affects project tasks.

Stakeholder Changes

Two kinds of stakeholder changes can affect a project. First, stakeholders, like project team members, may be removed from or added to a project. The project manager should ensure that any replacement, addition, or removal of a stakeholder is documented. Then the project manager should meet with the new stakeholder to ensure that they understand the project. The project manager also needs to document the new stakeholder's requirements.

EXAMPLE: A project stakeholder has left the company and been replaced by another stakeholder. In this case, the project manager will need to edit the stakeholder register and stakeholder management plan and notify the project sponsor and project team members about these changes.

Second, stakeholders may make change requests that affect project scope, time, cost, quality, or procurements. When a stakeholder change has been approved, the appropriate project documents need to be updated. A change in the stakeholder's requirements is technically a requirements change, as covered in the "Requirements Changes" section.

EXAMPLE: A new human resources manager is a stakeholder in a project to replace all computers in the human resources department. If the manager decides that video recording capability is important for all the computers, and this was not one of the original requirements, the project manager will need to evaluate the impact of this change to the project scope, schedule, and budget.

The project manager needs to make sure that the project team members understand how any stakeholder change will affect project communication and project scope.

Requirements Changes

A change to project requirements is most likely to affect its scope unless other constraints are carefully adjusted. Project requirements are specified by the sponsor and stakeholders and documented during the Initiating and Planning phases of the project, but new requirements often are identified during project execution. Sometimes previously identified requirements are never incorporated into the project. If a new project requirement is identified or a project requirement is removed, the project manager will need to analyze how this change will affect the project's scope, schedule, and budget.

A new requirement likely results in a change in the project scope and schedule as well as an increase in the project budget. Removing a requirement also changes the scope and schedule and likely decreases the project budget.

EXAMPLE: A project stakeholder asks the project manager to add a new feature to a software development project. The project manager will need to analyze the effects of this change on the project's schedule, budget, and scope. The project manager should meet with the project team members to gain their input on the effects of the new requirement. A new task or tasks will need to be added to the schedule to accommodate development of the new feature, and the project's budget will increase. If the new requirement is approved, the project scope will need to be expanded to include details about the new feature, and baselines will need to be adjusted.

Quality Changes

Quality is the level to which a project meets its specifications or meets the expectations of the project sponsor documented in the quality management plan. Quality changes occur when defects and enhancements are identified during monitoring and controlling, resulting in change requests.

Quality changes include changing parameters for deliverable quality, based on quality assurance and control measures or on changes to requirements. Quality requirements changes may affect the project's scope, budget, and schedule in a negative or positive manner, depending on the effort and resources needed to meet the new quality standards. By the same token, any change in scope, schedule, or budget can increase or decrease deliverable quality.

EXAMPLE: A plastics manufacturer is hired to produce a storage case for a new drone. During the Planning phase of the project, the drone manufacturer provided the plastics company and the project manager with very detailed case specifications, including appearance, color, internal slot sizes, and external size. In testing the prototype run of 15 storage cases, the drone manufacturer determines that the case is too weak to withstand drops without damaging the drone parts and therefore requests a stronger plastic. The project manager will need to determine what effects this specification change will have on the project's scope, schedule, and budget. More than likely, the project manager will need to consult with the plastics manufacturer's management and the project team to determine the full impact.

Budget Changes

Budget changes may originate from higher procurement costs, lower project team costs, longer task durations that affect project cost, reductions in the budget from the project sponsor, and so on. An increase in costs in one area may require trimming costs in other areas. By contrast, a decrease in costs may result in leftover funds to apply to other costs or to add to project reserves. If budget changes cannot be accommodated from the project reserves, they may change the project's scope or schedule.

When a budget change is requested, the project manager should assess its effect on other aspects of the project, informing the project team, stakeholders, and sponsor of the impacts of the proposed change. It is probably not necessary to share budget changes with all team members, except those who have budgetary or procurement roles. Once a budget change is approved, the cost baseline, project budget, and the cost management plan may need to be updated.

Like project schedules, project budgets are a predictive approximation of project costs made in advance and therefore are likely to change. Budget accuracy should be evaluated regularly by the project manager and communicated to project stakeholders.

EXAMPLE: A project manager is notified that all the bids for the new software needed for a large library remodel project are higher than originally estimated. Of course, the project manager will need to adjust the project budget. If reducing the number of features in the requested software is not possible, the project manager may need to find other areas and ways to cut costs. Options may include purchasing lower-quality shelving units for the library, decreasing the number of computers being purchased, hiring fewer contractors for the building remodeling, and so on.

Communication Changes

Communication changes are usually not as detrimental to project constraints as other project changes. These changes usually involve altering the type of communication required for a particular stakeholder or event. The project manager simply needs to document the change in the communication plan, notify affected team members, and implement version control. A communication change would only need to follow the formal change control process if it affected major constraints.

EXAMPLE: A stakeholder would like to start receiving project schedule reports. This change could be accomplished by adding the stakeholder to the distribution list for this report.

EXAMPLE: A new stakeholder on a project does not have access to the project team's video calls. Connecting the stakeholder to the rest of the team will require additional hardware, networking, and so on. Because this change affects the budget, it must go through the formal change control process.

Procurement Changes

Procurements undergo a formal process whereby the requirements are documented, bids are solicited, and vendors are selected before the actual procurements take place. Changes can be requested at any time during this process by either project sponsors or procurement vendors. However, a procurement change is less likely to be granted once a contract has been signed and production/delivery is imminent.

EXAMPLE: A project manager finds an error in the specifications for a part required in a project to manufacture a new wireless device. Because the project manager is already in negotiations with the selected vendor, she will need to amend the contract to document the changed specification. The selected vendor will need time to assess the effect of the change on the contract, including cost and schedule.

For any procurement change, the project manager will need to make sure that the vendor and the team members understand how the procurement change will affect the project, particularly the project schedule. If the change will affect the procurement cost, the project sponsor may also need to be informed.

Emergency Changes

Emergency changes are time-sensitive and needed to restore a service, prevent an incident, address a pressing need such as a legal requirement, and so on. If an emergency change is needed, the project manager should convene an emergency CCB meeting to discuss only the emergency change. Once approval is obtained, the project manager should walk the change through the remaining steps in the process to ensure that the change is implemented quickly.

EXAMPLE: A project team member discovers an error in an application being developed that could expose personally identifiable information to the Internet.

The team member has identified the code that needs repair, but a portion of the application was already released for beta review, and it contains the security issue. The project manager should implement the regression plan, document how long it will take to fix the problem, and immediately convene a CCB meeting to obtain approval for this emergency change.

Risk Events

If a risk was identified during the Planning phase, the budget should have contingency reserves allocated to cover the costs of responding to that risk. The solution may be as simple as adjusting the appropriate project constraints (such as scope, budget, or schedule) to address the risk. Such cases may not require formal approval from the CCB, but the project manager would still need to communicate the change, update the project documents, and perform version control and auditing as usual.

If a risk occurs that was not identified in the Planning phase, the project manager will need to address the effects of that risk event via the change control process covered earlier in this chapter. Risk and issue management are covered in detail in Chapter 4, "Risk and Issue Management."

Exam Preparation Tasks

As mentioned in the section "How to Use This Book" in the Introduction, you have a few choices for exam preparation: the exercises here, Chapter 17, "Final Preparation," and the exam simulation questions included in the Pearson Test Prep Software Online.

Review All Key Topics

Review the most important topics in this chapter, noted with the Key Topics icon in the outer margin of the page. Table 3-2 lists each reference of these key topics and the page number on which each is found.

Table 3-2 Key Topics for Chapter 3

Key Topic Element	Description	Page Number
Section	Discussion of project change control, change requests, and the change management plan	73
List	Steps in the change control process	73
Paragraph	Creating/receiving change requests	74

Key Topic Element	Description	Page Number
Figure 3-1	Example of a Change Request Template	75
Paragraph	Documenting change requests	74
Figure 3-2	Example of a Change Control Log	76
Paragraph	Conducting a preliminary review	77
Paragraph	Conducting impact assessments	77
Paragraph	Documenting change recommendations	78
Paragraph	Determining the decision-makers	78
Paragraph	Escalating to the change control board (CCB)	78
Paragraph	Documenting the change status	79
Paragraph	Communicating the change status	79
Paragraph	Updating the project plan	80
Paragraph	Implementing changes	80
Paragraph	Validating the change deployment	80
Paragraph	Communicating the change deployment	81
Paragraph	Discussion of project change management	81
Paragraph	Discussion and examples of product change versus project change	81
Paragraph	Discussion of managing scope creep and scope change	82
Paragraph	Discussion of scope creep	83
Paragraph	Discussion of scope change	84
Paragraph	Discussion and examples of project constraints	85
Paragraph	Discussion and examples of project influences	90

Define Key Terms

Define the following key terms from this chapter and check your answers in the glossary:

change request, change control, change management plan, change control log, change log, impact assessment, regression plan, change control board (CCB), product change, scope creep, scope changes, constraint, triple constraint, influence, constraint reprioritization

Review Questions

The answers to these questions appear in Appendix A. For more practice with sample exam questions, use the Pearson Test Prep practice test software online.

1. Which of the following scenarios would require formal change control? (Choose all that apply.)
   a. A team member completes tasks faster than estimated. As a result, the overall project schedule will be shortened.
   b. A stakeholder requests that a deliverable be released earlier than planned. As a result, the overall project schedule will be shortened.
   c. A procurement will be delivered later than the vendor originally promised. As a result, the overall project schedule will be lengthened.
   d. A stakeholder wants to change the materials being procured for a project with another, less expensive material. As a result, the overall project budget will be decreased.

2. What is the first step in the formal change control process?
   a. Conduct a preliminary review of the change.
   b. Create a change request.
   c. Determine the decision-makers.
   d. Document requests in the change control log.

3. What is the final step in the formal change control process?
   a. Validate the change implementation.
   b. Update the project plan.
   c. Communicate the change status.
   d. Communicate the change deployment.

4. Which plan, document, or entity should the project manager consult to identify the correct authority for approving the change?
   a. The project charter
   b. The change management plan
   c. The change control log
   d. The project sponsor

5. Which of the following does *not* describe a project constraint?
   a. If your organization's product is not released within 5 months, a major competitor will be first to market with a similar product.
   b. The project must include on-site training for the customer's staff, to be delivered 3 weeks in advance of project closure.
   c. The materials cost cannot exceed 20% of the budget.
   d. The product must run on the customer's existing point-of-sale terminals.

6. You are the project manager for a retail store redesign project. Two weeks into project execution, the project sponsor requests that you increase the width of the main aisles by 1 foot. This change is approved, and the project requirements are adjusted. Which influence is this an example of?
   a. Change request
   b. Scope creep
   c. Constraint reprioritization
   d. Another project

7. You are hired to take over as project manager for an existing project. On your first day, you discover that the project is over budget and behind schedule as a result of new requirements having been added to the project. The project's budget and schedule were not adjusted when these requirements were added. Which influence is this an example of?
   a. Change request
   b. Scope creep
   c. Constraint reprioritization
   d. Another project

8. What should a project manager perform to determine how a change might affect a project's scope, schedule, budget, quality, resources, and risks?
   a. Impact assessment
   b. Regression planning
   c. Constraint review
   d. Change implementation validation review

9. Which of the following is a cross-functional group that represents each business process and typically makes the decision to accept or reject a change during its monthly meeting?
   a. Subject matter experts (SMEs)
   b. Project stakeholders team (PST)
   c. Change control board (CCB)
   d. Steering committee (SC)

10. You are performing an impact assessment of a proposed change. Which statement accurately reflects the relationship between a proposed change and overall project risk?
    a. Overall project risk will increase if a change is approved.
    b. Overall project risk could decrease if a change is approved.
    c. Overall project risk would not be affected by changes to requirements.
    d. Overall project risk would not be affected by changes to budget.

This chapter covers the following topics:

- **Overview of Risk Management:** Understanding risks, threats, opportunities, issues, known risks, unknown risks, and interactions between risks, issues, and changes; the steps in the risk management process
- **General Risks:** New projects, new management, regulatory environment changes, digital transformation, infrastructure end of life, mergers and acquisitions, reorganizations, and major cybersecurity events
- **Risk Analysis:** Qualitative risk analysis, quantitative risk analysis, detectability, interconnectivity, simulation, impact analysis, and situational/scenario analysis
- **Common Risk Responses:** Contingency/fallback plans, project reserves, negative risk strategies, positive risk strategies, escalation, and workarounds
- **Roles and Responsibilities:** Points of escalation for risks, issue escalation paths, risk and issue owners, and contingency plan owners
- **Overview of Issue Management:** Developing and executing the issue management plan
- **Issue Resolution Plan:** Issue tracking, root cause analysis, response planning, contingency plans, outcome documentation, and assessing an issue's severity, urgency, and scope of impact

Risk and Issue Management

A *risk* is a potential event that could affect the project's execution or major aspects of the project, such as the budget, scope, or schedule. Negative risks are something the project wants to prevent, and positive risks are something the project wants to encourage. While risk is inevitable, it is not inherently bad; another term for a positive risk is *opportunity*.

Project risk management ensures that project risks (both negative and positive) are identified and analyzed during project planning so that response strategies can be planned. Projects can be affected by known risk events, but unknown risk events can also occur, and new risk events may be identified after the project begins work through periodic risk review. Risks are prioritized for response by using qualitative analysis, quantitative analysis, situational/scenario analysis, and impact analysis.

If the risk occurs and is not controlled by the response, or if an unforeseen risk happens, it becomes an issue. An *issue* is an event or condition that affects the project's quality, schedule, or execution and requires resolution. Risks are uncertainties, while issues are reality. *Issue management* ensures that issues are identified when they occur, analyzed to discover their cause and relative priority, communicated, resolved, and monitored.

Both risks and issues are assigned owners and tracked in logs. Highly significant risks and issues require contingency plans and escalation plans. Contingency plans direct risk or issue response, while escalation plans share risks and issues with stakeholders outside of the project's reporting structure.

This chapter covers the following objectives for the CompTIA Project+ exam:

1.4 Given a scenario, perform risk management activities.

1.5 Given a scenario, perform issue management activities.

NOTE Because risk management and issue management share concepts and techniques, this chapter merges some of the bullet points that CompTIA presents in separate objectives. Also, whereas CompTIA defines ***risk management*** strategies as a type of risk response, this book uses ***risk response***, *risk strategy*, and *risk management strategy* interchangeably to mean the project's approach to handling a given risk.

"Do I Know This Already?" Quiz

The "Do I Know This Already?" quiz allows you to assess whether you should read this entire chapter thoroughly or jump to the "Exam Preparation Tasks" section. If you are in doubt about your answers to these questions or your own assessment of your knowledge of the topics, read the entire chapter. Table 4-1 lists the major headings in this chapter and their corresponding "Do I Know This Already?" quiz questions. You can find the answers in Appendix A, "Answers to the 'Do I Know This Already?' Questions and Review Quizzes."

Table 4-1 "Do I Know This Already?" Section-to-Question Mapping

Foundation Topics Section	Questions
Overview of Risk Management	1–2
General Risks	3
Risk Analysis	4–5
Common Risk Responses	6–8
Roles and Responsibilities	9
Overview of Issue Management	10
Issue Resolution Plan	11

CAUTION The goal of self-assessment is to gauge your mastery of the topics in this chapter. If you do not know the answer to a question or are only partially sure of the answer, you should mark that question as wrong for the purposes of the self-assessment. Giving yourself credit for an answer you correctly guess skews your self-assessment results and might provide you with a false sense of security.

1. You learn that the resource needed to complete a project task will not be available during the scheduled time. However, you had anticipated this event and made plans to complete the task at a later date without changing the schedule's critical path. What does this describe?
   a. Schedule reserves
   b. Resource change
   c. Risk response
   d. Issue

2. What is another term for negative risks?
   a. Issues
   b. Vulnerabilities

c. Threats

d. Unknowns

e. Opportunities

3. All of the following general risk scenarios can pose both positive and negative risks for a project, *except* which one?

   a. Mergers and acquisitions

   b. Infrastructure end of life

   c. Regulatory environment changes

   d. Digital transformation

4. Which activity is performed during qualitative risk analysis?

   a. Assigning numeric probability scores to risks

   b. Running simulated scenarios with random values

   c. Prioritizing risks by their perceived level of impact

   d. Adding EMVs to a decision tree

5. Which process analyzes the statistical probability of a risk's occurrence?

   a. Risk identification

   b. Risk prioritization

   c. Qualitative risk analysis

   d. Quantitative risk analysis

6. When is a contingency or fallback plan executed?

   a. When a trigger occurs

   b. When a critical risk is logged

   c. When the risk owner decides it is necessary

   d. When an issue occurs

7. You are managing a project to create a new storage area network (SAN) for your company. One of the identified risks is that access to the network will fail. The sponsor decides to implement a redundant network backbone to ensure accessibility. Which risk strategy is this project using?

   a. Acceptance

   b. Enhancement

   c. Avoidance

d. Transference
e. Exploitation
f. Mitigation

8. What would be a valid risk strategy for *both* positive and negative risks?
   a. Acceptance
   b. Enhancement
   c. Avoidance
   d. Transference
   e. Exploitation
   f. Mitigation

9. Which role or individual monitors an Agile project's environment for an assigned risk trigger?
   a. The project manager
   b. The risk owner
   c. The product owner
   d. The scrum master

10. You are performing a project activity in which you remove workarounds and document outcomes while continuing to monitor the project environment. Which activity are you performing?
    a. Reviewing a risk response
    b. Closing a risk
    c. Closing an issue
    d. Preparing an issue for escalation

11. Which characteristic best describes a workaround?
    a. Temporary
    b. Ineffective
    c. Expensive
    d. Risky

Foundation Topics

Overview of Risk Management

Risk planning involves multiple processes that span the planning, executing, and closing phases of a project. All of the following ***risk activities*** are part of the risk management process:

1. **Plan risk management.** Create the risk management plan and determine the methodologies to be used for risk identification, analysis, tracking, and reporting. Identify key risk stakeholders.

2. **Identify risks.** Perform an initial risk assessment and create a risk register. (Initial risk assessments are covered in Chapter 10, "Planning Phase Activities." A sample risk register is included as Figures 13-10a, 13-10b, and 13-10c in Chapter 13, "Project Management Tools.")

3. **Perform risk analysis.** Analyze risks both qualitatively and quantitatively to document risk probability and impact, ranking, and urgency. Prioritize the risks by order of response and document this information in the risk register.

4. **Plan risk responses.** Determine the strategies to use for responding to each known risk, and document those strategies in the risk register. Develop fallback and contingency plans for highly critical risks. Assign owners to risks and finalize the risk register.

5. **Treat risks.** Beginning with the most critical risks, apply the appropriate strategies to reduce negative outcomes and increase positive ones. Escalate risks that fall outside the project's bounds. Monitor the project environment for risk triggers and contingencies.

6. **Monitor risks.** Maintain risk status and KPIs on the project dashboard. Prepare and distribute risks reports and risk communication. Perform periodic risk review to ensure planned responses are still appropriate and risk priority levels are unchanged. Add newly discovered risks to the register for analysis.

7. **Close risks.** Close resolved or treated risks on the risk log. Continue to monitor the project for the risk. Document lessons learned.

NOTE The risk management plan and risk management planning activities are covered at a high level in Chapter 10 as part of project planning. This chapter describes types of risk, the specific methods and techniques for analyzing risk, the options for responding to risks, risk roles, and the purpose and timing of risk escalation.

Connections Between Risks, Issues, and Changes

Before you can understand how issues, risks, and change requests relate to one another in a project, it is important to have a clear definition for each:

- **Issues:** Problems, events, conditions, or conflicts that occur unexpectedly in the life cycle and affect the project's objectives, schedule, tasks, scope, or other significant factor.
- **Risks:** Uncertain events or conditions that would have an effect (positive or negative) on at least one project objective if they were to occur. Risks are formally identified during project planning or as they are uncovered during project work.
- **Changes:** Corrective and preventative actions, defect repairs, updates, and modifications made to a project's parameters during execution. Changes are formally controlled through change management.

The best way to differentiate between the three is to understand their behaviors and where they fall during project execution:

- An ***issue*** is an uncontrolled event that has already occurred (or is occurring) during project execution, must be addressed for the project to proceed, and originated from a known or unknown risk.
- A ***risk*** is an event that may or may not happen but has a plan in place for it (unless it is unknown). If a risk occurs and its impact is controlled, it becomes a mitigated risk. If it occurs and its impact is uncontrolled, it is escalated to an issue.
- A change request is a project modification that is requested during the project, may or may not be approved, and must be analyzed fully before approval and implementation.

Remember that risks are events that *may or may not* occur, changes *will* occur after approval, and issues *have already* occurred. Risks and changes are logged before they occur (or are enacted), but issues can only be logged after they arise.

If a risk occurs but is managed and controlled by the planned response, then it is a risk event or a mitigated risk, not an issue. If a risk happens and the results are not controlled, it becomes an issue. Unknown risks that occur and cannot be controlled are also issues.

Responding to issues and risks can require changes to the project, and a change request to the project can generate new risks. Proposed changes to any aspect of the project's success criteria should trigger a risk assessment of the change. If changes to the project are not controlled, they may lead to new risks and cause issues to occur.

Resolving an urgent or high-priority issue may require making emergency changes to the project plan before formal change control can occur. If this happens, the change should be retroactively analyzed to ensure it did not in turn create unexpected risks.

Known Risk vs. Unknown Risk

While the ***risk register*** lists known risks, ***unknown risk*** lives in the project's blind spot. An unknown risk is an unforeseen event or condition that can affect project execution but was not anticipated or planned for. When unknown risks are found, they must be added retroactively to the risk register and analyzed so that a response can be planned. If an unknown risk materializes, it becomes an issue by default and is handled with a contingency plan or workaround. The goal of risk planning is to eliminate the majority of unknown risks.

A third risk category is the known unknown (or unknown known). The known unknown is a risk that the project manager is generally aware of but has so little information about that its impact cannot be assessed. Known unknowns are areas of risk uncertainty. The risk of a hurricane may be known, but not whether the next storm will be mild or a lethal Category 5 hurricane that will halt all work, or whether it will occur at the peak of project work. Potential planned responses might include both a week's contingency reserve in the schedule and a full employee evacuation plan.

General Risks

CompTIA identifies several common business scenarios that create risk for projects, both internal to the organization and external to the environment. When these scenarios occur in real life, active projects should perform a ***risk review*** to evaluate their impact. If the project is still being planned, you can apply brainstorming, what-if queries, and more quantitative forms of situational/scenario analysis (covered later in this chapter) to uncover relevant risks.

New Projects

Many organizations run multiple projects concurrently. The ongoing risk is that a new project will have a higher priority than an older one, causing resource loss or contention, lengthened timelines and delays, or decreased management support. An old project may be put on hold while a key resource is reallocated to the new one. The project's sponsor should remain its advocate and work with senior management to keep them informed of these impacts. A new project could also generate fresh resources (such as new team skills or subject matter experts) that could help ongoing projects. In a best-case scenario, incoming projects would inspire management to add resources to help old projects finish faster, thereby clearing the pipeline for new work.

New Management

New management at the senior level can bring a top-down change in priorities that directly affects a project's funding and support, or even ends it. New leadership may decide that existing projects exceed the current risk appetite or are no longer aligned with corporate values. (This author worked on a project that was completely halted in order for an incoming CEO to review and re-approve the charter before work could continue.) The positive risk is that new management could be more supportive of existing projects or change the organization's emphasis to enhance project work. A previously rejected project proposal may be granted approval. Projects undertaken for external clients are better shielded from these impacts, but all project managers and product owners should evaluate the extent to which a project relies on management support.

Reorganization

Reorganization occurs when a company restructures internal departments (such as merging, adding, or eliminating business units) or reassigns them to different leaders. In a simple reorganization, a key stakeholder may be replaced with a different member of senior management. A major reorganization may include layoffs and reduced headcount. The negative risks of reorganization are loss of a supportive sponsor and the loss of team members, especially those shared across functional departments. Otherwise, the risks resemble those of new management.

Mergers and Acquisitions

Mergers and acquisitions occur when two companies combine their assets to create a new business entity (merge) or when one organization is brought under the control of another (acquisition). As with reorganizations, a merger/acquisition may restructure or cut existing business units, cut staff, and change reporting structures. Unlike reorganization, a merger/acquisition may bring new staff and new resources for ongoing projects. Merged and acquired team members are often asked to adapt to new workflows and migrate to new technology systems. They could also be asked to get administrative approval to perform formerly independent tasks. Finally, a merger or acquisition can change the overall company culture, with hard-to-predict results.

Digital Transformation

Digital transformation moves formerly analog processes to technological solutions, moves business solutions to the cloud, or creates entirely new platforms via technology. Legal e-discovery, video conference calls, and digitized library archives are examples of past digital transformation. Digital transformation usually brings short- to medium-term disruption and long-term opportunity as new benefits of the technology are found. Another common example, migrating from on-premises computing to SaaS and IaaS, requires businesses to adapt, but also improves operational agility and resilience.

Digital transformation is not initiated at the project level, but project managers should strategically embrace it in the organization and remain alert to any challenges and competitive possibilities it brings. In addition to improving the tools directly used in project work, digital transformation can change project management itself, as seen in the shift from co-location to fully remote and geographically diverse teams.

Infrastructure End of Life

Legacy ***infrastructure end-of-life (EOL)*** system risks are created by hardware or software that is still used by your organization but no longer supported by the vendor. EOL risks are uniformly negative. Bugs and security flaws are no longer patched, and because end-of-support dates are public information, EOL systems are commonly targeted by attackers. If legacy infrastructure cannot be eliminated from your project, it must be managed proactively to reduce your exposure, such as moving legacy applications to virtual machines and removing legacy hardware from external-facing networks. The best way to manage EOL risk is to upgrade your technology and eliminate old infrastructure, regardless of cost; only in that sense can EOL present an opportunity.

Major Cybersecurity Event

A ***major cybersecurity event***, such as a successful ransomware attack, could temporarily or permanently block access to key network resources and files and severely impact project work. Network protection is outside the scope of a project, but project managers should be sure to document all of the project's essential digital assets and apply the risk responses dictated by the organization's security policies. The silver lining of a major incident is that it can impel senior management to invest in better training or security solutions that may protect the organization as a whole, making projects less vulnerable. A well-positioned IT project could take advantage of a major incident by developing a marketable security solution that could prevent future breaches.

Aside from cyber risks external to the project, projects can generate cyber risks themselves. Outside contractors may be granted access to more resources than required by the job role, or they could fail to have their access revoked after leaving project work. Poorly implemented workarounds for project issues might compromise authentication or authorization factors. Any of these risks could result in a network attack, loss of project assets, legal fines, loss of reputation, and schedule delays, so the project manager should pay attention to cyber-related risks from both within and outside the project.

Regulatory Environment Changes

The regulatory environment is the network of laws, standards, policies, and regulations that applies to all projects or to specific industries. Regulatory changes can affect a project by imposing new rules or by restricting activities that were previously allowed. The requirements for an ongoing project should be re-assessed when regulatory changes are implemented. The project plan should be reviewed for negative compliance risks, changes to the scope or schedule in response to new requirements, and changes to records management. However, because regulatory changes are announced months or years in advance and often have a phased rollout, organizations should have time to review their internal processes and to write procedures that guide compliance for new projects. Transitioning to new regulations is frequently managed as a formal project itself.

All regulatory changes are disruptive, but regulations can also be relaxed or removed to allow new project opportunities or remove burdensome requirements. Changing city zoning laws to allow accessory dwelling units (ADUs) to be built on single-family home lots would create a boom in local construction projects, while changes to banking regulations could allow the sale of a new type of financial instrument.

Risk Analysis

Risk analysis derives the key data that will drive response planning. The purpose of risk analysis is to determine the effects of risks on the project objectives so the most effective response can be planned. Because not every risk can (or should) be responded to, the risks with the highest chance of occurring and the highest projected ***risk impact*** are the first to have a response planned and a risk budget allocated. The four risk analysis techniques in this chapter are qualitative analysis, quantitative analysis, situational or scenario analysis, and impact analysis.

While risk should be primarily analyzed during planning for a predictive project, Agile projects should re-analyze project risks at the start of each new iteration. Projects of all types will need to re-analyze risk during formal change control and periodic risk review.

Qualitative

Qualitative risk analysis assigns descriptive terms such as low, medium, and high (or mild, moderate, and severe) to measure project risks by their likelihood and degree of probable impact. These ratings are calculated within a probability and impact matrix, which provides a risk score to guide risk responses.

This analysis also determines risk categorization and risk urgency. The category describes the area of the project it affects, such as "physical security" or "access control." Risk categories are derived from risk standards or from a template provided by the PMO.

A risk's *urgency* estimates the speed at which it could impact the project. An urgent risk is a near-term risk that requires a faster response than a less urgent risk. Factors that influence urgency include how long it would take to detect the risk, the time required to respond to the risk, risk symptoms or warning signs, and risk ratings. For example, a new law that affects the scope of all projects in your program is a highly detectable risk, but its urgency will depend on your organization's response time. If the law will take effect in 6 months and you estimate it will take at least 9 months to overhaul your project's processes and bring them into compliance, the risk is urgent despite its highly visible 6-month lead-in.

The rationale behind a qualitative assessment is derived from expert judgment, historical data from similar projects, industry standards, and case studies. Qualitative risk analysis is faster than quantitative analysis, but it's more subjective. It is often the only analysis used in small projects. When qualitative risk analysis is complete, each risk's probability and impact, ranking, urgency, and categorization information should be added to the risk register.

Detectability

Detectability is a qualitative measure that describes how easy it will be to recognize when a negative risk occurs. If it is likely that the risk event will be noticed and responded to while the project's quality is unimpaired or only slightly harmed, it is a high-detectability risk. If the risk is likely to occur without being noticed until quality is significantly or irreparably harmed, it is a low-detectability risk. If a project was a car, a high-detectability risk would be noticed during routine maintenance (a low oil level on the dipstick) or automatically detected by internal controls that provide a clear, timely alert (a warning light on the dashboard). A low-detectability risk would not be found until the engine stuttered and smoke began pouring out of the hood.

High-detectability risks can be intercepted before they significantly affect the project, but low-detectability risks are found only after the damage is done, often near the end of project work. Low-detectability risks pose the most danger and can cause significant rework or even product recalls. Unit testing, quality controls, expert judgment, defect management, quality monitoring, and control processes can all increase risk detectability.

Interconnectivity

Interconnectivity is a qualitative measure that refers to the relationship between risks. Interconnected risks influence each other to behave in different ways than if the same risks occurred in isolation. In other words, Risk A could have a ripple effect such that it greatly increases (or reduces) the likelihood or impact of Risk B. Project risks should be evaluated both alone and in aggregate using scenario analysis and historical data to find hidden connections. The more additional risks that a single risk is connected to, even if that risk is small, should factor into any risk planning. By detecting interconnected risks, project managers might be able to find a strategy that works for the risk grouping, rather than several individual risk responses, or develop tiered responses for both singular and grouped risks.

For example, the manager of an international project identifies a global pandemic and a supply-chain interruption as valid risks and adds them to the risk register. After analysis, the risk of a pandemic (Risk 1) is scored as "highest impact / lowest probability" and accepted, and the risk of a supply-chain interruption (Risk 2) is scored as "high impact / medium probability" and mitigated with a faster procurement timeline. However, pandemics are interconnected with multiple risks, including supply-chain disruption. If Risk 1 (the pandemic) is realized, the risk score for Risk 2 (supply chain) becomes "high impact / highest probability," changing its priority level. By contrast, a supply-chain disruption does not increase the likelihood of a pandemic.

Even risk responses should be analyzed for potential interconnections. A secondary risk is a new project risk caused by implementing a planned risk response. For example, applying a technical control to counter one network risk could inadvertently create a new application vulnerability, or it could create a secondary risk. Secondary risks should be planned for alongside their primary risk trigger.

Quantitative

Quantitative risk analysis is slower, more methodical, and more detailed than qualitative analysis. It also evaluates a risk by its probability and impact, but instead of using subjective values, it describes a risk's effects on project objectives in numeric terms, such as currency amounts, percentages of revenue, or calendar increments. Accurate quantitative analysis relies on high-quality data from similar risk scenarios and correctly chosen statistical models to produce confident results. The rationale behind a quantitative assessment is derived from expert judgment, interviewing, probability modeling, sensitivity analysis, expected monetary value analysis, and other modeling and simulation techniques. When quantitative risk analysis is complete, the risk register is usually updated with a prioritized list of quantified risks. The risk often equals the probability multiplied by the impact of the risk.

Expected monetary value (EMV), or risk exposure, is the product of a risk event's probability of occurrence and the gain or loss that will result. If the probability of a particular risk happening is 50% and the expected loss is $10,000, the expected monetary value of the risk (sometimes called the ***risk exposure***) will be $5,000 (0.5 × 10,000). If the impact of losing a web server for 1 day due to an attack is $100,000 and there is a 25% chance that it will happen in any given year, the risk of a single attack on the web server could be quantified as $25,000. EMV can be calculated using several tools, such as decision tree analysis.

The end result of ***risk quantification*** is also a list of prioritized risks. This ***risk prioritization*** ensures that risk response plans are developed for every identified risk based on its priority. Higher-priority risks will likely have detailed plans; medium-priority and low-priority risks may not have as detailed plans in the risk management plan. Ensuring that all risks have associated action plans will help the project team know what to do if they encounter a particular risk.

Simulation

Simulation, also called Monte Carlo simulation, is a quantitative risk analysis method that can use schedule and cost estimates to simulate real-life project results. Monte Carlo simulation gauges the probability of certain outcomes by running multiple risk scenarios using randomly generated variables that fall within a control range and then asking "what-if" questions of each scenario result. The aggregate results of thousands of simulations can be examined for trends, helping find the most probable results and worst-case results. A Monte Carlo simulation would help determine the likelihood of a project completing on time or on budget, the probability of a task being on the critical path, or the overall risk of a project. Because these values are derived from metrics, the estimates are quantitative.

Simulation is usually done with specialized software. Project managers should remember to adjust the simulation to take schedule path convergences into account, which are points in the schedule where many paths converge into one activity.

Impact Analysis

Impact analysis is the technique that actually produces the risk's impact calculation and scales it relative to the scores of other project risks. Impact analysis can use quantitative techniques only, qualitative techniques only, or semi-quantitative techniques. The important point to remember is that the probability/impact matrix, which is a key risk planning tool, is not tied to either methodology.

When impact and likelihood are combined, the result is variously referred to as a risk score, risk magnitude, or risk criticality. The quantitative measure of all risk in a project is also known as its risk exposure. All of these terms mean the size of the risk relative to the project it affects.

Probability vs. Impact

A ***probability and impact matrix***, also called a ***risk matrix***, is a tool used to assign the relative risk score. The matrix is a grid that scores each risk by comparing its likelihood on one axis against its impact on the other axis. The risk's assessed qualities are plotted onto the grid, which is pre-assigned with value ranges set by the risk management plan. Once the values are plugged in, the square where the risk lands shows the score for its criticality.

Probability and impact matrices can incorporate qualitative or quantitative analysis. They can also be used semi-quantitatively. Smaller and less complex projects may use a simple three-by-three matrix and qualitative values like "low, medium, high" or "uncommon, likely, very likely" to create matrices. These descriptive values can be assigned numeric operators to perform quantitative assessments. The scales are not universal; the percentages are determined by the project organization or PMO and reflect the risk appetite. From a mathematical standpoint, it may make more sense to assign "most likely" a 90% probability and "least likely" a 10% probability. However, the project using the scale in Figure 4-1 may consider the 50% chance of a risk as "high" for the purposes of calculating risk scores in order to keep the organization below a desired risk threshold.

Level Names	Level Values (%)	Level Values (numerical)	Description
Very High	70%	0.7	Very Likely
High	50%	0.5	Likely
Moderate	30%	0.3	Possible
Low	15%	0.15	Unlikely
Very Low	5%	0.05	Rare

Figure 4-1 Probability Value Scale

The following matrix displayed in Figure 4-2 uses a five-by-five map and sets each value on the likelihood axis as rare=1, unlikely=2, possible=3, likely=4, and very likely=5. The impact axis is set to very low=1, low=2, moderate=3, major=4, and extreme=5. The values are multiplied across each table and row to find numeric scores to represent the risk score.

		Level of Impact				
		Very Low 1	Low 2	Moderate 3	Major 4	Extreme 5
Likelihood	Very Likely 5	Medium 5	High 10	Very High 15	Critical 20	Critical 25
	Likely 4	Medium 4	High 8	High 9	Very High 16	Critical 20
	Possible 3	Low 3	Medium 6	High 9	High 12	Very High 15
	Unlikely 2	Low 2	Medium 4	Medium 4	High 8	High 10
	Rare 1	Low 1	Low 2	Low 3	Medium 4	Medium 5

Figure 4-2 Risk Probability/Impact Matrix

The organization decides to assign risk scores according to the values shown in Table 4-2 and to represent their risk appetite.

Table 4-2 Risk Scoring Model

Risk score	Value
1–3	Low
4–5	Medium
6–14	High
15–19	Very High
20 or above	Critical

Here's the formula for calculating the risk score:

Risk Score = Potential Impact × Probability of Occurrence

To find the score of a given risk, the project manager would calculate its probability and its projected impact and then compare those outcomes against the likelihood scale and impact scale in the risk management methodology. For example, suppose that the risk of a team member becoming ill during the project was assessed as likely and the impact was assessed as very low. The organization's matrix assigns a numeric value of 4 to likely and 1 to very low. Using the matrix in Figure 4-2, the risk score is found to be 4, which the organization considers to be a risk with medium criticality. This score will guide the risk response plan.

A risk heat map uses a probability/impact matrix to create a concise, understandable graphic of the project's risk exposure. Heat maps are useful for status reports and project dashboards. In the example risk heat map image displayed in Figure 4-3, supply-chain slowdowns (moderate/very likely) and ransomware attacks (possible/extreme) both have an orange threat level and therefore have equal priority for response planning. A team member's illness (likely/very low) would be addressed next; its placement on the map also shows at a glance how much risk it causes the project (not much). Finally, the file incompatibility is a green-zone risk and therefore likely to be accepted, not mitigated.

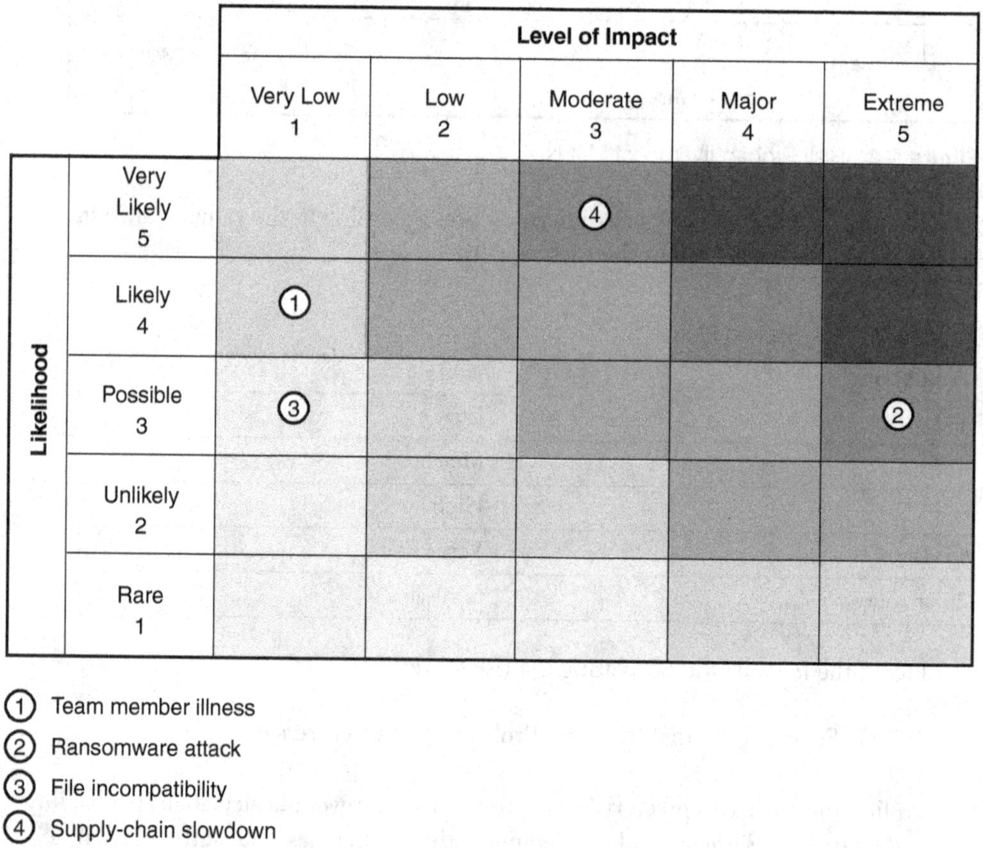

		Level of Impact				
		Very Low 1	Low 2	Moderate 3	Major 4	Extreme 5
Likelihood	Very Likely 5			④		
	Likely 4	①				
	Possible 3	③				②
	Unlikely 2					
	Rare 1					

① Team member illness
② Ransomware attack
③ File incompatibility
④ Supply-chain slowdown

Figure 4-3 Example Risk Heat Map

Situational/Scenario Analysis

A scenario is a coherent narrative that simulates a future project environment; it is used to calculate the most likely risks and outcomes of a project that executes under those conditions. This chapter lists general risk scenarios (new project, new management, digital transformation, and so on) that commonly affect projects and can be used to find specific potential threats and opportunities.

You can query project assumptions as if they were scenarios to uncover additional risks linked to the project. To perform this analysis, choose an assumption from the assumption log or charter and ask two questions: "Could this assumption be false?" and "If yes, would it significantly affect a project objective?" If both answers are yes, review your confidence in the assumption. If there is a moderate to strong possibility the assumption could be false, the associated risk should be logged and treated according to its priority.

Common Risk Responses

Risk management prepares a project to respond to risks in a controlled, proactive way. Project managers should understand the options for handling risk and how to choose the best response or responses. Risk responses are recorded in the risk register and periodically reviewed during project execution to ensure they are still valid. The most common methods for handling risk can be grouped into risk management strategies (proactive) and contingency or fallback plans (reactive). Risk management strategies vary based on whether the risk is positive or negative.

Executing a risk response, or responding to a risk, is sometimes referred to as risk treatment or treating a risk; a treated risk has been changed by one or more response actions. If a project risk occurs, it is said to be materialized or a ***realized risk***.

Risk Management Strategies

Once the identified risks are analyzed and prioritized, the project manager will work with senior stakeholders and subject matter experts (SMEs) to choose the appropriate risk response. Risk responses should be realistic, obtainable, proportionate to the risk, and cost-effective compared with the risk's estimated impact. The response will be influenced by the organization's risk appetite, risk threshold, and aggregate risk levels. ***Risk appetite*** is the amount of uncertainty that an organization is willing to take on to pursue project goals, while ***risk tolerance*** is the amount of risk the organization can take on before normal operations are affected. Senior management determines risk appetite, which can vary from project to project.

There is no set timeline for treating a risk. Preventative treatments or mitigations like buying insurance or encrypting hard drives on new project devices should be performed as soon as feasible, after which the risk would be closed and monitored. Other types of risk responses only need to be planned and will not require action unless the risk occurs.

Negative Risks

There are four primary responses for negative risks: avoidance (remove the possibility of the risk), mitigation (decrease the impact or probability of the risk), transference (use a third party to cushion the impact), and acceptance (do nothing and let the risk happen). Negative risk responses try to reduce the potential cost of all negative risk to an acceptable threshold.

Accept

Risk acceptance means to not take any action in response to the risk. Acceptance is a strategy for both negative and positive risks. Accepting a risk is not ignoring it; the project manager logs the accepted risk on the risk register and monitors it until the project closes. Acceptance is usually best for unlikely risks or risks where there is no suitable or cost-effective remediation. If the risk is likely but low-impact, organizations may plan to absorb its damage instead of preventing it.

EXAMPLE: Your project team will spend 2 weeks testing an application on various brands of mobile devices. The mobile devices must be kept in a semi-secure shared location. You identify the risk that some devices may be stolen by other employees or visitors. You do not have the authority or budget to increase physical security in the shared area. Because the devices do not contain sensitive data, are replaceable, and are only needed for 2 weeks, you accept the risk that some might go missing.

Avoid

Risk avoidance is a strategy for negative risks that tries to eliminate the activities or conditions that create the risk. This can mean removing a hazard from the project environment or altering a process to remove the chance of error. Reducing your risk exposure can also reduce the potential for reward, so risk avoidance should include a cost-benefit analysis. The most popular risk avoidance strategy is to edit the project parameters to remove the threat entirely.

EXAMPLE: A project has planned to use an overseas supplier for a key resource, but new political unrest in the region has made it likely the resource will have delivery delays or rapid price fluctuations. To avoid the risk, the project team may decide not to purchase from suppliers in politically unstable countries. They could also alter the project's requirements to use a domestically available resource. As another example, disconnecting an internal network from the Internet avoids the risk of cyberattack.

Mitigate

Risk mitigation is a strategy for negative risks that tries to reduce the probability of a risk and/or lower its projected impact to acceptable levels. Mitigation could include developing prototypes before committing to production, simplifying processes to reduce user error, encrypting project laptops, backing up data to the cloud, and adding security cameras. Mitigation is the "ounce of prevention is worth a pound of cure" strategy. Mitigation does not always prevent a risk from occurring, but it limits the effect of the risk if it does occur.

EXAMPLE: A new application development project identifies the risk that the web servers used by the project will become overloaded and cause performance issues. To mitigate this risk, the project team decides to deploy an upgraded web server farm before project work starts. They also recommend that all staff receive security awareness training to reduce the threat of phishing attacks that could compromise the server farm.

Transfer

Risk transference is a strategy for negative risks that shifts the risk's impact to a third party. This strategy almost always involves paying the other party to take on the risk. Insurance policies are a classic example of risk transference. It is important to note that transference protects your organization from a risk's impact, but does not eliminate the risk or reduce its probability. Also, certain types of risk can never be transferred, notably the risk of non-compliance with laws or regulations.

EXAMPLE: Company A hires Company B as a subcontractor to perform project work. Because this industry is volatile, there is a slight risk that the subcontractor could go out of business before the project is complete. Company A requests that Company B purchase a payment bond, which is a financial instrument that will pay Company B's employees and suppliers for their work on Company A's project if Company B goes bankrupt. This transfers the impact of Company B's insolvency to the issuer of the bond and away from Company A.

Table 4-3 demonstrates how negative risk responses affect the likelihood and impact of a given risk (assuming each response was successful).

Table 4-3 Effect of Negative Risk Responses on Likelihood and Impact

Risk Response	Reduces Risk Likelihood	Reduces Risk Impact
Acceptance	No	No
Avoidance	Yes	Yes
Mitigation	Sometimes	Yes
Transference	No	Yes

Positive Risks

Positive risk management strategies try to find and enhance opportunities to increase the project's return on investment (ROI), shorten its timeline, reduce its costs, or bring new projects and partnerships to the organization. The four positive risk strategies are acceptance (do nothing), enhancement (encourage the opportunity), exploitation (seize the opportunity), and sharing (divide the opportunity).

Accept

As with negative risks, acceptance is a strategy for positive risks whereby the project manager does not take any action in response to the risk. Acceptance means declining the chance and letting what may happen, happen. This strategy makes sense for opportunities that seem unlikely or (as with negative risks) are not cost-effective to pursue.

EXAMPLE: A major vendor is promoting their latest technology with a contest. Projects that use the technology can submit a 10-page press kit to the vendor with the winning project to be featured on the vendor's website. Your project uses the technology, but because there is a low chance of winning and the benefit is not clear, you decide not to spend time or resources preparing an entry.

Enhance

Risk enhancement is a strategy for positive risks whereby the project manager identifies the key drivers behind a risk and adjusts them to increase the odds of the risk occurring. It can also mean adjusting the project's parameters to take advantage of a positive risk after it occurs, increasing its impact. Enhancement is the opposite of mitigation.

EXAMPLE: Your project team members are attending a trade show in advance of your new product launch. They discover that the show is hosting a VIP add-on event where attendees can pitch their projects directly to investors. You use project reserves to buy the team members tickets to the VIP event, enhancing the opportunity to find a new sponsor or new markets for the product.

Exploit

Risk exploitation is a strategy for positive risks whereby the project team takes steps to ensure that the risk occurs. This is the opposite of risk avoidance. High-impact opportunities should be exploited when possible.

EXAMPLE: Your project team identifies a single task in the critical path that would complete the product one month early if they had one additional team member. The cost savings will exceed the cost of hiring the resource. You exploit the opportunity by adding the extra resource, ensuring the project will finish early and under budget.

Share

Risk sharing is a strategy for positive risks whereby partial ownership of the risk is allocated to a third party. Sharing is a valid strategy when the team or organization wants to benefit from an opportunity that they cannot enhance or exploit on their own.

EXAMPLE: Your team has identified a project with a high potential ROI that would require Agile development practices. Because your project team has no Agile experts, the team decides to partner with a company that specializes in Agile development so that both companies can earn revenue from the product.

Development of Contingency/Fallback Plans

Contingency plans are based on certain events occurring, known as ***risk triggers***. Also called a fallback plan, the contingency plan is usually part of the risk register and is funded with contingency reserves. The project manager and/or the risk owner should develop a contingency plan for all high-impact and high-priority risks with the most disruptive potential, including positive ones. Contingency plans are the backup for when the planned response does not adequately reduce or embrace the risk. The plan should record the drivers behind the trigger event or condition and clarify when and how to respond, including the following:

- A description of the trigger
- The response owner and key roles associated with the plan
- Advance work required to prepare the plan (such as ordering supplies)
- Actions that should be taken in response to the trigger and the sequence in which response steps should be performed
- How the response should be communicated to the necessary stakeholders

For example, if a project's key deliverable is a physical prototype that must be shipped to a trade show, shipping error is a critical risk. To avoid the risk, a team member could be chosen to transport the prototype in person. A contingency plan could be holding a duplicate prototype in reserve and designating a second team member as backup transportation. To prepare the plan, you would create the duplicate, budget travel funds, get buy-in from the team, and draft an emergency contact protocol. The risk trigger would be any incident that stopped the first team member from getting to the trade show on time with a working prototype. If no incident occurred, no fallback would be needed and the risk would be closed.

NOTE Remember that both mitigation plans and contingency plans address risk, but a mitigation plan is executed when a risk is identified and before it occurs. A contingency plan is only executed after it is triggered by a risk event or condition.

Project Reserves

Project reserves are funds that are set aside during planning to cover unexpected costs or to fund planned risk responses. The two types of reserves are ***contingency reserves*** (for known risks) and ***management reserves*** (for unknown risks). Both contingency and management reserves are part of the budget requirements, but only contingency reserves are included in the project's cost baseline.

A contingency reserve is portioned from the project's budget and established by the project manager. The amount to reserve is usually determined from probability and impact calculations. If an identified risk occurs, then the portion of the reserve that was allocated for that risk will be spent. Contingency plans are funded from contingency reserves. These reserves might also fund costs incurred by a change request, as scope changes are usually a recognized risk.

A management reserve is mainly used when unforeseen work is needed to complete the project or when a previously unknown risk or issue threatens the project. The reserve is allocated from the organization's funds, not the project's, and spending these reserves requires approval from management. Unlike contingency reserves, they are not controlled by the project manager and are not part of the budget baseline.

Roles and Responsibilities

Roles, in the context of issues and risks, are not project roles like sponsor or developer. Risk and issue roles convey a stakeholder's scope of accountability for an issue or risk. The primary roles are risk owner and issue owner. There is a strong overlap between their responsibilities, but where risk ownership can mean watchful waiting, issue management is an active process by default. For example, both risks and issues have points of escalation defined in their respective management plans. Escalating a risk once could mean transferring it away from the project, but an issue can need repeated escalation to be resolved.

Risk Ownership

Each risk in the risk register must be assigned an owner who has the ability to monitor the risk, detect a risk occurrence, and execute the risk response if necessary. Some projects may have the ***risk owner*** select the risk response instead of the project manager. This role uses the risk budget, documents all risk response actions taken and their outcomes, and communicates the risk response status to interested stakeholders and the project manager. If the risk is closed, the owner monitors the project environment for reoccurrence. The project manager can also be a risk owner, but effective risk management can require subject matter expertise beyond project management.

If a response action requires more than one person, the risk owner coordinates their efforts. The risk owner can delegate the activities of a risk response (but not the accountability for the risk) by assigning the *risk action owner* role to another individual.

Issue Ownership

Like risks, all issues should have owners. If a known risk occurs and the response plan reduces it to an acceptable impact, the risk event can remain with the risk owner. If an unknown risk occurs, or if a known risk is not mitigated, the risk event becomes an issue that requires issue management. The issue owner could be the same as the risk owner (for known risks), but it may sometimes be necessary to transfer a critical issue to a more experienced team member for problem-solving.

The issue owner is accountable for following the issue resolution plan or issue contingency plan or else escalating the issue. If a resolution plan does not exist, this role works with the project manager to develop one. If the issue requires a workaround, the issue owner should create it or ensure it is created, communicate it to the project manager, and monitor the workaround for secondary issues. Because issues are active, the issue owner should keep the project manager aware of its status so the ***issue log*** and issue dashboards remain current.

Points of Escalation

With ordinary risk management, stakeholders or team members who find evidence of an active risk are responsible for notifying the project manager or the person listed as the owner in the risk register. Urgent risks should be communicated directly to the project sponsor as well. Sometimes risk analysis will uncover risks that should be communicated outside the project's boundaries or otherwise escalated. The risk management plan should list ***escalation points***, which describe the circumstances when a risk should be escalated and the responsible roles or individuals to whom the risk should be handed off. This can be another project's manager, a functional manager, or the member of senior management with authority over the risk's scope. Here are some common escalation points:

- Finding a project-level risk with a probability/impact score or estimated monetary value above a certain threshold, such as a critical risk or a potential impact that exceeds 30% of reserves
- Finding a project-level risk that shares dependencies with another project
- Finding a business-level risk that affects another functional department, another project or program, enterprise operations, or shared services
- Planning a risk response that exceeds the project manager's authority, such as a response that requires action from legal counsel or the human resources department

Escalation may require the project manager to obtain the sponsor's or senior management's approval for the risk response, or it may transfer the risk ownership away from the project and into the enterprise risk plan. The project manager should document how, when, and to whom the risk was escalated and the outcome, and the escalation status should be logged in the risk register and the risk report.

EXAMPLE: Your organization and several industry competitors all sell your products in the same third-party marketplace. This is also your company's main retail sales channel. A team member learns from an industry contact that a direct competitor wants to acquire the third-party marketplace. Because the risk affects your entire organization's sales strategy, it is an enterprise-wide risk and an escalation point. You identify risks that threaten retail sales as an escalation point owned by the VP of sales and risks that threaten market share as an escalation point owned by the CEO. You escalate the risk to both.

Escalation Path

Issue escalation is used when a project team identifies an issue that affects the project but is not being handled. The project team will need to identify to whom the issue should be escalated. They also need to identify the escalation point, meaning the parameters or conditions that result in an issue being escalated. Issues can be identified at any level of the organization and should be resolved at the lowest possible level. If an issue cannot be resolved, it must be escalated to ensure it comes to the attention of appropriate parties. This procedure promotes the visibility of longstanding unresolved issues.

Issues can have multiple escalation points if the impact continues unabated, forming a tiered escalation path. ***Escalation paths*** can be defined by the PMO and provided as part of the issue management plan. The plan should include both escalation criteria (a description of the escalation point) and the escalation contact.

An escalation path for a project-level issue is described in Chapter 7, "Communication and Meeting Management," and illustrated in Table 7-3.

Overview of Issue Management

No risk can be perfectly managed or anticipated, and every project will experience issues. Issue management has several of the same activities as risk management but primarily happens during the Executing phase. At a high level, the steps are as follows:

1. **Identify and document issues.** Create an issue log to track all issues, active and resolved, along with the issue owner and details of the issue response. (An example of an issue log is presented in Figure 13-11 in Chapter 13.)
2. **Review issues.** Analyze the issue and prioritize it by its severity, urgency, and impact to the project and the organization. Perform root cause analysis for repeat issues and major issues. Escalate issues along the escalation path, if applicable.
3. **Resolve issues.** Communicate issues to key stakeholders inside and outside the project. Create and apply a resolution plan and assign action owners. Execute a contingency plan, if triggered, and install appropriate workarounds. Resolve the issue.
4. **Close issues.** Continue to monitor the project environment for a new occurrence of the issue. Remove workarounds. Update the project management plan and document outcomes for lessons learned.

> **NOTE** Depending on the issue's severity, not all steps may happen in this order, and some steps may iterate. If a contingency plan exists for an urgent issue, it should be executed as soon as the issue is detected, and root cause analysis should be deferred until the issue is mitigated.

Issue Resolution Plan

Issues are addressed with an ***issue resolution plan***. If the issue arose from a logged risk, the resolution plan will begin with the risk treatment that was assigned during planning and then be adapted to the actual (not the estimated) circumstances of the issue. If no plan exists, the project manager will need to work quickly with project team members to create one. The plan should include the issue owner, a description of the issue, a description of the resolution actions, the opening date, the required budget, and a target resolution date. The plan should describe any workarounds that were implemented.

It is important to add a target resolution date to ensure that issues do not permanently float in the backlog. Even if the date is pushed back, having one assigned will keep the issue on the calendar.

Issue Tracking

The primary tool for tracking issues is the issue log, as shown in Figure 13-11. All stakeholders should understand the issue tracking methodology being used and know where to find the central issue log. All relevant internal stakeholders, particularly the project team and issue owners, should have full access to the issue log so they are able to review, add, or update issues as they arise.

Project managers should also ensure that the project team understands the difference between issues and action items, which are tracked separately from issues:

- Issues usually require multiple resources and considerable time to resolve. They are issues because they delay or hinder some factor of the project.
- Action items should require few resources—often only a single resource—and usually less than 1 week to resolve. These items should not cause delays in the project.

Action items should not be added to the issue log unless they are part of a logged issue's response.

> **NOTE** Agile methodologies like scrum categorize issues as impediments, which are defined as any internal or external factor that slows a team's work and delays execution.

Executing the Contingency Plan

Issues that were previously identified as risks, or that fall into a pre-identified category of risk, may already have a contingency plan in place. The contingency plan should be executed as soon as it is triggered by an issue, even if the issue is not severe. It may be necessary to analyze and prioritize the issue before deciding if it is important enough to execute the contingency plan. However, you would always execute a contingency plan *before* analyzing its root cause. It is more important to mitigate the impact of the issue than to allow it to go unchecked while you look for a cause.

Contingency plans may resolve a time-bound issue, as in the example of the failed delivery used earlier in this chapter. However, they are not the same as an issue resolution plan. Full issue resolution includes tracking, ownership, analysis, escalation (if appropriate), and documentation of outcomes.

Root Cause Analysis

Root cause analysis looks for the key drivers behind a risk, issue, or impediment, which could be a defect, an assumption, a variance, or an unknown risk. If you address an issue without fixing the root cause, it will continue to crop up, draining project resources and slowing the schedule. If an issue was caused by an unknown risk, it is important to find the source of the risk to eliminate or reduce it in future projects.

Project managers might gravitate toward analyzing only issues where the origin is unknown, but it is equally (if not more) important to analyze recurrent issues, even if their cause seems apparent. If the same issue has recurred multiple times after being resolved each time, then prior resolution plans could have made bad assumptions about the root cause. Organizations can require root cause analysis for all high-priority issues or issues with a high monetary impact or scope to prevent reoccurrence.

A root cause may not be obviously connected to an issue without analysis. Several common quality management tools and techniques are used to find a root cause, including Pareto charts (Figure 14-2), run charts (Figure 14-3), scatter diagrams (Figures 14-4 to 14-6), and fishbone or Ishikawa diagrams (Figure 14-8), as provided later in the book in Chapter 14, "Quality and Performance Charts." Techniques like situational/scenario analysis, interviews, brainstorming, and troubleshooting can be less formal but effective for issues that do not generate hard data. After generating a list of potential root causes, the project manager can treat each one to see if the problem is eliminated. One root cause can produce multiple issues, so root cause analysis has a good return on the time spent investing in it.

EXAMPLE: A power outage occurs at a remote location where project work is taking place. This risk was anticipated, and an alternate power source had been supplied in advance. The power outage was assumed to be a normal fluctuation of the power grid. However, two more power outages occurred within the month. The project manager should start a root cause analysis to try to prevent future occurrences.

Issue Prioritization

Issue prioritization means setting the order in which issues will be addressed. The priority score is derived from a combination of five factors: the severity, the impact on the project, the impact on the organization, the urgency, and the escalation status.

Each of these factors can be defined with qualitative values like low, medium, and high or critical, major, minor, and minimal. The issue management plan or risk management plan should have a predefined scale with clearly defined criteria to compare against the factor and find its score.

After the factors are weighed, the resulting priority score will define the timeline for the response. Again, each project or organization will have internal standards for correlating a priority score with a response timeline. The following is an example of a scale:

- **Urgent**: Immediately stop normal operations and address the issue until it is resolved or escalated.
- **High**: Begin work on the issue within 24 hours and allocate 50% of working hours to resolving it.
- **Medium**: Begin work on the issue within 3 business days and devote 20% of working hours to resolving it.
- **Low**: Schedule a time to begin working on the issue after higher-priority issues are complete or defer the issue to the backlog.

Unlike risks, issues cannot be analyzed in advance. However, it is vital to have a plan for identifying the highest-priority issues to protect project operations and the larger organization. Without a way to score issues relative to each other, people tend to prioritize only the issue in front of them.

Issue Severity

The severity factor of an issue describes the issue's impact on the system's end users or client. An issue that disabled one of the product's central requirements or locked end users' access would have the highest severity rating, as would any issue that caused a safety hazard. An issue that affected a minor requirement and had a successful workaround would have a minor severity rating. A cosmetic flaw that did not affect usability, such as an incorrect color or font selection, would be the least severe, as it has negligible impact on the user.

Urgency

The urgency factor describes the time it will take for an issue to significantly impact your business or project. Urgency is usually measured by how much time should elapse before the issue is addressed, with the most urgent issues requiring immediate attention. Issues that are time-sensitive or that will cause cascading issues the longer they are unaddressed are also urgent. Highly urgent issues must be resolved within hours, in the same business day, or within 24 hours, while low-urgency issues can be resolved on a relaxed timeline.

Impact to Project

The impact to project factor evaluates the effect of the issue on the scope, quality, budget, or schedule. A high-impact issue could delay a task in the critical path by 2 weeks or cause it to exceed its budget by 10%. A low-impact issue would be absorbed by schedule or contingency reserves and have no risk to product quality. An issue with the highest impact rating would mean the project might not be completed, such as the loss of a critical resource with no replacement.

Scope of Impact to Organization

The scope of impact to organization factor evaluates whether operations in the project's organization are affected by the issue and, if so, what percentage of the organization is affected. An issue with low impact to the organization would only affect a small percentage of people. It could also mean an issue with organization-wide effects that were not noticed by most users. An issue with high impact affects the largest percent of the organization, such as an issue that disables all access to the employee parking garage.

Issue Escalation

The escalation factor takes into account how far the issue has already been elevated along the escalation path. An issue that has already been escalated to the third tier of response, usually senior management, will have a priority weighting far above an issue that has not been escalated at all.

Workarounds

Workarounds are temporary solutions intended to keep some aspect of project work moving forward until the issue affecting it is resolved and the normal or official process can be restored. A workaround can be included in an approved risk response or contingency plan, or it might be developed on the spot to bypass an unexpected roadblock. Active workarounds should be documented in the issue resolution plan to help ensure they are removed when they are no longer needed. If the workaround addresses a defect, it should also be described and tracked in the defect log. A workaround is not inherently negative, but because it was not part of the original requirements or quality planning, it could have unforeseen effects on the project.

IT project managers in particular should log and monitor technological workarounds implemented in response to product defects or code errors. If a minor issue is continually added to the backlog instead of being resolved, long-standing workarounds can become embedded in the product and affect future deliverables. Workarounds are a common response to application defects, but continually bypassing a nonfunctional feature to use a temporary replacement or an obscure solution (such as hitting the Escape key to exit an unresponsive page) can create a quality or security issue.

Outcome Documentation

Once an issue is closed, its outcome should be documented in the issue log along with all actions taken to address the issue, the stakeholders involved, its impact on the project (such as costs or schedule delays), and any changes it caused to the project. These factors should also be included in the next project status report, along with an issue summary. If the project management plan was impacted by an issue, the budget, schedule, defect log, or other affected documents should be updated to include the issue's impact. Issue impacts and outcomes should be included in the next project status report.

Finally, all project issues should be added to the lessons learned documentation. This document should include a writeup of significant issues and the findings of a root cause analysis, along with a performance assessment of the issue response. If root cause analysis revealed an issue that could reoccur, it may need to be added to future risk registers. When the project is closed, the issue log itself should be added to the archives maintained by the organization.

Exam Preparation Tasks

As mentioned in the section "How to Use This Book" in the Introduction, you have a few choices for exam preparation: the exercises here, Chapter 17, "Final Preparation," and the exam simulation questions included in the Pearson Test Prep Software Online.

Review All Key Topics

Review the most important topics in this chapter, noted with the Key Topics icon in the outer margin of the page. Table 4-4 lists each reference of these key topics and the page number on which each is found.

Table 4-4 Key Topics for Chapter 4

Key Topic Element	Description	Page Number
List	Risk management process	109
List	Definitions of issues, risks, and changes	110
Section	Describes known and unknown risks	111

Key Topic Element	Description	Page Number
Paragraph	Defines risk review	111
Paragraph	Describes risk analysis	114
Paragraph	Defines qualitative risk analysis	114
Paragraph	Describes detectability	115
Paragraph	Describes interconnectivity	116
Paragraph	Defines quantitative risk analysis	116
Paragraph	Describes simulation	117
Paragraph	Defines impact analysis	117
Section	Describes risk management strategies	121
Paragraph	Defines contingency plan and risk triggers	125
Paragraph	Describes risk ownership	127
Paragraph	Describes issue ownership	127
Paragraph	Describes points of escalation	127
Paragraph	Describes escalation path	128
List	Issue management steps	129
Paragraph	Describes issue resolution plan	129
Paragraph	Describes issue tracking	130
Paragraph	Defines root cause analysis	131
Paragraph	Defines issue prioritization	131
Paragraph	Describes workarounds	133
Section	Describes outcome documentation	134

Define Key Terms

Define the following key terms from this chapter and check your answers in the glossary:

project risk management, risk management, risk response, risk planning, risk activities, issue, risk, risk register, unknown risk, risk review, digital transformation, infrastructure end-of-life (EOL), major cybersecurity event, risk analysis, risk impact, qualitative, detectability, interconnectivity, quantitative risk analysis, risk exposure, risk quantification, risk prioritization, risk management plan, simulation, impact analysis, risk exposure, probability and impact matrix, risk matrix, situational/scenario analysis, realized risk, risk appetite, risk tolerance, risk acceptance, risk avoidance, risk mitigation, risk transference, risk enhancement, risk exploitation, risk sharing, contingency plans, risk triggers, project reserves, contingency reserves,management reserves, risk owner, issue log, escalation points, escalation paths, issue resolution plan, root cause analysis, workarounds

Review Questions

The answers to these questions appear in Appendix A. For more practice with sample exam questions, use the Pearson Test Prep practice test software online.

1. Which general risk scenarios are *most* likely to require the project team to adapt to new technologies and new workflow processes? (Choose two.)
   a. Business acquisitions/mergers
   b. Digital transformation
   c. New management
   d. Regulatory changes
   e. Reorganizations

2. After discovering midway through the project that its operational center is located in a flood plain, the project manager buys additional insurance using funds from management reserves. What best describes this scenario?
   a. A contingency plan was followed.
   b. A workaround was found.
   c. A negative risk response was implemented.
   d. A root cause was analyzed.
   e. An issue was responded to.

3. You are hired to take over managing a project. You are concerned that the original risk planning process did not identify all the project risks. What should you do?
   a. Perform a risk review.
   b. Prepare a risk report.
   c. Perform risk quantification.
   d. Review the current risk prioritization.

4. A team member discovers that a current project at your company could be completed much faster by using a certain proprietary technology. If you approach the technology's manufacturer with a plan to work together for a percentage of the profit, which risk strategy are you employing?

   a. Risk exploitation

   b. Risk enhancement

   c. Risk sharing

   d. Risk acceptance

5. During a project meeting, a stakeholder reports that the venue for a planned project event may not be available and the prepaid deposit might be lost. This was not anticipated as a project risk. Where should this new information be documented *first*?

   a. Risk register

   b. Escalation plan

   c. Action items

   d. Issues log

6. A project team is using expert judgment and reviewing lessons learned to assign impact and likelihood scores to all project risks. Which process are they completing?

   a. Situational analysis

   b. Qualitative risk analysis

   c. Quantitative risk analysis

   d. Risk prioritization

7. A commercial bakery hires a recipe consultant to create a dessert line. During development, the consultant discovers a new production technique that would reduce the bakery's operating costs by 20%. The bakery's project manager gains approval to expand the project's scope and formally train all production staff in the new technique. Which risk response strategy was used?

   a. Acceptance

   b. Enhancement

   c. Transference

   d. Exploitation

8. Which of the following is *not* performed as part of issue management?
   a. Assigning probability scores
   b. Removing workarounds
   c. Adding workarounds
   d. Analyzing root causes
   e. Assigning priority scores

9. Which statement is correct regarding risks, issues, and/or changes?
   a. A planned risk response should not affect the project's scope.
   b. Issue response should be proactive, not reactive.
   c. Most risks and issues are documented during project planning.
   d. Both risks and issues can trigger the change control process.

10. A project manager has prepared a document that lists three members of your organization and three future scenarios that would trigger communication with these individuals. What does this describe?
    a. Scenario analysis
    b. An escalation point
    c. Root cause analysis
    d. A contingency plan

This chapter covers the following topics:

- **Overview of Project Schedule Development:** Provides introductory information regarding project schedules
- **Story Estimation/Story Points:** Includes themes, epics, stories, and tasks
- **Upcoming Milestones and Activity Identification:** Discusses milestones, durations, start/finish dates, and sprint goals
- **Sequencing:** Covers dependencies and successor/predecessor relationships
- **Resource Loading:** Includes resource loading, resource smoothing, and resource leveling
- **Schedule Baselining:** Discusses the schedule baseline
- **Estimating Techniques:** Covers analogous estimating, parametric estimating, three-point estimating, alternatives analysis, contingency reserves/buffers, and critical path analysis
- **Schedule Maintenance:** Includes buffer utilization, critical path analysis, impacts to cadence, forecasting, publication and sharing, sprint planning, and backlog prioritization
- **Revise the Baseline vs. Rebaseline:** Discusses revising the baseline and rebaselining

CHAPTER 5

Schedule Development and Management

One of the main limitations for any project is the schedule, which is established during the project's planning phase and can be changed only through formal change control. If task durations take longer than originally estimated, either more resources will need to be provided or the project end date will have to be changed. If critical tasks are delayed or milestones missed, the entire project may be at risk. Project managers therefore need to manage project schedules carefully. Schedule development should answer the following questions:

- How long should a given task take to accomplish? How much work can be performed in a unit of time?
- Which tasks cannot start or finish until one or more other tasks starts or finishes? Which tasks can happen at any time, and which must be performed in a certain order?
- Which tasks must occur at a fixed point in the schedule, and which could be moved without affecting project work?

Project ***schedule management*** (referred to in some standards as *time management*) ensures that project work is completed when it should be. It begins with defining the units of work and creating a work breakdown structure, defining and sequencing the project activities, estimating the activity resources and durations, and then developing the actual schedule. These documents become part of the schedule management plan, which is part of the project management plan. After the schedule is established, the project manager is responsible for controlling it for the duration of project execution. Project schedule control allows project managers to recognize variances from the project plan and take corrective actions.

For predictive projects, the entire project schedule is developed during planning and can only be changed via change control. However, for adaptive projects, the overall project deadline is known, and the team works together during each cycle (sometimes called sprint, iteration, or increment) to determine the schedule for the current cycle.

This chapter covers schedule development, identifying sprint goals and milestones, story estimation, defining epics and tasks, task sequencing, resource loading, and schedule maintenance.

NOTE Because the project schedule and project budget are closely related, project managers must thoroughly understand the relationship between the completion of project tasks and the consumption of project funds. Project cost control is covered in Chapter 6, "Quality, Cost, and Performance Management."

This chapter covers the following objectives for the CompTIA Project+ exam:

1.6 Given a scenario, apply schedule development and management activities and techniques.

NOTE CompTIA's objective 1.6 lists scheduling tools as a bullet point. In an effort to consolidate content, all scheduling tools are discussed in Chapter 13, "Project Management Tools."

"Do I Know This Already?" Quiz

The "Do I Know This Already?" quiz allows you to assess whether you should read this entire chapter thoroughly or jump to the "Exam Preparation Tasks" section. If you are in doubt about your answers to these questions or your own assessment of your knowledge of the topics, read the entire chapter. Table 5-1 lists the major headings in this chapter and their corresponding "Do I Know This Already?" quiz questions. You can find the answers in Appendix A, "Answers to the 'Do I Know This Already?' Questions and Review Quizzes."

Table 5-1 "Do I Know This Already?" Section-to-Question Mapping

Foundation Topics Section	Questions
Upcoming Milestones and Activity Identification	1, 6, 9
Estimating Techniques	2, 3, 7
Overview of Project Schedule Development	4
Sequencing	5, 10
Schedule Maintenance	8

CAUTION The goal of self-assessment is to gauge your mastery of the topics in this chapter. If you do not know the answer to a question or are only partially sure of the answer, you should mark that question as wrong for the purposes of the self-assessment. Giving yourself credit for an answer you correctly guess skews your self-assessment results and might provide you with a false sense of security.

1. What is a task relationship called if task B relies on the completion of task A and should start after task A is complete?
   a. Dependency
   b. Predecessor
   c. Critical path
   d. Float

2. What is the critical path?
   a. The sequence of tasks comprising the project path that takes the shortest amount of time
   b. The sequence of tasks comprising the project path that takes the longest amount of time
   c. A list of all the tasks needed to complete a project
   d. The approved version of the project schedule

3. What is the method for determining the LS and LF of project tasks?
   a. Starting with the first task(s), the project manager performs a backward pass through all the tasks.
   b. Starting with the first task(s), the project manager performs a forward pass through all the tasks.
   c. Starting with the last task(s), the project manager performs a backward pass through all the tasks.
   d. Starting with the last task(s), the project manager performs a forward pass through all the tasks.

4. What is the WBS used to determine?
   a. Project costs
   b. Project tasks
   c. Project risks
   d. Project changes

5. What is a task called if it must be completed prior to starting the next task?
   a. Dependency
   b. Predecessor
   c. Critical path
   d. Float

6. What are milestones?
   a. Significant events in a project
   b. The tasks in the project path that take the longest amount of time
   c. Acceptance criteria used to ensure that project tasks are completing deliverables within the quality control guidelines
   d. Points in a project when the project manager must obtain formal approval prior to proceeding with the project

7. What is used to calculate each task's ES, EF, LS, and LF?
   a. SV
   b. Forecasting
   c. Critical path
   d. SPI

8. Which of the following does *not* occur during sprint planning?
   a. The team uses burndown charts to gather requirements.
   b. The team decides on the sprint duration.
   c. The team selects the target backlog that will be addressed during the sprint.
   d. The team estimates the tasks.

9. Why should project milestones be noted on the project schedule?
   a. To ensure that proper communication occurs
   b. To ensure that dependent tasks start on time
   c. To ensure that time is allocated for the milestone to be completed
   d. To ensure that the project is reviewed by the CCB

10. A project task cannot be started until its predecessor task finishes. Which type of task relationship is this?
    a. Start-to-start (SS)
    b. Start-to-finish (SF)
    c. Finish-to-finish (FF)
    d. Finish-to-start (FS)

Foundation Topics

Overview of Project Schedule Development

It would be impossible to schedule project work without first defining *which* specific actions should be performed by the team to achieve the project's goal and how those actions relate to all of the other project tasks. Whether the project is predictive or Agile, the first part of project scheduling is to break down (or ***decompose***) the project's end goal into manageable components using a top-down approach. These components are broken into deliverables, which are further divided into units of labor that can be scheduled, tracked, sequenced, and assigned to time frames and resources.

In traditional project management, the project manager begins schedule management by creating the ***work breakdown structure (WBS)***, which is a hierarchical listing of the activities or work packages that must be completed during the project. The smallest unit of a WBS is called a work package. Each work package within the WBS should have a unique identifier to help link the work packages with their costs, schedules, and resources. The ***WBS dictionary*** is a companion document to the WBS and provides detailed information about each WBS component, including the identifier, description, and scheduling information. Experts and team members will often need to weigh in so the deliverables can be accurately decomposed into all the required activities.

The top level of the WBS is the project itself, and the second level of the WBS is usually the project's main phases. The third level contains the project deliverables, and the fourth level is the individual tasks to create the project deliverables. However, keep in mind that an organization may have an established WBS template that follows a structure designed for the organization's specific needs.

The WBS ends when the project manager has defined the individual ***work packages***, which are the smallest units of work in the WBS. Each work package is then assigned a control account and a unique identifier. These assignments make it easy to provide work package tracking of scope, budget, actual cost, and schedule.

EXAMPLE: Table 5-2 shows the WBS for a charity dinner event. This event is broken into six main components: Planning & Supervision, Dinner, Room & Equipment, Guests, Staff, and Speakers.

Table 5-2 Example of a Work Breakdown Structure

1.0	Charity Dinner						
		1.1	Planning & Supervision				
				1.1.1	Planning		
				1.1.2	Budget		
				1.1.3	Coordination		
		1.2	Dinner				
				1.2.1	Menu		
				1.2.2	Shopping List		
				1.2.3	Shopping		
				1.2.4	Cooking		
				1.2.5	Serving		
		1.3	Room & Equipment				
				1.3.1	Site/Room		
				1.3.2	Tables/Chairs		
				1.3.3	Settings/Utensils		
				1.3.4	Decorations		
				1.3.5	Cooking Equipment		
		1.4	Guests				
				1.4.1	Guest List		
				1.4.2	RSVPs		
				1.4.3	Name Tags		
				1.4.4	Special Needs		
						1.4.4.1	Dietary Needs
						1.4.4.2	Accessibility
		1.5	Staff				
				1.5.1	Shoppers		
				1.5.2	Cooks		
				1.5.3	Servers		

		1.5.4	Hosts
		1.5.5	Setup/Takedown
1.6	Speakers		
		1.6.1	Invite/Accept
		1.6.2	Transport
		1.6.3	Coordinate Topics
		1.6.4	Backups for No-Shows
		1.6.5	Thank You Notes

In this example, the 1.4 Guests deliverable includes four main tasks:

- 1.4.1 Guest List
- 1.4.2 RSVPs
- 1.4.3 Name Tags
- 1.4.4 Special Needs

Task 1.4.4 Special Needs is further divided into two subtasks:

- 1.4.4.1 Dietary Needs
- 1.4.4.2 Accessibility

The project manager may have anticipated all of these tasks or may have worked with other experts to determine the tasks. For example, the Dietary Needs task (1.4.4.1) would likely be added during dinner planning when the menu planners ask about it, and the Accessibility task (1.4.4.2) would likely be added when planning the room reservation and audiovisual equipment for the event.

Keep in mind that full decomposition of project tasks may not be possible at the early stages of the project. The project team will not work to decompose a deliverable until they all agree on the full scope of that deliverable. ***Roll wave planning*** is a method whereby planning for future deliverables occurs when the project is closer to that deliverable being needed. This technique uses detailed planning for closer activities and high-level planning for activities that will be performed in the future. As the project progresses and requirements become clearer, more detailed planning is done for the work packages at lower levels of the WBS.

The WBS must represent the entire project's work, including the full scope of the project and all purchases or procurements.

At this point, predictive and Agile frameworks diverge in practice and terminology, but both types of projects must have and use a WBS. Predictive frameworks develop the WBS during project planning and adhere to it for the duration of project work unless it is modified with formal change control. In Agile methods, the product backlog is the equivalent of the WBS. Even when Agile projects include a document named the WBS, the specific work packages are defined or refined at the beginning of each iteration or sprint rather than at the start of project work. Agile also prefers the terms *epic* and *task*, discussed in the next section.

After all work is documented in the WBS (or product backlog), the project manager will use the results to schedule all activities for the project or sprint. Creating the schedule is probably one of the most time-consuming tasks for any project because of the amount of coordination required in the process. As a general rule, all of the following must be completed before project execution begins, usually in the order given:

1. Determine the tasks.
2. Determine the project's milestones.
3. Determine each task's durations and start/finish dates.
4. Set predecessors and dependencies.
5. Sequence and prioritize the tasks.
6. Determine the critical path.
7. Allocate project resources to the individual tasks (perform resource loading).
8. Set the schedule baseline.
9. Set the quality gates.
10. Set the governance gates.

Quality gates and governance gates are covered as phase gate reviews in Chapter 11, "Executing Phase Activities."

NOTE Please do not get too hung up on terms like *activities*, *tasks*, and *work packages*. Often these terms are used interchangeably. The only important factor you need to keep in mind for the certification exam is that the activity (or work package or task) is the basis for estimating the time, resources, and money needed to complete that activity. Whether this book is referring to an Agile method, a predictive method, or general project management, it will use the terms *task* and *activity* interchangeably to mean the lowest defined level of project work.

Story Estimation/Story Points

In most projects, the project manager moves from identifying the activities to sequencing the activities. However, for Agile projects, story estimation is the process whereby activities are identified.

Agile project management includes four principles: themes, epics, stories, and tasks. A ***theme*** is an area of focus that helps an Agile team keep track of their organizational goals. Themes occur over a longer period of time and are usually developed by upper management, although two-way communication is vital in an Agile environment.

Epics

An Agile ***epic*** is a body of work that can be broken down into user stories based on the needs/requests of customers or end users. Epics are generally 1–3 months and are usually developed by the business analyst, the product owner, the project manager, and key stakeholders.

Stories

A ***user story*** is the smallest unit of work in an Agile framework. Storytelling allows the project manager to be more effective because it works toward a better relationship with stakeholders. It's an end goal, not a feature, expressed from the software user's perspective. A user story is an informal, general explanation of a software feature written from the perspective of the end user or customer. Stories occur during a 1- or 2-week sprint, but multiple stories can be handled during a sprint if there are multiple teams. Team members develop the stories. Team members are individuals selected as part of the project team. They take the epics that were developed by the business analyst, product owner, project manager, and stakeholders and turn them into user stories.

Story points are maintained in the product backlog and are usually estimated prior to the sprint planning meeting. They provide a measurement point within a user story. User stories should be expressed in a user + need + purpose format. For example, if a project is developing a banking application, a customer user story may state, "As a banking customer, I want to view loan balances so that I can pay my monthly payment or choose to pay a higher amount." In this example, the user's need and purpose are stated so that the team can easily complete the goal.

Tasks

A ***task*** is any work item that needs to be completed within the given time frame. Sometimes tasks are further divided into subtasks. Tasks generally require only a day or a couple of days and are developed and completed by the team.

Figure 5-1 shows the relationship between the four Agile story estimation principles.

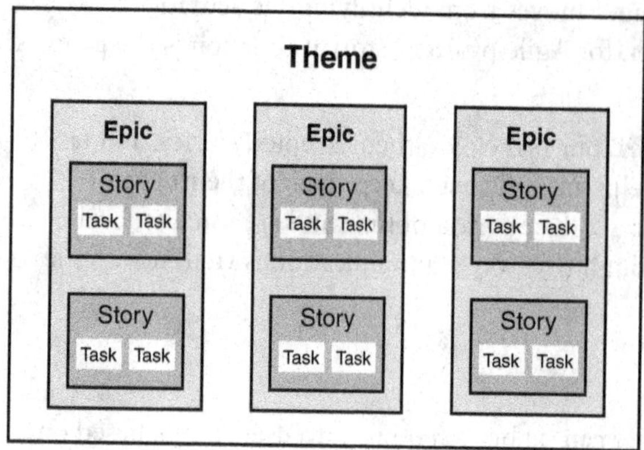

Figure 5-1 Story Estimation Principles

In Chapter 3, "Change Control Process Throughout the Project Life Cycle," a custom jewelry application was discussed. Carrying over that scenario into this discussion, a breakdown example of the different principles would be as follows:

- Theme
  - As a premier jewelry store, we want to provide our customers with jewelry pieces of their dreams.
- Epic
  - We want our customers to be able to design custom pieces using our application.
- Stories
  - As a customer, I want to choose from a list of design options for each jewelry type.
  - As a customer, I want to see a 3-D preview of my finished custom jewelry piece.
  - As a customer, I want to save my custom jewelry design so that I can purchase it later.
  - As a customer, I want to upload a photo of myself so that I can have a virtual try-on.
  - As a customer, I want to view my saved custom jewelry design so that I can purchase it.
  - As a customer, I want a chat option so that I can get help during the design process.

- Tasks (not comprehensive)
  - Document the different jewelry types.
  - Within each jewelry type, document the design options.
  - Give each design option a unique ID.
  - Capture 3-D images of the jewelry type design options.
  - Create descriptions that accompany the design options.
  - Implement a hierarchy for design option selections. Start with jewelry type (ring, bracelet, necklace, earrings, and so on) and then get into the granular selections (gem type, gem shape, additional selections, and so on).

Upcoming Milestones and Activity Identification

Once the WBS is completed, the project manager must be sure to identify all activities (tasks) and project milestones. In some cases, these tasks may come directly from the WBS. If subtasks need to be included, the project manager creates a task list of all the tasks needed to complete the project. Each task must have a unique name and should be tracked back to a WBS component. Each task should match with the work packages in the WBS. Multiple tasks may be assigned to a work package.

A ***milestone*** is a significant project event that indicates when a phase of the project work is complete. Milestones are incorporated into the project schedule, but they do not have durations because they are not actually project tasks. Rather, milestones are points in time that are reached as a project progresses.

Even though milestones do not actually have their own durations, the project's sponsor, stakeholders, and team members should be notified when milestones are met, missed, or moved so that all parties have a realistic view of the project's status. For example, if the first 20% of work on a project should bring the project to its first milestone, the project manager must report on that milestone once the schedule shows that 20% of the work is done. Reporting whether the milestone was met (hit on time), exceeded (hit early), or missed (not yet hit) gives valuable insight into how well the project is performing.

Milestones are included at a high level in the project charter and are part of the project schedule. They should be noted on the project schedule so that the project manager will know when to report the achievement (or failure) of a project goal. If scheduled tasks slip, milestone dates may need to be adjusted.

The ***milestone list*** identifies all project milestones and indicates whether each milestone is mandatory. A mandatory milestone is one that must occur, such as procurement delivery. An optional milestone is one that may or may not occur and is often based on historical information or past projects.

Durations and Start/Finish Dates

Once the tasks are documented, the project manager needs to determine each task's *duration*—how long the task will take to complete. It is important that the project manager work with the project team to establish these task duration estimates. Once the task durations are created, the project manager can begin to assign actual start and finish dates to each task.

Sprint Goals

Tied to milestone and activity identification is a sprint goal. A scrum sprint is a short, timeboxed period when a scrum team works to complete a set amount of work. A sprint defines the current iteration length and usually lasts 1–4 weeks. A ***sprint goal*** is an overarching objective that the scrum teams plan to complete during the sprint.

Sequencing

Once the project's goal is broken down into defined tasks or work packages, and project milestones and/or sprint goals are identified, the project manager can put the tasks into the sequence (called a path or pathway) in which they need to be completed. Prioritizing tasks ensures that if two tasks have a conflict, the task with the higher priority will be given the necessary resources. ***Sequencing*** is the process whereby the dependencies and relationships of tasks are determined so that the order of tasks is documented.

While sequencing and prioritizing tasks, the project manager will develop a schedule that likely has multiple paths to completion. These paths become an important factor in determining the critical path, which is discussed later in this chapter.

Dependencies

Now that the task list is complete (or as close to complete as it can be made at this time), the project manager must determine task predecessors and dependencies. A ***predecessor*** is a task that must be completed prior to starting the next task. A task that follows the predecessor, called a ***dependency***, relies on the completion of the earlier task.

EXAMPLE: For our charity dinner WBS, the project team cannot create the shopping list (task 1.2.2) until the menu has been determined (task 1.2.1). In addition, cooking the dinner (task 1.2.4) cannot be completed until after someone has done the shopping (1.2.3), obtained cooking equipment (task 1.3.5), and hired the cooks (task 1.5.2).

You need to understand five terms used regarding dependencies for the PK0-005 exam: hard logic (mandatory), soft logic (discretionary), external, internal, and issue escalation.

Mandatory or ***hard logic dependencies*** are those that must occur in a certain order based on the project needs. For example, the food for the event must be purchased before it can be prepped for the event.

Discretionary *or* ***soft logic dependencies*** are those that can be completed in any order in the project. This does not mean that the activities are not completed separately. It just means that they do not need to be in sequential order. For example, the equipment can be purchased while the staff is being selected and hired.

External dependencies are those that involve project activities and non-project activities and lie outside the project team's control. For example, the food cannot be prepared if the event venue is without power or if the equipment that was selected is not delivered on time.

Internal dependencies are those that involve project activities and are under the control of the project team. For example, the shopping list cannot be determined until the menu is chosen.

These four terms are combined to create four dependency types: mandatory external, mandatory internal, discretionary external, and discretionary internal.

Issue escalation is the process whereby a decision-making process is followed to ensure that project issues are resolved in a timely manner. In the context of project schedules, scheduling issues would be escalated to the scheduling authority and project manager. Issues that could negatively impact the critical path, defined later in this chapter, should be given a higher priority than ones that affect a project task with a documented float, also defined later in this chapter.

Successor/Predecessor Relationships

Tied to dependencies are successor and predecessor relationships. When two or more project tasks share a dependency or logical relationship, a predecessor activity comes before any dependent activities, and a ***successor*** activity comes after the activity on which it is dependent.

Project task relationships are defined in one of four ways:

- ***Finish-to-start (FS)***: The predecessor activity must finish for the successor activity to start.

- **Finish-to-finish (FF):** The predecessor activity must finish for the successor activity to finish.
- **Start-to-start (SS):** The predecessor activity must start for the successor activity to start.
- **Start-to-finish (SF):** The predecessor activity must start for the successor activity to finish.

The FS relationship is the most common relationship in most projects.

Because many project tasks may involve different project team members, it is important to ensure that the project team is notified when tasks start and finish. The completion of a task should always be a communication trigger. Notification ensures that team members who are working on dependent successor tasks can start their tasks on time.

It is important to start and finish tasks on the critical path on time, in order to prevent project delays. Monitor tasks on the critical path closely.

Resource Loading

After all tasks have been identified, sequenced, and scheduled, the project manager needs to allocate the resources required to perform each activity. Resources can refer to materials, personnel, equipment, or supplies. All resources must be listed for each task in the project schedule.

Resource loading is the process whereby a project manager determines the hours of work a resource is available to the project and then utilizes these resources to complete project activities. This might sound like a very straightforward process, but it often is not.

A project manager needs to ponder the following questions regarding the team:

- Is the team member allocated only to this project? Or will the team member be shared in any way (between projects or between the project and their regular job)?
- What is the maximum number of hours per day (or hours per week, and so on) that this team member will be available to the project?
- Of those hours, what is the number of hours of work the team member can realistically be expected to complete?

The project team members may have interruptions, meetings, breaks, and other things to pull them off a task. Project managers should estimate somewhere between 65% and 75% utilization of team member time. For example, a team member available to the project 8 hours a day will likely accomplish between 5 and 6 hours of project work per day.

Physical resources are a bit easier when it comes to resource loading. Machinery, assembly lines, and other manufacturing processes often have a documented hourly or daily rate. Project managers should also consider any documented downtime for machinery for repairs and regular maintenance. Another factor is the need for qualified operators for some machinery (for example, skilled network hardware installers, backhoe operators, and drone operators).

All resources must be documented in a resource breakdown structure, which breaks down allocated resources hierarchically by category and type. The time during which those resources are available is listed in the resource calendar, which shows the resources needed for each of the project tasks. The project manager may also need to document ordering and shipping lead times for physical resources that could take days or weeks to deliver. For example, if a new IT project requires purchased equipment to be available on a certain date during the project, the project manager must determine from the vendor exactly how long it will take for the equipment to be delivered after the order is placed. While all of this information is found in the procurement documentation, it must also be documented in the resource calendar for easy reference while developing the project schedule.

The project manager uses resource calendars to match resources with the various project tasks and durations documented in the WBS. Using resource optimization techniques such as resource leveling and resource smoothing, the project manager can develop the project schedule. ***Resource leveling*** adjusts the task's start and finish dates based on resource constraints and might increase the original critical path. ***Resource smoothing*** adjusts the activities within their float amounts so that the resource requirements do not exceed the limits of available resources.

Estimating Techniques

Project managers use the same estimating techniques in estimating activity durations for the schedule and in estimating costs for the budget. In predictive projects, all estimates are completed at the beginning of the project. In adaptive projects, estimates are made with each sprint, iteration, or increment. As an adaptive project progresses, estimates will become much more accurate because activities have been completed upon which the project manager can base future estimates.

Estimating activity durations uses information from the WBS and requires an understanding of the skill level needed for each activity. If the project manager is unfamiliar with the activities and the time each activity will take, they should seek help from an expert.

The estimating techniques project managers should understand include analogous estimating, parametric estimating, three-point estimating, alternatives analysis, and critical path analysis.

Analogous Estimating

Analogous estimating uses historical data from a similar activity or project. This is the least costly and time-consuming method, but it is also less accurate. If this estimating is used in an adaptive project, the estimate becomes more accurate as the project progresses because the project manager can see the actual project results from previous sprints, iterations, or increments.

Parametric Estimating

Parametric estimating uses an algorithm to calculate duration. Often this algorithm takes into consideration historical data and project parameters. This is more accurate than analogous estimating, but it is more costly and time-consuming.

Three-Point Estimating

Three-point estimating uses the most likely (tM), optimistic (tO), and pessimistic (tP) estimates in a formula to calculate the activity duration. This method is used when there is a bit of uncertainty and risk in the project and its activities' durations.

With this estimating method, two formulas can be used:

- **Triangular**: Gives the three estimates equal weighting.
  - Formula: (tO + tM + tP) / 3
- **PERT or Beta**: Gives the most likely estimate a bit more weighting.
  - Formula: (tO + 4tM + tP) / 6

This estimating technique is more accurate than other types of estimating due to its consideration of risk. However, the effort for this technique is much higher because the project manager must collect three data points for each task. Subject matter experts (SMEs) must give estimates on task completion, including their optimistic duration estimate, most likely duration estimate, and pessimistic duration estimate. Then those values are plugged into the formula.

Let's look at an example: Suppose a developer tells you as project manager that a particular coding task takes 22 hours for a single developer. However, the developer also states that it could take as little as 15 hours and as much as 25 hours. You would then plug those values into the formulas as follows:

Triangular: (15 + 22 + 25)/3 = 20.7 hours

PERT or Beta: (15 + 88 + 25) = 21.3 hours

For a single, short-duration task, this isn't much of a difference. But over the project life cycle, it could end up being a huge difference in total project duration.

Alternatives Analysis

Alternatives analysis is also a part of activity duration estimation. It allows a project team to look at the different alternatives to weight resource, cost, and duration variables to determine the best approach. Let's look at a few examples of what this means.

Suppose a team has two developers, but each is better at different activities. Team member 1 may take a longer time to complete activity 1 than team member 2, with both members taking the same amount of time to complete activity 2. In this case, it is a better decision to assign team member 2 to activity 1 and team member 1 to activity 2.

Suppose a project needs a specific type of machinery, and the machinery can either be purchased or rented. Many factors could affect this decision, including cost differences, duration needed, and future needs (even in other projects). Often the decision to rent or buy could be heavily influenced by factors outside the project itself.

Determine Contingency Reserves/Buffers

Reserve analysis is used to determine the amount of contingency and management reserves needed. Think of these reserves as a buffer or padding that gives the project schedule a little wiggle room.

Contingency reserves are the extra durations estimated specifically for handling identified risks (known unknowns). ***Management reserves*** are the durations held by management for unforeseen work within the project scope (unknown unknowns). Contingency reserves are included in the schedule baseline and clearly identified. Management reserves are documented but not in the schedule baseline.

Critical Path Analysis

With the sequences, priorities, and durations of the tasks determined, the project manager is ready to find the critical path for the project. The ***critical path*** represents the project path that will take the longest amount of time to complete. This critical path also defines the shortest possible duration for a project. If any tasks on the critical path take longer than originally estimated, the project end date will change, and the activity time will need to be cut or compressed if the project is to remain on the approved schedule baseline. If the schedule baseline needs to be changed, a change request may need to be submitted.

To calculate the critical path, the project manager determines the duration of each path by adding the task durations within each project path. The path with the longest duration is considered the critical path.

EXAMPLE: Figure 5-2 shows a sample project with tasks designated as A through P. The duration (D=) of each task is listed above the task.

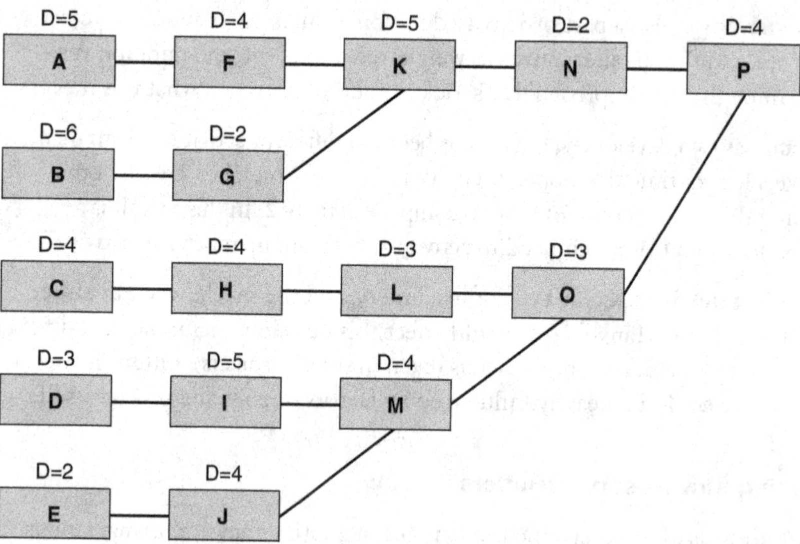

Figure 5-2 Example of a Path Grid

The diagram in Figure 5-2 is a common chart type used to calculate the critical path of a project and show the task dependencies. In this example, task N depends on the completion of task K, while task K depends on the completion of tasks F and G.

The chart in Figure 5-2 holds a total of five project paths:

- A–F–K–N–P
- B–G–K–N–P
- C–H–L–O–P
- D–I–M–O–P
- E–J–M–O–P

To determine the critical path, the project manager adds the durations for each task within each path to obtain the following values:

- A–F–K–N–P = 5 + 4 + 5 + 2 + 4 = 20
- B–G–K–N–P = 6 + 2 + 5 + 2 + 4 = 19
- C–H–L–O–P = 4 + 4 + 3 + 3 + 4 = 18
- D–I–M–O–P = 3 + 5 + 4 + 3 + 4 = 19
- E–J–M–O–P = 2 + 4 + 4 + 3 + 4 = 17

Based on those calculations, the critical path for this project is A–F–K–N–P. Depending on the units used, this could be 20 days or 20 hours. For this example, we will use days, with each day being an 8-hour workday.

After determining the critical path, the project manager can calculate the ***early start (ES)***, ***early finish (EF)***, ***late start (LS)***, and ***late finish (LF)*** for each task. These values will be entered into a grid and used to calculate the ***float*** (also called ***slack***). Float is the difference between the LS and ES values for a task, and it shows which tasks have some leeway for moving versus tasks with fixed points in the schedule. Figure 5-3 shows an example of a task grid.

Early Start	Duration	Early Finish
	Activity	
Late Start	Float	Late Finish

Figure 5-3 Task Grid for Determining Critical Path

The calculations can start from 0 or from 1, following the standard set by the project management office (if any). No matter which value is used, the calculations are basically the same. For this example, the project starts at 0.

The ES is the earliest start date for each task, and the EF is the earliest finish date for each task. The method used for calculating ES and EF is often referred to as a ***forward pass***. For the first task in any critical path, the ES will be 0 (or 1). The EF for the first task in any critical path is the same as the duration. Task A, the first task in our example (refer to Figure 5-2), has a duration of 5 days, giving it an ES of 0 and an EF of 5.

To calculate ES and EF for other tasks in the critical path, the ES is the same as the EF value of the previous task. The EF of the task is the duration of the task added to the ES of the task. In this example, the ES for task F is the same as the EF of task A (5). Task F's duration (4) added to its ES (5) results in a calculation of 9 days for task F's EF.

Calculating ES can get tricky if a task depends on multiple predecessors. An example is task K in Figure 5-2, which is dependent on both task F and task G. Calculating the ES and EF of task K is impossible without knowing the EF of task B and task G. For task B, the ES is 0, and the EF (duration) is 6. For task G, the ES is 6, and the EF is 8. Now the project manager must compare the EF of task F (9) to the EF of task G (8). The ES of a dependent task is the latest date of its predecessors. In this case, 9 is greater than 8; therefore, task K will have an ES of 9.

The project manager will continue with this method until all tasks have ES and EF values. Once these values are complete, it is possible to determine the LS and LF for each task and calculate the float. Tasks with a float of 0 are critical tasks; they must be started and completed on time because they allow no movement in the schedule.

To start calculating LS and LF, the project manager starts with the last task(s) and performs a ***backward pass*** through all the tasks, determining each task's late start and late finish. The LS and LF for the last task are the same as the ES and EF for that task. In our example, task P should have ES and LS values of 16 and EF and LF values of 20.

Working backward, a task's LF is equal to the LS of the task after it. So task N's LF is 16. To get a task's LS, subtract the duration from the LF. For task N, the LS is 14.

Task O is also a predecessor of task P and will give us a chance to compute float. The LF for task O is the LS of task P, which is 16. The LS for task O is 13 (LF minus duration). To calculate float, compare the ES and LS for the task. Task O's ES is 12 and LS is 13. Therefore, float for this task is 1, meaning that this task could lag by 1 day without negatively affecting the project.

TIP Wondering why task O's ES is not the same as task L's EF? It's because task O also depends on task M. If task O depended only on task L, task O's ES would be 11. However, because it is also dependent on task M, task O's ES is the later value (12). The same principle applies to the ES for tasks K, M, and P.

The project manager will keep performing these steps until the LS and LF fields are complete. Figure 5-4 shows the completed critical path grid for this example.

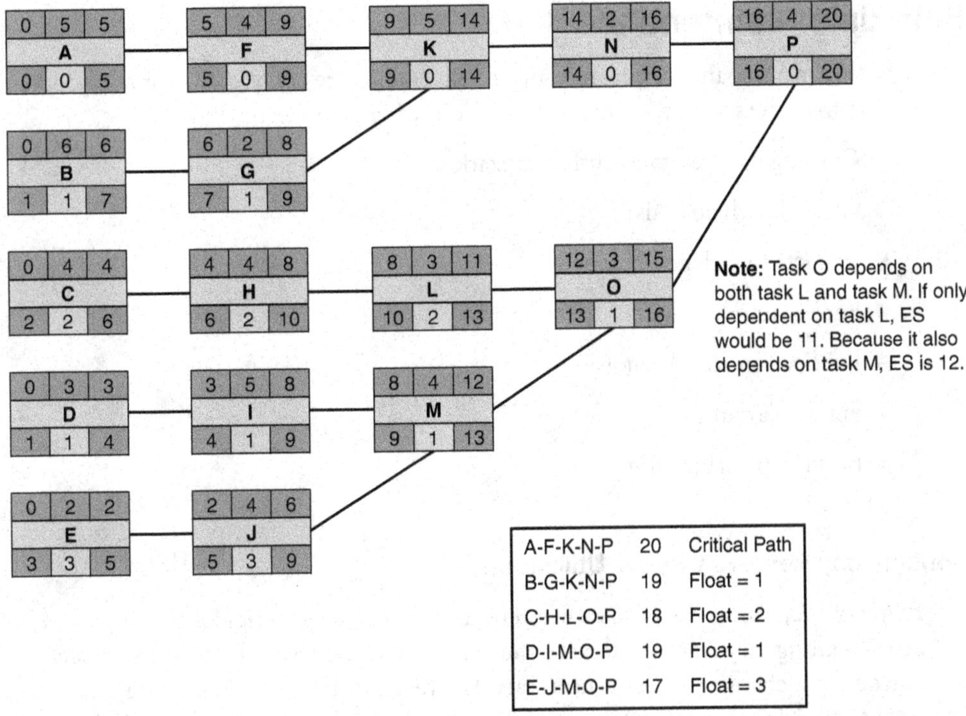

A-F-K-N-P	20	Critical Path
B-G-K-N-P	19	Float = 1
C-H-L-O-P	18	Float = 2
D-I-M-O-P	19	Float = 1
E-J-M-O-P	17	Float = 3

Figure 5-4 Critical Path Calculations

Completing critical path calculations is time-consuming. Many project management tools include templates to help project managers with these calculations. But no matter which method is used, the critical path calculations are an important part of creating the schedule. To ensure that you fully understand this process, practice working out critical path calculations with various examples.

Schedule Baselining

The ***schedule baseline*** is the approved version of the project schedule. A project's time management is always measured against the original schedule baseline. The project schedule can be adjusted only through the formal change control process.

NOTE The Project+ objectives from CompTIA listed Scheduling Tools in the schedule management objective and then later again in the project tools objective. Instead of covering them here, the authors have decided to cover scheduling tools with the other project tools in Chapter 13.

Schedule Maintenance

Schedule maintenance occurs as project deliverables are completed. For this process, project managers need to understand the following activities:

- Contingency reserves/buffer utilization
- Critical path analysis
- Impacts to cadence
- Forecasting
- Publication and sharing
- Sprint planning
- Backlog prioritization

Contingency Reserves/Buffer Utilization

Buffer utilization is the process whereby a project manager decides to use part of the contingency reserve. Because the contingency reserve is part of the project schedule, no change request is necessary. However, if the buffer is used for a task on the critical path, the critical path (discussed in the next section) will lengthen, meaning the overall project deadline will move to a later date. Any contingency usage should be tracked and reported to the project team, stakeholders, and project sponsor.

Management reserves may also be used. However, management reserves are not reflected in the schedule baseline. The project manager will need to adjust the schedule if management reserves are utilized.

Critical Path Analysis

Schedule maintenance involves monitoring the tasks on the critical path to ensure that the durations for these tasks do not increase. Figures 5-2 and 5-4 both show different versions of a critical path grid. In both examples, if tasks A, F, K, N, or P are delayed, the project itself will be delayed because these tasks form the critical path.

As long as tasks C, H, L, O, and P are delayed no more than 2 days, the overall product will not be delayed because the float for path C–H–L–O–P is 2 days. However, if one of those tasks is delayed more than 2 days or if the overall delay of that path is more than 2 days, then C–H–L–O–P would become the new critical path.

Project managers should carefully update the project schedule as tasks are completed, keeping a careful watch on the critical path and the float for the other paths.

EXAMPLE: A project manager is notified of a delay in the shipment of the cabinetry needed for a new data center facility. Many of the project's tasks can continue without being affected by the cabinetry delay. However, the IT department work area cannot be completed until the cabinetry is installed. The project manager will need to adjust dependent tasks (counter installation and machinery installation) for the shipment delay. All of these steps are part of the original schedule change. The project manager needs to assess the schedule to see if the cabinetry installation is part of the critical path. Even if the cabinetry installation is not part of the original critical path, the project manager should also assess if the delay causes a new critical path to emerge. This type of schedule change could also result in a budget increase if the original installers will not be available for the delayed delivery date and the new installers have a higher rate of pay.

When a change such as this occurs, the project manager should meet with the project team members responsible for the dependent tasks, to gain their input on the effects of the change. Getting team member feedback will often ensure that nothing is forgotten or omitted from consideration.

Impacts to Cadence

Cadence is the sequence of project tasks that create a pattern for the team to follow to understand what they are doing and when they will be done with it. This term is specifically used in Agile projects.

Agile projects include four types of cadence:

- Daily cadence emphasizes execution daily. The individual developer is primarily involved in this technical work.
- Iteration (or flow) cadence occurs when individuals come together to decide which items will be taken up as they interact and communicate.
- Delivery is made in release cadence, which can occur after multiple iterations, every iteration, or on-demand.
- Meeting cadence refers to the frequency of team meetings or how often recurring meetings are held.

Events that interrupt or impact project cadence can result in schedule delays. High-functioning teams get into a rhythm, and often interrupting this rhythm affects the schedule more than expected. Project managers should be aware of the cadence and attempt to analyze any issues that may impact cadence before discussing them with the team.

Forecasting

Forecasting is all about looking at the current schedule status and determining if you are on schedule, ahead of schedule, or behind schedule.

To understand forecasting the schedule, project managers must understand several terms:

- **Planned value**: The budgeted cost for the work scheduled to be done. This is the portion of the project budget planned to be spent at any given point in time.
  - Formula: Budget of the project × percentage of work that should be complete (planned complete)
- **Actual cost**: The money spent for the work accomplished. This simply requires that the project manager add up the costs for the project to the point in time.
- **Earned value**: The percent of the total budget actually completed at a point in time.
  - Formula: Budget of the project × percentage of work that is complete (actual complete)

Let's look at examples of these three terms in a scenario:

- Planned value (PV)
  - You have a project to be completed in 12 months. The budget of the project is $100,000. Six months into the project, the schedule says that 50% of the work should be completed. What is the project's PV?
  - PV = 50% × 100,000 = $50,000
- Actual cost (AC)
  - You have a project to be completed in 12 months. The budget of the project is $100,000. Six months into the project, $60,000 has been spent. You find that only 40% of the work has been completed so far. What is the project's AC?
  - AC = $60,000
- Earned value (EV)
  - You have a project to be completed in 12 months. The budget of the project is $100,000. Six months into the project, $60,000 has been spent. You find that only 40% of the work has been completed so far. What is the project's EV?
  - EV = 40% × 100,000 = $40,000

Now let's actually explain how PV, AC, and EV are used to measure project performance in terms of schedule.

Planned value (PV) is used to calculate ***schedule variance (SV)*** and ***schedule performance index (SPI)***. ***Actual cost (AC)*** is used to calculate cost variance (CV) and cost performance index (CPI). ***Earned value (EV)*** is used to calculate SV, CV, SPI, CPI, estimate at completion (EAC), and to-complete performance index (TCPI). For schedule maintenance, project managers only need to understand SV and SPI.

SV lets a project manager know if the project is ahead of schedule or behind schedule in dollars. The formula for SV is as follows:

SV = EV – PV

When the SV calculation is performed, the results are either positive, negative, or zero.

If SV is positive, the project is ahead of schedule. If SV is negative, the project is behind schedule. If SV is zero, the project is on schedule.

Schedule performance index (SPI) shows how the project is progressing compared to the planned project schedule. The formula for SPI is as follows:

SPI = EV / PV

When the SPI calculation is performed, the results are either greater than one, less than one, or zero. If SPI is greater than one, the project is ahead of schedule. If SPI is less than one, the project is behind schedule. If SPI is zero, the project is on schedule.

Publication and Sharing

Project managers should be cautioned from publishing and sharing all the project schedule editions. Some schedules show individual activities, including the resource(s) assigned. While this type of information is valuable to the project manager and project team, it might end up being information overload to project stakeholders or even the project sponsor.

The most popular schedule type that is shared is the milestone chart. (Note: This and other scheduling tools are covered in Chapter 13.) The Gantt chart is also very popular to share.

Giving too much schedule information to stakeholders or the project sponsor may lead to questions that the project manager does not have time to answer. The old adage that "less is more" usually applies to any project documentation. Limit what you publish and share with general audiences.

Sprint Planning

Sprint planning is the process that decides the specific work to be handled in the upcoming sprint. The product owner, the scrum master, and the entire project team attend the sprint planning meeting. Other project stakeholders may also be invited to the sprint planning meeting.

During the sprint planning meeting, the team decides on the sprint's duration. The Scrum Alliance (an organization that helps with scrum standards) suggests 30-day sprints, but the duration can be as short as 1 week. As a guideline, the duration selected for one sprint should be the duration used throughout the project. During the sprint planning meeting, the project team selects the target backlog that will be addressed during this sprint. Once those targets are known, the team will need to clarify the requirements of this sprint.

In addition to the sprint duration, the team needs to determine the sprint goal and where the team is going to start. Then comes the what, the how, and the who:

- **What**: The owner gives the objective of the sprint and what backlog items contribute to that goal. The scrum team decides what can be done in the coming sprint and what they will do during the sprint to make that happen.
- **How**: The team plans the work necessary to deliver the sprint goal. Negotiation between the development team and product owner decides the sprint plan based on value and effort.
- **Who**: The team decides who will complete the activities needed to obtain the objective.

The team returns to sprint planning after the end of each sprint, until all the backlog items are completed or removed. Because the team specifies how much work they can do in each sprint, sprints do not necessarily map out to portions of a project. For example, the product owner cannot expect every sprint to get one-quarter of the work done just because that amount was accomplished in the first sprint.

Backlog Prioritization

The backlog is a list of work for the project team that is derived from the roadmap and its requirements. ***Backlog prioritization*** is the process whereby the owner identifies the priority of the tasks on the backlog, including the sequence of the tasks. The most important items are shown at the top of the product backlog list so the team knows what to deliver first.

The owner is the ultimate authority on backlog priorities. However, the team should have influence over this decision.

Revise Baseline vs. Rebaseline

Looking at the terms ***revise baseline*** and ***rebaseline***, one might think they mean the same thing. Some project managers out there likely use them interchangeably. However, revising the baseline is different from rebaselining.

At the beginning of a project, the project manager documents project requirements. Depending on the development approach (predictive or adaptive), the entire project scope or maybe only the scope of the current sprint, iteration, or increment may be documented. But from that point forward, the work that must be completed is known (even if it isn't broken down into individual tasks yet).

The initial project schedule is referred to as the schedule baseline. While the schedule baseline in predictive projects is fairly complete, adaptive projects often do not fully build the schedule.

Often, during the project life cycle, stakeholders come to the project manager with change requests. A new feature may be needed, or maybe a particular deliverable is needed sooner. Requested changes must go through the change control process. If a change is approved that affects the project schedule, scope, or budget, it is time to revise the baselines. Changes include scope changes, quality changes, team changes, or any other change that deviates from the parameters set forth in the original project plan. Revising the baseline retains historical information and is dependent on documented change requests and results in revision (change begets change).

In projects where the schedule is not fully assessed and documented, it is normal to rebaseline the schedule baselines over time as sprints, iterations, or increments are completed and new planning occurs. Also, multiple-phase projects will often only fully develop the schedule baseline for the current phase. The next phase of planning will complete that plan's schedule, which is added to the previous phase's schedule to rebaseline.

Predictive projects generally do not rebaseline the baseline as often as adaptive projects do. But rebaselining is much rarer than revising the baselines. With a rebaseline, the historical information is not preserved. This is infrequently done, but it is typically done when low-quality information is used to estimate and there is no value in preserving the historical information.

NOTE Projects have a scope baseline, schedule baseline, and cost baseline. All three of these baselines can be revised or rebaselined.

Here is an easy way to remember it: *Revising* means that something has changed and the original baseline needs changing (but you still want to refer to it). *Rebaselining* means creating a new baseline and forgetting about the original.

Exam Preparation Tasks

As mentioned in the section "How to Use This Book" in the Introduction, you have a few choices for exam preparation: the exercises here, Chapter 17, "Final Preparation," and the exam simulation questions in the Pearson Test Prep Software Online.

Review All Key Topics

Review the most important topics in this chapter, noted with the Key Topics icon in the outer margin of the page. Table 5-3 lists each reference of these key topics and the page number on which each is found.

Table 5-3 Key Topics for Chapter 5

Key Topic Element	Description	Page Number
Paragraph	Explains WBS	145
Figure 5-1	Story Estimation Principles	149
Paragraph	Explains Agile themes	149
Paragraph	Explains Agile epics	149
Paragraph	Explains Agile user stories	149
Paragraph	Explains Agile tasks	149
Paragraph	Explains milestones	151
Paragraph	Explains dependencies	152
Paragraph	Explains successor/predecessor relationships	153
Paragraph	Explains analogous estimating	156
Paragraph	Explains parametric estimating	156
Paragraph	Explains three-point estimating	156
Paragraph	Explains alternatives analysis	157
Paragraph	Explains critical path analysis	162
List	Explains planned value (PV), actual cost (AC), and earned value (EV)	164
Paragraph	Explains schedule variance (SV) and schedule performance index (SPI)	165

Define Key Terms

Define the following key terms from this chapter and check your answers in the glossary:

schedule management, decompose, work breakdown structure (WBS), WBS dictionary, work packages, roll wave planning, theme, epic, user story, story points, task, milestone, milestone list, sprint goal, sequencing, predecessor, dependency, mandatory dependencies, hard logic dependencies, discretionary dependencies, soft logic dependencies, external dependencies, internal dependencies, issue escalation, successor, finish-to-start (FS), finish-to-finish (FF), start-to-start (SS), start-to-finish (SF), resource loading, resource leveling, resource smoothing, analogous estimating, parametric estimating, three-point estimating, alternatives analysis, reserve analysis, contingency reserves, management reserves, critical path, early start (ES), early finish (EF), late start (LS), late finish (LF), float, slack, forward pass, backward pass, schedule baseline, buffer utilization, planned value (PV), schedule variance (SV), schedule performance index (SPI), actual cost (AC), earned value (EV), sprint planning, backlog prioritization, revise baseline, rebaseline

Review Questions

The answers to these questions appear in Appendix A. For more practice with sample exam questions, use the Pearson Test Prep practice test software online.

1. Which of the following is completed as part of project time management?
   a. Sequencing activities
   b. Creating the work breakdown structure
   c. Estimating costs
   d. Identifying risks

2. A project has the tasks shown in Figure 5-5, with the durations shown in the following table.

Task	Duration
Task A	10 days
Task B	3 days
Task C	2 days
Task D	4 days
Task E	3 days
Task F	2 days

Task G	4 days
Task H	5 days
Task I	3 days
Task J	4 days
Task K	1 day
Task L	3 days
Task M	2 days

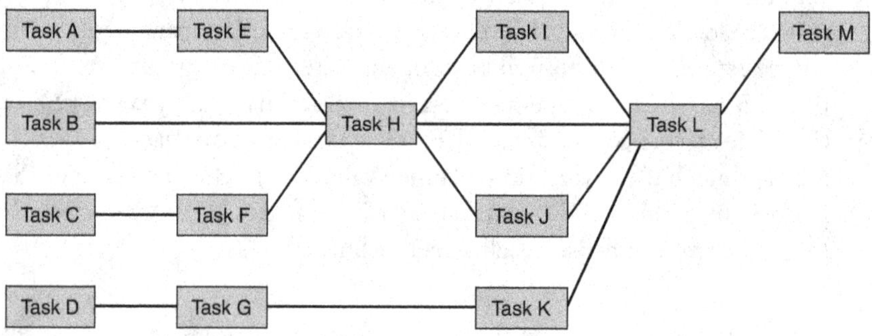

Figure 5-5 Project Tasks

Which path is the critical path for this project?

a. A–E–H–I–L–M

b. A–E–H–J–L–M

c. C–F–H–I–L–M

d. C–F–H–J–L–M

3. Continuing the scenario in question 2, what is the early start (ES) of task E, assuming that the ES of task A is 0?

a. 1

b. 2

c. 3

d. 10

4. Continuing the scenario in question 2, what is the early finish (EF) of task E, assuming that the ES of task A is 0?

a. 13

b. 11

c. 10

d. 9

5. A team member contacts you regarding an event on the project calendar that has no duration. What is this event?

    a. Float

    b. Milestone

    c. Slack

    d. Dependency

6. What is the float for a task?

    a. The sequence of tasks comprising the project path that takes the longest amount of time

    b. The difference between the ES and EF values for the task

    c. The difference between the LS and LF values for the task

    d. The difference between the LS and ES values for the task

7. Which two values are used to determine the float of a project task?

    a. LS and LF

    b. LF and EF

    c. LS and ES

    d. LF and ES

8. Which values are determined during a forward pass?

    a. ES and LS

    b. ES and EF

    c. EF and LF

    d. LS and LF

9. What technique might increase the critical path?

    a. Resource smoothing

    b. Forward pass

    c. Resource leveling

    d. Backward pass

10. A project stakeholder is concerned that certain project tasks are slipping and will affect the project's final completion date. Which project document will help you determine if this is true?
    a. Critical path
    b. Resource calendar
    c. Cost baseline
    d. Schedule baseline

11. You are the scrum master for an Agile project. You need to schedule the sprint planning meeting for this project. Who must attend this meeting? (Choose all that apply.)
    a. Team members
    b. Product owner
    c. Scrum master
    d. Stakeholders

This chapter covers the following topics:

- **Key Performance Indicators and Objectives and Key Results:** Includes coverage of key performance indicators, objectives, and key results used to determine project performance
- **Cost and Schedule Performance:** Covers earned value management, cost variance, schedule variance, estimate at completion, and to-complete performance index
- **Verification and Validation:** Covers verification and validation
- **Sprint Review:** Explains sprint review
- **Retrospective/Lessons Learned:** Includes retrospective and lessons learned coverage
- **Audits and Inspections:** Discusses audits, inspections, and governance gates/quality gates
- **Test Plan and Testing Cycles:** Includes test plan, testing cycles, and testing types
- **Post-implementation Support/Warranty Period:** Covers support and warranty
- **Service Level Agreement:** Discusses service level agreements

Quality, Cost, and Performance Management

Performance management compares raw data gathered from actual project performance against the baselines defined in the project management plan, yielding detailed information about work performance. The results are integrated into project reports and used to control the project's changes, scope, schedule, costs, quality, risks, and procurements.

Project ***quality management*** ensures that the project quality satisfies the needs of the project. It includes creating the quality assurance plan (which is part of the project management plan), performing quality assurance, and controlling quality. Any quality control issues may require a project change to maintain the deliverable quality set forth in the project management plan.

Project cost control involves monitoring the project's costs and managing changes to the ***cost baseline***, which is the approved project budget. The project budget starts as the cost baseline; however, unlike the cost baseline, the project budget can be changed through formal change control.

This chapter covers the following objectives for the CompTIA Project+ exam:

1.7 Compare and contrast quality management concepts and performance management concepts.

"Do I Know This Already?" Quiz

The "Do I Know This Already?" quiz allows you to assess whether you should read this entire chapter thoroughly or jump to the "Exam Preparation Tasks" section. If you are in doubt about your answers to these questions or your own assessment of your knowledge of the topics, read the entire chapter. Table 6-1 lists the major headings in this chapter and their corresponding "Do I Know This Already?" quiz questions. You can find the answers in Appendix A, "Answers to the 'Do I Know This Already?' Questions and Review Quizzes."

Table 6-1 "Do I Know This Already?" Section-to-Question Mapping

Foundation Topics Section	Questions
Introduction	5
Key Performance Indicators and Objectives and Key Results	9
Cost and Schedule Performance	6, 7, 8
Verification and Validation	11
Sprint Review	2
Retrospectives/Lessons Learned	3
Audits and Inspections	1, 4
Test Plan and Testing Cycles	10
Post-Implementation Support/Warranty Period	12
Service Level Agreement	13

CAUTION The goal of self-assessment is to gauge your mastery of the topics in this chapter. If you do not know the answer to a question or are only partially sure of the answer, you should mark that question as wrong for purposes of the self-assessment. Giving yourself credit for an answer you correctly guess skews your self-assessment results and might provide you with a false sense of security.

1. Which project schedule component provides acceptance criteria to ensure that project tasks are completing deliverables within the quality control guidelines established during project planning?
   a. Critical path
   b. Governance gates
   c. Milestones
   d. Quality gates

2. During the scrum retrospective, who should document and prioritize actions and lessons learned prior to starting the next sprint?
   a. Team member
   b. Product owner
   c. Scrum master
   d. Project manager

3. When should a scrum retrospective be held?
    a. Before every sprint
    b. After every sprint
    c. After the last sprint
    d. Before the first sprint
4. Which communication trigger is the result of verifying compliance with project requirements?
    a. Gate review
    b. Project milestone
    c. Project change
    d. Project audit
5. What activity involves monitoring the project's costs and managing changes to the cost baseline?
    a. Cost control
    b. Reserve analysis
    c. Forecasting
    d. Critical path
6. What is the formula for calculating planned value (PV)?
    a. (% of completed work) × budget
    b. EV – AC
    c. (planned % complete) × budget
    d. EV / AC
7. What does the formula AC + ETC calculate?
    a. EAC for work, including both CPI and SPI
    b. EAC for work performed at current CPI
    c. EAC for work performed at current rate
    d. EAC using calculated ETC
8. What does a TCPI greater than 1 indicate?
    a. The project is within its scheduled time.
    b. The project is outside its scheduled time.
    c. The project is over budget.
    d. The project is under budget.

9. Which KPI is used to show the value a project has earned from the money spent to date?
   a. CPI
   b. AC
   c. PV
   d. EV

10. Which testing type determines the point at which the application or device falters?
    a. Unit testing
    b. Smoke testing
    c. Stress testing
    d. Performance testing

11. Which term measures project deliverable quality against the requirements baselines and the quality benchmarks?
    a. Verification
    b. Validation
    c. Auditing
    d. Performance testing

12. Which of the following can be provided by an internal source after an internal application development project to ensure that the application remains operational and often includes a patching process?
    a. Verification
    b. Post-implementation support
    c. Warranty period
    d. Validation

13. Which of the following is between a service provider and customer and includes service metrics that the provider should meet?
    a. Verification
    b. Warranty
    c. SLA
    d. Validation

Foundation Topics

Overview of Quality, Cost, and Performance Management

Quality, cost, and performance management are closely tied together for project managers. Quality management ensures that the quality of the deliverables is verified based on the quality management plan. Cost management ensures that the cost of the project is managed as close to the initial budget or cost baseline. Performance management ensures that the project performs as expected and measures performance against the initial baselines.

Key Performance Indicators and Objectives and Key Results

Project managers should periodically assess project performance based on key performance indicators (KPIs) and objectives and key results (OKRs). These KPIs and OKRs allow the project manager to communicate project performance metrics with stakeholders and the project sponsor in a way that makes sense. Project managers should ensure that these metrics are captured and documented on a timely basis to ensure that project issues can be noted earlier so that corrective actions can be taken.

Key Performance Indicator

A ***key performance indicator (KPI)*** is a measure that evaluates the success of a project or deliverable in meeting objectives for performance. The U.S. Department of Defense (DoD) refers to these as ***key performance parameters (KPPs)***. KPIs and KPPs are usually documented in the project dashboard.

NOTE A few of the KPIs/KPPs were discussed in Chapter 5, "Schedule Development and Management." We will be covering them again in this chapter to bring all of the KPIs/KPPs together.

Table 6-2 shows KPIs and KPPs that project managers typically provide in the dashboard. (Note that PV, AC, EV, CV, CPI, SPI, and SV and their formulas are explained later in this chapter.)

Table 6-2 Key Performance Indicators/Key Performance Parameters

KPI or KPP	Description
Planned value (PV)	The planned cost for the amount of work that is currently completed.
Actual cost (AC)	The actual money spent to date on a project.
Earned value (EV)	The value a project has earned from the money spent to date.
Cost variance (CV)	The budget deficit or surplus at any given point in time.
Cost performance index (CPI)	The ratio of earned value to actual cost.
Schedule performance index (SPI)	The ratio of earned value to planned value.
Schedule variance (SV)	The difference between the earned value achieved to date by the project and the planned value for that date.
Return on investment (ROI)	The total dollar/time return the project sponsor will receive for the project. ROI is calculated using one of two formulas: (change in operations cost) / (costs of project) (change in revenue) / (costs of project)
Cost of managing processes	An overview of time and resources spent on supervising and managing the project.
Overdue project tasks (also called ***crossed deadlines***)	The number of project activities that are overdue. A calculated percentage of project activities that go past their due date is compared to all completed project activities.
Missed milestones	Indicates whether a project is running ahead of schedule, on time, or behind schedule.
Percentage of tasks completed	Indicates how far along the tasks are toward completion.
Resource utilization	Measures how the team members' time is used while working on the project. Specifically, this measurement shows how much time team members are spending on billable activities compared to the time spent on non-billable tasks, such as meetings.
Percentage of projects completed on time	Helps demonstrate the overall project success for an organization.
Percentage of canceled projects	Shows how sustainable an organization's projects are. Projects risk cancellation from internal factors such as lack of budget or sponsor support, or external factors such as regulatory or environmental issues. If too many projects are canceled, the organization should change its approach to project management or focus on different types of projects.

NOTE Missed milestones are noted in the milestone list, which identifies all project milestones and indicates whether each milestone is mandatory. See Chapter 5 for details on milestones.

Other KPIs or KPPs may be added based on the organization's needs. Project managers should ensure that the project sponsor and stakeholders understand what each measurement means.

Objectives and Key Results

For any KPI that will be monitored, the objectives of monitoring that KPI should be documented as well as the desired key results that are needed. Objectives and key results (OKRs) are all about goal setting in an Agile project. Each OKR has an objective and up to five results based on that objective.

An ***objective*** states the goal, but unlike KPIs, the objective does not need to be measurable. It simply gives a goal and why the goal is important. A ***key result*** is a measure based on the objective that shows how the project manager knows the objective is achieved. Objectives are the *what*, while key results are the *how*.

Let's look at an example. Suppose organizational management is concerned that projects tend to take longer than originally estimated. Management has asked that the project management office (PMO) work to improve schedule performance for all future projects. As a result, the PMO develops an objective that states, "Ensure timeliness of all projects." Then the PMO works to develop the following key results:

- Increase on-time completion percentage to 75%.
- Decrease time spent on projects by 10%.
- Increase earned value management accuracy to 60%.
- Reduce resource conflicts per project to below 3.

The example provided shows a project objective based on an organizational objective. It then gives stated key results that are measurable to support the objective.

Cost and Schedule Performance

Project ***cost control*** allows project managers to recognize variances from the project plan in time to take corrective action. Because the project budget and project schedule are closely related, project managers must understand the relationship between the consumption of project funds and the actual project work being completed.

To calculate any KPI or variance from the budget or the schedule, project managers must first have the project's budget and cost baseline. The budget is compared to the cost baseline to find any deviations. As mentioned previously, the project budget may vary as project changes are approved, but the cost baseline does not unless it is formally revised or rebaselined.

To perform cost control, the project manager uses the cost baseline to measure the project's expenditures against its achievements. These calculations show a time-phased view of the budget. But before beginning the cost control calculations, the project manager must derive the planned value, earned value, and actual cost of the work as compared against the cost baseline:

- **Planned value (PV):** Indicates the budgeted cost for the work scheduled to be done. This is the portion of the project budget that was planned to be spent by a given point in time. To find this value, you multiply the budget by the percentage of work that *should be complete*. The following formula computes PV:

(planned % complete) × budget

- **Earned value (EV):** Shows the value a project has earned from the money spent to date. The following formula computes EV:

(% of completed work) × budget

- **Actual cost (AC):** The money spent to date on a project. Calculating AC requires no formula; it is simple addition.

These values quantify the project's progress to date and help analyze how close to budget the project is running.

NOTE These calculations were covered in Chapter 5. However, there they were used in schedule variance and performance calculations. In this chapter, we will go into all the performance calculations.

In Chapter 5, a scenario was provided to look at these three values. Let's look at that scenario again:

- Planned value (PV)

- You have a project to be completed in 12 months. The budget of the project is $100,000. Six months into the project, the schedule says that 50% of the work should be completed. What is the project's PV?
- PV = 50% × 100,000 = $50,000

- Actual cost (AC)
  - You have a project to be completed in 12 months. The budget of the project is $100,000. Six months into the project, $60,000 has been spent. You find that only 40% of the work has been completed so far. What is the project's AC?
  - AC = $60,000
- Earned value (EV)
  - You have a project to be completed in 12 months. The budget of the project is $100,000. Six months into the project, $60,000 has been spent. You find that only 40% of the work has been completed so far. What is the project's EV?
  - EV = 40% × 100,000 = $40,000

Earned Value Management

Earned value management (EVM) uses scope, schedule, and resource measurements to assess the project's performance using one of four EVM formulas:

- **Schedule variance (SV): The** difference between the earned value and the planned value.
- **Cost variance (CV): The** budget deficit or surplus at any given point in time.
- **Schedule performance index (SPI):** The ratio of earned value to planned value.
- **Cost performance index (CPI): The** ratio of earned value to actual cost.

The SV and SPI values answer the question, "Is the project behind or ahead of schedule?" The CV and CPI values answer the question, "Is the project over or under budget?"

To perform cost control, the project manager uses the cost baseline to measure the project's expenditures against its achievements. These calculations show a time-phased view of the budget. Before beginning the cost control calculations, the project manager must derive the planned value, earned value, and actual cost of the work as compared against the cost baseline.

In some cases, a project manager may need to understand *burn rate*, which is simply the rate at which the project budget is being spent. The burn rate is an inverse of CPI.

The SV, CV, SPI, and CPI are all calculated from the PV, EV, and AC. Table 6-3 shows the formulas used to calculate all of the EVM values.

Table 6-3 Earned Value Management (EVM) Value Calculations

EVM	Formula
Planned value (PV)	(planned % complete) × budget
Earned value (EV)	(% of completed work) × budget
Schedule variance (SV)	EV – PV
Cost variance (CV)	EV – AC
Schedule performance index (SPI)	EV / PV
Cost performance index (CPI)	EV / AC
Burn rate	1 / CPI

Cost Variance

First, let's explain how PV, AC, and EV are used to measure project performance in terms of cost. Cost variance (CV) lets a project manager know if the project is ahead of or behind budget in terms of *dollars*. CV is calculated as follows:

CV = EV – AC

A positive CV indicates that the project is under budget for the amount of work completed, and a negative CV indicates that the project is over budget for the amount of work completed. A value of 0 indicates that the cost for the work completed is on budget.

The cost performance index (CPI) lets a project manager know if the project is ahead of or behind schedule in terms of *time*. The formula for CPI is as follows:

CPI = EV / AV

A CPI greater than 1 indicates that the project is over budget, and a CPI less than 1 indicates that the project is under budget. A value of 1 indicates that the budget is proceeding exactly as planned.

EXAMPLE: A project manager has a project to be completed in 6 months for a total cost of $50,000. The schedule says that 3 months into the project, 50% of the work should be completed. PV is calculated as follows:

PV = 50% × $50,000

PV = $25,000

However, the project manager determines that only 40% of the work was completed during these 3 months. EV is then calculated as follows:

$$EV = 40\% \times \$50,000$$

$$EV = \$20,000$$

The AC is the amount spent to date, which the project manager determines is $20,000. With these values, the project manager can compute the variances.

CV is calculated as follows:

$$CV = \$20,000 - \$20,000$$

$$CV = 0$$

For this example, the project is on budget for the amount of work completed.

CPI is calculated as follows:

$$CPI = \$20,000 / \$20,000$$

$$CPI = 1$$

For this example, the project is on budget.

Finally, the burn rate is calculated as follows:

$$\text{Burn rate} = 1 / 1$$

$$\text{Burn rate} = 1$$

A burn rate greater than 1 indicates that the project is consuming the budget faster than planned and will exhaust the budget before all the work is completed. A burn rate of less than 1 indicates that the project is consuming the budget slower than planned and will be completed within the budget. A burn rate of 1 indicates that the project is consuming the budget as planned and will be completed on budget. For this example, the project is on budget.

Schedule Variance

Next, let's review how PV, AC, and EV are used to measure project performance in terms of schedule (as this was discussed in the previous chapter). Schedule variance (SV) lets a project manager know if the project is ahead of or behind schedule in terms of *dollars*. The formula for SV is as follows:

$$SV = EV - PV$$

The results of the SV calculation are either positive, negative, or 0. If the SV is positive, the project is ahead of schedule. If the SV is negative, the project is behind schedule. If the SV is 0, the project is on schedule.

The schedule performance index (SPI) lets a project manager know if the project is ahead of or behind schedule in terms of *time*. The formula for SPI is as follows:

SPI = EV / PV

The results of the SPI calculation are greater than 1, less than 1, or 0. If the SPI is greater than 1, more work has been completed than planned, and the project is ahead of schedule. If the SPI is less than 1, less work has been completed than planned, and the project is behind schedule. If the SPI is 0, the planned amount of work was completed in the planned amount of time, and the project is on schedule.

EXAMPLE: Returning to the project in the cost variance section, where the PV = $25,000, the EV = $20,000, and the AC = $20,000, you can use the following formulas to compute the schedule variance.

SV is calculated as follows:

SV = $20,000 – $25,000

SV = –$5,000

Because the result is a negative value, the project is behind schedule.

SPI is calculated as follows:

SPI = $20,000 / $25,000

SPI = 0.8

Because the value is less than 1, less work has been completed than planned.

Estimate at Completion

When there is a change to the total project cost (usually because the project needs additional funds if it is to succeed), the project manager may find it necessary to forecast a new ***estimate at completion (EAC)*** that is different from the project budget or cost baseline. Essentially, the EAC represents how much money the project will have cost once the new changes are factored into the cost baseline.

To calculate the EAC, the project manager needs to calculate an ***estimate to complete (ETC)*** value, which provides an approximate idea of how much money will be required to complete the remaining balance of project work. Whereas the EAC estimates the total hypothetical project cost, the ETC estimates how much the remaining work will cost. The project manager may also want to compare a range of EAC values for more accurate forecasting. Table 6-4 shows other EAC formulas that can help to factor in various scenarios based on current performance.

Key Topic

Table 6-4 Estimate at Completion (EAC) Value Calculations

EAC	Formula
EAC using calculated ETC	AC + ETC
EAC for work performed at current rate	AC + (budget – EV)
EAC for work performed at current CPI	Budget / CPI
EAC for work including both CPI and SPI	AC + [(budget – EV) / (CPI × SPI)]

EXAMPLE: Returning to the earlier scenario, the following values are determined based on the given parameters:

Budget = $50,000

AC = $20,000

EV = $20,000

CPI = 1

SPI = 0.8

Suppose the project manager determines that the ETC for the remainder of this project is $30,000. The EAC using calculated ETC would be as follows:

EAC = $20,000 + $30,000

EAC = $50,000

This forecast shows no change in the final project cost. However, to derive a range of forecasts, you should also calculate EAC using the three other formulas that represent the EVM values:

EAC for work performed at current rate = $20,000 + ($50,000 – $20,000)

EAC for work performed at current rate = $50,000

EAC for work performed at current CPI = $50,000 / 1

EAC for work performed at current CPI = $50,000

EAC for work including both CPI and SPI = \$20,000 + [(\$50,000 – \$20,000) / (1 × 0.8)]

EAC for work including both CPI and SPI = \$20,000 + [(\$30,000) / (0.8)]

EAC for work including both CPI and SPI = \$20,000 + \$37,500

EAC for work including both CPI and SPI = \$57,500

The forecast budget remains the same for most of these calculations, except the calculation that includes both CPI and SPI. This result will not always be the case, as the CPI and SPI may or may not match in projects.

To-Complete Performance Index

The project manager may need to measure the required cost performance for the remaining budget. With this calculation, the project manager must have a specific goal in mind, such as the project budget or one of the EAC values. The EAC value should be used if it is apparent that the cost baseline is no longer viable. To measure this value, the project manager will need to compute the ***to-complete performance index (TCPI)***, using one of the following formulas:

TCPI using current budget = (Budget – EV) / (Budget – AC)

TCPI using EAC value = (Budget – EV) / (EAC – AC)

EXAMPLE: Returning to the earlier scenario, we first compute TCPI using the original cost baseline:

TCPI = (\$50,000 – \$20,000) / (\$50,000 – \$20,000)

TCPI = 1

Deciding that the EAC calculation with CPI and SPI gives a better forecast, the project manager determines the TCPI by using the other formula, as follows:

TCPI = (\$50,000 – \$20,000) / (\$57,500 – \$20,000)

TCPI = \$30,000 / \$37,500

TCPI = 0.8

A TCPI greater than 1 indicates that the project is under budget, and a TCPI less than 1 indicates that the project is over budget. A value of 1 indicates that the budget is proceeding exactly as planned. For this project, the first TCPI value shows that the project is proceeding as planned, but the second TCPI value shows that the project is over budget.

NOTE Do not just memorize these formulas—practice using them. Come up with your own project scenarios and then complete these calculations. The "Review Questions" section at the end of this chapter also holds some examples.

Verification and Validation

Verification measures the quality of the project's deliverables against the requirements baseline and the quality benchmarks established during initiation and planning. ***Validation*** measures how well the end result of the project (or sprint) performs for the customer or the intended audience. Verification measures accuracy, and validation measures acceptance. Verification is an internal activity performed within the project by a team member, while validation is external approval from the owners and/or users of the product. Verification and validation apply equally to every project regardless of the framework and either can result in deliverable rework or rejection. Table 6-5 summarizes the differences between verification and validation in a project.

Table 6-5 Project Verification Versus Project Validation

Verification	Validation
Internal; performed by project team and testers (including project managers)	External; requires interaction between product and audience
Measures how well requirements were matched	Measures how well requirements were captured
Measures performance in the project environment	Measures performance in the real world
Concerned with accuracy	Concerned with acceptance
Derived from sprint reviews, retrospectives, audits, inspections, and software testing	Derived from service level agreements, warranties, and post-implementation support

Sprint Review

A sprint review is about project accomplishments and stakeholder feedback. The sprint review takes place prior to the sprint retrospective. The sprint review discusses what the project is producing, while the sprint retrospective discusses how the results of the project are produced. The sprint review is about alignment between the team and stakeholders. The sprint review produces an updated backlog.

A sprint review should answer three main questions:

1. What went well during this sprint?
2. What went wrong during this sprint?
3. What changes could be made to improve the next sprint?

At the end of the sprint review, the scrum master should document and prioritize actions and lessons learned prior to starting the next sprint. Keep in mind that the sprint review is all about providing continuous feedback and adapting the project requirements to meet the project's goals. It focuses on improving the product, not the team.

Retrospective/Lessons Learned

Retrospectives are used in Agile projects at the end of each sprint and at the end of the project. Retrospectives foster open communication. ***Team retrospectives*** have a team focus on celebrating, learning, and improving their relationship on a regular basis.

Sprint retrospectives occur at the end of a sprint to assess the team's work processes and to brainstorm improvements. This meeting happens throughout the life of a project and often occurs every 2 weeks. At the end of every sprint, the team holds a ***scrum or sprint retrospective***. The team members and scrum or sprint master meet to discuss the sprint that has just concluded and to note any changes that could help make the next sprint more productive. This meeting is similar to the "lessons learned" meeting in many project management methodologies and is a verification activity. The goal of this retrospective is continuous improvement. The output of this retrospective is a workflow improvement list for the team.

Release retrospectives concentrate on the release of a product or service. Retrospectives may be done by one team, involve multiple teams, or include a cross-departmental group. This is a verification activity. Each retrospective identifies which practices are successful and which need to change. The team discusses potential changes and then makes a plan to implement the top one or two ideas. Retrospectives focus on the team, not the product.

Lessons learned is a process in which project participants provide input on what the team learned. The project manager then documents and analyzes this input so that the organization can apply these lessons the next time it undertakes a similar project. Therefore, while retrospectives can occur throughout the project, lessons learned typically only occur at the end of a project or phase. Retrospectives aim at improving the current project, while lessons learned aim at improving future projects.

Audits and Inspections

An ***audit*** verifies that project deliverables comply with the guidelines set forth in the project management plan, in order to validate the performance of the project. Audits are usually performed to validate a project's scope, quality, and regulatory compliance, but they also can verify cost or schedule compliance, identify new risks, and determine whether a risk is about to occur.

Project audits offer two main benefits:

- Obtaining tangible data about specific components, to determine how the project is aligning with its objectives
- Motivating team members and stakeholders, who see audits as evidence of managerial oversight

Audit results should be analyzed carefully to determine whether the project is performing as expected. If any issues are discovered, they should be documented as part of the audit report. Based on the audit results, the project manager should work with the project team to identify any corrective actions that could improve issues identified by the audit.

When the audit report is completed, the project manager should distribute the results of that audit to the recipients listed in the project's communication plan. Typically, these reports will be shared with project team members, the project sponsor, and any project stakeholders that request audit results. Communicating the audit results with the project sponsor and stakeholders allows them to analyze the results and provide any applicable feedback. Communicating the audit results with the project team members ensures that they understand any audit findings that may affect their project tasks or schedule. Audits are defined in the subsidiary plans of the project management plan: quality audits are defined in the quality management plan, cost audits are defined in the cost management plan, and so on.

EXAMPLE: The project management plan for a manufacturing project includes regular audits to ensure that the parts being produced fit within certain design specifications and cost ranges. If the audit shows that none of these values are outside the required standards, the project manager sends a normal audit report. However, the communication plan includes an audit trigger that instructs the project manager to hold a meeting with certain team members if values fall outside the quality or cost specifications, to discuss what adjustments need to be made to the project to address these issues.

While inspections are similar to audits, ***inspections*** are not considered as formal as audits and often just complete a checklist to ensure that deliverables meet certain conditions. Inspections are generally carried out to verify either project governance, compliance, or quality.

Governance Gate/Quality Gate

Project managers may establish ***quality gates*** during schedule development. Quality gates are usually a checklist of parameters and acceptance criteria that determines whether a deliverable meets the quality control guidelines established during project planning. Quality gates are most often carried out between project phases, but they can also be completed during other transitional periods. Once all the measurable parameters are matched, the quality gate is unlocked, and the project can proceed. Quality gates are often completed at the end of an Agile iteration.

EXAMPLE: An organization requires a third-party service at a certain point in a project. Service levels were previously negotiated with the third party and documented in a formal service level agreement (SLA). The project manager knows that the appropriate service level is vital to project success. As soon as the service is available, the project manager should set a quality gate to test the available service level to ensure that it meets the promised levels.

NOTE SLAs are discussed later in this chapter.

A ***governance gate*** is similar to a quality gate in that it marks acceptance criteria for the project tasks, but a governance gate is more about client sign-off, management approval, or legislative approval. The key word here is *approval.* A governance gate should be set up whenever the project manager must obtain formal approval prior to proceeding with the project activities.

EXAMPLE: An organization needs a state governing body to approve certain aspects of a project as complying with a new regulation. The project should include a governance gate (or multiple governance gates, depending on complexity) to ensure that the appropriate approval is obtained. Setting the governance gate ensures that the project can be revised to meet governance criteria if its initial approval is denied.

Inspections or audits can be completed at the governance or quality gate to ensure that the parameters have been met to proceed through the gate.

Test Plan and Testing Cycles

Application development projects develop code throughout the project. All code that is developed should be thoroughly tested to ensure that the code is free from error and includes the appropriate security controls. A ***test plan*** defines the types of tests that should occur, when those tests should be completed, and who should complete them. Test cycles are defined start and end dates for particular tests. Some of the tests that can be performed are covered in the following sections.

Unit Testing

Application code is typically developed in pieces or modules of code that are later assembled to yield the final product. Each module should be tested separately in a procedure called ***unit testing***. Having development staff carry out this testing is critical, but using a different group of engineers than the ones who wrote the code can ensure that an impartial process occurs. This is a good example of the concept of separation of duties.

Smoke Testing

Smoke testing, also called ***build verification testing*** or ***build acceptance testing***, checks that the most crucial functions of an application work but does not delve into finer details. Smoke testing is the preliminary check of the application after a build and before a release.

Regression Testing

Regression testing takes place after changes are made to the code to ensure the changes have reduced neither functionality nor security. Regression testing should be built into the change control process for any application development project.

Stress Testing

Stress testing is the process of determining the ability of a computer, network, application, or device to maintain a certain level of effectiveness under unfavorable conditions. Think of this as a process to determine the point at which the performance of the code or device being tested is negatively affected.

Performance Testing

Performance testing is a nonfunctional software testing technique that determines how the stability, speed, scalability, and responsiveness of an application hold up under a given workload. Performance testing tests against a given workload, while stress testing continues to increase the given workload to determine the point at which the application or device falters.

User Acceptance Testing

User acceptance testing ensures that the end user is satisfied with the functionality of the software. Acceptance testing must be completed for each set of users identified by separate user stories, as each user story will have different requirements for the project.

Post-Implementation Support/Warranty Period

After an application or system has been released, support will need to be provided to the users of the application or system. This includes updates or hot fixes that are released. During the ***warranty period***, the vendor must fix all software defects within the agreed time period. Generally, a warranty period is for products or resources that are provided by a vendor. ***Post-implementation support*** can be provided for both internally released products and those purchased from a vendor. However, most vendor post-implementation support is for a defined time period. Thereafter, support from the vendor must be purchased.

Often an additional warranty period can be purchased from a vendor. A cost-benefit analysis should be performed to determine if the costs of the additional warranty are less than the risk to the application or system. If the cost outweighs the risk, the organization may choose to implement some other security mitigation rather than purchasing the additional warranty.

Depending on the vendor, post-implementation support can begin immediately after deployment or once the system is in operation and the warranty period has expired. Project managers are responsible for ensuring that post-implementation support and warranty are detailed in any procurement agreement.

Service Level Agreement

A service level agreement (SLA) is a contract between a service provider and its customer. The SLA sets specific metrics for different aspects of the service, including quality, availability, and responsibilities. SLAs are also covered in Chapter 8, "Project Procurement and Vendor Selection."

Exam Preparation Tasks

As mentioned in the section "How to Use This Book" in the Introduction, you have a few choices for exam preparation: the exercises here, Chapter 17, "Final Preparation," and the exam simulation questions in the Pearson Test Prep Software Online.

Review All Key Topics

Review the most important topics in this chapter, noted with the Key Topics icon in the outer margin of the page. Table 6-6 lists each reference of these key topics and the page numbers on which each is found.

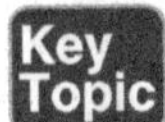

Table 6-6 Key Topics for Chapter 6

Key Topic Element	Description	Page Number
Table 6-2	Key Performance Indicators/Key Performance Parameters	180
Table 6-3	Earned Value Management (EVM) Value Calculations	184
Table 6-4	Estimate at Completion (EAC) Value Calculations	187
Table 6-5	Project Verification Versus Project Validation	189
Paragraph	To-complete performance index (TCPI) formulas	188
Paragraph	Verification versus validation	189
Paragraph	Audit explanation	191
Paragraph	Quality gate	192
Paragraph	Governance gate	192
Paragraph	Unit testing	193
Paragraph	Smoke testing	193
Paragraph	Regression testing	193
Paragraph	Stress testing	193
Paragraph	Performance testing	194
Paragraph	User acceptance testing	194

Define Key Terms

Define the following key terms from this chapter and check your answers in the glossary:

performance management, quality management, cost baseline, key performance indicator (KPI), key performance parameter (KPP), planned value (PV), actual cost (AC), earned value (EV), cost variance (CV), cost performance index (CPI), schedule performance index (SPI), schedule variance (SV), return on investment (ROI), cost of managing processes, overdue project tasks, crossed deadline, missed milestones, resource utilization, objective, key result, cost control, earned value management (EVM), estimate at completion (EAC), estimate to complete (ETC), to-complete performance index (TCPI), verification, validation, retrospectives, team retrospective, sprint retrospective, scrum or sprint retrospective, release retrospective, lessons learned, audit, inspection, quality gates, governance gate, test plan, unit testing, smoke testing, build verification testing, build acceptance testing, regression testing, stress testing, performance testing, user acceptance testing, warranty period, post-implementation support

Review Questions

The answers to these questions appear in Appendix A. For more practice with sample exam questions, use the Pearson Test Prep practice test software online.

1. Which of the following is included in project schedules to ensure that required approvals are obtained?
   a. Governance gate
   b. Quality gate
   c. Work breakdown structure
   d. Milestone

2. Your team has just completed the first sprint of a four-sprint project. What must you do prior to starting the next sprint?
   a. Hold a sprint planning meeting.
   b. Create the user stories.
   c. Hold a daily scrum meeting.
   d. Hold a scrum retrospective.

3. You have been hired to take over as project manager for a new research project. You need to assess the project to ensure that it is complying with project requirements and quality metrics. What should you do?
   a. Place a formal change request.
   b. Perform a gate review.
   c. Update the risk register.
   d. Perform a project audit.

4. You have a project to be completed in 12 months, and the total cost of the project is $1,000,000. Six months have passed, and the schedule says that 40% of the work should be completed. What is the project's planned value (PV) at this point?
   a. $600,000
   b. $100,000
   c. $900,000
   d. $400,000

For questions 5–10, refer to the following scenario: You have a project to be completed in 12 months, and the total cost of the project is $1,000,000. Six months have passed. On closer review, you find that only 40% of the work has been completed so far, but the schedule indicates that 60% of the work should be complete.

5. The project has spent $600,000. What is the project's actual cost (AC) at this point?
   a. $100,000
   b. $1,000,000
   c. $600,000
   d. $400,000

6. What is the project's earned value (EV) at this point?
   a. $600,000
   b. $400,000
   c. $1,000,000
   d. $240,000

7. What is the project's schedule variance (SV) at this point?
   a. $200,000
   b. –$200,000
   c. $100,000
   d. –$100,000

8. What is the project's cost variance (CV) at this point?
   a. $400,000
   b. $0
   c. $200,000
   d. –$200,000

9. What is the project's schedule performance index (SPI) at this point?
   a. .5
   b. 1
   c. 1.5
   d. .67

10. What is the project's cost performance index (CPI) at this point?
    a. 1
    b. 1.5
    c. .67
    d. .5

This chapter covers the following topics:

- **Assess Methods of Communication:** Understanding synchronous and asynchronous, written and verbal, formal and informal, and external and internal communication
- **Develop Communication Platforms/Modalities:** Considering communication types (status updates, issues, and so on), methods/platforms (email and dashboards), and recipients (project manager, team lead, and team member)
- **Manage Project Communication:** Overcoming communication challenges, language barriers, time zones/geographical factors, technological factors, and cultural differences, maintaining the integrity and security of communication records, and archiving
- **Control Project Communication:** Escalating communication issues and revising the communication plan
- **Meeting Roles:** Understanding facilitators, scribes, and attendees/target audiences
- **Meeting Tools:** Understanding the benefits of agenda setting/publishing, timeboxing, action items, meeting minutes, and follow-ups
- **Meeting Types:** Includes collaborative meetings (workshops, focus groups, joint application development/joint application review sessions, and brainstorming), informative meetings (demonstrations/presentations, stand-ups, and status meetings), and decisive meetings (refinement, task setting, and project steering committee meetings)

CHAPTER 7

Communication and Meeting Management

Communication is the lifeblood of project work; in fact, Project Management Institute (PMI) has estimated that project managers spend 90% of their working time in communication. For this reason, the ability to facilitate effective, efficient communication is one of the most important skills the project manager can have. In addition, communication technologies must be chosen carefully based on the needs of the stakeholders. Factors that can affect the choice of a communication technology include how urgently the information is needed, the availability of a communication technology, its ease of use, the project environment, and the sensitivity or confidentiality of the information.

Communication is formally governed by the communication plan, the escalation plan, the stakeholder engagement plan, and the records management plan. Because CompTIA considers communication development a crucial part of project planning, these plans are covered in Chapter 9, "Project Life Cycles, Discovery/Concept Preparation Phase, and Initiating Phase Activities," and Chapter 10, "Planning Phase Activities." For the purposes of this chapter, you only need to know that the communication plan lists the tempo, format, and channels for distributing project information throughout the project's Executing and Closing phases. The project manager is responsible for knowing when and how involved parties should be kept in the loop and how records should be maintained.

This chapter also covers the various communication factors and modes, common challenges to team communication, and the purposes of meeting-specific roles. Finally, it discusses the three main categories of project meetings, their target audiences, and their intended outcomes and purposes.

This chapter covers the following objectives for the CompTIA Project+ exam:

1.8 Compare and contrast communication management concepts.

1.9 Given a scenario, apply effective meeting management techniques.

"Do I Know This Already?" Quiz

The "Do I Know This Already?" quiz allows you to assess whether you should read this entire chapter thoroughly or jump to the "Exam Preparation Tasks" section. If you are in doubt about your answers to these questions or your own assessment of your knowledge of the topics, read the entire chapter. Table 7-1 lists the major headings in this chapter and their corresponding "Do I Know This Already?" quiz questions. You can find the answers in Appendix A, "Answers to the 'Do I Know This Already?' Questions and Review Quizzes."

Table 7-1 "Do I Know This Already?" Section-to-Question Mapping

Foundation Topics Section	Questions
Assess Methods of Communication	1–2
Develop Communication Platforms/Modalities	3
Manage Project Communication	4–6
Control Project Communication	7
Meeting Roles	8
Meeting Tools	9
Meeting Types	10–11

CAUTION The goal of self-assessment is to gauge your mastery of the topics in this chapter. If you do not know the answer to a question or are only partially sure of the answer, you should mark that question as wrong for the purposes of the self-assessment. Giving yourself credit for an answer you correctly guess skews your self-assessment results and might provide you with a false sense of security.

1. What is considered the most effective method of communication?
   - a. Written communication
   - b. Formal communication
   - c. Nonverbal communication
   - d. Face-to-face communication

2. You are hired to take over an active project. Based on the previous project manager's notes, you are concerned about conflict between two team members. What is the best method of determining whether the team members can successfully communicate without impeding project work?
   - a. Hold separate face-to-face meetings with each of the team members.
   - b. Hold a single face-to-face meeting with both team members.

c. Send an email to each of the team members.

d. Hold a single virtual meeting with both team members.

e. Carefully observe how the team members interact during meetings.

3. Which tasks would a project manager perform when developing communication platforms for the project? (Choose all that apply.)

   a. Purchase a new enterprise license for a chat application.

   b. Establish internal communication accounts for external contractors.

   c. Tailor the platform to the needs of the project.

   d. Secure the credentials for the social media account used for project communication.

4. All members of a virtual project team speak the same language but live in various areas around the world. What are the two most likely communication issues the team will need to address?

   a. Language barriers and cultural differences

   b. Geographical factors and cultural differences

   c. Language barriers and geographical factors

   d. Geographical factors and personal preferences

5. A project manager is struggling to find an acceptable time for international team members to have a video conference. Scheduling the meeting at 1:00 p.m. EST might allow London team members to join (6:00 p.m. GMT) but would exclude New Delhi team members by falling at 11:30 p.m. IST. Which communication challenge must be resolved?

   a. Cultural differences

   b. Technological factors

   c. Geographical factors

   d. Time zone factors

6. The application your project is designing will have several proprietary features that must be protected. A stakeholder has requested access to a report that includes confidential development information, but they are not approved to receive it. What should you do?

   a. Consult with the project sponsor to verify that the stakeholder needs the information.

   b. Deny the stakeholder's request.

c. Grant the stakeholder access and note the change in the communication plan.

d. Give the stakeholder a redacted copy of the report, removing the confidential data.

7. A business analyst frequently drops by your team member's office to convey the customer's questions about the project. As a result, the team member stops work and spends time researching answers that she does not immediately have. What would help her stay on task with fewer interruptions? (Choose two.)

   a. Timeboxing

   b. Escalation plan

   c. Communication plan

   d. Stakeholder engagement plan

8. Which project document or artifact is created by the meeting's scribe?

   a. Meeting agenda

   b. Meeting minutes

   c. Printed media

   d. Status report

9. Some speakers linger too long over their topics in the weekly status meeting and do not leave enough time for the final Q&A session. What would ensure the full agenda is covered in a meeting?

   a. Timebox

   b. Action item

   c. Communication plan

   d. Follow-up

   e. Cadence

10. Which meeting type would describe a daily stand-up?

   a. Collaborative

   b. Recurring

   c. Decisive

   d. Informative

11. Which type of meeting would *not* be used to capture new product requirements from attendees?

    a. Focus group

    b. JAD session

    c. Brainstorming

    d. Demonstration

Foundation Topics

Assess Methods of Communication

Every time information is exchanged, whether through a quick cubicle drop-in or a formal written announcement, communication has occurred. Table 7-2 summarizes the major attributes of communication. From these factors, you can predict the advantages and drawbacks of each communication method and choose the one best suited to each situation.

Table 7-2 Communication Factors and Communication Tools

Communication Factors	**Types**
Direction (flow)	Push, pull, interactive
Timing	Synchronous, asynchronous
Mode	Verbal, nonverbal, written
Formality	Formal/official, informal/unofficial
Audience	Internal, external, general, restricted
Communication Tools	**Examples**
Medium	*How* information is packaged: as a written report, slide presentation, phone call, text message, oral conversation, email, press release, or memo
Platform/channel	*Where* information is transmitted: through video conferencing software, social media, telephone, project dashboards, fact-to-face meetings, or chat applications

In its most basic form, ***communication*** is the flow of information (message) from a source (communicator) to an audience (receiver). The message is encoded in a communication medium, travels via a channel, and is transmitted during a communication session. The information in the message can include ideas, instructions, or emotions. The flow can travel in three directions:

- ***Push communication***: The communicator sends (pushes) a communication to an audience. In-app notifications, press releases, and sent emails are push communication.
- ***Pull communication***: The audience seeks out (pulls) a communication from a source provided by the communicator. Websites, project dashboards, and retrieved emails are pull communication.

- **Interactive communication:** Communication flows back and forth between two or more people at the same time (bidirectional or simultaneous). Participants take turns being communicator and audience. Live meetings, instant messenger chats, and phone calls are interactive communication.

Push and *pull* indicate how communication is transmitted and received, not the medium being used. Sending a written report through email is push communication, while posting the same report to an intranet for stakeholders to download is pull communication.

Noise is any factor (not just sound) that interferes with communication, such as bad acoustics, participants cross-talking over a speaker, distractions, electronic interference, and poor video quality.

Synchronous and Asynchronous Communication

Synchronous communication means that participants receive and exchange information in a communication session in real time. Interactive communication is synchronous, with all parties continually listening and responding to each other (as with face-to-face communication). ***Asynchronous communication*** has a delay, meaning the communicator and the audience enter the communication session at separate times. Push and pull communications are both asynchronous.

Synchronous communication allows rapid feedback; communicators can tailor their message on the fly to meet the audience's needs. For example, a listener might ask the speaker to repeat an unclear phrase or define a term. When handled well, synchronous communication creates a continual improvement loop. If not well facilitated, it can create noise and obscure information with confusing cross-talk or distracting chatter.

Synchronous communication is the quickest way to exchange ideas, making it the choice for urgent issues and emergencies, conflict resolution, and brainstorming. It supports more nuanced discussions than does asynchronous communication. Most communication in an Agile project should be synchronous. On the downside, it needs all parties to be free to communicate at the same time and requires additional technology (such as cameras or mobile devices) to overcome geographic distance.

The strength of asynchronous exchange is that it can be accessed when convenient to the audience and revisited on demand. Audience size does not degrade message clarity, and the recipients can be anywhere in the globe. It also provides a built-in record of the communication. However, it limits the audience's ability to respond, provides no feedback to the communicator, and slows knowledge transfer. Asynchronous messages can sound the alert in an emergency but will not help resolve it.

Written, Verbal, and Nonverbal Communication

Written communication is anything text-based, including voice dictation, emails, chats, reports, press releases, and handwritten notes. It produces a record and is integral to project management. All official project communication must be written. Written text is the most formal and precise communication, but it is weaker at conveying emotional content. While written facts are not likely to be misinterpreted, written tone is, and a badly phrased or hastily written email cannot be recalled once sent.

Verbal or oral communication includes phone calls, live speech, sign language, and meetings. It is the fastest and most unconstrained way for team members to interact, build relationships, and share tacit knowledge. Because verbal communication is ephemeral, it should be logged or documented in a written follow-up to be saved in the communication ***archive*** when it covers significant project issues.

All verbal communication is accompanied by ***nonverbal communication***: body posture, tone of voice, speaking volume, and gestures that all augment (or directly contradict) the words being spoken. Project managers need to be able to read nonverbal cues to effectively manage conflict and understand the emotions that drive interactions among team members or stakeholders.

Formal and Informal Communication

Formal communication is frequently based on a predefined template or standard adapted to a specific need. It is used for any official communication that represents the project or the organization, including press releases, reports, project kickoff meeting briefings, company memos, and internal policies. Formal communication is powerful in that it channels decision-making for the project, but inflexible in that it cannot deviate from its purpose or format and remain effective.

Informal communication includes all unstructured information flows: written, verbal, or nonverbal. Casual emails, text messages, hallway discussions and ad hoc discussions, nods and waves, smiles, scowls, and gestures continually outpace formal communication. Because it requires no preparation or effort, informal communication is the easiest way to convey critical project knowledge or train team members. Whereas formal communication is used to create project documentation, informal communication drives the decisions made before they enter formal channels. Agile methodologies rely more heavily on informal communication than do predictive projects. Note that many modes, like email, can be formal or informal, depending on the message's content.

External and Internal Communication

Internal communication takes place within the project, team, program, organization, or group of stakeholders, whereas ***external communication*** travels outside the organization to customers, vendors, or the general public. Like formal communication, external communication will usually follow a specific format or template and require authorization to release, such as a blog post or ad campaign.

Internal communication can also be categorized by hierarchy. Vertical communication travels up or down the organizational chart (for example, from project manager to board member or from product owner to team member). Horizontal communication occurs between peers with the same level of authority.

Sensitivity and criticality rules govern how information should be shared both internally and externally. General communication can be distributed to any audience, while restricted communication (such as a statement of work) may require that the external recipient sign a non-disclosure agreement. Project managers should also provide a way for team members to communicate internally and privately about issues like personal conflict.

Develop Communication Platforms/Modalities

The ***communication management plan*** (or ***communication plan***) includes guidelines for communication types (status updates, issues, and so on), methods/platforms (email and dashboards), and recipients (project manager, team lead, and team member). Once the platforms are chosen, the project manager is responsible for configuring them to support project work and ensuring that team members have access. The project manager may also need to set up private channels for team communication only.

The communication plan should include tools that keep team members aware of each other's activities, especially in software development projects. It should be easy to see the in-progress status of each module, artifact, or document, and they should be accessible in a joint repository such as GitHub. The team should only use communication channels that your organization supports; for example, some companies block the use of third-party cloud drives due to security issues.

Other development tasks for project communication include the following:

- Setting up access to internal systems (like SharePoint) for external contractors
- Distributing an emergency contact list that all project members can access offline
- Verifying that social media accounts (and their credentials) are documented in the communication plan

NOTE Project dashboards and common project communication modalities, such as email, are covered in detail in Chapter 13, "Project Management Tools."

Manage Project Communication

Project managers must understand all communication methods and mediums in order to determine which are best for any situation that may arise. These choices are influenced by many factors, as discussed in detail in this chapter.

NOTE Project managers should be aware of general differences in communication between Agile and Waterfall or predictive projects. Communication tends to be more open, informal, synchronous, and unconstrained in Agile projects; stakeholders communicate constantly throughout project execution and have open access to team members. Waterfall projects limit stakeholder communication to specific times, channels, and cadences, and they isolate team members from direct stakeholder feedback. In Agile, the project manager will be more concerned with moderating multiple communication channels, and in Waterfall, the project manager will focus more on preparing communications for regular distribution to stakeholders.

Overcoming Communication Challenges

The primary factors that affect project communication are language barriers, geographic separation and time zone differences, technological factors, and cultural differences. Project managers must also be prepared for interorganizational and intraorganizational differences, communication plan requirements, and plain old personal preference. Understanding these influences can help a project manager pinpoint issues that are delaying or interrupting tasks and choose the best solution. Taking the time to overcome, or at least mitigate, these barriers can improve communication quality, increase the team's internal cohesion and trust, facilitate knowledge transfers, improve productivity, and decrease overall development time.

Language Barriers

The effects of language barriers are usually easy to anticipate. If project team members or stakeholders do not share a common language, the project manager will have to provide translation or interpretation services. Solutions may involve translating documents, employing interpreters for verbal communication, or using visual methods of communication and training. If the issue is fluency level, adding closed captioning for live speakers and subtitles for recorded audio can greatly improve comprehension. Another strategy is for the affected team members to learn some basics of the other language(s) needed, which is also an excellent means of team building. Even though mastery of the other language is rarely achieved, just learning the basics can help with simple communication. Having a bilingual team member is also feasible, but constantly translating for the team can become a strain and might delay project work.

While verbal language barriers seem obvious, projects may also involve hearing-impaired personnel. Sign language interpreters may be needed. Some deaf or hearing-impaired people read lips, but that does not help if they speak or read in a different language from other people with whom they need to communicate.

Time Zones and Geographical Factors

As with language barriers, it is fairly easy to anticipate how time zones and geography will affect project communication. The communication plan should always document the time zone and area for team members or stakeholders who are not co-located. The project manager should be mindful during scheduling to ensure that time and location will not affect tasks or dependencies; this includes accounting for regional holidays. The communication plan should list methods of sharing meeting results with absent members if time zones conflict with their ability to attend.

EXAMPLE: A project manager and most of her team are based in New York, NY, USA, on Eastern Standard Time (EST), UTC–5. Other team members reside in New Delhi, India, on India Standard Time (IST), UTC +5.5, and in London, England, on Greenwich Mean Time (GMT), UTC +0. The project manager might schedule the weekly team meeting as a half-hour video conference at 8:00 a.m. EST (6:30 p.m. IST, 1:00 p.m. GMT) so that the New Delhi team members do not have to work late into the evening. Another option would be to schedule a daily remote stand-up from her home at 7:00 a.m. EST for the international team only (5:30 p.m. IST and 12:00 p.m. GMT), and have a second daily stand-up for the New York team at 10:00 a.m. EST. The project manager could share any issues reported by the international team members during the second, local stand-up.

The primary challenge of geographically separate teams is that it can limit most interactions to slow, asynchronous methods like email, decreasing communication frequency and quality. To compensate, encourage team members to interact more frequently and to try multiple synchronous channels, such as phone calls, Skype, Slack, and chat. All team members should know when they can communicate with remote coworkers and which channels to use. Some communication tools can trigger an alert if a team member sends a message or schedules a meeting outside of the recipient's working hours.

Be sure to remember that geographical factors affect team members differently. Team members in different countries, or even different parts of the same country, might face very different weather or traffic conditions that affect travel, procurement, or meetings. A project manager in the northeastern U.S. may need to convert all in-person meetings to video conferences during winter to minimize weather hazards.

Technological Factors

Given how much project communication relies on technology, it can be daunting to contemplate the many ways it can interfere with communication instead. A weak technical infrastructure can make it difficult for team members to coordinate their work on joint tasks or solve problems. ***Technological factors*** include faulty or aging equipment, unreliable utilities, accessibility issues, user discomfort, and security.

The project manager should document any known technological issues and attempt to resolve or bypass them. For example, all video calls should include a dial-in number so that team members can join by phone if their Internet connection is interrupted. If a user is uncomfortable with a tool or application, determine whether the problem is lack of training or accessibility. Not everyone can see in color or type text messages on a mobile device. Shrinking device sizes, in particular, affect both older populations and the visually impaired. Documenting which communication platforms team members or stakeholders do not like or cannot use is just as important as documenting their preferences.

Security is a crucial technological factor. Devices issued to personnel may need security controls to protect the organization's assets, but the project's needs may conflict with the organization's security policies. Security controls may need to be disabled or overridden temporarily to let a team member complete a specific task, but they should be restored when the task is complete. For example, the organization's security policy may block computers from transferring data through USB connections, making it impossible to back up the hard drives on remote team members' laptops to external media. The project manager should find a secure workaround, such as an approved online backup accessed through a secure cloud gateway.

Finally, as a project manager, you must stay proficient with project management software and Agile tools and adapt to new tools as they are added by the organization. To meet these challenges, you may want to acquire an entry-level technical certification or set aside a training budget for personal skills development. As a proficient modern project manager, you need to keep up with technical complexities so that you can effectively handle projects from start to finish.

Cultural Differences

Cultural differences influence how a person thinks about, hears, and sees the outside world as well as how they interpret communications. Culture can refer to a country or region of origin but also to cultures of affinity based on shared interests and attitudes. It is the project manager's job to perceive and translate cultural differences among stakeholders and team members and to bridge communication gaps.

Cultural differences can affect communication in several ways:

- ***Cognitive constraints*** are largely unconscious worldviews that influence perception. Common sources are religious beliefs, literacy level, educational background, gender, and economic status.
- ***Behavioral constraints*** are the unspoken rules that affect verbal and nonverbal communication. Examples include making eye contact, directly discussing an issue versus talking around it, interrupting a speaker, and encroaching on someone's "bubble" of personal space.
- ***Emotional constraints*** are deeply held beliefs regarding the display of emotion. They affect whether people find it acceptable to cry, yell, speak boldly, act humbly, or display any strong emotion in the workplace—and how they react when other team members do so.

EXAMPLE: A project involves teams in two different countries. A team member in one country always agrees to the deadlines set by her manager in the other country, but she frequently misses them without explanation. The project manager consults an expert who explains that the team member's local culture considers it rude to tell a superior "no," even if the superior's request cannot be met. The cultural expert is hired to train both teams on how to communicate clearly and set feasible goals.

Cultural differences can exist within the same building, or even within the same team. Interorganizational differences are the differences between organizations, and intraorganizational differences are the differences within an organization. Different divisions within an organization may have very different communication requirements (such as the communication medium, platform, or cadence), which project managers need to recognize and anticipate.

EXAMPLE: All stakeholders receive an emailed status update prior to the weekly meeting. Over a couple of meetings, it becomes apparent that one stakeholder is not reading the status updates, because he often asks questions about topics that were addressed in the email. The project manager questions the stakeholder privately and discovers that he thinks the status emails are not significant. The stakeholder works in a department that must meet stringent requirements for legal discovery, and he believes that a real status update email would be encrypted. Because the updates were in plaintext, the stakeholder thought they could not contain important project information.

Remember that remote team members can feel excluded from an established on-site culture. The best way to overcome this issue is to encourage frequent meetings and verbal communication and ensure that remote members have as much access to project documentation as on-site members. If possible, bring remote members on site for at least one visit per project.

Maintaining Communication Records

All significant project communication (including written notes captured from meetings as well as official documents) should become part of the permanent project record. These archived documents become a valuable repository and knowledge base for future projects, and they also provide a paper trail for procurements. This does not mean that every single email or chat generated during project work is stored; only important messages need to be retained. Everyday updates between team members sent via text messages are just normal conversations, but you would archive an email requesting the change board to authorize a change that affects the project.

A project manager has three key responsibilities regarding records:

- **Security**: Preventing unauthorized access to restricted information.
- **Integrity**: Ensuring that all relevant records are captured in their most accurate form and not altered in transit or storage.
- **Archiving**: Retaining each type of record for the correct length of time in the required format(s) and using the approved storage method(s).

> **NOTE** Directives for when and how to store communication records are part of the records management plan developed during project initiation, not the communication plan. Other project management standards may place management of communication records in the communication plan. However, CompTIA's objectives state that a separate records management plan should provide this guidance.

Communication Security

Security means to protect communication records from unauthorized access, corruption (loss of integrity), or theft. Your specific security practices will be governed by both the project's records management plan and your organization's data control policies. Authorization for access can be assigned to an individual or to a project function or job role. To provide confidentiality, you should not allow individuals to access project records for which they do not have authorization. Some information may go on the general project dashboard, while some status reports may have an approved email distribution list; project tools can also assign varying levels of access at the user level. When a project communication is classified for sensitivity, the label should include a data owner. Requests to access restricted records should be approved by the data owner, not the project manager (unless they are also the data owner). Data classification and labels are covered in Chapter 16, "Foundational IT Concepts and Operational Change Control for IT Project Management."

Confidentiality can be provided by encrypting electronic data in storage, in usage, and in transmission as well as by securing physical storage (such as a locked filing cabinet). To ensure availability, all valid users must have access to the service. While it may be difficult to account for all service outages, project managers should identify service outages that could occur as risks and then document alternative solutions for the team members.

Communication Integrity

Integrity means to maintain the consistency, accuracy, and trustworthiness of a record. Integrity can be addressed through technical or analog means. Your records management plan may require that important project communications be digitally e-signed (such as contracts) or encrypted in storage. Digital signatures can prove message integrity as well as nonrepudiation (sender/receiver validation). Hashes can verify that a communication was not altered when it was transmitted or downloaded.

Individuals should not be able to edit project records after they are stored or to hide project communications from the record. Sometimes project communications are not so much hidden as they are redirected; you may need to limit the ways in which communications are exchanged in order to keep major project communication funneled through the primary platforms and channels authorized for project use, making them easier to capture.

Most projects result in a plethora of documentation, usually distributed in printed form, which requires version control and strategic distribution. Project managers should retain a list of printed media that pertains to the project, noting who owns the master files or should receive copies. Recording this information will help ensure that all interested parties receive documentation when it becomes available and that documentation is not lost if a team member suddenly leaves a project.

Communication Archiving

Archiving means to maintain records in storage until their life cycle ends and they can be destroyed. In larger organizations, archives will be managed by the PMO. As with security, your archiving practice will be dictated by the records management plan and your organization's record retention policies. The latter governs all contracts, legal records, documents containing sensitive or proprietary information, and communication that should be retained for legal reasons (such as performance reviews). The record retention policies will clarify which types of records should be retained and for how long, as well as the correct storage and disposal methods. Meanwhile, the records management plan documents which project communications must be archived and who has the source documents. It also clarifies the format required for storage (such as printed copies of emails or notarized physical copies of agendas).

Control Project Communication

All team members and stakeholders should have access to the communication plan and use it to guide formal and informal communication. However, communication issues are inevitable in any project. Poor communication can lead to differences in expectations, decreased productivity, or scope creep. If unchecked, communication issues can escalate into outright conflict. Common sources of conflict and conflict resolution techniques are covered in detail in Chapter 11, "Executing Phase Activities."

Escalating Communication Issues

An ***escalation plan*** for project communication is much like an IT help desk escalation plan: its goal is to direct issues that threaten a milestone or impede project work to the appropriate tier in the hierarchy for resolution. While an issue log or risk log attempts to solve a problem directly, escalation redirects an issue into another channel for resolution. The escalation plan can be maintained as a section of the communication plan, or it can be kept as a separate document, but both should be accessible to the team. If a category of issue can be escalated multiple times, the plan includes the escalation path.

An escalation plan should include categories of potential issue scenarios, a role or person who owns the response, a decision trigger to show when to escalate, and severity levels. Some escalation can be lateral (from one team member to another with specific skills). Also, different scenarios may need different sensitivity levels. For example, the project manager might want the team to know how to escalate a problem with the development environment, but not how to escalate vendor issues. However, team members should know the appropriate way to escalate a problem with a coworker rather than deal with it directly. Table 7-3 shows an example of a partial escalation matrix.

Table 7-3 Example of an Escalation Matrix

Scenario	Trigger	Level 1	Contact	Level 2	Contact	Notes
Development environment	Team cannot open authoring tool. Team cannot get into ticketing system.	15–30 minutes downtime	Yusef Parker, operations team lead	More than 30 minutes or more than three incidents per week	Tanesha Lee, operations manager	Notify PM before escalating to Ms. Lee
Accounts receivable	License payments not sent on time; seats expiring.	One late payment per month over three months	Account manager (cc: Sam Williams after third contact)	Two or more late payments per month, warning email from vendor	Pat Cornick, VP of operations	

An escalation plan reduces friction, redundancies, and delay by ensuring only the relevant people are contacted with issues. One frequent scenario is when team members field questions from stakeholders. In most cases, stakeholder communication should be funneled through the project manager, scrum master, or other team leader instead. A good project manager or scrum master will shield team members from overly frequent inquiries from customers or stakeholders that interrupt team progress.

Project managers should understand when to let a situation try to resolve itself versus escalating the issue (and bringing conflict) before it damages the project. The first step should be to try to resolve the issue locally. If a sincere effort doesn't work, document the impact to the project and verify the correct authority with your manager. In the preceding example, your project is affected because your accounting department is not renewing your software licenses on time. It would be inappropriate and counterproductive to escalate immediately to the vice president. However, if multiple payments are missed and your first attempts to correct the issue with the accountant do not work, then you should loop in your manager, Sam Williams, each time you contact the accountant. If the issue continues, it should be escalated to the person with the authority to fix the accounts receivable process, because overseeing the payments is taking your time away from project work.

NOTE Escalation in this context is not the same as conflict escalation. Conflict management is covered in Chapter 11.

Revising the Communication Plan

Like all project management documents, the communication plan is a living document that will change during execution. It is commonly revised when the project adds or loses a stakeholder or ends a phase. The project manager may adjust the meeting cadence in response to stakeholder feedback or update a stakeholder's preferred communication method. After verifying that the communication goals will remain the same after the change is implemented, you should revise both the communication plan and the project schedule to reflect any schedule changes. If stakeholder communication data (such as email address) changes, it should be updated in the stakeholder register as well. The stakeholder register and the communication plan are both detailed in Chapter 10.

Meeting Roles

Meeting roles are not permanently assigned like project roles; they are assumed for the duration of a meeting to help meet its goals. The project manager usually sets the agenda and the guest list, sends the meeting invitations and follow-up, and tracks attendees who were assigned action items. However, the project manager is not supposed to facilitate or record every meeting. If at least one other person can be support staff, the project manager can pay full attention to the actual meeting activities. The people assigned to fill meeting roles can be external to the team or even to the organization. Specialized meetings, like focus groups and joint application development (JAD) sessions, may require a trained facilitator hired from outside the company.

Scribe

Smaller meetings and well-established Agile meetings, like scrum meetings, can rely on their participants to take notes and update their own project dashboards. A scribe captures the results of more formal meetings in writing, creating documents to be archived with project communications and/or distributed to the team. The scribe does not have to be a member of the team, or even have product knowledge. When used, a scribe records action items, follow-ups, meeting minutes, annotations to the meeting agenda, brainstorming session results, and the results of official meetings that should be entered into project records.

Facilitator

A facilitator maintains the vision for the meeting and is responsible for it meeting its goals. This person controls everyone's participation, guiding the group and keeping activities in line with the agenda. If communication gets noisy or stagnant, the facilitator solicits contributions and encourages attendees to consider all points of view. In smaller meetings, this person documents the meeting results and future action items, but more involved meetings will use a scribe so that the facilitator is free to focus on meeting management.

While this is not a definitive list, here are some techniques of successful facilitation:

- Choose a supportive locale with adequate facilities.
- Prepare an agenda and define concrete, realistic goals, matching activities to the meeting's goals.
- Schedule food and regular rest breaks.
- Model active listening and objectivity.
- Tone down aggressive communication and head off conflict.
- Redirect teams to focus on key topics or tasks, not digressions.
- Allow the team's work to guide the outcome rather than directing their work.

Attendees/Target Audience

Attendees or target audiences are the team members and stakeholders attending the meeting. The terms *audience*, *participant*, *attendee*, and *target audience* are interchangeable in this context. Attendees should never be selected through a "may as well add them to the invite list" approach; it is important to weigh the time commitment of a meeting against the attendee's schedule. Attendees who should attend a meeting, but cannot due to schedule constraints, should review the meeting minutes. In practice, the attendee's role and responsibilities in the meeting will depend entirely on the type of meeting.

Meeting Tools

A meeting is a structured communication form. Although meetings can have widely varying formats and purposes, there are common tools, techniques, and artifacts to govern the structure and ensure that a meeting executes according to its plan. Among these tools are timeboxing, agenda-setting, meeting minutes, action items, and follow-ups.

Timeboxing

A ***timebox*** is a predetermined time frame allocated to one unit of work or goal. Timeboxes are typically fractions of the overall schedule; their purpose is to keep a process moving by allocating just enough time to advance (or, hopefully, finish) a task without delaying future work. However, the timebox method halts work when the clock runs out, finished or not. In Agile and other adaptive approaches, a timebox refers to the sprint duration or the length of time an activity will take (such as one week or one month). Work not finished at the end of the timebox is added to the backlog or reprioritized into a new timebox.

When applied to communication, a timebox is allotted to a unit of communication or an agenda item, such as introductions or presentations, so that meetings do not run over or omit presenters. A meeting scheduled to run from 2:00–2:30 p.m. is timeboxed, as is an agenda item that gives Charlotte 15 minutes to present a slideshow.

Agenda-Setting/Publishing

A ***meeting agenda*** is a document that provides the topics of discussion and activities planned for a meeting. (The exception is daily scrum meetings, stand-ups, and other meetings with a set format.) An agenda keeps the meeting on track, facilitates timeboxing, makes sure that meeting goals are achieved, and creates a communication record. Agendas are prepared (or set) and distributed (or published) in advance of the meeting, but they can be revised after the meeting to reflect any items that were added or omitted before they are archived.

Meeting Minutes

The ***meeting minutes*** are a record of what was discussed and decisions that were made during a meeting. The minutes should be published formally for review by project stakeholders. Meeting minutes can simply summarize key points of discussion or provide a full written recap of what was discussed, who discussed it, who was present, which items need follow-up, and which decisions were made. Minutes are particularly important when key team members are invited but unable to attend, or when the meeting's attendance and outcome should be logged for regulatory purposes. They create a record of project decisions and are a valuable resource for generating lessons learned documentation.

Brief, informal minutes can be taken by a scribe or team member and should be distributed to participants and relevant stakeholders. When possible, minutes should be distributed on the same business day as the meeting unless they require formatting to meet a standard. They are typically sent as an email but can be logged to project dashboards or sent in chat channels according to the communication plan.

Remember that the agenda is there to guide the meeting, and the minutes are created to record what happened during the meeting. Because impromptu meetings are variable, they will not have an agenda. If an important project decision is made during an impromptu meeting, you should record and publish meeting minutes in lieu of an agenda.

Action Items and Follow-Ups

An ***action item*** is a previously unknown or unassigned task that is identified as a requirement during the course of a meeting. Action items are assigned to team members (the ***action item owners***) along with a completion goal or time; they are usually expected to be completed by the next meeting. Action items differ from issues in that they should require few resources—often only a single resource—and usually take less than one week to resolve. These items should not cause delays in the project.

A follow-up is an after-action following an action item that seeks to update its status or resolve it. To follow up after meetings, a chat or email is sent to request a status update on the action item or to resolve it. If sent in written form, the follow-up may summarize a list of the issues introduced in the meeting, along with the people responsible for each. The best time to send a follow-up email or chat is right after the meeting to help ensure that the attendees follow through with their action items and to ensure no action items were forgotten. The project manager or team member can also schedule a follow-up meeting to collect the status of action items and update the project status report.

Meeting Types

Scheduled meetings occur regularly, while impromptu meetings arise by chance or as project conditions change. Some meetings are triggered by the project's phase, such as the kickoff or closure meetings. Whatever their cause, all project meetings serve one of three purposes: to create value, to share information, or to find consensus, and they can be classified as collaborative, informative, or decisive meetings, respectively. Some events may blend types; for example, a two-day all-hands meeting could combine a presentation (informative meeting) with a tabletop exercise (collaborative meeting).

In collaborative meetings, all attendees have equal control over and input into the meeting's outcome, regardless of their place in the organization's hierarchy. Decisive meetings also empower their attendees, but senior management and sponsors may drive the outcomes. Informative meetings are mostly driven by the presenter and facilitator, and attendees have little control over the meeting's format. (While daily stand-ups are a collaborative exchange of information, their format cannot be varied.)

Collaborative Meetings

Collaborative meetings bring a group together to work in unison to achieve a specific goal. The purpose is usually to generate value, such as customer feedback, prototypes, new ideas, or a solution to a problem. Collaborative meetings are primarily creative, and information flows in multiple directions. They work best when they are conducted in person and are kept small enough that everyone can communicate clearly and stay on task. Meetings with more than a dozen participants benefit from periodically forming small breakout groups for targeted discussion. The main formats are workshops, focus groups, brainstorming sessions, and joint application development/review (JAD or JAR) sessions.

Workshops

Workshops are centered around a scheduled activity that all attendees should perform, such as a tabletop exercise or strategic planning session. Facilitated workshops are used to quickly define requirements (or some other aspect of the project) and reconcile the differences. This type of meeting requires a stakeholder balance, particularly if the project manager suspects that members will have opposing viewpoints. For example, accounts payable and accounts receivable may each think a different component of a financial application needs to be completed first. Workshops need a facilitator who can keep the group moving along but does not try to affect the decisions being made. While the project manager may facilitate a smaller group, it is often best to separate these roles because the project manager should be the voice of the project and may have to negotiate conflicting requirements.

For a workshop to succeed and not waste participants' time, all attendees should take part in the activity (except for scribes). Project managers and facilitators should take care not to let the workshop spin into a presentation or demonstration led by one person or dominated by a small group. All lessons learned and group findings should be provided in written form as soon as possible after the workshop concludes.

Focus Groups

The purpose of a ***focus group*** is to conduct in-depth research within a small audience to better define a market or a set of requirements. It brings together SMEs and attendees, who may or may not be stakeholders, and gathers the attendees' expectations and ideas around a particular project or result. Focus groups work best when they are limited to five to twelve participants, plus at least one facilitator and one SME. In between answering prepared questions, the attendees take open discussion time to share examples of use cases and give their views on success criteria.

Focus groups can also recruit external participants to represent a theoretical customer. In this style of group, the mock customers are presented with a product demo or concept, and the facilitator documents their honest reactions in a controlled way.

After viewing the demo, the participants discuss the product's pros and cons among each other. They may have one or more rounds of discussion, each facilitated (but not guided) by the moderator, before taking a final survey or other assessment. This style yields real-world insight into the product's likely reception in the marketplace, and the conversational style allows more insight into opinions than surveys or other tools.

Brainstorming

Brainstorming is a popular technique that inspires creative, associative, nonlinear thinking from the participants. Brainstorming is fast, informal, and usually fun; its purpose is to rapidly generate a large number of ideas in a short amount of time and then distill them into a workable list relating to an open-ended scenario or problem to solve, such as project risks or alternate approaches to a design issue. After the list is generated, its line items are analyzed to find the most feasible and discard the least workable. Like workshops, brainstorming sessions typically include SMEs, stakeholders, and team members. They also require facilitation to keep the meeting on track and constrained to its designated time block. Uncontrolled brainstorming sessions can waste time and generate more chaos and noise than value.

Joint Application Development/Joint Application Review Sessions

Joint application development (JAD) sessions, sometimes called joint application reviews, are a type of workshop in which the customer and the project team collaborate on software product design and review prototypes as they are developed. They were invented in the 1970s as a faster way to gather requirements and specifications than interviews, and they are easily adapted to both Agile and predictive projects.

The mandatory JAD roles are the facilitator, an executive sponsor, SMEs, business users, and a scribe. The executive sponsor is the ultimate decision-maker who owns the results. Each JAD session has a defined set of objectives, an agenda, documentation, and a schedule of activities and exercises. Because JAD sessions can run from a full day to a week or more, they require an outlay of time and budget, can be difficult to coordinate, and can become overly complex for nontechnical users. Their advantage is generating prototypes with direct customer involvement and less rework or rejection.

Informative Meetings

Informative meetings are meant to convey project details, persuade an audience, or provide training in a process or tool. Meetings in this category place more limits on back-and-forth interaction between the presenter and attendees. Information primarily flows one way, from the presenter to the attendees, except during questions or feedback. Stakeholders and team members are expected to evaluate the information as it is presented, minimize chatter, and ask questions only during designated timeboxes so that the meeting stays on track. The meeting should produce an informed audience that can form opinions about how much value the product or initiative poses.

Unlike collaborative meetings, informative meetings can be easily scaled to hundreds or even thousands of participants by renting a convention facility or providing a virtual meeting link. They are an effective way to coordinate knowledge, sell products, or roll out new products or company initiatives. However, they run the risk of low audience engagement.

Demonstrations/Presentations

Demonstrations show the functions or features of the product or project results. They are one of the most valuable ways for Agile projects to align actual project results with the customer's requirements and gather the feedback needed to guide the next iteration or sprint. This type of meeting requires more discussion time to go over the customer's reaction and would be followed by a product refinement meeting. Regular demonstrations should be scheduled in the communication plan. However, demonstrations apply to any project methodology and are a primary avenue for product sales.

Presentations share information about the project or product, usually in the form of slides, charts, graphics, project dashboards, audio-visual files, graphs, and project documents. Presentations are used to share schedule and budget progress (or lack of progress), threats/opportunities, issues, burndown charts, and so on. Online webinars are a classic example of an externally focused presentation.

Stand-Ups

Daily stand-up meetings are a key Agile tool and a core component that makes the Agile team align rapidly to shifting requirements. Stand-ups require that the project team members report on their individual progress and align their daily priorities at a high level. Each team member takes turns reporting the prior day's accomplishments and pain points. They may note issues that need later follow-up, but the strength of a stand-up is its brevity: the goal it to limit the session to 15 minutes. Stand-ups were originally developed as part of the scrum methodology, but because they are an easy, flexible format that adapts to any type of project, they can be part of any project framework.

Status

Project ***status meetings*** are scheduled in the communication plan, which should also include a template for their agenda and an attendee list. They are not intended to resolve issues or discuss any one point in depth but rather to align project knowledge. They should present a summary of the progress made since the last report, such as milestones reached or deliverables completed. Status meetings are ideal for low-information stakeholders who want to be kept informed but are not responsible for project work.

Decisive Meetings

Decisive meetings are held to make a decision about the project's next steps and then formulate the action to take. They may require additional project documents related to the flexion point, such as change request forms or the issue log, the project scope baseline, or the schedule. They also require a clear agenda so that everyone who enters the meeting knows its purpose and their personal level of authority over the decision. It is important to document the action items generated from these meetings and distribute them to the correct team members so that the decision is carried out.

Because decision requires consensus, the meeting should be small enough to facilitate open discussion. It is unlikely that a large number of people all have the power to weigh in on a project decision; the project documents should list the person with final decision-making authority if there is no easy consensus.

Change control board meetings, which were covered in Chapter 3, "Change Control Process Throughout the Project Life Cycle," are a type of decisive meeting.

Refinement

Refinement meetings, also referred to as backlog refinement meetings, are a scrum meeting type that decomposes the highest priority backlog items into user stories for inclusion in the next sprint. They also help the team prioritize the backlog in the first place and to insert new items by their relative priority. Items near the bottom of the list are least relevant, may be vaguely worded ("This seems like a good idea at some point"), and may be pruned away during refinement.

Task Setting

Task-setting meetings decide which tasks or activities the team will focus on in the next timebox and then assign the tasks to the appropriate team member. This can be done during a daily scrum meeting or whenever a new action item is found. If tasks are set during an ad hoc meeting, the manager should send a follow-up communication to document the request.

Sprint planning meetings, also referred to as iteration planning meetings, are task-setting meetings in which the project team decides how much of the backlog can be delivered in the forthcoming iteration.

Project Steering Committee Meeting

Also referred to as a stakeholder board meeting, a ***project steering committee meeting*** is held regularly to ensure project success and goal achievement and to provide governance from start to finish. Its purpose is to identify the next steps that will keep the project moving forward successfully. If the organization includes a PMO, it will be part of this meeting. The project steering committee usually controls the project's budget and is authorized to make project decisions that are outside the project team's authority.

NOTE Do not confuse project steering committee meetings with project status meetings, although the same people may attend both. Status meetings are informative, whereas the project steering meetings are decisive.

Exam Preparation Tasks

As mentioned in the section "How to Use This Book" in the Introduction, you have a few choices for exam preparation: the exercises here, Chapter 17, "Final Preparation," and the exam simulation questions in the Pearson Test Prep Software Online.

Review All Key Topics

Review the most important topics in this chapter, noted with the Key Topics icon in the outer margin of the page. Table 7-4 lists each reference of these key topics and the page number on which each is found.

Table 7-4 Key Topics for Chapter 7

Key Topic Element	Description	Page Number
Table 7-2	Communication Factors and Communication Tools	206
Section	Synchronous and asynchronous communication	207
Section	Written, verbal, and nonverbal communication	208
Section	Formal and informal communication	208
Section	External and internal communication	209
Paragraph	Manage project communication	210
Paragraph	Overcoming communication challenges	210

Key Topic Element	Description	Page Number
Section	Control project communication	216
Table 7-3	Example of an Escalation Matrix	217
Section	Meeting roles	218
Section	Meeting tools	219
Paragraph	Collaborative meetings	222
Paragraph	Informative meetings	223
Paragraph	Decisive meetings	225

Define Key Terms

Define the following key terms from this chapter and check your answers in the glossary:

communication, push communication, pull communication, noise, synchronous communication, asynchronous communication, archive, nonverbal communication, formal communication, informal communication, internal communication, external communication, communication management plan, communication plan, technological factors, cognitive constraints, behavioral constraints, emotional constraints, escalation plan, timebox, meeting agenda, meeting minutes, action item, action item owners, collaborative meetings, focus group, brainstorming, daily stand-up meetings, status meetings, decisive meetings, refinement meetings, task-setting meetings, project steering committee meeting

Review Questions

The answers to these questions appear in Appendix A. For more practice with sample exam questions, use the Pearson Test Prep practice test software online.

1. In a typical focus group, which interactions produce the most value for the product owner?
   a. Interactions between the moderator and the target audience
   b. Interactions between the SME and the moderator
   c. Interactions among the target audience members
   d. Interactions between the SME and the target audience

2. Your project team members all work in the same building. They prefer informal communication like chat applications and in-person desk meetups. Which communication method are they using?

   a. Synchronous communication

   b. External communication

   c. Verbal communication

   d. Asynchronous communication

3. You are the project manager for a software development project. When the project started, all team members were in a single location in the U.S. Three team members left and were replaced by team members in Spain. All the team members work on the same schedule. Not everyone speaks English. What should be your primary concern regarding project communication?

   a. Cultural differences

   b. Language barriers

   c. Geographical factors

   d. Relationship building

4. Your records management plan requires that all meeting agendas be archived in an online repository. You find your remote meetings will sometimes fail to cover all agenda items, or they will add items not originally listed. Which options would preserve communication integrity? (Choose two.)

   a. Use a document naming convention.

   b. Use a secure connection to upload the agendas to the internal repository.

   c. Use a scribe.

   d. Use version control.

5. Project managers need to recognize when technological factors influence project communication. Which of the following is an example of this influence?

   a. One team member has been hired as a contractor for this project.

   b. One team member works in a different country than the other members.

   c. One team member speaks English as a second language.

   d. One team member has unreliable Internet access.

6. You are the project manager for your company. All of the team members for your current project are employees of other departments. You have asked for daily verbal status updates as part of the scrum meeting. A couple of the team members also want to submit written weekly project status reports, as required by their departmental supervisor. Which communication influence is occurring?
   a. Cultural differences
   b. Confidentiality constraints
   c. Intraorganizational differences
   d. Interorganizational differences
7. Why is it *most* important to capture accurate written notes following a verbal meeting in which an important project decision was made? (Choose two.)
   a. To preserve communication integrity
   b. To preserve communication criticality
   c. To facilitate archiving records
   d. To preserve communication security
   e. To facilitate consensus
8. In response to an unplanned service outage, your company records a public service announcement that plays automatically when a customer calls your help desk. How would this communication be classified?
   a. Formal, synchronous, internal, push
   b. Formal, asynchronous, external, pull
   c. Formal, asynchronous, external, push
   d. Formal, synchronous, internal, pull
9. Which artifact is the primary output of a decisive meeting?
   a. Product mockup
   b. Action item
   c. Dashboard information
   d. Status report
10. Which outcome would indicate that a workshop with 20 attendees was poorly facilitated?
   a. The product backlog was not discussed.
   b. The agenda was bound by timeboxes.
   c. All attendees left their seats to move around the room.
   d. The meeting was informative.

This chapter covers the following topics:

- **Resource Procurement Overview:** Understand the steps for resource procurement.
- **Resource Procurement Methods:** Understand the advantages and disadvantages of building, buying, leasing, subscriptions, and pay-as-you-go procurements.
- **Exploratory Documents:** Understand the purposes of a request for proposal (RFP), request for information (RFI), request for quote (RFQ), and request for bid (RFB).
- **Vendor Evaluation Techniques:** Choose vendors based on best value vs. lowest cost, cost-benefit analysis, market research, competitive analysis, qualifications and prequalified vendors/sellers, demonstration, technical approach, physical and financial capacity, and vendor references.
- **Contract Considerations and Types:** Understand common contract formats and mutually binding documents, including time and materials, unit-price, fixed-price, and cost-plus contracts; master service agreements (MSAs), purchase orders (POs), terms of reference (TOR), and statements of work (SOWs); maintenance agreements, warranties, and vendor service level agreements (SLAs); non-disclosure agreements (NDAs), non-compete clauses, cease-and-desist letters, memorandums of understanding (MOUs), and letters of intent (LOIs).

CHAPTER 8

Project Procurement and Vendor Selection

At some point, most projects will need to purchase labor, goods, services, materials, and/or equipment from a third party to conduct project work and complete their deliverables. If a resource cannot be created or sourced internally, it must be formally procured. The procurement process describes how to find, assess, contract, and manage vendors for outside resources. It includes creating proposals for quotes, bids, and proposals, choosing among competing vendors, assessing vendors for fitness, and choosing the contract with the best cost-benefit ratio. Once a contract is signed, additional documents may be required to initiate an order for goods or authorize labor to begin.

Project managers must understand multiple contract types, including unit-price contracts, fixed-price contracts, cost-plus contracts, and purchase orders, as well as mutually binding agreements that govern relationships with contractors and partners. Warranties, maintenance agreements, and service level agreements ensure the quality of the procurement after purchase. Other common documents, including non-compete clauses and non-disclosure agreements, protect the organization's interests in the market.

Individual procurements are managed by vendor documentation, which includes payment and delivery terms and the specifications for the procurement. Large projects may require multiple procurement contracts. Vendor documents are created according to the procurement management plan, which is part of the overall project management plan.

This chapter covers the following objective for the CompTIA Project+ exam:

1.11 Explain important project procurement and vendor selection concepts.

"Do I Know This Already?" Quiz

The "Do I Know This Already?" quiz allows you to assess whether you should read this entire chapter thoroughly or jump to the "Exam Preparation Tasks" section. If you are in doubt about your answers to these questions or your own assessment of your knowledge of the topics, read the entire chapter. Table 8-1 lists the major headings in this chapter and their corresponding "Do I Know This Already?" quiz questions. You can find the answers in Appendix A, "Answers to the 'Do I Know This Already?' Questions and Review Quizzes."

Table 8-1 "Do I Know This Already?" Foundation Topics Section-to-Question Mapping

Foundation Topics Section(s)	Questions Covered in This Section
Resource Procurement Overview	1
Resource Procurement Methods	2
Exploratory Documents	3–5
Vendor Evaluation Techniques	6–8
Contract Considerations and Types	9–10

CAUTION The goal of self-assessment is to gauge your mastery of the topics in this chapter. If you do not know the answer to a question or are only partially sure of the answer, you should mark that question as wrong for purposes of the self-assessment. Giving yourself credit for an answer you correctly guess skews your self-assessment results and might provide you with a false sense of security.

1. Which procurement steps would need to occur before a vendor is selected? (Choose all that apply.)
   a. Perform a make-or-buy analysis.
   b. Issue a purchase order.
   c. Evaluate the vendor's physical capacity.
   d. Assess the procurement needs.

2. Which option is a service that accumulates costs at a specified rate only as the service is being used?
   a. Subscription
   b. PAYG
   c. CPAF
   d. Lease

3. Which vendor documentation should be issued if the purchaser is unsure of which specifications to look for in a procurement?
   a. Request for quote
   b. Invitation for bid
   c. Request for proposal
   d. Request for information
4. What best describes the purpose of issuing a request for quote (RFQ)?
   a. Soliciting price quotations from prospective sellers of common products or services, such as computers or building materials
   b. Requesting that a potential seller provide information related to the desired product or to the seller's capabilities
   c. Soliciting sealed bids from prospective sellers of products or services
   d. Outlining what the terms for a service agreement will be between the parties if the vendor is selected
5. Which vendor documents would be given to prospective sellers to obtain price quotes? (Choose two.)
   a. RFI
   b. PO
   c. RFP
   d. MSA
   e. RFB
6. Which vendor characteristic or attribute will create the fastest turnaround time for issuing a contract?
   a. References
   b. Cost effectiveness attributes
   c. Qualifications
   d. Prequalification status
7. Which option is one of the most accurate ways to fully assess the capabilities of the vendor and evaluate a proposed software or hardware solution?
   a. Market research
   b. Prequalification status

c. Demonstration

d. Technical approach

8. The project manager is not sure what constitutes reasonable prices for an upcoming procurement. Which tool could be used to perform market research that will aid in vendor selection?

a. Cost-benefit analysis

b. Competitive analysis

c. Request for quote

d. Financial capacity analysis

9. Which contract type establishes a lump sum to be paid for the work performed?

a. Fixed price

b. Unit price

c. Cost plus

d. PAYG

10. Which document should be used to ensure that vendors and contractors do not share details of the project with unauthorized parties?

a. TOR

b. LOI

c. MSA

d. NDA

Foundation Topics

Resource Procurement Overview

A ***procurement*** is any product or service that is needed by the project team—from equipment to software to office supplies. Purchases from contractors, providers, and so on (known collectively as ***vendors***) follow a formal procurement process:

1. Pre-existing contracts and prequalified vendors are assessed during the Discovery phase.
2. The project manager performs the appropriate make-or-buy analysis and makes a preliminary assessment of procurement needs during the Planning phase.
3. Once the decision is made to acquire a procurement or service, the project manager documents the details of the desired product or service and the source selection criteria for a vendor.
4. An exploratory document such as a request for information (RFI), request for bid (RFB), request for proposal (RFP), or request for quote (RFQ) is issued by the project manager or by the organization's procurement team.
5. Potential vendors who return the documents are assessed using a number of techniques, including market research, a cost-benefit analysis, their technical approach, and their physical and financial capacity to provide the procurement. In simpler scenarios, cost may be the sole deciding factor. More complex scenarios may require an evaluation committee to reach a decision.
6. One bidder ultimately becomes the selected source and then evolves into the contracted supplier or seller. This part of the procurement process finalizes the mutually binding vendor documents, such as a contract or master service agreement (MSA), non-disclosure agreement (NDA), and/or warranty.
7. If needed, the project manager generates statements of work (SOWs) and purchase orders (POs) to initiate the work or buy the material as well as monitors both vendor performance and the quality of the incoming work or material.
8. The organization's procurement team and/or the project manager issues payments, enforces the vendor rules of engagement, maintains procurement records for auditing and reporting, and monitors or closes contracts.

Any of these steps may need to be repeated during project work if new resource needs are identified or if vendors are unable to fulfill their contracts. Because vendor documents are legally binding, they may need to be reviewed and approved by individuals outside the project team's structure. Vendor artifacts can be handled through the appropriate accounting personnel or by authorized project team members, as long as they are freely available to each.

Resource Procurement Methods

After assessing the project's resource needs and identifying gaps, the first decision the project manager makes is whether to build, buy, lease, or subscribe to the resource. Because procurements rely on the supply chain, you should carefully plan to ensure they arrive before they are needed. If one exists, the project management office (PMO) will know future project needs and can provide information regarding existing contracts, both of which may affect procurements for a new project.

Build

A project may require specialized equipment or computers that are not available to buy with all the necessary features or are cost-prohibitive to acquire commercially. A common example of when it may be better to build is when the project needs a specialized high-end computer with a large amount of video RAM, high graphics capabilities, fast memory, and solid-state storage. After a make-or-buy analysis, it may be determined that the best solution is to build the hardware or software for the project. If so, then the labor hours and the cost of parts or components need to be added to the schedule and budget, and a team member will need to be free to assemble and/or configure the item(s).

Buy

Some procurements are easily purchased in the marketplace, such as wiring, mobile devices, computers, laptops, networking hardware, and applications. Some procurements may only come from a specialized vendor, or even involve solutions that do not yet exist. These scenarios favor buying over building.

A purchase of durable goods, equipment, facilities, real estate, and/or vehicles incurs both capital expenses and ongoing maintenance for the organization. The procurement becomes a business asset that may appreciate or depreciate, be sold for a profit or loss, incur additional taxes, or alleviate a tax expense. These down-the-line considerations should be factored into any decision to buy. They are also partly responsible for the shift from on-premises IT infrastructures to cloud-based and service-based models, which replace the overhead of maintaining equipment with consumption-based pricing.

Lease

Some procurements should be leased because they are only needed for a short period, as with construction or specialty equipment, or are only available to rent, as with office space. Although this decision would not be made at the project level, converting a capital expense (a purchase) to an operational expense (a lease) may also create a financial advantage for the organization. The terms of a lease contract usually make the renter the responsible party for damage, maintenance, and repairs to leased equipment or facilities, which should be factored into the cost estimate.

Because a lease agreement usually has time parameters associated with it, the project manager should ensure that the procurement is used effectively to minimize lease costs. An idle leased resource means wasted funds. On the other hand, you should make sure not to lease equipment for so long that its monthly cost exceeds its up-front purchase price. Even in this case, the convenience of a lease may outweigh the cost of upkeep, as with a leased vehicle.

Subscription/Pay-as-You-Go

Subscriptions and pay-as-you-go procurements typically apply to cloud and data services, technical devices that deprecate rapidly, vehicles, and professional services. Like leased procurements, they are operational expenses that reduce the organization's up-front costs and maintenance load. For example, rather than owning a fleet or leasing cars for business travel, an organization could use a car-sharing service that charges an annual access fee and has outlets in major cities. Unlike a lease, a subscription does not usually require the subscriber to maintain the resource. The primary benefit of a subscription is ease of use and low entry costs compared with buying the resource.

While they are presented as one topic by CompTIA, there is a key difference between subscriptions and pay-as-you-go services. A ***subscription*** incurs a monthly or annual flat fee, regardless of how often the service or product is used during the subscription period (unless it is a usage-tiered subscription). By contrast, a ***pay-as-you-go*** (PAYG) service is billed by consumption, and it accumulates costs at a specified rate for every minute or unit of value consumed. Amazon Web Services (AWS) cloud resources are a common pay-as-you-go use case. AWS offers more than 200 cloud services, each of which has its own pay-as-you-go pricing system. It is important that someone on the project team monitors PAYG consumption for services used by the team and shuts down idle workloads to avoid wasting funds on unused resources.

Exploratory Documents

A portion of the project budget is usually allocated to small, one-time expenses that do not require a contract. However, most project procurements go through a formal bid process whereby vendors are given the chance to submit written bids, quotes, or proposed solutions for the procurement. The appropriate procurement exploratory document will vary depending on whether the procurement is common and easily sourced versus complex, specialized, or otherwise difficult to acquire. Some types of procurement may be sourced from prequalified vendors only.

Of the four exploratory documents, the RFP is the most formal and requests the most information from a vendor, followed by the RFI. The RFQ and RFB are very similar, as both of these indicate that a purchase is imminent and are primarily concerned with pricing.

Request for Proposal

A ***request for proposal (RFP)*** is issued to "solicit" a highly skilled solution or a complex procurement. Completed RFPs help the buyer make the most informed comparison between vendors. The RFP itself should be detailed enough that bidders can make an accurate estimate of the cost and effort. It should include information on the requesting organization, relevant project information, the project scope, bidder qualification requirements, timelines, and guidelines for submitting the proposal. For example, if the proposal requires a solution narrative, the guidelines should state how many pages of text, photographs, and diagrams are desired.

A supplier becomes qualified only after its RFP is received. Received RFPs may be evaluated by an in-house team or committee with enough experience to evaluate each vendor's approach to the work and the financial issues associated with the purchase. The winning proposal may not be the cheapest solution.

When creating an RFP, project managers should keep the following tips in mind:

- Clearly define the evaluation criteria to ensure that both the in-house selection team and the potential suppliers understand all the areas to be evaluated.
- Conduct reference calls and site visits to ensure that the prospective vendor is competent and capable of providing the product or service.
- Send all requests for communication to one person to prevent multiple individuals from having to answer proposal questions.

Promises made in the RFP should be incorporated into the contract to ensure that they remain part of the vendor's commitment. The end result of a successful RFP is a ***procurement agreement*** or contract.

Request for Information

A ***request for information (RFI)*** does not directly solicit a quote or bid; it is used when the buyer wants to gather more details about potential solutions or does not fully understand the marketplace. An RFI focuses not on the project but on the vendor's products or services, prior work, skills, and/or experience. This approach allows the buyer to preselect providers with the capability to submit a winning proposal. It also helps vendors remove themselves from consideration if they cannot meet the project's needs.

The RFI should state who is issuing the RFI, to which project the RFI applies, the RFI reference ID, the date of issuance, the WBS level of the project scope to which the RFI applies, the priority of the RFI, any specific queries or questions for which the issuer needs a response, and the deadline for responding to the RFI. After all RFIs are returned and analyzed, the next step is to issue a request for proposal, bid, or quote.

The project manager should be aware when an excessive number of RFIs are being implemented. Too many RFIs could indicate incomplete contract or project documents or an incomplete study of the project's procurement needs. Excessive RFIs can result in project delays as well as additional costs.

Keep in mind these points regarding RFIs:

- RFIs are used when specifications cannot be finalized because of incomplete information or lack of understanding.
- RFIs help narrow the vendor pool.
- RFIs do not complete the contract.

Request for Quote

A ***request for quote (RFQ)*** is issued to request price quotations from prospective sellers of common, readily available products or services. The project manager already has detailed specifications for the product or service being sought and is primarily interested in comparing prices among vendors. RFQs are issued only to vendors with which the buyer has previously worked; therefore, the suppliers are qualified prior to receiving the RFQ. Because so much information regarding the product or service is already known, the RFQ is mainly about pricing. The result of an RFQ is a procurement agreement or contract; keep in mind that the quote may be valid only for a set period, such as 30 days.

The RFQ process is considered transparent and easily understood. Project managers should ensure that the awarding criteria and weights document the following details:

- Product functionality or range of services
- Initial price
- Total cost of ownership (TCO)
- Risks with the product or service
- Risks with the vendor
- Ability to meet requirements

Request for Bid/Invitation for Bid

A ***request for bid (RFB)***, also called an invitation for bid (IFB*)*, is used when the buyer seeks price quotes or bids from several sellers. The buyer chooses the most attractive bid and awards the contract to that seller. In some organizations, the differentiator between RFQs and RFBs is that RFQs are only sent to preselected sellers, while RFBs are sent to any vendor. As with an RFQ, the end result of an RFB is a procurement agreement or contract.

Both RFBs and RFQs can be returned as sealed bids. A sealed bid ensures that no one can see the completed bids prior to the deadline for selection. This process is preferred for government contracts, where vendors should be selected strictly by price and without favor or bias. The bidding system opens after the submission deadline, and RFQs are reviewed by the selection team for awarding of the contract.

Vendor Evaluation Techniques

How does a project manager "decide" when a flurry of seemingly qualified vendors respond to requests for quotes or bids? In addition to describing the procurement process and providing templates and forms, the ***procurement management plan*** gives selection criteria to use for choosing vendors and procurement sources. Project managers may need to evaluate the vendors for their fitness as well as evaluate how well the procurement fits the project scope. This can be done alone or with the help of a vendor evaluation team.

Note that the quality assurance plan frequently contains vendor criteria and minimum acceptable standards for services, and it should also be consulted when you are evaluating proposals or vendors. Both management plans are described in Chapter 10, "Planning Phase Activities." Remember, also, that contracts are legal documents, and projects in some industries must meet a legal obligation to treat all vendors equally and choose a contract without bias.

Best Value vs. Lowest Cost

Project managers should compare both the overall value of a proposal and its bottom-line cost when comparing bid documents. Unless the budget is so tight that only the cheapest solution will do, a project may benefit from choosing the bid with the higher bottom line if it offers better value, even if the value is more qualitative than quantitative. The lowest-cost selection approach works best when choosing between multiple vendors who are supplying the same product, like printer paper.

EXAMPLE: Two companies offer the same 3-D printer, but the better value bid includes an extended warranty for a slightly higher per-unit price. Another company may estimate higher labor costs for a project that will be billed hourly, but it also has positive reviews from clients whose opinion you trust.

Cost-Benefit Analysis

A ***cost-benefit analysis*** compares the benefits provided by a procurement against the cost to acquire or own it. The evaluated cost includes both direct costs and indirect costs. Examples of indirect costs could be the costs of training, installation, additional utilities, or lost employee productivity while migrating to a new solution, while direct costs could be acquisition price and licensing. Benefits could include increased output, added capacity, reduced labor or maintenance costs, reduced supply chain costs, and reduced taxes or fees. The benefits should be quantified as much as possible for evaluation purposes and then forecast over the expected timeline of the procurement's use. If the projected benefit exceeds the projected costs, the purchase (or project) is a good investment.

Cost-benefit analyses are used to evaluate whether a project should move from discovery to initiation and to assess whether a risk response outweighs a risk's impact. When applied to vendors, a cost-benefit analysis could determine whether vendor A's proposal or vendor B's proposal has the highest cost-to-benefit ratio, or whether it would be better to produce a resource in-house versus procuring it.

EXAMPLE: You are evaluating proposals to lease construction machinery for 2 years. Vendor A will provide the machinery for $500,000 per year, but will not include servicing or repairs. Vendor B will provide the machinery for $690,000 per year, along with on-site maintenance from its technicians and a guaranteed repair time of 48 hours. You estimate that if the machinery goes out of commission for 3 or more days, the impact would exceed $250,000. Depending on the likelihood of the loss event, vendor B's proposal would have the higher cost-benefit ratio.

EXAMPLE: You are analyzing whether to spend $300,000 to acquire a new system that would expand your capacity to take on project work and is projected to increase revenues by $200,000 per year. The system would cost $50,000 annually to maintain after the first year. In the first 2 years, the procurement will cost $350,000 and generate revenue of $400,000. If the system has an expected lifespan of 2 years or more, it may be a good investment.

The project management plan should include the organization's preferred framework and formulas for making cost-benefit analyses for project proposals, procurements, vendor bids, and risk responses.

Market Research

Market research is conducted early in the vendor selection process or whenever the project manager needs to obtain an unfamiliar resource for an ongoing project. Its purpose can be to find a vendor that offers a niche product or service, to help evaluate a vendor who has submitted a proposal or quote, or to determine which vendor(s) have the largest footprint and strongest reputation in the project's field.

Market research can be passive or active, and it can be a paid service or self-initiated by the project manager. Blogs, whitepapers, and research journals can help you find industry experts, as can conferences and in-person networking events. Commercial market research firms sell access to their newsletters and to targeted industry data; purchasing these products can give you a better understanding of your target industry's scope and capabilities so that you can gain an understanding of what a vendor could provide.

If you have received a quote from an unfamiliar vendor, you should examine their online presence and read any customer reviews or referrals left on social media. Market research can also help you uncover general industry trends and financial data that can guide the criteria for an RFP or project scope. Issuing an RFI is always a reliable way to gather industry intelligence and attract relevant vendors.

Competitive Analysis

Once you have gathered your raw data through market research, you can convert it into actionable intelligence by using ***competitive analysis***, which involves identifying the competitors who could be vendors for a particular procurement and using research to reveal their strengths and weaknesses. In particular, it compares and contrasts how each vendor seems to perform in the marketplace.

To begin the analysis, you should identify groups of data points that are common to all your vendors who are relevant to your project, such as market share, year founded, gross revenues, number of countries within the customer base, number of unique website visits per month, or number and types of product offerings. The data points should be gathered into a matrix for one-to-one comparison and then ranked according to the attributes most relevant to you. The matrix could become an organizational asset that is continually updated as vendors grow, change, or enter or leave the market.

Qualifications

Qualifications are client-defined characteristics that make a vendor a good fit for some types of project work. In some cases, vendors must demonstrate their fitness to meet a qualifying standard before you can send them a request for a quote or proposal or issue a contract. Qualifying a vendor means to pre-screen them against a set of criteria, usually by publishing an open vendor invitation with a detailed description of the standards to be met. Vendors whose applications are approved will be shortlisted for proposals and fast-tracked for new contracts or purchase orders. Qualified vendors are sometimes referred to as prequalified vendors, but the terms mean the same thing.

Some of the qualifications can be subjective standards, such as the longevity of their company or the expertise of the staff. More often, prequalification is used to build a list of vendors who can handle complex or high-risk procurements or who will help your project meet regulatory requirements. They may be insured against a certain level of liability or have the correct third-party certification to handle hazardous materials or to protect health data. You may also want to prequalify vendors with special characteristics to meet future project needs, such as veteran-owned businesses or vendors with security clearance.

Prequalified Vendors/Sellers

A list of prequalified vendors is maintained by your organization's procurement team or PMO. Because these sellers have already been vetted and are known to meet minimum qualifications, using them can shorten the bid process considerably. ***Prequalified vendors/sellers*** provide a known level of quality and have a vested interest in maintaining a good relationship. It is worth taking the time to prequalify vendors if you frequently issue the same types of RFQs and RFBs for recurring project work, or if your projects require vendors who hold specialized licensure.

Technical Approach

A technical approach evaluation can be performed after a vendor responds to an RFP with a proposed solution. This approach uses predetermined criteria to assess the vendor's ability to meet project requirements, and it assigns a numeric score to the result. Subject matter experts and/or procurement staff who understand the technical requirements perform the evaluation separately and then compare results. This approach does not evaluate vendors against each other but rather rates them solely against the project's scope. Vendor bids must all be rated using the same evaluation criteria for this approach to succeed.

Demonstration

Demonstrations may be needed to fully assess the capabilities of the vendor or of the procurement. A product demo is one of the most accurate ways to evaluate proposed software or hardware solutions. The vendor can provide a demonstration in a controlled setting or in an environment that simulates the project's conditions, such as dropping a ruggedized laptop onto a concrete floor. It can also be used to observe the procurement in use to compare it against another potential procurement. A demonstration can be public, such as a conference presentation, but when you are in the final stages of evaluating one or two vendors for a contract, you should request a private individualized demo.

Physical and Financial Capacity

Capacity evaluations verify that the vendor can produce the project deliverables at scale and to schedule. This is particularly important in projects where a large number of the same procurements are being manufactured to order or sourced from the vendor. Physical capacity can refer to having the right size production facility, sufficient staff to provide the man-hours, and access to shipping and delivery services, but it can apply to any unit of measure defined by the contract. For example, your project needs an estimated 400 hours of coding in one week to finish a sprint, but the vendor only employs eight developers. The vendor would need to force 10 hours of usable code daily from each developer, assuming none of them needed to eat or leave their desk while at work—an obvious risk. You should also ask about the vendor's "burst capacity" and verify they could handle a sudden influx of work from existing clients while still meeting your deliverables schedule, or even scale up if you needed to increase your unit production mid-project.

Financial capacity refers both to the vendor's financial stability and to their ability to hire subcontractors and buy the raw materials needed for your procurements. You should have a CPA or other professional examine any financial statements the vendor provides and estimate their profitability. If the vendor is large or publicly traded, you can acquire their 10-K filings, credit agency ratings, and audited financial statements. Bankruptcy filings or liens against the vendor's property would obviously indicate severe liquidity issues. Pending lawsuits, while not an immediate red flag, may help you pinpoint future cash flow issues if a settlement were issued. Rapid turnover of key staff (demonstrated by job postings) could indicate mismanagement of some kind.

References

Project managers can request references from the vendor's other customers to attest to the quality of the vendor's work. It is especially important to do so before signing a contract for services, which depend on the vendor's skill and integrity and are harder to quantify than a physical procurement. Testimonials on the vendor's website or social media page may not reflect the true customer experience. A vendor might agree to provide you with a letter written by a former client, but the most valuable reference is one you can contact yourself. Questions should not center around the details of the project but around the vendor's performance with regards to cost, schedule, and quality. Even if their project experienced some turbulence, learning how the vendor handled obstacles could raise caution flags or indicate a solid choice.

Contract Considerations and Types

Once a vendor has been evaluated and chosen, the contract is awarded. An agreement or ***contract*** is a ***mutually binding document*** that spells out the conditions of the transaction between two parties. Such documents include fixed-price contracts, unit-price contracts, cost-reimbursable contracts, and time-and-materials contracts. The type of contract is selected based on the needs of the project. Multiple suppliers and contract types may be required for a single project.

Project managers should work with management and the PMO to determine the best type of contract for each procurement. A purchasing specialist or department may also be needed. Many organizations have internal guidelines for this process. The organization's legal representatives should help draft mutually binding documents in case these documents are needed in civil suits. In larger organizations, the accounting department typically provides the support needed to ensure that all procurements are completed correctly. Vendor artifacts can either be handled by the accounting personnel or authorized project team members, as long as they are freely available to each.

Time and Materials

With a ***time-and-materials (T&M) contract***, the vendor buys the materials necessary to complete project work and bills their labor at a flat hourly rate. The buyer reimburses the seller for their labor and for the actual cost of the materials, which can include physical supplies, subcontracted labor, and direct costs like vehicle mileage. The contract does not specify how many hours of labor or units of material will be required, usually because these details are not known when the contract is executed. Payment is based on billable time and all allowed costs.

To prevent this type of contract from overrunning your budget, you should establish not-to-exceed values, time limits, and caps on material costs. Because they are open-ended, T&M contracts are usually best for simple projects that have small monetary values or time frames.

EXAMPLE: A T&M contract is used to hire a team of brick masons for a project to develop new housing over a multiyear period. The contract means the masons can work and be paid whenever a house is ready; their contract will not penalize the project if they have to stay idle during two weeks of bad storms.

Unit Price

With ***unit-price contracts***, the seller charges the buyer a flat fee for a single unit of a procurement. The same cost is charged for each unit produced, and the final total is based entirely on the number of units completed or purchased. This type of contract makes for easy accounting but does not allow the project manager to negotiate a volume discount.

EXAMPLE: A vendor charges $500 per unit of procurement. If the project manager executes a purchase order for 30 units, the cost will be $15,000. If the project manager buys 2 units, the cost will be $1,000.

Fixed Price

A ***fixed-price contract*** establishes a lump sum to be paid for the work performed. Although a firm fixed-price (FFP) contract sets the payment in stone after the contract is signed, this type can be modified slightly with a fixed-price incentive fee (FPIF) or fixed-price with economic price adjustment (FP-EPA) contract.

- ***Firm fixed-price (FFP) contract:*** The price for the procurement is set at the outset and cannot change unless the scope of work changes. The vendor absorbs any cost increase that occurs due to performance issues. Changes to the procurement specification will result in increased costs. This is the most popular type of contract.

  EXAMPLE: A project needs to purchase seven desktop computers that will be used for graphics applications. An FPP contract is used because the specifications are known and the computers are in stock or available within a relatively short period.

- ***Fixed-price incentive fee (FPIF) contract*:** As with FFP, the price for the procurement is set at the outset. However, a clause adds financial incentives for the vendor to achieve goals related to cost, schedule, or performance. The incentive includes a price ceiling, and the final cost is determined after the work is complete.

  EXAMPLE: A project needs to purchase a storage area network (SAN). The selected vendor has projected six weeks to make the SAN available for use. If the project needs the SAN sooner, the project manager could use an FPIF contract in hopes that a financial incentive will speed up the vendor's process.

- ***Fixed-price with economic price adjustment (FP-EPA) contract*:** Multiyear procurement contracts can take fluctuating commodity costs, such as inflation, into account with an economic price adjustment. Usually, the economic adjustment clause is tied to a specific financial index.

  EXAMPLE: A long-term project involves building houses in a new neighborhood. Phase 1 will construct 50 homes in the first year of the project. Phase 2 will build 100 homes in the second year. Phase 3 will complete 200 homes in the third year. An FP-EPA contract would be the best choice for the lumber supplier because this type of contract can be adjusted to account for rising lumber costs in the third year.

Cost Plus

With ***cost-plus* contracts**, the buyer prioritizes speed and/or quality over price. The seller is reimbursed for all of their incurred costs and awarded an extra amount intended to reduce project uncertainty. The major types of cost-plus contracts are cost plus fixed fee (CPFF), cost plus incentive fee (CPIF), and cost plus award fee (CPAF).

- ***Cost plus fixed fee (CPFF) contract*:** The vendor receives payment for all allowed costs plus a fixed fee, which is a percentage of the estimated costs. The payment does not change unless the project scope changes.

  EXAMPLE: A high-risk project to develop medical equipment requires the services of a medical research firm. Because the project has many unknowns that will become clear only as the research progresses, the project manager and vendor may decide to use a CPFF contract to protect the research vendor in case no successful device can be brought to market.

- ***Cost plus incentive fee (CPIF) contract*:** The vendor receives payment for all allowed costs plus a bonus based on meeting performance goals for schedule, delivery, or cost savings. In this contract, the vendor could earn extra money by delivering the product under budget.

EXAMPLE: In the medical project from the previous example, a CPIF contract could be used instead of the CPFF to encourage the vendor to develop a prototype device as early as possible. The vendor would receive the incentive fee if they delivered the device ahead of schedule.

- ***Cost plus award fee (CPAF) contract*:** The vendor receives payment for all allowed costs and an award fee based on a subjective evaluation of their performance. An award fee is used when performance goals are qualitative or cannot be defined before the contracted work begins.

  EXAMPLE: In the medical project from the previous example, a CPAF contract would allow the project team to award the vendor if they developed the device according to contract and also discovered a new marketable use for it that exceeded its previous scope.

Master Service Agreement

> **NOTE** Use of the term "master" is ONLY in association with the official terminology used in industry specifications and standards, and in no way diminishes Pearson's commitment to promoting diversity, equity, and inclusion, and challenging, countering and/or combating bias and stereotyping in the global population of the learners we serve.

A ***master service agreement (MSA)*** is a broad contract that is established when two parties begin an ongoing business relationship that will encompass multiple projects, including future projects that are not yet defined. The external party could provide an ongoing service as a vendor or independent contractor, or could act more like a partner for the project's organization. Having this pre-existing framework in place protects each entity's business rights while streamlining the negotiations for each new contract or project.

While the specific areas covered by the MSA can vary by industry or organization, its purpose is to establish the terms and conditions that govern each party's actions and responsibilities. It can establish the governance terms for sensitive data handling, confidentiality, warranties, payment terms, limitations of liability, dispute resolution or arbitration, venue of work, product delivery terms, and work standards. It can also include agreements for handling future conditions, such as ownership of jointly developed intellectual property or royalties earned from the results of project work.

The MSA authorizes the project's environment, but not project work. Once the project is ready to begin work, the project organization will submit a statement of work, terms of reference, scope of work, or purchase order tailored to the new project's scope, depending on contract terms. This subsidiary contract will be appended to the MSA and will authorize project work. In some industries the project authorization will be called a work order.

EXAMPLE: A global oil producer that plans to cap several disused oil wells in the next decade signs an MSA with an environmental engineering firm. Each oilfield reclamation will be handled as a separate project with a separate contract and SOW, all to be executed under the terms of the MSA.

Purchase Order

A ***purchase order (PO)*** is a customer's request to receive specific goods or services from a contracted vendor. When a PO is issued to a vendor after a contract is signed, it initiates the work or begins the transaction. The contract sets the price, but the PO authorizes the transaction to pay for the purchased resource or service. The PO states the financial agreement, terms, method of delivery, delivery date, quantity needed, and so on, and is binding for the purchaser. Depending on organizational policies, project managers may need to issue POs only for purchases over a certain amount.

Once the product or service is delivered, the vendor issues an invoice that references the PO number. This practice allows accounting procedures to track the full transaction.

Contracts and POs are often confused. A procurement contract and a PO are both legally binding documents. A contract establishes an agreement to purchase something at some point, while the order is fulfilled through one or more POs.

Terms of Reference

A ***terms of reference (TOR)*** document is similar to a statement of work, but it is more commonly used when contracting for services to be rendered than defining a procurement. It defines the expectations for the project, including standards for the contractor's performance, the respective responsibilities of the buyer and the contractor, the expected results and deliverables of the assignment, and a schedule for delivery. The purpose of a TOR is to establish a common framework and scope, specifying how work should be executed to meet the terms of a contract. TORs are often subsidiary documents; they are rarely issued as standalone contracts.

Statement of Work

A ***statement of work (SOW)*** can be issued before or after a contract is signed. When issued during procurement, it gives a description of the procurement item or the project so that prospective sellers know its specifications and can determine whether they can meet the specifications. The SOW lays out the terms of the work to be provided to the organization by the vendor or contractor. It can include quantity needed, quality specifications, performance data, performance period, the duration of work and the work location, and any other requirements.

EXAMPLE: For a project to produce training materials for an IT course, the contract will spell out the terms and conditions of the project, including payment information. The SOW will contain specific details about the required end product, including any graphics, videos, virtual machine–based practice labs, and assessment questions that will be part of the product.

When issued after a contract is signed, a SOW can group multiple related products or services that the vendor will provide as part of a single procurement. It can also be issued after a master service agreement is in place, in which case each SOW authorizes a new project to take place under the existing terms and conditions established in the MSA.

Maintenance Agreements and Warranties

The value of any contract hinges on its ability to enforce the terms for the procurement's quality level and expected performance. Maintenance agreements, service level agreements, and warranties provide quality assurance and lower the financial risk of a procurement. All provide a degree of protection, but they have different purposes as well as different terms of coverage and delivery methods.

Warranty

A ***warranty*** offers purchase protection that begins the moment a purchase is completed. A warranty can be included in the vendor contract, but some procurements may come with multiple separate warranties issued by the manufacturer, especially for a complex procurement like a server farm that includes servers, routers, and other devices. The warranty guarantees the purchased item will operate as described for a certain period of months or years. If it fails within that period, the warranty issuer must repair it, replace it with a comparable product, or issue a refund. Warranties may exclude certain types of failures or damages caused by misuse and not by product defects. When extended warranty coverage is offered, you should be careful to run a cost-benefit analysis first; paying for a 5-year warranty on a product you expect to replace within 3 years is not a sensible use of funds.

Warranties are more often associated with tangible, defined products like devices and software applications than with subscriptions. Software warranties guarantee that bugs, errors, and defects will be patched or repaired by the developer in a timely way. Larger organizations may use third-party products to track warranties and process claims, including warranties for IT assets.

Maintenance Agreement

A ***maintenance agreement*** establishes the ongoing services that a vendor will provide after you begin using the procurement. Unlike with a warranty, maintenance does not mean the product is malfunctioning or failing in an unexpected way. Just as a car requires regular tune-ups, the procurement might require maintenance to ensure both high performance and the expected lifespan. The agreement lays out the conditions under which both the vendor and buyer must operate, including service level requirements and hourly rates to be paid to the maintenance provider. In fact, hiring an unauthorized third party to maintain the procurement may void its associated warranty, meaning that the vendor would not be liable or offer a remedy if the procurement ever did malfunction.

A service contract combines features of a warranty with a maintenance agreement. A service contract specifies the terms and conditions by which a vendor will support, troubleshoot, repair, or replace a procurement, regardless of whether the issue stems from user error or device malfunction. One example would be a 3-year service contract for a computer manufacturer that provides remote diagnosis, chat and phone support, and finally, on-site repair services for the owner.

Vendor Service Level Agreement

Service level agreements (SLAs) were covered in Chapter 6, "Quality, Cost, and Performance Management," in terms of a project offering, but they are commonly associated with external procurements. An SLA is a promise that a procured service will meet a specific level of quality and availability and will offer a specific remedy if it does not. SLAs can be separate contracts or subsections of larger contracts. If some project services are provided by a department within the organization, an intra-departmental SLA can ensure that the promised services have a formal agreement in place.

The SLA should describe the parameters of the service provided, the promised performance level (such as 99.99% available uptime 365 days/year), the steps for reporting issues, the issue-resolution parameters, and repercussions if the provider fails to meet the service terms. It should include an escalation plan that defines minor, significant, and major disruptions to the service, plus reporting requirements and customer support options for each level. For example, minor issues might need to be reported through an online portal with a response time of 48 hours, while major disruptions might be guaranteed live phone support from a senior engineer within 1 hour.

Project managers should verify that the parameters of the SLA will satisfy the project's needs. One potential remedy for a provider failing to uphold its SLA is to offer a discount or credit toward future services instead of fully restoring performance; essentially, this would mean the project pays less overall but receives an inferior service that might not support its requirements.

It is possible for subscription services (like cloud services) and software to be covered by both a warranty and an SLA. In this situation, the product is guaranteed to work or be replaced/refunded (warranty) and has a path to report and cure future potential defects (SLA). A warranty is desirable because a vendor might modify the SLA for an ongoing subscription, while the terms of a warranty are fixed at the time of purchase.

Non-Disclosure Agreement

A ***non-disclosure agreement (NDA)*** is a type of confidentiality agreement in which the selected vendor and their personnel agree not to disclose any details about your project to outside parties. NDAs are often used when the vendor needs to know certain details about the project to formulate an accurate bid, quote, or proposal, but the project sponsor wants that information to remain private. They also apply to project work after a contract is signed, particularly if the project is bringing a new product or design to market. For example, an NDA may state that a contracted developer cannot disclose any information about the design of your proprietary hardware, even after the project that utilizes the hardware is complete.

An NDA is not itself a confidential document. It establishes the type of confidential information to be protected without actually revealing details, lists the parties that are covered by the agreement, and also specifies the types of information that are *not* covered by the NDA. In the preceding example, the NDA could cite "unpublished computer code, design definitions and specifications, flow diagrams and flowcharts, formulas and algorithms, and system and user documentation" as protected confidential information.

Non-Compete Clause

In some cases, NDAs may need to incorporate a ***non-compete clause*** or a separate *non-compete agreement* to prevent a vendor or contractor from pursuing a similar project with the buyer's direct competitors within a specified time period. The time period for enforcement of the non-compete clause should be included in the contract, along with any penalties tied to the agreement. Non-compete clauses also protect existing customer and client lists; meaning that, for example, a contractor may speak with your client while performing job duties for your project, but is prohibited from contacting that client for a side project for a year.

Other Common Documents

While the following vendor-centric documents are not listed in the exam objectives, they are commonly encountered during project management.

Cease-and-Desist Letter

A ***cease-and-desist letter*** is sent to a person or entity to order them to stop doing something immediately (cease) and never do it again (desist). Common cause for a cease-and-desist letter is alleged infringement of the claimant's intellectual property, copyrights, trademarks, or patents. The letter can include a demand for compensation or a request for attribution. While not legally enforceable, the letter can threaten legal action if the alleged misconduct does not stop. A cease-and-desist letter from a legal representative usually carries more weight than one issued from the project sponsor.

Letter of Intent/Memorandum of Understanding

A ***letter of intent (LOI)***, sometimes called a ***memorandum of understanding (MOU)***, is a mutually (but not legally) binding document that describes a forthcoming agreement between two or more parties. It is usually issued as a temporary precursor to a formal contract and is implemented to state that the parties are in the process of negotiating terms for the contract. The project manager should ensure that the LOI or MOU has a limited time frame and that the formal contract is implemented as quickly as possible. An LOI or MOU carries a degree of seriousness and implies that a binding contract is in the works. Alternatively, an MOU or LOI might be signed between two parties that are unable to enter into legally binding contracts together, such as agencies within the same state government.

Exam Preparation Tasks

As mentioned in the section "How to Use This Book" in the Introduction, you have a few choices for exam preparation: the exercises here, Chapter 17, "Final Preparation," and the exam simulation questions in the Pearson Test Prep Software Online.

Review All Key Topics

Review the most important topics in this chapter, noted with the Key Topics icon in the outer margin of the page. Table 8-2 lists each reference of these key topics and the page number on which each is found.

Table 8-2 Key Topics for Chapter 8

Key Topic Element	Description	Page Number
List	Overview of resource procurement process	235
Paragraph	Overview of resource procurement methods	236
Paragraph	Overview of request for proposal (RFP)	238
Paragraph	Overview of request for information (RFI)	239
Paragraph	Overview of request for quote (RFQ)	239
Paragraph	Overview of request for bid (RFB)	240
Paragraph	Overview of vendor evaluation techniques; description and examples of various vendor evaluation techniques	240
Paragraph	Overview of time-and-materials contract	245
Paragraph	Overview of unit-price contract	246
Paragraph	Overview of fixed-price contract	247
Paragraph	Overview of cost-plus contract	247
Paragraph	Overview of master service agreement; discussion of purchase orders (POs) and terms of reference (TOR)	249
Paragraph	Overview of statement of work (SOW)	249
Paragraph	Overview of maintenance agreements, warranties, and vendor service level agreements (SLA)	251
Paragraph	Overview of non-disclosure agreement (NDA) and non-compete clause	252

Define Key Terms

Define the following key terms from this chapter and check your answers in the glossary:

procurement, vendors, subscription, pay-as-you-go, request for proposal (RFP), procurement agreement, request for information (RFI), request for quote (RFQ), request for bid (RFB), procurement management plan, cost-benefit analysis, market research, competitive analysis, qualifications, prequalified vendors/sellers, contract, mutually binding document, time-and-materials (T & M) contract, unit-price contracts, fixed-price contract, firm fixed-price (FFP) contract, fixed-price incentive fee (FPIF) contract, fixed-price with economic price adjustment (FP-EPA) contract, cost plus fixed fee (CPFF) contract, cost plus incentive fee (CPIF) contract, cost plus award fee (CPAF) contract, master service agreement (MSA), purchase order (PO), terms of reference (TOR), statement of work (SOW), warranty, maintenance agreement, service level agreements (SLAs), non-disclosure agreement (NDA), non-compete clause, cease-and-desist letter, letter of intent (LOI), memorandum of understanding (MOU)

Review Questions

The answers to these questions appear in Appendix A. For more practice with sample exam questions, use the Pearson Test Prep practice test software online.

1. You are the project manager for a project to design and build sets for a Broadway musical. You need to obtain a motorized mechanism that will allow certain parts of the stage to rotate 360 degrees automatically. You are unsure of the specifications for this procurement or which solution would be best. Which procurement document should you use?

   a. RFQ

   b. RFI

   c. RFP

   d. RFB

2. You are the project manager for a project with multiple procurements, and you need to purchase the equipment to implement a lab network. This equipment includes servers, routers, and cabling. You already have details about the exact equipment models and specifications needed for the project. Which procurement document should you issue?

   a. RFI

   b. RFP

c. RFQ

d. PO

3. Which document is usually issued after an analysis of the RFI is complete?

a. Contract

b. Purchase order

c. MSA

d. RFP

4. You are purchasing a procurement for your project at a contract price that was negotiated with the vendor. If the procurement is delivered early, the vendor will receive a bonus. Which type of contract did you implement?

a. FFP

b. FPIF

c. FP-EPA

d. T&M

5. Divisions within your large corporation often work together on projects. Your project will obtain a procurement from another division of your company. The other division has agreed to provide the procurement for the cost of its materials plus its labor. Which type of contract will be used for this procurement?

a. CPAF

b. CPIF

c. CPFF

d. T&M

6. While managing a project that includes a new patent granted to your company, you discover that another company is working on a project that will infringe upon your company's patent. What should you invoke to inform the other company of the issue?

a. Letter of intent

b. Non-disclosure agreement

c. Cease-and-desist letter

d. Non-compete clause

7. You have contracted a portion of a new mobile app to be developed by a third party. You need to ensure that personnel from that company do not share any details of this project with anyone. Which document should you use?
   a. Cease-and-desist letter
   b. Non-disclosure agreement
   c. Terms of reference
   d. Statement of work

8. Your company has located a potentially qualified vendor for a procurement that should be manufactured to spec. However, you need to do more due diligence and ensure that the vendor's factory is large enough to handle your order volume on schedule. What should you request or "evaluate"?
   a. Capacity
   b. Request for proposal
   c. References
   d. Technical approach

9. Your organization has an established MSA with a university's biomedical research department. You manage a series of highly confidential projects aimed at developing new biological therapies based on the university's research. You are ready to kick off a new project. Which document, if any, is required to begin project work?
   a. RFP
   b. NDA
   c. SOW
   d. None; the MSA is sufficient authorization

10. As the project manager, you are concerned that some equipment currently being purchased will not last for the duration of the project, which is 3 years. Which of the following should you check?
    a. Purchase order
    b. Maintenance agreement
    c. Warranty
    d. Physical and financial capacity

This chapter covers the following topics:

- **The Project Life Cycle:** Understand the purpose of the Discovery, Initiating, Planning, Executing, and Closing phases for a project or phase.
- **Discovery Phase Activities:** Conceptualize the project, define the business case, define the current vs. future state, and estimate the return on investment; understand the importance of prequalified vendors, predetermined clients, preexisting contracts, capital expenses (CapEx), and operational expenses (OpEx).
- **Initiating Phase Activities:** Define the project's objectives, success criteria, preliminary scope and requirements, high-level risks and assumptions, summary milestones, summary budget, and key stakeholders; create a stakeholder register, develop a responsibility assignment matrix, establish communication channels, begin records management, review existing artifacts, determine a solution design, define access requirements for project work, obtain charter sign-off, and perform kickoff.

Project Life Cycles, Discovery/Concept Preparation Phase, and Initiating Phase Activities

This chapter introduces the five stages of the project life cycle and covers the first two phases in detail, along with their key activities and documents. It also touches briefly on alternative models for project management—specifically project knowledge areas and performance domains.

The purpose of the Discovery phase, or concept preparation, is to build a business case by describing a potential project and its justification, determining its feasibility, and estimating its potential for gain. The project's sponsor completes most of this work. This phase defines the desired outcomes the project could bring about and lays out the rationale for a preferred solution. It establishes whether prior contracts or agreements apply to this project's work that would shorten development time or add constraints.

If a business case is approved, the proposal becomes a project and moves into the Initiating phase. The new project's scope, major risks, assumptions/constraints, objectives, and success criteria are described at a high level in the project charter. The project manager identifies key stakeholders and determines their areas of responsibility. This phase sets the stage for successful project work by establishing communication channels and the records management plan, choosing a solution design for IT projects, and formally kicking off the project. When the sponsor signs off on the charter, the project officially moves into the Planning phase.

This chapter covers the following objectives for the CompTIA Project+ exam:

2.1 Explain the value of artifacts in the discovery/concept preparation phase for a project.

2.2 Given a scenario, perform activities during the project initiation phase.

"Do I Know This Already?" Quiz

The "Do I Know This Already?" quiz allows you to assess whether you should read this entire chapter thoroughly or jump to the "Exam Preparation Tasks" section. If you are in doubt about your answers to these questions or your own assessment of your knowledge of the topics, read the entire chapter. Table 9-1 lists the major headings in this chapter and their corresponding "Do I Know This Already?" quiz questions. You can find the answers in Appendix A, "Answers to the 'Do I Know This Already?' Questions and Review Quizzes."

Table 9-1 "Do I Know This Already?" Section-to-Question Mapping

Foundation Topics Section	Questions
The Project Life Cycle	1
Discovery Phase Activities	2–5
Initiating Phase Activities	6–10

CAUTION The goal of self-assessment is to gauge your mastery of the topics in this chapter. If you do not know the answer to a question or are only partially sure of the answer, you should mark that question as wrong for purposes of the self-assessment. Giving yourself credit for an answer you correctly guess skews your self-assessment results and might provide you with a false sense of security.

1. During which phase(s) of the project life cycle do you actively control the project's expenditures? (Choose as many as apply.)
   - a. During the Initiating phase
   - b. During the Planning phase
   - c. During the Executing phase
   - d. During the Closing phase

2. Which statement *best* describes a project artifact?
   - a. Lessons learned documents archived from prior projects
   - b. Any project document template provided by the PMO
   - c. A quantifiable deliverable produced by project work
   - d. Any tangible document, output, product, or template used in project work

3. When is the project's potential for financial gain first calculated?
   a. During the Discovery phase
   b. During the Initiating phase
   c. During the Planning phase
   d. Prior to beginning the project life cycle

4. You need to estimate the total dollar return that the project sponsor will receive for a project. Which value should you calculate?
   a. CV
   b. ROI
   c. EAC
   d. CapEx
   e. OpEx

5. Which of the following would describe an operational expense? (Choose two.)
   a. Paying a per-meeting charge to add landline access to your video conferencing platform
   b. Buying 100 VoIP handsets to replace landlines in your office
   c. Upgrading the server hardware in your data center to increase video quality
   d. Paying a monthly utilities bill for Internet and phone services in your office

6. During the Planning phase of a project, you are given the document shown in Figure 9-1. What type of document is this?

Ref	Task Description	Board	Steering Group	Project Sponsor	Project Manager	IT/Business Analyst 1	IT/Business Analyst 2	IT/Business Analyst 3	Departmental Manager	Departmental User 1	Departmental User 2	Departmental User 3
1	Requirements Specification											
1.1	User Interviews	I	I	C	A/R	R	C	C	C	C	C	C
1.2	Consolidate Requirements	I	I	C	A/R	R	C	C	C	C	C	C
1.3	First Draft of Requirements	I	I	I	A/R	R	C	C	I	I	I	I
1.4	Review Draft Requirements	I	I	A/R	I	I	I	I	A/R	C	C	C
1.5	Amend Draft Requirements	I	I	A	A/R	C	C	C	A/C	C	C	C
1.6	Sign Off Requirements	I	A	A	R	I	I	I	A	I	I	I

Figure 9-1 Project Document

a. RTM
b. WBS
c. RAM
d. CRM

7. Which document officially authorizes a project manager to spend funds and acquire resources?
   a. Business case
   b. Project charter
   c. Procurement management plan
   d. Budget baseline

8. Which document is produced during the process of identifying stakeholders?
   a. Stakeholder register
   b. Stakeholder engagement plan
   c. Responsibility assignment matrix
   d. Communication plan

9. Which job role or entity provides the most subject matter expertise and guidance during the solution design process?
   a. Business analyst
   b. Network engineer
   c. Product owner
   d. PMO
   e. Architect

10. Your project is well into the Planning phase when you add three new team members. As the project manager, you need to make sure they understand their duties and the project goals. What should you do?
    a. Distribute the final WBS to the new team members.
    b. Upload their tasks to the project dashboard.
    c. Hold a second kickoff meeting.
    d. Pair the new members with senior team members to act as mentors.

Foundation Topics

The Project Life Cycle

No matter which methodology or framework guides them, all projects and their phases have a similar trajectory: they are planned, they begin work, they execute under supervision, and they deliver a result, at which point they roll into a new phase or formally end. While named frameworks like PRINCE2 and DevOps have their own definitions for each project stage, the universal activities of any project can be intuitively grouped into five ***phases*** that CompTIA calls the project life cycle: Discovery, Initiating, Planning, Executing, and Closing.

The phases are described in detail across the next few chapters but are summarized as follows:

- **Discovery**: Project conceptualization. This phase creates a business case to describe the proposed project and estimates its benefits, risks, and results. It ends when the project is rejected or initiated.
- **Initiating**: Project authorization. This phase creates the project charter and defines the project's major characteristics, maps stakeholders and their responsibilities, and analyzes the project environment.
- **Planning**: Project development. This phase defines the final scope (for Waterfall projects) or sprint goals (for iterative/adaptive projects) and creates plans to formally manage procurements, communication, stakeholders, tasks and schedules, resources, risks and issues, changes, quality, and testing.
- **Executing**: Project work. This phase creates the project deliverables and validates them against scope and quality requirements while the project manager validates cost, budget, and schedule performance against baselines.
- **Closing**: Project termination. This phase delivers an accepted product or deliverable to the project sponsor, creates closure documentation, and releases resources to prepare the next project or phase.

Figure 9-2 shows an illustration of how the project management phases interact.

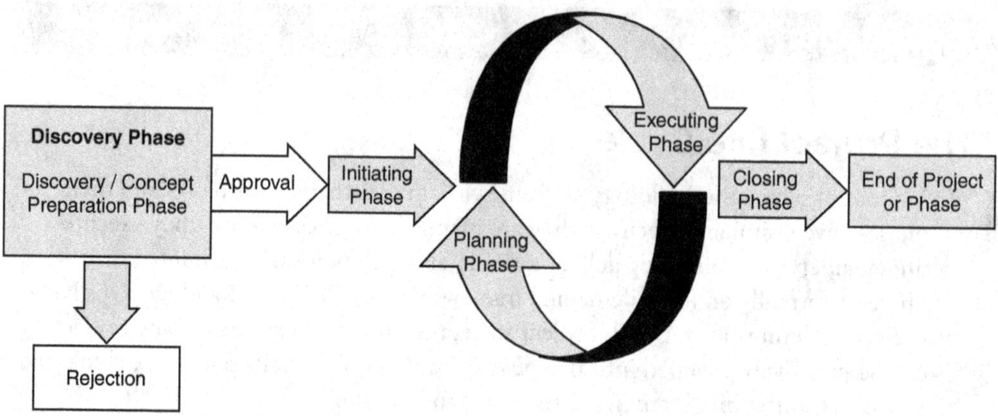

Figure 9-2 Project Management Phases

> **NOTE** If you've been studying project management for a few years, you might wonder how a major phase of project work could vanish. CompTIA previously started its life cycle with Initiating, not Discovery, and included a phase named Monitoring and Controlling that ran parallel to the Executing phase. Nothing has truly vanished; the current model simply groups all monitoring and controlling with project execution, and it is still a key part of the project manager's job.

Although these phases are often listed or drawn in a linear manner, they are not always performed in a linear fashion. For example, if a few deliverables are created during project execution, it may be necessary to go back and modify the plans that were created as part of the Planning phase. It's also important to remember that Agile and iterative projects will constantly initiate into new phases and add requirements for the next scope while the current sprint executes.

Other Project Management Models

CompTIA's published objectives for the Project+ exam include this statement: *The lists of examples provided in bulleted format are not exhaustive lists. Other examples of technologies, processes, or tasks pertaining to each objective may also be included on the exam, although not listed or covered in this objectives document.*

This chapter briefly covers project management topics that are covered in *A Guide to the Project Management Body of Knowledge (PMBOK® Guide)* but not in the current Project+ objectives—specifically project knowledge areas and performance domains.

The authors chose to include them in case the student encounters them in other project management literature.

Knowledge Areas

Knowledge areas are a foundational topic in the *PMBOK® Guide—Sixth Edition*. Where project phases describe how a project progresses through its life cycle, *project knowledge areas* describe how all of the project's processes are grouped into similar specializations. A project's process has both a phase and a knowledge area. For example, the process of developing the project charter belongs to the Initiating phase and the project integration knowledge area. These are all useful ways of thinking about a project manager's duties. The 10 project knowledge areas are as follows:

- **Project integration**: Identifies and coordinates all the processes and activities in a project
- **Scope management**: Ensures all work required by the project is complete and falls within the defined project scope
- **Time management**: Ensures that the project delivers on time and that the schedule is adjusted to compensate for risks and issues
- **Cost management**: Ensures that the project costs are monitored and completed within the approved budget
- **Quality management**: Ensures that the performance of the project deliverables meets the client's requirements
- **Resource management**: Ensures that the project team is organized and that the correct physical resources are available when required by project work
- **Communication management**: Ensures that project information is properly created, distributed, and stored
- **Risk management**: Ensures that threats and opportunities are identified, analyzed, and controlled, and that risk responses are planned in advance
- **Procurement management**: Ensures that any products or services needed from a third party are acquired while meeting legal and regulatory requirements
- **Stakeholder management**: Documents the expectations and project impact on any people, groups, or organizations that will be affected, engages key stakeholders, and manages expectations

Performance Domains

Performance domains are introduced in the *PMBOK® Guide—Seventh Edition*. This streamlined model groups all project activities into eight areas of focus: Teams, Stakeholders, Development Approach and Life Cycle, Planning, Project Work, Delivery, Measurement, and Uncertainty. Like knowledge areas, these domains are not time-bound and apply to project work that occurs at any stage of the project life cycle. They replace the linear progression of a life cycle with constant iteration that more resembles real-life project management. This is not a concept you will see in Project+, but it may help you to look at project management from different conceptual angles and guide your further studies.

Discovery Phase Activities

The *Discovery phase* (or *concept preparation phase*) is project pre-work that results in a proposal. This phase is strategic, and its primary output is the business case. Proposals that are rejected in discovery—too risky, not a good fit for the company's brand, or not feasible under current conditions—die on the vine, while approved business cases are developed into project charters.

Unless the project is being prepared at a client's request, it may have to compete with other project proposals. The project selection committee or project steering committee decides whether a business case warrants green-lighting the project.

Business Case or Business Objective

A project can be undertaken for market demands, organizational needs, customer requests, technological advances, legal requirements, ecological impacts, or social needs. Whatever its purpose, a project also needs a rationale. The ***business case*** is a strategic document that outlines the scope, audience, and purpose for the proposed work and establishes the value it could bring. A well-researched business case can show that a project is worth the investment or prevent an expensive failure. It is a strategic document.

The first part of the document is usually an executive summary that provides a top-level synopsis of the problem, the proposed solution, the justification, and the expected benefit, but it skips the analysis behind these decisions. That analysis, along with the estimates of all project financials, would be included in the body of the business case. Depending on the size of the project, the business case could include the following elements:

- **Description**: A narrative of the project and its key stakeholders, with a high-level view of the scope, deliverables, timeline, major milestones, and budget
- **Justification**: The reason the organization would benefit from the project or face risk if no action was taken

- **Mission statement**: How the project meets the organization's vision statement and values
- **Goals and objectives**: The anticipated future state that the project will bring about
- **Problem statement**: The current state of the issue to be addressed by the project, whether it is a detriment or an opportunity
- **Analysis**: A root cause analysis, a cost-benefit analysis, an estimated return on investment, or any other analysis that predicts the outcome of the project's work, whether positive or negative
- **Proposed solutions**: Alternative approaches to the recommended solution (which could include no solution at all, thus bypassing the opportunity) and their strengths and limitations
- **Recommended solution**: The solution that was analyzed as most likely to succeed

Many of these elements will be refined and formalized in the project charter, which is covered in detail later in this chapter.

Return on Investment Analysis

In the business case/objective, an estimated ***return on investment (ROI) analysis*** calculates the profit the project sponsor will make from the project, although the formulas can also calculate a project's realized gains. The ROI can be expressed as a currency amount (net profit) or as a percentage, and it is usually annualized, or calculated as a return over 1 year, even if the profit was accrued in multiple or partial years. Any positive ROI percentage means a gain.

EXAMPLE: Your house was appraised by a realtor who said it would sell as-is for $300,000. You spent $24,000 on a kitchen remodel (including dinners out) and then sold your renovated house in the same month for $346,000. Assuming that the $24,000 kitchen upgrade was the reason your house gained $46,000 in value, the net profit is found by subtracting the investment cost from your gain, yielding the true impact of the investment.

In this scenario you spent $24,000 and gained $46,000, which means you got back your $24,000 investment and earned a net profit of $22,000:

Value of Investment – Cost of Investment = Net Profit

$46,000 – $24,000 = $22,000 (net profit)

To find your ROI, subtract the gain or value of the investment from the cost of the investment, divide the result by the cost of the investment, and multiply the result by 100:

$$\frac{(\text{Value of investment} - \text{Cost of Investment}) \times 100}{\text{Cost of Investment}}$$

$$\frac{(\$46{,}000 - \$24{,}000) \times 100}{\$24{,}000}$$

$$\$46{,}000 - \$24{,}000 = \$22{,}000$$

$$\$22{,}000 / \$24{,}000 = 0.916 \times 100 = 91.6\% \text{ ROI}$$

If the net profit is known, you can divide it by the cost of the investment and multiply the result by 100 to find ROI:

$$(\text{Net Income or Profit} / \text{Cost of Investment}) \times 100$$

$$\$22{,}000 / \$24{,}000 = 0.916 \times 100 = 91.6\% \text{ ROI}$$

Next, assume that instead of selling your house immediately, you sold it 2 years later for the same price (ignoring real-life cost factors for this example). That means the 91.6% ROI was earned in 2 years. A simple way to calculate your annualized return would be to divide the total ROI by 2, for an annualized return of 45.8%. This technique allows you to compare the ROIs of projects with dissimilar time frames against each other to find the better prospect, such as a 3-month project against a 1-year project.

Projects do not need to earn revenue to be worthwhile. Actual ROI calculations for a project must also account for qualitative and intangible values gained by project work. A project can bring value by reducing ongoing costs and preventing expensive failures or by encouraging brand recognition. Even if a project is estimated to have a substantial negative ROI, that might be the unpleasant side effect of nonnegotiable improvements, such as addressing a workplace hazard or avoiding legal penalties for noncompliance. A positive ROI is only one of many factors behind a successful business case. Also note that there are many formulas for ROI calculation, most of which are outside the scope of the exam.

Current State vs. Future State

Half of a project proposal is describing the problem to solve or opportunity to chase; the other half is visualizing its benefit. The analyst will describe the current state of the issue addressed by the project and contrast it, point by point, with the target state achieved through project success. This journey helps create a compelling business case. A ***current state*** analysis can solidify a nebulous project idea or clarify an issue. The analysis can focus on gaps, bottlenecks, and weaknesses in current processes, such as lack of automation or missed revenue caused by outdated software, or on opportunities for expansion or improvement.

The ***future state*** should describe the desired improvement, not actions or implementations. In fact, narrowing your focus to one solution early on may blind you to better ways of achieving your goals. You should compare the same metric across states and describe the future state as outcomes, such as "Sales leads are increased by 42%," and not as proposed solutions, such as "Sales team is migrated to Salesforce." Solutions go in the analysis portion of the case. The result of your current/future state analysis should be concise and clear, as shown in Figure 9-3.

Business Unit	Current State	Future State
IT Help Desk	Live customer support only available from 8:00 AM - 8:00 PM PST for all incident levels 48% of tickets are escalated to a supervisor for resolution	**Customers have 24/7 access to a live engineer for Level 2 and Level 3 incidents** **Under 20% of tickets are escalated for supervisor resolution** **Cost savings: $200,000 in first quarter**

Figure 9-3 Comparison of Current State Versus Future State for a Process Improvement Project

Remember, the *gap* is the difference between the current state and your projected future state, and *gap analysis* compares current performance with desired performance to find feasible strategies and actions. These actions are eventually translated into a workable project. You will learn more about gap analysis in Chapter 11, "Executing Phase Activities."

Prequalified Vendors

If you need a vendor with a particular skill set or a vendor who can fast-track a large purchase order, you can ask your PMO or procurement department for a list of prequalified providers. As discussed in Chapter 8, "Project Procurement and Vendor Selection," a ***prequalified vendor*** has already been evaluated for their ability to supply goods or services. The prequalified vendor list is usually a spreadsheet or a database that allows you to find vendors by their characteristics. Each vendor record should include recent contact information and a description of the services, materials, or activities they are qualified to provide, like surveying or permitting. Some records might also include pricing, especially if the vendor prequalified by agreeing to sell their materials or labor at a discounted rate.

A project can require you to use another organization's vendor list instead of your own. For example, a construction project on brownfield land needs a contractor from the government's list of prequalified vendors who can certify that the brownfield remediation is performed to code. An independent contractor would have to apply and be approved as a qualified vendor before they could respond to your request for proposal (RFP) or request for bid (RFB).

Predetermined Client

A ***predetermined client*** is a client that has an existing, mutually binding agreement with the project organization and has agreed to partner with it to develop project initiatives. Projects that arise from agreements with predetermined clients may not need to develop a business case and instead might go directly to project initiation, with the contract as the basis for the project charter.

Preexisting Contracts

A preexisting contract might be a resource for your project or a constraint, depending on whether it refers to a vendor contract or a client contract. Active contracts with vendors mean that your organization already has a procurement relationship in place, so you can bypass the effort of finding a new vendor. Active contracts with clients mean that your project is developed for a specific audience, as under the terms of a master service agreement (MSA). The client may have an existing ***statement of work (SOW)*** or terms of reference (TOR). Both of these contract types were covered in Chapter 8.

Client SOW

A ***client statement of work (SOW)*** is a narrative description of a product, service, or result that your project should deliver for the client. This SOW may be the entire scope of the project or just a portion of it.

Client TOR

A ***client terms of reference (TOR)*** is a document that defines the tasks and duties required of your project and the project's client, and it highlights the project background and objectives at a high level. The document also states the planned activities, expected inputs and outputs, project budget, working schedules, and job descriptions.

Capital Expenses vs. Operational Expenses

Capital expenses (CapEx) are investments in durable assets, such as land, buildings, or vehicles, that have a useful life measured in years. A capital expense is a business asset that may appreciate or depreciate, be sold for a profit or loss, and incur or offset taxes. ***Operating expenses (OpEx)*** are costs for consumables or short-term assets that do not appreciate, depreciate, or require long-term management. OpEx expenses include repairs, services, utilities, salaries, office supplies, and rent.

Capital and operating expenses are usually drawn from different budgets and have different accounting codes. If you need to acquire capital assets for your project, you will need to know how to correctly account for the source of funds. Because capital assets will benefit the organization for years after the project ends, they may be sourced from the organization's budget, not the project's.

Initiating Phase Activities

The Initiating phase officially starts the project. During this phase, the organization selects a project manager, and the project sponsor and/or project manager defines the initial scope, financial resources, and stakeholders. The focus of this phase is to establish the charter, align stakeholder expectations with the project's scope and objectives, and identify existing artifacts that will affect project planning, such as open contracts. This stage ends with an official sign-off by the project sponsor and a project kickoff meeting. Once the charter is authorized, the project manager can begin spending funds and acquiring project resources.

NOTE Don't be confused by terminology. Approval in the Discovery phase means that a project is cleared to begin developing a formal charter, but not to spend money. Approval in the Initiating phase means that the project's sponsor approves of the charter, scope, objectives, success criteria, and design in its current form and has freed project resources to begin work.

Develop the Project Charter

The ***project charter*** becomes the cornerstone of the project and its central authority. In addition to authorizing the project itself, it defines the project manager's authority and the project reporting structure for decision-making. The charter is usually developed by the project manager, which can be a lengthy process for a large project. It includes and expands on the business case from the Initiating phase. The charter also provides the project's purpose, goals, and objectives, the requirements, high-level assumptions and constraints, high-level risks, success criteria, a summary milestone schedule, key stakeholders, a summary budget, and an initial key stakeholder register.

The project charter is also the starting point for the many documents that go into the project management plan (discussed in the next chapter). Project managers should understand how components of the project charter relate to later project documents. The charter itself is not refined after sign-off; instead, project management documents grow where the charter leaves off. For example, high-level risks go into the risk register, which helps develop the risk management plan. The preliminary scope is refined to produce the detailed scope statement, not a detailed project charter scope.

Existing organizations will begin with a software-provided template or an existing project charter to modify. A standard (not definitive) charter table of contents for an IT project is shown in Figure 9-4.

Table of Contents	Section 2 - Proposed Solution
Section 1 - Request Definition	2.1 Core Team / Stakeholders
1.1 Leadership Structure	2.2 Stakeholder Analysis
1.2 Business Background	2.3 Technical Design
1.3 Problem Statement	2.4 Cost Estimates
1.4 Business Objective	2.5 Expected Delivery Schedule
1.5 Solution Boundaries / Scope Definition	2.6 Project Assumptions
1.5.1 In Scope	2.7 Charter Approval
1.5.2 Out of Scope	Appendix
1.6 Market/Operational Research	Users and Use Case Summary
1.7 Business Needs	Non-Functional Requirements
1.8 Benefits and Success Metrics	Compliance and Security Checklist
1.9 Request Definition Approval	User Experience Design (High Level)

Figure 9-4 Example of a Project Charter's Table of Contents

Because the charter is the basis for the project, the project manager and the project team should analyze the charter each time they create or update major project documentation.

The following subsections describe the project objectives, success criteria, preliminary scope statement, and other key charter components.

Project Objectives

The objectives listed in the business case should be reviewed and expanded in the charter to incorporate any new information. An effective project goal or objective follows the SMART criteria:

1. **Specific**: The goal should be specific such that it exactly details the goal that should be achieved.

2. **Measurable**: The goal should be quantifiable to easily determine whether the goal has been achieved.
3. **Achievable**: The goal should be one that is within an individual's control and is achievable.
4. **Relevant**: The goal should be aligned with the project's vision.
5. **Time-bound**: The goal should have an established target date as to when it should be completed by the individual.

Project Success Criteria

A successful project delivers its objectives while meeting constraints and requirements—particularly requirements for scope or quality. One measure of a successful project is whether it meets with the client's or sponsor's approval and has its deliverables accepted during the project closure meeting. Success criteria list the metrics that will validate its goals. The sponsor's feedback is critical when developing the success criteria. Success metrics can help defend a deliverable to a balky client or pinpoint the issues with a deliverable or a project if it is rejected.

Preliminary Scope Statement

Like the business case, the ***preliminary scope statement*** defines the work that must be performed and, importantly, which work falls outside the project's parameters. It is sometimes called the ***high-level scope***. It usually includes a description of the project, its major deliverables, its acceptance criteria, key milestones, and exclusions from scope.

You may feel like the project has been thoroughly scoped by now, and you're not even to the Planning phase. To clarify the scope journey: the business case includes the initial scope for the purposes of justifying a project. The charter expands that scope into the larger preliminary scope statement. The project manager will analyze requirements and create a detailed scope statement during project planning, which is added to the scope baseline and eventually includes the individual work units that must be completed for the project. However, the charter's scope remains preliminary because, before more analysis is performed, not all parts of the scope have been uncovered.

Other Charter Components

The ***high-level risks*** are part of the project charter. As described in Chapter 4, "Risk and Issue Management," a risk describes any uncertain event that may have a positive or negative effect on the project's objectives. Risks are more formally defined in the Planning phase. As additional risks are defined or discovered during the initial risk assessment, they are added along with the high-level risks to the risk register.

The approved *business case* is included along with an initial key stakeholder list.

The preliminary milestone schedule might be part of the scope or a separate section in the charter. Milestone dates will move as the schedule is defined, but unless the scope changes, the definition of each milestone should remain consistent.

While *high-level assumptions* and *high-level constraints* have been mentioned in other chapters, they are covered here now as a key charter concept. An ***assumption*** is a factor that is considered to be true for the purposes of planning a project, and a *constraint* is a limiting factor that will affect how project work is created or delivered or which solution is chosen. Here is an example of each:

- **Assumption:** A typical deliverable for the project will take approximately 2 weeks to complete.
- **Constraint:** There is only enough budget to hire five team members to work on the project.

Lessons learned repositories can help project managers find assumptions that apply to the new charter but have not yet been articulated in the current project.

An ***organizational chart*** may be included to show reporting relationships.

A preliminary budget is included to show the funds that are available for project work and to estimate the total costs, along with an initial breakdown of costs by area (materials, salaries, rent, and so on).

The purpose or justification should be included. Key stakeholders and their authority in the project belong in the charter. The stakeholder register (developed in the Initiating phase) becomes part of the project management plan.

Identify and Assess Stakeholders

While key fiscal stakeholders such as the sponsor and business analyst are listed in the business case, a formal ***stakeholder register*** captures everyone involved with the project after it is initiated. The list could include client contacts, team members, subject matter experts, functional managers who control shared resources, important vendors, and internal resources such as the accountant and procurement officer. You may want to brainstorm with the sponsor to find everyone relevant to or interested in your project. Some stakeholders will be grouped by job role, such as the customer service team. The stakeholder register is later used to create the responsibility matrices, the WBS, the stakeholder engagement plan, and the communication plan.

Early versions of the register can simply include names, titles or job roles, contact information, and project role (such as internal/external). This information should be captured before you build task assignments and scheduling documents like the work breakdown structure (WBS). As you move into project planning, you should continue to build the register by interviewing stakeholders and noting their requirements, their expectations for project work, and their areas of expertise. Preferred communication method(s) should be noted in the communication plan, but the project manager may also note them in the register because team members may use it to contact stakeholders. Direct interviews are the best way to build a responsibility assignment matrix (RAM) and a RACI (responsible, accountable, consulted, and informed) chart (both covered later in this chapter) and the engagement strategy.

Finally, you should assess high-level or high-involvement stakeholders to ensure they are receiving the correct level of attention and inclusion. Several project management techniques are used to assess key stakeholders and determine who needs prompt attention versus tactful disengagement. The salience model is a qualitative assessment tool where you rank each stakeholder by their power, legitimacy, and urgency:

- *Urgency* is defined as a stakeholder's need for immediate attention.
- *Legitimacy* defines whether a stakeholder's involvement is appropriate.
- *Power* is defined as a stakeholder's impact and influence over major project decisions.

The characteristics overlap into nine models, depending on whether stakeholders have one, two, or all three qualities. The resulting score helps drive the stakeholder engagement plan. An urgent, powerful, and legitimate stakeholder (3) should be included in all decision-making meetings, whereas a stakeholder without any salience score could be directed to project dashboards but eliminated from meeting schedules. A legitimate stakeholder (1) who lacks power or urgency might still need to be consulted; this stakeholder could represent an end user from the department that will use your developed application.

Another tool, the power/interest grid, is a simple x/y axis that lets you plot stakeholders by their level of authority and their level of interest (low, medium, or high). Interest represents their active involvement, while power is their ability to change project execution (impact). Once they are plotted on the x/y axis, you draw the power/interest grid over the chart (see Figure 9-5) to see the recommended engagement model.

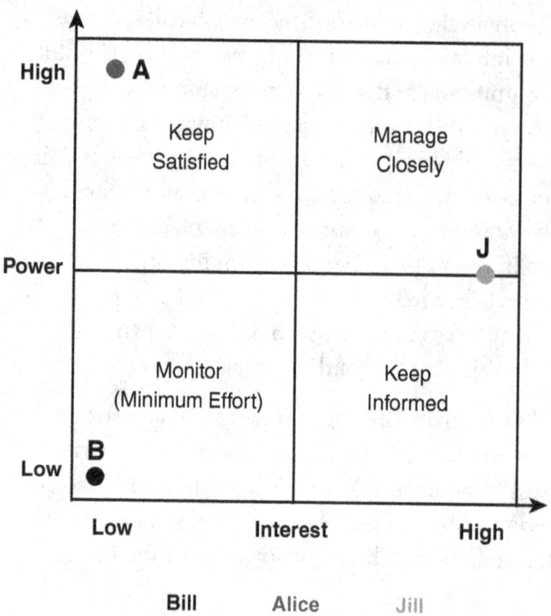

Figure 9-5 Example of a Stakeholder Power/Interest Grid

In this model, Bill has low power and interest, Jill has the most interest but only moderate power, and Alice has the highest level of power over the project but almost no interest in keeping up with its work. All of this information can guide stakeholder engagement, covered in the next chapter.

Establish Accepted Communication Channels

Even though the project has not yet kicked off, the active stakeholders need to know when and how to communicate with the project manager and each other. The project manager should set guidelines for how communication should flow. External clients, in particular, should know which internal stakeholders to contact. At this stage, it is vital to loop all decision-making through the project manager so that requirements aren't lost and scopes don't creep. It is also good to remove unneeded people from the email distribution list, reducing their frustration and inbox volume.

This is a good time to resolve issues from prior sprint communications. If work was delayed by constant contact between the team and a difficult client, you could instruct the team to redirect ad hoc queries to a designated point person. Alternatively, you could let the team and the client work together to find the lowest-impact solution. Choosing a specific way to communicate is less important than adapting a plan to project. More formal rules for communication, like meeting cadence and distribution lists for status reports, will be established during Planning; this activity simply sets ground rules.

As previously discussed in Chapter 7, "Communication and Meeting Management," it is the project manager's job to choose or configure the platforms that will funnel most nonverbal communication (email, chats, dashboards, and message forums). You should remind stakeholders of any policies that limit communication to a designated platform, such as Skype or Microsoft Teams.

Develop a Responsibility Assignment Matrix

Just as stakeholders need to know when and how to communicate, they need to know who to consult about a project task, who has ownership of an activity or phase, and which tasks do (or do not) concern them. While high-level responsibilities are listed in the charter, the ***responsibility assignment matrix (RAM)*** maps all resources to their areas of ownership, oversight, or task assignments using the stakeholder list.

A RAM can be broken down to the level of detail required by the project. For example, you could create a cross-functional RAM that shows which portions of project work are to be performed by each separate project team. However, the most common use of a RAM is to show task-level assignments. One of the most useful ways to depict a task-level RAM is in a RACI chart.

Responsible, Accountable, Consulted, and Informed Chart

The ***responsible, accountable, consulted, and informed (RACI) chart or RACI matrix*** tracks stakeholder and team roles and responsibilities against project activities. For each task, the project manager assigns one of four values:

- **Responsible (R)**: Who does the work to complete the activity?
- **Accountable (A)**: Who signs off on the activity or verifies its completion?
- **Consulted (C)**: Who provides input, expertise, or guidance regarding the activity?
- **Informed (I)**: Who needs to know a given activity's status?

EXAMPLE: A hotel meeting room must be booked for a project workshop. Rachel (R) must call the hotel and reserve the room. Before she does, she emails Chen (C) to ask how many people the room should accommodate. After Chen responds, Rachel makes the reservation and forwards the reservation to the project manager, Andrea (A). Andrea marks the task as complete and emails the booking information to the client (I).

In a typical RACI matrix, a grid lists the project activities down the left-hand column. Then each project stakeholder or team member is listed in an individual column, with R, A, C, and/or I designated below the name or role. Incidentally, the terms *responsible*, *accountable*, *consulted*, and *informed* should be thoroughly defined so that no one misunderstands their level of oversight for a task. Everyone should know the established channels for communication task status.

Table 9-2 shows a RACI matrix template. The **Activity** column corresponds to a task number in the WBS, while the **Role** columns are project stakeholders and team members.

Table 9-2 RACI Matrix Template

Activity	Role 1	Role 2	Role 3	Role 4	Role 5
Activity 1.1	R, A	I	C, I		
Activity 1.2	I		R, A	C	I
Activity 2.1	I	C	R	A	
Activity 2.2	R		A	C, I	I
R = Responsible	A = Accountable		C = Consulted		I = Informed

Each activity should have only one *accountable* person, which may or may not be the same as the responsible one. Having one accountable role means there is never a question about who has the authority to sign off on a task. It also means that if the responsible person doesn't do the work, the accountable person has to find a solution or workaround. The accountable person might be the project manager, or they may just report the task's status to the project manager. The C and I designations do not have assignment limitations. Informed roles can be notified during regular communications or through their preferred channel.

Although CompTIA's objectives introduce the RAM as an Initiating phase task, a task-level RACI for a Waterfall project will only be complete once the WBS is finalized during project planning. If the project is iterating or Agile, the RACI chart may be tied to user stories or sprints.

Develop a Records Management Plan

A ***records management plan*** uses tools and procedures to manage creation, use, retention, and disposal of documents and data, both physical and electronic. It governs how records are handled within the project and across the organization, and it is usually part of enterprise governance. If the organization does not have a records management plan in place, the project manager should apply best practices. Here are the most important steps for the project manager:

- Apply the existing records management plan and policies to new project records.
- Make project documents centrally available and track their location and ownership.
- Ensure all stakeholders understand how, when, and why to retain project records and data.
- Establish and communicate project-level standards, such as file naming conventions and document tagging within shared cloud drives.

You will need to verify the team's understanding of and, most likely, train them on these policies. Stakeholders should know what qualifies as a project record versus ephemera. For example, emails that contain a business decision or key project data should likely be retained. Dashboard views would not, because their underlying data is stored elsewhere. You might not need to photograph every diagram drawn on a physical whiteboard during a meeting, but you might need the team to follow a security policy and erase all boards before leaving a shared meeting room, all of which should be communicated.

Records that are typically managed in a project include the following:

- Communications with stakeholders, handouts, meeting minutes and status reports, and written reports captured from verbal decision-making
- Documents created through project work, such as solution design documents and blueprints
- Documents created through project management, such as the charter and all project management plan components
- Legally binding documents, purchase orders, invoices, receipts, and contracts
- Electronic data records, code modules, source code, and copies of project deliverables

Refer to Chapter 7 for a more granular review of how electronic and physical project records should be maintained. Enterprise-level tools such as electronic document and records management systems (EDRMS) and content management systems (CMS) are covered in Chapter 16, "Foundational IT Concepts and Operational Change Control for IT Project Management," along with other project-specific technologies.

Define Access Requirements

For IT projects, team members might need to interact with business-critical production systems or sensitive records to build project deliverables. Early stages might use a dummy data set or sandbox, but smoke testing will require live data and environments. Data access rules will already be defined in the organization's IT security policy, but the policy alone will not be enough to account for all of a project's variables. The project manager should meet with the project's solution architect, the network engineer, the functional manager of any affected departments, and other subject matter experts (SMEs) with direct knowledge of the relevant systems and data before work begins. These roles can judge the level of access to grant the team and choose the best technical way to do so. Access should be assigned according to the principle of least privilege, which means that only the minimum required permissions should be assigned. Permissions should be logged and audited, and the access should be revoked promptly when work is complete or after the project or phase is closed. The access list should be maintained in project documentation. You should also log which user accounts have administrative access or creation privileges to shared project tools, such as dashboards and project scheduling software.

Some project management documents might contain confidential or restricted information owned by the client. If a stakeholder or team member needs to access those documents, it should be noted in the communication plan when the record is labeled.

Data classifications, access controls, data security, and IT security policies are all covered in more detail in Chapter 15, "Environmental, Social, and Governance (ESG) Factors and Compliance, Data Security, and Privacy Considerations."

Review Existing Artifacts

Artifact is the term for any tangible document, output, product, or template used in project management, or any tangible output produced from project work. Artifacts can be electronic (like emails and recorded conference calls) or physical (like paper files). The term does not imply a document is old.

The current project's artifacts are the business case, open and ongoing contracts with clients or suppliers, and prequalified vendor lists. You should be familiar with all of these, especially if you just inherited the project. Your other priority is to study documents from prior projects, especially if they were delivered to the same client, had a similar scope or solution design as the new project, or were completed by the same team. Because these records will provide context and give you valuable insight into the upcoming project work, you should gather them as early as possible during project initiation.

The most relevant artifacts to review would be the charter, lessons learned and other closeout documents, the WBS, risk registers, change and issue logs, and budget and cost baselines. For instance, reviewing prior risk assessments can help you better identify risks or more accurately estimate their impact, while reviewing the success of risk strategies can help you fine-tune future responses. Over time, prior solution designs become valuable repositories of tested architectures that could be modified for new proposals. It is even sometimes possible (if not always desirable) to repurpose portions of a charter or other project documentation, particularly if the new project's parameters (such as key stakeholders and meeting cadence) are the same.

Finally, it is good practice to periodically review your own prior projects to find areas where your own management processes could be tuned or improved.

Determine Solution Design

Solution design, as a separate step, originated as part of the Design phase of the Software Development Life Cycle (SDLC), which we covered in our discussion of project methodologies in Chapter 1, "Project Characteristics, Methodologies, and Frameworks." While it is a named step in other frameworks (such as SAFe), it is also a key step for IT projects in any framework. The ***solution*** refers to the technological components (such as APIs), supported and dependent technologies, interfaces, and hardware that will deliver the finished project into the client's environment. A project may require one product or many as its solution.

EXAMPLE: The project's client wants a new inventory management system that will run on their existing warehouse workstations. In this scenario, the solution is the end-to-end design that will blend third-party components, newly written code, standard APIs, and custom modules into a product that will deliver all required features in their environment.

Determining which solutions are needed and how they will interact with existing infrastructure is primarily the job of the architect. This role might be the solution architect, the enterprise architect, the infrastructure architect, or another senior IT architect. The architect must work with the business analyst to make sure the client's business requirements and environment are clearly understood; the better the up-front analysis, the better the result. The result should also be maintainable and scalable to the client's future needs.

The process of solution design has two main outputs: a high-level conceptual design and a low-level technical blueprint. The high-level design describes how the proposed solution will operate and interact with existing constraints such as firewalls and bandwidth limits. It incorporates two types of client requirements: functional and nonfunctional. ***Functional requirements*** are tangible things the solution must do or mandatory ways it must behave for the end user, such as providing a sharable link in a shopping cart or adding a live chat function. ***Nonfunctional requirements*** are intangible ways the solution will deliver value, such as compliance, scalability, performance, and reliability. Requirements are formally captured in the requirements documentation and tracked in the requirements traceability matrix. Although CompTIA places solution design in the Initiating phase, further requirements may be captured during scope refinement in the Planning phase.

The low-level blueprints are a technical roadmap developed by the architect, senior developers, and specialized roles such as user experience (UX) designers once the high-level design is final. The low-level design breaks down the solution into components that can be developed in sprints or iterations. The low-level blueprints are sometimes referred to as the solution design documents.

Choose Project Framework or Methodology

Be sure not to confuse designing a solution with choosing a project framework or methodology (such as scrum, Waterfall, or PRINCE2). However, if a framework has not been preselected, the Initiating phase is the best time to adopt a new one or to tailor existing processes to the specific needs of the new project. One of the factors that influences your choice of project management method is its tolerance for change or flexibility. This flexibility must be gauged based on the environment within which the organization operates and the risks the organization is willing to take. A high tolerance for change means greater risks. Agile has a high tolerance for change, while Waterfall has a much lower tolerance. Frameworks were covered in Chapter 1.

Conduct Project Kickoff Methods

A ***kickoff meeting*** signals the official start of a project or iteration. It should be attended by the project sponsor, key stakeholders, the team, and the project manager. Its main purpose is to set expectations and establish communication. Ideally, a kickoff is held in person, but if attendees must be remote, they should be able to participate with real-time audio and video conferencing. The agenda should briefly cover the scope and purpose of the project and share high-level milestones and/or the project roadmap without going too far into project details. The focus is on aligning team members to the project work, including the following:

- The methodology and approach
- Roles and responsibilities of stakeholders and team members
- Client expectations (for external clients) and communication channels

Agile projects frequently begin a project or phase with a preexisting team. In many Waterfall and hybrid methodologies, the team might not be acquired until later in the project planning. In that scenario, you should plan a second kickoff meeting that brings the entire team together. A team kickoff should ensure each team member understands their role in the project and has the chance to ask questions and identify needs. The project manager should immediately follow up on any needs identified during the kickoff meeting, such as a skills gap or resource requirement.

NOTE Some project management standards say that the kickoff meeting should occur during or after project planning, just prior to executing. In practice, the best time for the kickoff to happen is before project work begins. Remember, though, that for the purposes of this exam, CompTIA places kickoff activities at the end of project initiation, signaling the start of the Planning phase.

Exam Preparation Tasks

As mentioned in the section "How to Use This Book" in the Introduction, you have a few choices for exam preparation: the exercises here, Chapter 17, "Final Preparation," and the exam simulation questions included in the online Pearson Test Prep Software Online.

Review All Key Topics

Review the most important topics in this chapter, noted with the Key Topics icon in the outer margin of the page. Table 9-3 lists each reference of these key topics and the page number on which each is found.

Table 9-3 Key Topics for Chapter 9

Key Topic Element	Description	Page Number
Section; list	Overview of the project management life cycle	263
Figure 9-2	Project Management Phases	264
Paragraph	Overview of the Discovery phase	266
Paragraph; list	Overview of the business case or business objective	266
Paragraph; formulas	Discussion and examples of return on investment (ROI) analysis	267
Section	Discussion of current state versus future state	268

Key Topic Element	Description	Page Number
Figure 9-3	Comparison of Current State Versus Future State for a Process Improvement Project	269
Paragraph	Discussion of prequalified vendors	269
Paragraph	Discussion of preexisting contracts, client SOWs, and client TORs	270
Paragraph; examples	Discussion of capital expenses (CapEx) and operational expenses (OpEx)	271
Section	Discussion of project charter development	271
Figure 9-4	Example of a Project Charter's Table of Contents	272
Paragraph; list	Overview of project objectives	272
Paragraph	Overview of the preliminary scope statement	273
Section	Identify and assess stakeholders	274
Section	Establish accepted communication channels	276
Paragraph	Develop a responsibility matrix (RAM)	277
Table 9-2	RACI Matrix Template	278
Paragraph	Develop a records management plan	278
Paragraph	Define access requirements	280
Paragraph	Review existing artifacts	280
Paragraph	Determine solution design	281
Section	Discussion of kickoff meeting	282

Define Key Terms

Define the following key terms from this chapter and check your answers in the glossary:

phases, business case/objective, return on investment (ROI) analysis, current state, future state, prequalified vendor, predetermined client, statement of work (SOW), client statement of work (SOW), client terms of reference (TOR), capital expenses (CapEx), operating expenses (OpEx), project charter, preliminary scope statement, high-level scope, high-level risks, assumption, organizational chart, stakeholder register, responsibility assignment matrix (RAM), responsible, accountable, consulted, and informed (RACI) chart or RACI matrix, records management plan, artifact, solution design, solution, functional requirements, nonfunctional requirements, kickoff meeting

Review Questions

The answers to these questions appear in Appendix A. For more practice with sample exam questions, use the Pearson Test Prep practice test software online.

1. Which project phase begins when the sponsor signs off on the charter?
   a. The Planning phase
   b. The Discovery phase
   c. The Initiating phase
   d. The Executing phase

2. Which artifact is used to determine whether a given person should be consulted before work begins on a project task?
   a. WBS
   b. RACI chart
   c. Organizational chart
   d. Project charter

3. What is *most* likely to ensure that team members and stakeholders understand the overall project goals and their part in the project?
   a. Stakeholder register
   b. Responsibility assignment matrix
   c. Kickoff meeting
   d. Status meeting

4. Project A has a 1-year time frame and an estimated ROI of 29%. Project B has a 2-year time frame and an estimated ROI of 54%. Which project has a better estimated ROI?
   a. Project A
   b. Project B
   c. Projects A and B will be equally profitable.
   d. The answer cannot be determined from this information.

5. Which of these statements are project assumptions? (Choose two.)
   a. The first release of the product will not support the Android platform.
   b. The customer base for the product will be primarily English speakers.
   c. The product must meet the Apple Store's requirements for data security.
   d. The in-house team has the required skills to develop the product.

6. Project work is delayed when the lead developer cannot access sensitive records stored on a secured server owned by the client. The records are needed for stress testing, but the developer does not know who to contact to request access. During which Initiating process did this problem begin?
   a. When determining the solution design
   b. When defining the access requirements
   c. When establishing the communication channels
   d. When developing the records management plan

7. In which scenario should a proposed project *most* likely be rejected?
   a. When no predetermined client exists for the product
   b. When the estimated ROI shows a revenue loss
   c. When the project scope is undefined
   d. When the target market for the product is unknown

8. You are developing a shipping application that is only compatible with UPS, USPS, FedEx, and DHL tracking numbers. The business analyst reports that the client wants the application to display an error when an invalid tracking number is entered. What does this scenario describe?
   a. A constraint
   b. A client environment
   c. A functional requirement
   d. A nonfunctional requirement

9. When would be the best time to review existing artifacts from a similar project that was completed in the last year for the same client?
   a. When developing the WBS
   b. When developing the project charter
   c. When preparing the project's lessons learned
   d. When determining the project's solution design

10. What would you analyze to help create a persuasive business case? (Choose all that apply.)
    a. The gap
    b. The scope
    c. The requirements
    d. The ROI
    e. The lessons learned from previous projects

This chapter covers the following topics:

- **Plan the Project Scope:** Gather requirements, finalize the scope, and create the scope management plan
- **Define Units of Work:** Define tasks and work packages, create a work breakdown structure (WBS), and establish the backlog and iteration plan
- **Develop a Project Schedule:** Assign project tasks to timelines and dates and establish sprint cadences
- **Plan Resource Management:** Assess the resource pool, estimate preliminary procurement needs, assign project resources, and train project team members
- **Plan Project Communication:** Define communication needs, set a meeting cadence, choose meeting formats, develop a communication plan, and develop a stakeholder engagement plan
- **Determine Budget Considerations:** Determine budget requirements versus available funds and calculate project reserves
- **Develop a Quality Assurance Plan:** Develop a quality assurance plan, test plan, and requirements traceability matrix
- **Plan Risk Management:** Perform an initial risk assessment, develop the risk register, and plan risk responses
- **Develop a Project Management Plan:** Develop subsidiary management plans, define the minimally viable product, define milestones, and set baselines for cost, schedule, and scope
- **Develop a Transition/Release Plan:** Plan for operational training, going live, and handoff of operations to internal or external clients

Planning Phase Activities

The Planning phase defines what the project's work will be, how it will be completed, and how resources will be allocated to its activities. The project manager will refine earlier documents to finalize the project's scope, requirements, schedule, work packages, costs, quality requirements, resource needs, risks, communication methods, and procurements. The final budget, scope, and schedule become project baselines that will measure performance in the Executing phase.

For predictive frameworks, the Planning phase sets the scope, resource assignments, and schedule for the project. For adaptive, iterative, and incremental frameworks, the Planning phase establishes the backlog, cadence, and release plans. These frameworks may use roll or rolling wave planning to set schedules and assign resources in regular increments. A transition plan establishes how the project will deliver its results to end users and transfer knowledge and assets from the developers to operations and maintenance. The main result of this phase is the completed project management plan, including its subsidiary plans and documents, which provide both governance and a living roadmap of all project work.

Project work begins when the first pass of the Planning phase is complete. Because projects are rarely linear, project managers will continually review and modify planning documents, especially as changes occur.

NOTE Except where called out, the planning activities and plans in this chapter assume a traditional predictive framework, especially for scope development. All project managers should know these concepts. The activities and plans used primarily by adaptive, incremental, and iterative frameworks are noted where they significantly differ from predictive approaches.

CompTIA does not provide a definitive list of project management plan components. This chapter covers the plans and artifacts that appear in project management standards, including a few not listed in the CompTIA objectives (which CompTIA states are not comprehensive). Table B-1 of Appendix B, "Master Table of Project Management Artifacts, Documents, and Plans," lists all project management plans, artifacts, and documents mentioned in this textbook. Remember that component names may vary across standards, such as *communication plan* versus *communication management plan*.

The Planning phase establishes the total project scope and objectives and then develops the actions required to successfully achieve the project's goals. The project manager develops the project management plan and all of its subsidiary plans, registers, and documents. The key planning activities (which can occur in any order or in parallel) are as follows:

- Developing the detailed scope statement and scope management plan
- Gathering detailed requirements and establishing a requirements management plan
- Defining the units of work (WBS or backlog)
- Assessing the resource pool and planning procurement needs
- Assigning project resources and training team members
- Developing the schedule and setting the cadence of releases
- Determining the budget needs and reserves
- Developing the quality assurance plan and test plan
- Developing the risk management plan and performing an initial risk assessment
- Developing the communication plan and stakeholder management plan
- Establishing the project baselines and subsidiary management plans
- Developing the transition/operational handoff plan

IMPORTANT NOTE Because this book follows CompTIA's objective order, many of the plans and activities in this chapter were covered in depth in prior chapters (particularly activities such as scheduling, work package identification, and risk identification). However, this chapter shows you how they fit into the flow of planning activities and reframes them in terms of overall project management.

This chapter covers the following objective for the CompTIA Project+ exam:

2.3 Given a scenario, perform activities during the project planning phase.

"Do I Know This Already?" Quiz

The "Do I Know This Already?" quiz allows you to assess whether you should read this entire chapter thoroughly or jump to the "Exam Preparation Tasks" section. If you are in doubt about your answers to these questions or your own assessment of your knowledge of the topics, read the entire chapter. Table 10-1 lists the major headings in this chapter and their corresponding "Do I Know This Already?" quiz questions. You can find the answers in Appendix A, "Answers to the 'Do I Know This Already?' Questions and Review Quizzes."

Table 10-1 "Do I Know This Already?" Section-to-Question Mapping

Foundation Topics Section	Questions
Plan the Project Scope	1–2
Define Units of Work	3
Develop a Project Schedule	4
Plan Resource Management	5
Plan Project Communication	6
Determine Budget Considerations	7
Develop a Quality Assurance Plan	8
Plan Risk Management	9–10
Develop a Project Management Plan	11–12
Develop a Transition/Release Plan	13

CAUTION The goal of self-assessment is to gauge your mastery of the topics in this chapter. If you do not know the answer to a question or are only partially sure of the answer, you should mark that question as wrong for the purposes of the self-assessment. Giving yourself credit for an answer you correctly guess skews your self-assessment results and might provide you with a false sense of security.

1. What should a project manager define before establishing a project schedule, setting goals and targets, and allocating resources to the project?
   a. Project budget
   b. Milestones
   c. Work breakdown study
   d. Detailed scope

2. Which document, artifact, or tool includes a project description, acceptance criteria, description of key deliverables, exclusions, estimated budget, preliminary schedule, constraints, and assumptions?
   a. Business case
   b. Detailed scope statement

   c. Requirements management plan
   d. Quality assurance plan

3. Which component is *not* part of the scope baseline?
   a. WBS dictionary
   b. Scope statement
   c. WBS
   d. RTM

4. Which of the following activities take place during project schedule development? (Choose all that apply.)
   a. Determine start and end dates for each activity.
   b. Allocate resources over the project's duration.
   c. Define the project's milestones.
   d. Estimate the complete time frame for the project.

5. What is the purpose of a preliminary procurement needs assessment?
   a. To identify missing resources
   b. To perform a gap analysis
   c. To inventory the available resources
   d. To better understand the requirements

6. A stakeholder informs the project manager that she wants to receive a text message when a project milestone is reached. Where should this detail be recorded?
   a. Resource management plan
   b. Stakeholder register
   c. Communication plan
   d. Project schedule

7. What is the purpose of performing a reserve analysis?
   a. To determine how much a schedule delay would cost the project
   b. To determine the CapEx expenditures for the project
   c. To find under-allocated and benched resources
   d. To hold funds against cost uncertainties

8. All of the following would be included in the quality assurance plan, except for which one?
    a. A schedule for testing
    b. Quality standards
    c. Quality targets
    d. The timing and cadence for testing

9. Which process creates the first version of the risk register?
    a. Risk reporting
    b. Risk assessment
    c. Risk review
    d. Risk response planning

10. What is the first step in risk management?
    a. Identifying project risks
    b. Identifying risk roles and responsibilities
    c. Estimating contingency reserves
    d. Establishing the risk management plan

11. All of the following baselines are established during project planning, except for which one?
    a. Cost baseline
    b. Schedule baseline
    c. Resource baseline
    d. Scope baseline
    e. Performance measurement baseline

12. What *best* describes the purpose of establishing a minimum viable product during project planning?
    a. To establish a "definition of done"
    b. To gather early feedback from customers
    c. To perform smoke testing before releasing to market
    d. To determine which functional requirements drive the solution design

13. Which project activity would be governed by the transition plan?
    a. Transferring control of an active project to a new project manager
    b. Capturing critical knowledge from an outgoing team member
    c. Providing training to the customer's staff
    d. Preparing for a project closeout meeting

Foundation Topics

Plan the Project Scope

The project scope statement is a formal statement that includes project justifications, scope description, acceptance criteria, deliverables, exclusions, constraints, and assumptions. The scope statement and detailed requirements both aid the project manager in creating the work breakdown structure (WBS). Taken together, the WBS, the WBS dictionary, and the detailed scope statement form the scope baseline that is used to control the rest of project work (in predictive projects) or the sprint or iteration.

The ***scope management plan*** describes how the scope will be defined, developed, monitored, controlled, and verified. It is one of the main components of the project management plan. Because scope, requirements, and quality are closely linked during the Planning phase, it is important to understand how they interact:

- *Requirements* describe what the product owner intends to achieve or have from the product, how it should behave, and the qualities it should have.
- *Scope* includes all of the activities that should be performed in order to develop the product that satisfies the requirements.
- *Quality* defines whether the required outcome(s) were delivered by the project's output.

Remember that in predictive projects, *all* approved requirements are used to define the project scope. In adaptive projects, the scope is defined only by the requirements that apply to the *current* sprint, iteration, or increment.

For Agile projects, the scope for the sprint or iteration should also include the definition of done. Because requirements are continually added to the backlog, the definition of done establishes the criteria for releasing a product, deliverable, or output, with the understanding that no release will include all of the planned features.

Gather Requirements

The requirements of a project include any stakeholder needs and specifications for the project. Often these requirements must be negotiated using decision-making techniques. Requirements are documented during the development of the scope management plan and are included in requirements documentation. The requirements documentation is used to develop the requirements traceability matrix (refer to Figure 13-12). Each requirement, once defined, should be assigned a unique ID that is used to track it against the ***test plan***, the defect log, the quality assurance plan, and the requirements traceability matrix.

The ***requirements management plan*** describes how requirements will be analyzed, documented, and managed. The types of requirements to gather apply to every aspect of the project, including business requirements, functional and nonfunctional requirements, transition requirements, and solution requirements.

Requirements are gathered during the Planning phase for predictive projects and then finalized. They are continually gathered and refined during adaptive projects. At the beginning of the project or phase, the project manager or product owner will capture only enough requirements to begin the first round of development.

Develop a Detailed Scope Statement

The ***detailed scope statement*** is a document that defines all the elements of the project's scope. It is used as a reference for all future project work and acts as a basis for all current project work. The scope is developed from the preliminary scope in the project charter and refined throughout the planning process. Some elements, like the description and objectives, will probably not be substantially changed from the charter. The milestones, requirements, and budget will all be more granular by the end of project planning, and a detailed WBS will be attached once complete.

At the end of planning, the project scope statement will contain the following items:

- A description of the project, its objectives, and acceptance criteria
- Key deliverables (within scope) and exclusions (outside of scope)
- Project assumptions and constraints
- Risks
- Estimated budget
- Estimated schedule
- Project milestones
- Requirements documentation
- WBS or backlog

Remember that many of these fields are *preliminary* in the charter (such as preliminary acceptance criteria and preliminary scope) and *detailed* in the final scope statement (such as detailed acceptance criteria and detailed scope).

In predictive projects, the scope statement must be formally approved by the project sponsor and can be changed only through formal change control procedures.

Define Units of Work

Defining the units of work that need to be performed to meet all of the project requirements begins with the detailed scope statement and the detailed requirements. Once these are in place, the project manager can define the actual tasks that team members will perform. Agile, iterative, and hybrid methodology projects begin work with a high-level epic or theme in place, and then they continually extract and refine requirements. These requirements are captured in user stories and stored in the backlog. The WBS and the backlog must both be developed before the project's schedule can be finalized and its budget established. For more information about the WBS and backlog, refer to Chapter 5, "Schedule Development and Management,"

Work Breakdown Structure

As described in Chapter 5, the work breakdown structure (WBS) is a hierarchical listing of the activities or work packages that will create the project's required deliverables. It includes a WBS dictionary, which describes each WBS component in detail. Refer to Table 5-2 to view an example WBS.

Backlog

The ***backlog*** is the Agile or adaptive equivalent of a WBS. It is a list of work for the development team that is derived from the roadmap and its requirements. It is first developed during project scope planning and then used to hold all of the initial project requirements. Requirements can be prioritized, dropped, revised, and created throughout project work. User stories can also live in the backlog. Because each user story represents an increment of functionality or a deliverable output, user stories in a backlog are roughly equivalent to work packages in a WBS. Each represents the lowest level of decomposition for the requirement.

The owner identifies the priority of the items on the list. The most important items are shown at the top of the product backlog so the team knows what to deliver first.

Develop a Project Schedule

The schedule presents project activities with the planned start/end dates, durations, milestones, and resources used. For the project to be accurate, project managers must determine the activities needed, the resources required to complete the activities, and the resource calendars regarding resource availability.

The ***project schedule*** shows project activities with their planned start/end dates, durations, milestones, and resources. The project schedule is usually maintained in project management software and updated as activities are started and finished. This tracking ensures that dependent activities are started on time.

Developing a project schedule, the subject of Chapter 5, can only occur once the WBS (or backlog) is complete and project resources have been assessed. Once developed, the predictive project schedule is a top-down plan that can only be changed through formal change control. Two other aspects of schedule planning, cadence and iterations, are unique to adaptive projects.

Project managers use the same estimating techniques to calculate activity durations for the schedule and costs for the budget. In predictive projects, all estimates are completed at the beginning of the project. In adaptive projects, estimates are made with each sprint, iteration, or increment. As an adaptive project progresses, estimates will become much more accurate because activities have been completed upon which the project manager can base the future estimates.

Estimating activity durations uses information from the WBS and requires an understanding of the skill level needed for each activity. If the project manager is unfamiliar with the activities and the time each activity will take, the project manager should seek help from an expert. Also, keep in mind that activity durations can be affected by the law of diminishing returns (increasing the resources at some point no longer positively affects the duration), too many resources, technology advances, and team motivation.

Establish Cadences

Cadence is the sequence of project tasks or events that create a pattern for the team to follow to understand what they are doing and when they will be done with it. This term is mostly applied to Agile projects, although it can mean any regularly scheduled occurrence, such as a meeting cadence. Daily cadence emphasizes execution daily. Iteration (or flow) cadence occurs when individuals come together to decide which items will be taken up as they interact and communicate. Delivery is made in release cadence, which can occur after multiple iterations, every iteration, or on-demand.

Any event that interrupts or impacts project cadence can result in schedule issues. High-functioning teams get into a rhythm, and often interrupting this rhythm affects the schedule more than expected. Project managers should be aware of the cadence and attempt to analyze any issues that may impact cadence before discussing them with the team.

Iteration Plan

For adaptive projects, the project manager will create a high-level ***iteration plan***, which describes the outcomes or backlog features that will be delivered in each upcoming iteration, along with an approximate timeline. The iteration plan is continually refined as the backlog is reprioritized and requirements change. The iteration cadence is usually 2-week sprints, but there is no set length of time assigned to an iteration. Project team members will mutually agree to the planned length after considering the size and the complexity of the project and adding up the story points to be gotten through.

Plan Resource Management

Project managers need to determine resource availability, including both human and physical resources. You will need human resources with certain knowledge and skills. All team members should have an outline of their skills recorded in the resource management plan. For physical resources, you may have the resources or you may need to perform a make-or-buy analysis before deciding to purchase or rent them. The majority of resource planning is covered in Chapter 2, "Team and Resource Management," while procurements are covered in Chapter 8, "Project Procurement and Vendor Selection."

Assess the Resource Pool

To plan ***resource management***, you will need the detailed requirements and the WBS, along with the resource management plan. Starting from there, you will assess the resource pool to determine which resources are available, which might be in contention, and which are not present in the organization. The project's ***resource pool*** includes the personnel, equipment, services, supplies, and funds needed to complete the project. Each resource will need a ***resource calendar*** that defines the days and hours each resource will be available. This process also determines what the project needs in procurements and the strategy for obtaining them, including delivery methods, bid documents, and contract types.

Once the assessment is performed and gaps are identified, the project manager may need to create a procurement plan.

Conduct Preliminary Procurement Needs Assessment

Assessing the resource pool will typically locate gaps in physical or human resources needed for all project tasks. The project manager should perform a gap analysis to determine whether the gap can be reduced with skills-based training, as well as what the project needs in procurements and the strategy, including delivery methods, bid documents, and contract types.

A procurement plan or procurement strategy is developed after assessing a project's procurement needs and performing a make-or-buy analysis that points toward using an outside vendor. The procurement plan should contain a description of the procurements, critical dates, vendor options, criteria for choosing a vendor, associated risks, and financial analyses, as described in Chapter 8. The organization's procurement specialists, the PMO, or the procurement management plan will provide guidelines for writing the procurement plan.

Assign Project Resources

You will use the resource calendar, the ***resource breakdown structure***, the WBS, and the schedule to begin assigning project resources to project tasks. This process ensures that team members, physical resources, and procurements are assigned to the project activities. You will need to make your resource calendar a shared resource with other functional departments or other projects within the organization to reduce contention; in some cases, you may have to negotiate with other managers to obtain the right resources for the right task durations.

Project resources are assigned in the WBS and the project schedule. Resource loading is the process whereby a project manager determines the hours of work a resource is available to the project and then utilizes these resources to complete project activities. While this might sound like a very straightforward process, it often isn't. You have to consider that you have team members (human) and physical resources. A project manager needs to ponder the following questions regarding the team:

- Is the resource allocated only to this project? Or will the resource be shared in any way (between projects or between the project and their regular job)?
- What is the maximum number of hours per day this resource will be available to the project (or whatever unit you use, such as hours per week)?
- Of those hours, what is the number of hours of work you can realistically expect a team member to complete?

Team members are not robots. Project managers can expect interruptions, meetings, breaks, and other things to pull a team member off a task. As a general rule, project managers should estimate somewhere between 65% and 75% utilization of team member time for project tasks. For example, a team member available to the project 8 hours a day will optimistically accomplish 5–6 hours of project work per day.

Train Project Team Members

If project team members do not have the right skills to perform project work, it is often more cost-effective to put them through internal or external training to bridge the resource gap. Pairing them with other team members who can mentor them is slower but sometimes enough to reduce the skills gap. In cases where it is not, online training, boot camps, and in-house training can all bring a team member up to speed.

Determine Budget Considerations

The ***budget*** is the cost estimate for the project. It includes a breakdown of the costs for individual WBS work packages, procurements, and any scheduled activities. As the WBS or backlog is developed, the project manager uses it to estimate the costs associated with all project activities to determine the project budget. Because budgets are based on cost estimates, project managers should constantly analyze actual costs and compare them to the budgeted costs. The project manager develops the cost management plan, estimates the project's costs, and determines the budget during the Planning phase.

The project manager is responsible for tracking the budget throughout the project. If the budget is insufficient for completing the project, the project manager will have to ask the project sponsor to provide more funds or alter the project parameters using change control.

The sum of all costs from the initial budget estimate is referred to as *total estimated costs* (TEC). This value is used in various budget calculations, reserve analyses, and early project documents. By the time project work is complete, the project manager will have compiled the *total project costs*, which is all costs specific to a project that were incurred from project initiation through project closure. Total project cost becomes a historical figure used in future project budget estimates.

Calculate Reserves

Reserve analysis is a method of calculating the amount of funds that should be held in contingency against any cost uncertainties, expressed as a percentage of the total project budget. These reserve amounts are calculated using the probability and impact calculations from risk analysis. Another calculation method is to add up the expected monetary value (EMV) of all risk responses and reserve that amount. The contingency reserve is part of both the cost baseline and budget requirements. Unused contingency reserves are returned to the sponsor during project closure, unless the project management plan states differently.

The management reserve is also part of the project's budget requirements, but it is *not* included in the cost baseline. This reserve amount is determined by the project sponsor and senior administration, and the funds become an official part of the project's budget only if they are used.

Develop a Quality Assurance Plan

Using the project scope and requirements documentation, the project manager develops the ***quality assurance (QA) plan***, also referred to as the ***quality management plan***. This documents the process for performing quality audits and describes the quality metrics that should be applied to the project's deliverables. The quality assurance plan answers such questions as the following:

- How are you going to implement your organization's quality standards in the project?
- Which external standards (regulatory, industry-specific, or voluntary) must the output satisfy?
- Which KPIs and KPPs are the quality targets?
- Which deliverables must be audited for quality?
- Who is responsible for managing the quality assurance processes?
- How will defects be measured, logged, and remediated?
- How will you approach the customer if the quality is not acceptable?

The project manager will use the tools and techniques outlined in the quality assurance plan to help monitor KPPs and KPIs. Quality control issues that are identified may require a project change to ensure that deliverable quality is maintained as set forth in the project management plan. Control charts, fishbone diagrams, flowcharts, Pareto charts, and histograms are among the tools that help monitor quality, and they are covered in Chapter 14, "Quality and Performance Charts."

Develop the Test Plan

Whereas the quality assurance plan describes the specifications that the project's deliverables must meet to be accepted, the *test plan* describes how the specification will be tested and verified. The test plan is developed as part of the overall quality assurance plan for projects and products that must meet measurable quality standards. Whether the output is an application module or a highly regulated good such as motors and medication, the test plan is essential to proving that the quality metrics have been met.

EXAMPLE: You are developing a web application for a client. The quality assurance plan lists the requirement that cart checkout errors should fail gracefully and return the user to the prior page with their session information cached. The test plan describes conditions and scenarios for simulating cart failure from different causes and verifying that each scenario will resolve with a graceful failure. If the requirement is not met during testing, it will be listed in the defect log and added to the defect repair queue or the backlog, depending on its priority.

The test plan and its components were covered in Chapter 6, "Quality, Cost, and Performance Management."

Plan Risk Management

Risk management is a comprehensive, multipart strategy for all areas of the project. The project manager creates the risk management plan, identifies risks, performs qualitative and quantitative risk analysis, and plans risk responses during the Planning phase and then monitors and controls risks during project execution. The main risk management activities that take place during the Planning phase are developing the risk management plan and performing an initial risk assessment.

The risk management plan contains risk-related templates and describes *how* the project will evaluate and handle risks, including formulas, risk categories and definitions, estimation techniques and methods, risk roles, and the risk budget. The risk management plan should include the following details:

- **Risk methodology:** Lists the approaches, tools, and data sources to be used for risk management, including document templates, estimating techniques, and standards for rating impact and probability.
- **Roles and responsibilities:** Defines the risk management team members and their responsibilities.
- **Risk budget:** Estimates the funds reserved in the budget for risks. Contingency reserves cover known risks, and management reserves cover unknown risks.
- **Risk categories:** Groups risks by their potential causes, such as external, internal, or technological.
- **Risk probability and impact:** Defines the likelihood and effect of each risk based on the risk analysis.
- **Stakeholder tolerances (risk appetite):** Defines key stakeholders' tolerance for known risks and/or the organization's overall risk appetite, usually documented as a currency amount.

- **Reporting:** Defines how risk activities will be documented, analyzed, and communicated, along with document templates.
- **Tracking:** Documents how risk activities will be tracked and audited.

Once all risk planning steps are completed and all decisions are documented, the risk management plan is finalized and becomes part of the project management plan.

Perform an Initial Risk Assessment

Risk identification is the process of determining in advance which risks may affect a project and documenting them for analysis and response. The more accurately risks are identified before the project begins work, the better the project manager will be able to prepare responses to mitigate them or act quickly if a risk occurs. The project manager will work with the project team and stakeholders to analyze all aspects of a project—including cost, schedule, quality, personnel, scope, stakeholders, and procurements—to determine any anticipated risks.

Here are some of the information-gathering techniques that can be used to find project risks:

- **Brainstorming:** With the help of a facilitator, have stakeholders brainstorm a list of project risks. Preset risk categories or a risk breakdown structure may help with this process.
- **Interviewing:** Encourage team members, stakeholders, and subject matter experts to identify risks.
- **Root cause analysis:** Review lessons learned documents to find problems with similar prior projects, determine the causes that led to those problems, and then develop preventive actions for these causes in the current project.
- **Delphi technique:** Develop a risk list based on expert opinion.

The ***initial risk assessment*** will be used to create the risk register, which is the document that charts all risks identified throughout the project. Any new risks discovered during the Executing phase are added to the risk register as well. Figures 13-10a through 13-10c in Chapter 13, "Project Management Tools," show a sample risk register.

After the initial risk assessment is complete and an initial version of the risk register is developed, the project manager will analyze their impact and plan responses using the methods outlined in Chapter 4, "Risk and Issue Management."

Plan Project Communication

The groundwork for project communication was laid in the Initiating phase by establishing project communication channels, identifying stakeholders, building a stakeholder register with their preferences and expectations, and analyzing their impact on the project. It culminates in the communication plan, which ensures that all necessary information will be shared at the right time to the correct audiences and in the correct format. Some projects may also need a strategy to guide engagement with stakeholders.

Plan Stakeholder Engagement

Small projects with mostly internal stakeholders may simply combine the stakeholder register with the communication plan to manage project communication. Larger, high-risk, and formal projects should have a ***stakeholder engagement plan*** (or ***stakeholder management plan***). Both qualitative and strategic, it helps the project manager manage stakeholder expectations for project performance, anticipate disruptions, meet their needs, and build productive relationships. The plan could include a prioritized list of stakeholders, their goals or interest in the project, their engagement needs by approach, method, and frequency, and their attitude toward the project. Figure 10-1 shows a sample stakeholder engagement plan.

Stakeholder	Project goals/interest	Influence	Interest	Stance	Engagement Type	Strategies
Project steering committee	Budget, governance	High	High	S	Manage closely	Set expectations regarding milestone challenges.
Sponsor	Drives project	High	High	S	Manage closely	Prefers phone calls for all budget info; otherwise include in communications in all existing channels
Procurement team	Verifies compliance with procurement/bidding guidelines	Medium	Low	N	Consult	Exclude from routine project communications. Add fiscal quarter deadlines to project schedule.
Operations team	Will provide transitional support to end users for 3 months prior to transition	Low	High	N	Keep informed	Contact at least 2 months before go-live to schedule orientation and training. Keep educated about the change. Conduct 'Look and feel' workshop.
Internal end users	Highly vested in changes to the UI and workflow	Low	High	S	Keep informed	Publish updates on company intranet and send monthly email. Conduct 'Look and feel' workshop.

Stance: S=supportive, N=neutral, U=unaware, R=resistant

Figure 10-1 Example of a Stakeholder Engagement Plan

The power/interest grid shown in Figure 9-4 and the salience model (both covered in Chapter 9, "Project Life Cycles, Discovery/Concept Preparation Phase, and Initiating Phase Activities") plot stakeholders by their interest, urgency, legitimacy, and power. The results can define the engagement approach (such as manage closely, keep informed, or keep satisfied). Some projects might classify stakeholders as supportive (S), neutral (N), unaware (U), or resistant (R) and develop strategies for each type. Are they a cheerleader, or do they consistently ignore your emails? The reason behind the classification can yield strategies to address them. If a group of resistant stakeholders feels they are not being consulted enough, you could add them to a quarterly call with the steering committee. Neutral or unaware stakeholders could be invited to a custom product demo to increase their investment in the project's outcome and awareness of its benefits.

NOTE Some project management standards use a unified stakeholder engagement and communications plan (SECP), but for the purposes of this book, they are presented as separate concepts.

Communication Style

Adjusting not only the communication method but also the communication style to fit each stakeholder will help reduce friction and enhance productivity, especially with highly salient and key stakeholders. The Dominant, Influence, Steadiness, Cautious (DISC) method of categorization helps project managers to assign a communication mode based on four behavioral styles:

- **Dominant personality:** Dominant individuals, also referred to as *direct* or *controlling*, require communications that are brief and compelling. Basically, these people prefer just the facts, without a lot of details.
- **Influencer personality:** Influencers are very social, preferring back-and-forth communication. Influencers want details, and in turn they provide a lot of feedback.
- **Steadiness personality:** Stakeholders with the steadiness style are calm, cool, and collected. These stakeholders will be loyal once they are convinced of the need for the project, and they thrive on sincere appreciation.
- **Cautious personality:** These stakeholders are task-oriented and prefer that other people send an email or call to set up an appointment instead of dropping by. This personality type may require face-to-face meetings with detailed documentation in writing so they can verify your conclusions on their own.

Develop a Communication Plan

The communication plan describes how formal project communications will be planned, structured, implemented, and monitored. It should list the anticipated types of communication, their purposes, the cadence, and their expected modes (such as written or verbal). Audits, project changes, risk reviews, milestones, schedule changes, gate reviews, status meetings, and kickoffs are all regular ***communication triggers***, while reports and meetings are common methods of communication. Some projects may need both internal and external plans: one to manage internal project communications and one to manage outreach with a group of public stakeholders, such as a community affected by a large-scale municipal project.

The communication plan should document any stakeholder requirements not included in the stakeholder register or engagement plan. Common fields include frequency of communication, level of report detail, communication types, and location. The plan can be organized by listing each stakeholder and all of their required communications or by listing each planned communication type (such as steering committee meeting, weekly status report, or risk review) and the applicable audience. Most project management software will let you build the plan both ways and toggle between the views. In the example tool that created the table in Figure 10-2, clicking the "Stakeholder or Group" field would expand a list of all individuals in that field, along with their contact details, and allow you to edit, add, or remove members.

Type	Stakeholder or Group	Purpose/ Outcome	Communication Method	Timing & Frequency	Confidential
Steering board meeting	Steering board members	Status updates, decision-making on budget and change control	Physical meeting	Monthly	Y
Monthly all-hands meeting	Extended project team	Status update, alignment	Physical meeting plus Zoom for remote	Monthly	N
Company-wide project status update	Upper management	Informative, alignment	Email	Monthly	N
Schedule updates	Extended project team	Alignment, task-setting	Dashboard, kanban, email	Daily (dashboard, kanban), weekly (email)	N
Project status meeting (client)	PM, product owner, customer	Review status of deliverables, alignment, project planning	Verbal meeting (Zoom)	Weekly	N
Risk review meeting	PM, product owner, risk owners	Review status of current risks and open or close risks	Physical meeting plus Zoom for remote	Monthly	N

Figure 10-2 Example of a Communication Plan

The project manager should account for all types of messages and provide guidance on methods for emergency communications, change communications, project status communications, quality assurance communications, budget communications, schedule communications, and so forth. The communication plan should be published and shared with team members so that everyone knows how information is being distributed. Once the plan is final, the project manager should schedule out each of the meetings and add calendar reminders to send reports, emails, or updates at the scheduled frequency.

Some project communications may have confidentiality constraints, such as information that can require security clearance or a non-disclosure agreement (NDA). This situation is typical with projects related to the development of new technology or involving government entities. The communication plan should have a category for restricted-audience communication, and it should list the confidentiality level of each stakeholder. The project manager will need to document the different levels of confidentiality as well as which types of communication fit into each level. An access control list may need to be built to filter communications to only the correct stakeholders. The project manager might also designate criticality levels (such as *normal*, *urgent*, and *critical*) and provide guidelines for applying these levels to project communication.

Meeting Cadence and Methodologies

Meeting ***cadence*** refers to the frequency of team meetings, or how often recurring meetings are held. The cadence of the communication plan will vary depending on the framework governing your project and the type of work being done. Some Agile methodologies have meetings that follow specific formats (the daily stand-up, sprint retrospective, and sprint planning meeting being major examples). Traditional predictive projects that set project tasks at the outset would rarely need a daily meeting of the full team; a weekly alignment cadence makes more sense, with daily ad hoc meetings among team members as needed. No communication should be scheduled so frequently that it interferes with the actual creation of deliverables or causes communication fatigue.

Develop a Project Management Plan

The majority of the project planning documentation is created during the Planning phase of a project. The ***project management plan*** describes how the project will be executed, monitored, and controlled. This document consolidates a number of subsidiary plans and baselines. The project manager compiles the project management plan, which is made up of the management plans, all baselines, and milestones. For adaptive projects, it includes a blueprint of the minimally viable product.

The project management plan is not a single document or plan. As previously stated, CompTIA does not provide a comprehensive list of project management plan documents, which can vary by project size and methodology. Figure 10-3 shows a list of standard project management plan components that would be included in a typical predictive project and an Agile or hybrid project.

Project Area	Project Management Plan or Component: Waterfall	Project Management Plan or Component: Agile or Hybrid
Scope	Detailed scope statement, WBS, WBS dictionary, scope baseline, scope management plan	Product scope statement, backlog, scope baseline, scope management plan
Requirements	Detailed requirements, requirements management plan, requirements traceability matrix	Detailed requirements, requirements management plan, requirements traceability matrix
Quality	Test plan, quality assurance plan, transition/release plan	Test plan, quality assurance plan, transition/release plan
Risks	Risk register, risk management plan, issue log	Risk register, risk management plan, issue log
Schedule	Project schedule, schedule baseline, schedule management plan	Project schedule, schedule baseline, schedule management plan, iteration plan
Resources	Resource calendar, resource management plan, procurement plan	Resource calendar, resource management plan, procurement plan
Communication	Communication plan, stakeholder engagement plan, stakeholder register	Communication plan, stakeholder engagement plan, stakeholder register
Costs	Approved budget, budget baseline, cost management plan	Approved budget, budget baseline, cost management plan

Figure 10-3 Components of a Sample Project Management Plan

Establish Baselines

The ***project baseline***, also called the *performance measurement baseline*, is made up of the three subsidiary baselines established at the end of project planning: the cost baseline, schedule baseline, and scope baseline. Once these baselines are approved, they become the standard to compare with the project's actual performance in these three areas, unless they are formally altered during change control. For this reason, approving the baselines is one of the last steps in the Planning phase:

- ***Cost baseline***: The cost baseline is the sum of all project cost estimates plus the contingency reserve.
- ***Schedule baseline***: The schedule baseline is the approved version of the project schedule, or the project's total duration.
- ***Scope baseline***: The scope baseline is the approved version of the project's scope. It includes the WBS, the WBS dictionary, and the detailed scope statement. Formal scope changes will be made against this baseline.

Remember that the project budget and the project cost baseline are not the same. The project budget is the complete pool of funds available to cover project expenses and includes the management reserves, which the cost baseline does not. In earned value management, the cost baseline is the budget at completion (BAC).

Establish Milestones

Milestones are the major project events, such as iterations or releases. While high-level milestones are part of the project from the beginning of the charter, more specific milestones can be developed and all milestones assigned a target date once the project schedule is complete. The milestone list identifies all project milestones and indicates whether each milestone is mandatory. A mandatory milestone is one that must occur for project work to go forward, such as a procurement delivery. An optional milestone is one that may or may not occur and is often based on historical information or past projects.

Establish Minimum Viable Product

A ***minimum viable product (MVP)*** or ***minimally viable product*** is a release that is complete enough to function according to requirements but does not include all of the planned features. Releasing an MVP can help validate a product idea early in the development cycle. In software industries, the MVP can bring rapid user feedback to the product team, which can be used to iterate and improve the product to include features that customers want. If the early adoption fails, the product can be scrapped without the loss of too much effort. The MVP is a key concept for incremental and iterative projects, especially the scrum framework.

To create the MVP, the desired feature list is pared down to the basic functional requirements that will produce a workable design, and the rest of the requirements are transferred to the backlog. Alternatively, the product owner pulls a user story from the backlog, and the product team creates a functional mockup based on that story. It contains only enough features to determine whether the approach being taken will meet the objectives, and it is used as an internal proof of concept.

Develop Subsidiary Management Plans

Subsidiary management plans are developed during the Planning phase and usually do not change. They may be adapted from similar projects or provided as templates by the PMO. Not every project will need every plan listed here, especially smaller projects, and some projects may merge related plans.

Remember that subsidiary project management plans provide governance. They describe how to perform a set of project processes (such as quality assurance) and how to handle the process's artifacts in a measurable and controlled way. The artifacts created by those management plans, such as the risk register, also become part of the subsidiary plan, and by extension the overall project management plan.

This section includes some subsidiary management plans that are not mentioned elsewhere in the CompTIA Project+ objectives. For a list of every project management plan component and project document in this book, refer to Table B-1 in Appendix B, "Master Table of Project Management Artifacts, Documents, and Plans."

Change Management Plan or Change Control Plan

The change management plan or change control plan (covered in Chapter 3, "Change Control Process Throughout the Project Life Cycle") describes how change requests are initiated, approved, validated, and communicated. Depending on the change, you may need to refer to another subsidiary plan to update associated artifacts and perform all actions triggered by the change, as illustrated in Figure 10-4.

EXAMPLE: A client requests a new feature to be added to the product's scope. The request itself will be handled according to the change management plan, but if it is approved, the scope management plan will define how to update the scope baseline, requirements, WBS, and WBS dictionary. In other words, the client requests the scope change, the change management plan tells you how to handle the request, and the scope management plan tells you how to correctly insert the change into project documentation and align the rest of the project accordingly.

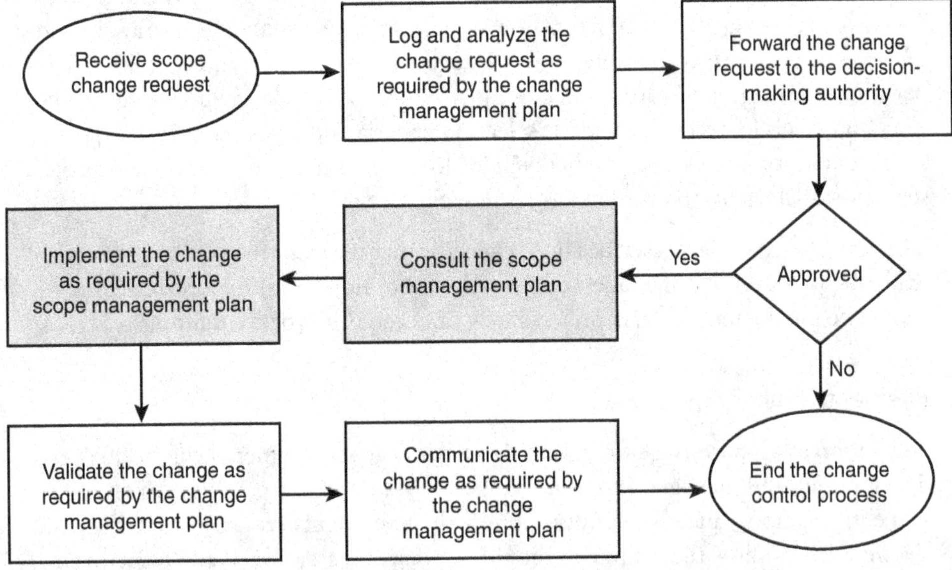

Figure 10-4 Interaction Between the Change Control Plan and Subsidiary Management Plan

Cost Management Plan

Project cost management ensures that the project expenditures fall within the approved budget. The ***cost management plan*** specifies how the project costs will be estimated, structured, monitored, and controlled. It defines units of measure (such as labor weeks or labor hours), the process and formulas to use for estimating costs, variance thresholds, templates and formats for cost reporting, rules for performance measurement, and the approved process for developing budgets and monitoring costs.

Issue Management Plan

The issue management plan, previously covered in Chapter 4, describes how issues should be logged, treated, resolved, and monitored after resolution. It should include an issue log template and identify points of escalation for different issue categories and severity levels, as well as the metrics used to prioritize issues. Smaller projects may combine the risk and issue management plans, but risks and issues should always be identified and tracked separately. Remember that the issue resolution plan is developed to address an active issue using guidance from the issue management plan and/or the risk management plan.

Procurement Management Plan

Managers of smaller projects will work with the organization's procurement team to acquire resources or to manage bids, proposals, or contracts. Larger projects may need a formal procurement management plan with guidelines set by the organization or PMO. This plan documents how to perform procurement activities, including assessing the project's resource needs, acquiring equipment and supplies, hiring personnel, managing vendors, and closing contracts. It should include procurement roles and levels of authority, vendor selection criteria and assessment techniques, procurement timelines, prequalified vendor lists, and guidelines for relevant project scenarios, such as paying vendors in foreign currencies.

The procurement plan describes how a specific project resource will be procured, while the procurement management plan describes how procurement activities should be conducted. Smaller projects may only require procurement plans.

Requirements Management Plan

The ***requirements management plan*** describes how requirements will be analyzed, documented, and managed through changes. It is sometimes combined with the scope management plan. Regardless of how the documents are organized, the plan should describe how requirements should be elicited, categorized and prioritized, documented, and added to a requirements traceability matrix. The plan also sets the standards or tools to be used to track, report, trace, and validate the requirements against project deliverables and quality requirements. Adaptive projects can use the requirements management plan to define how the backlog will be handled.

Resource Management Plan

The ***resource management plan*** describes how both team members and physical resources should be allocated, managed, and released at the end of project work. For human resources, this plan provides the organizational chart, training requirements, onboarding and offboarding processes, project roles and responsibilities, and the methods used to document skill levels and resource types. For physical resources, this plan describes how materials should be acquired, transported, distributed, stored, and disposed of. For example, a project that generates construction waste or decommissioned computer hardware will need a procedure for each type of disposal.

Schedule Management Plan

The schedule management plan describes how the schedule should be developed, monitored, and controlled. It specifies the scheduling tool and methodologies used to estimate activities, units of measure, variance thresholds, and the approved EVM measurement techniques, if used. It should include the process for updating the schedule when required and provide guidelines for rebaselining. The schedule management plan can also be used to plan iterations and releases and their durations.

Develop a Transition/Release Plan

Transition plans govern how a project transfers its results from the development team to the operations team or the client-owner. A transition owner will be assigned to the plan and be responsible for overseeing its activities. The plan will usually include a transition schedule (including a go-live date), product documentation, a training plan, an asset transfer plan, a deployment plan, a rollback plan, maintenance requirements, service level agreements (SLAs) and warranties, and a list of the activities required for a successful handoff.

Transition plans are executed when an adaptive product is complete or at the end of a predictive project that delivers software or a service. For IT-based projects, the result of a sprint or project is released to the operations team, which owns the deployment platforms and processes.

NOTE Predictive projects may use the terms *release plan* and *transition plan* synonymously to describe the process of releasing a product to the client. An adaptive project's iteration plan (covered earlier in this chapter), which is used for scrum, Agile, and other incremental and iterative frameworks that roll out usable deliverables in staged releases, is also referred to in project management literature as a release plan. However, adaptive release plans also need to include the elements of a transition plan to support the team that will be using the released deliverable.

Regardless of the project type, delivering any final result requires the orderly transfer of knowledge and assets. The release/transition plan becomes part of the project management plan, and its activities are performed during the close of the project or iteration.

Operational Training

Training should be provided in advance of the go-live date, but close enough to release that the recipients can remember the information once they are responsible for the product. For adaptive projects with multiple releases, the project team should train the operations team prior to each new release to ensure they understand the latest features and functions.

Operational training should include a full set of product documentation, a list of all assets required to run the product (such as administrative credentials or databases), requirements for operating, patching, and maintaining the product, a maintenance schedule, and a development team contact to answer questions after training. Training sessions may need to continue after the operational handoff, as the users master the basic functions and are ready to advance.

Go Live

After all testing, data migrations, training, and other preparations are complete, the product can go live according to the deployment portion of the transition plan. The ***go-live date*** or ***release date*** is when the development team deploys the product or deliverable in the client environment. This is the first date of public availability to the customer, and it is typically a project milestone. The development team should be prepared to execute a rollback strategy if issues arrive during deployment.

Operational Handoff

After going live, the product or release will be running in the end environment using the customer's real data under the control of the operations team. At this point it is formally handed off to the team that will operate and maintain it for internal and/or external end users. This team will be responsible for patches, maintenance, and end user support. A clearly defined ***operational handoff*** ensures that all individuals involved with the product know when their responsibilities end or begin. Handoff includes turning over any assets (physical or intangible) required to operate the product according to the asset transfer plan, including administrative credentials.

Operations should note any issues during the handoff period and communicate them to the project team as soon as possible. Once the handoff is complete, any subsequent issues with the product are the responsibility of the client. Operational handoff is also a common project milestone.

Audience Tailoring

An ***internal audience*** refers to product recipients in the same organization as the project team, as for an internally developed application or service. An ***external audience*** refers to product recipients who are outside the project organization. The transition process should be tailored for each client type. All clients, but external clients in particular, should understand the warranties and SLAs that support the product, ongoing service fees and/or licensing costs, maintenance schedules, and the escalation path for issues. Product documentation for external users is typically more robust and may include multiple user manuals—specifically one for general end users and another for administrative end users. Training external users may require on-site visits.

Transitioning to an internal audience can involve less formal communication and can use internal company resources, such as wikis or intranets, to deliver training and product documentation. An internal dashboard or ticket system might be used to resolve transition issues or provide a countdown during handoff. However, no transition plan element should be omitted when the audience is internal.

Exam Preparation Tasks

As mentioned in the section "How to Use This Book" in the Introduction, you have a few choices for exam preparation: the exercises here, Chapter 17, "Final Preparation," and the exam simulation questions included in the Pearson Test Prep Software Online.

Review All Key Topics

Review the most important topics in this chapter, noted with the Key Topics icon in the outer margin of the page. Table 10-2 lists each reference of these key topics and the page number on which each is found.

Table 10-2 Key Topics for Chapter 10

Key Topic Element	Description	Page Number
Paragraph	Defines the detailed scope statement	296
Paragraph	Explains units of work	297
Paragraph	Describes the work breakdown structure	297
Paragraph	Describes backlog	297
Section	Explains developing a project schedule	297
Paragraph	Describes cadence	298
Paragraph	Explains milestones	310
Section	Describes determining budget considerations	301
Paragraph	Explains the project's resource pool	299
Paragraph	Explains assigning project resources	300
Section	Describes developing a quality assurance (QA) plan	302
Paragraph	Explains performing an initial risk assessment	304
Figure 10-2	Example of a Communication Plan	307
Figure 10-3	Components of a Sample Project Management Plan	309
Paragraph	Describes the project baseline	309
Paragraph	Explains minimum viable product (MVP)	310
Section	Describes developing a transition plan	313

Define Key Terms

Define the following key terms from this chapter and check your answers in the glossary:

scope management plan, requirements management plan, detailed scope statement, backlog, project schedule, cadence, iteration plan, resource management, resource pool, resource calendar, resource breakdown structure, budget, quality assurance (QA) plan, quality management plan, test plan, risk identification, initial risk assessment, stakeholder engagement plan, stakeholder management plan, communication triggers, cadence, project management plan, project baseline, schedule baseline, scope baseline, minimum viable product (MVP), minimally viable project, cost management plan, requirements management plan, resource management plan, transition plans, operational training, go-live date, release date, operational handoff, internal audience, external audience

Review Questions

The answers to these questions appear in Appendix A. For more practice with sample exam questions, use the Pearson Test Prep practice test software online.

1. You are the project manager for a project to redesign the shelving solutions for your company's jewelry products. These solutions will be sent to retail stores. As part of the project planning, you work with the team to brainstorm potential pitfalls to the project. Which risk activity is this group working on?
   a. Risk quantification
   b. Risk analysis
   c. Risk review
   d. Risk identification

2. Which of the following are created or captured during the Planning phase of a project? (Choose all that apply.)
   a. Budget and schedule
   b. High-level requirements and risks
   c. Deliverables
   d. Detailed scope
   e. Baselines

3. For which of the following questions would you need to consult the communication plan?
   a. Which urgent actions need to occur within the next week?
   b. Which topics will be discussed at the next project steering committee meeting?
   c. Which stakeholders should receive a particular report?
   d. When will the next status report meeting take place?

4. Which of the following elements should be included in a transition plan? (Choose all that apply.)
   a. Deployment plan
   b. Asset transfer plan
   c. Rollback plan
   d. Training plan

5. You have identified one stakeholder on your project as a dominant personality type. You need to relay some project information to this stakeholder. This stakeholder prefers face-to-face communication, except in emergency situations. Which type of communication should you use?
   a. Provide just the facts in an email.
   b. Provide lots of detail in an email.
   c. Provide lots of detail orally.
   d. Provide just the facts orally.

6. You have just taken over a project in the planning stage. Most of the team members are unfamiliar to you, and you do not know who has the skill level to complete a task on the RACI chart. Which documents could you consult to answer this question? (Choose two.)
   a. WBS dictionary
   b. Stakeholder register
   c. Resource management plan
   d. Resource breakdown structure
   e. Stakeholder engagement plan

7. Which project document serves as the guide to the project team to ensure that the project's result meets the project sponsor's requirements?
   a. Project schedule
   b. Scope statement
   c. Quality assurance plan
   d. Scope baseline

8. You just examined the requirements documentation and you are currently reviewing a list of the project team members, their skill sets, and their scheduled activities. Which process does this describe?
   a. Conducting a needs assessment
   b. Performing a gap analysis
   c. Assigning project resources
   d. Defining units of work

9. Which aspect of project management is *not* involved in quality assurance?
   a. Risk management
   b. Regulatory compliance
   c. Scope management
   d. Stakeholder management

10. How is the length of an iteration timebox determined?
    a. The total number of user stories is divided by the team's speed at completing the stated tasks.
    b. The iteration timebox is fixed at 1 week.
    c. The iteration timebox is fixed at 2 weeks.
    d. The team mutually agrees to the length after considering the size and the complexity of the project.

This chapter covers the following topics:

- **Execute Tasks According to the Project Management Plan:** Introduces project execution and the tasks that must be carried out to complete the project
- **Monitor and Control Project Work:** Explains how project monitoring and controlling are related to project execution
- **Manage Vendors:** Covers vendor management, including enforcing vendor rules of engagement, monitoring performance, and approving deliverables
- **Conduct Project Meetings and Updates:** Discusses the importance of project meetings and updates during project execution
- **Tracking/Reporting:** Explains tracking and reporting as part of project execution, including team touch points, risk reporting, external status reporting, overall progress reporting, gap analysis, and ad hoc reporting
- **Update the Project Budget:** Covers updating the project budget as project tasks are completed
- **Update the Project Timeline:** Covers updating the project timeline/schedule as project tasks are completed
- **Manage Conflict:** Discusses conflict as it relates to project execution and the methods for dealing with conflict, including smoothing, forcing, compromising, collaborating/negotiating, avoiding, and confronting
- **Coordinate a Phase-Gate Review:** Explains phases, phase gates, and phase-gate reviews in a multiphase project
- **Implement Organizational Change Management:** Explains how organizational change can affect a project, including the types of changes and impacts/responses

Executing Phase Activities

The Executing phase completes the work defined in the project management plan. During this phase, the project manager coordinates personnel and other resources and manages stakeholder expectations. The major portion of the project's budget will be expended during this phase.

In the Executing phase, the project manager directs the project work, quality assurance, and communications. In addition, the project manager develops and manages the project team as well as conducts procurements.

The main output of this phase is the project deliverables, which are the unique work packages defined in the work breakdown structure (WBS).

This chapter covers the following objective for the CompTIA Project+ exam:

2.4 Given a scenario, perform activities during the project execution phase.

"Do I Know This Already?" Quiz

The "Do I Know This Already?" quiz allows you to assess whether you should read this entire chapter thoroughly or jump to the "Exam Preparation Tasks" section. If you are in doubt about your answers to these questions or your own assessment of your knowledge of the topics, read the entire chapter. Table 11-1 lists the major headings in this chapter and their corresponding "Do I Know This Already?" quiz questions. You can find the answers in Appendix A, "Answers to the 'Do I Know This Already?' Questions and Review Quizzes."

Table 11-1 "Do I Know This Already?" Section-to-Question Mapping

Foundation Topics Section	Questions
Execute Tasks According to the Project Management Plan	1
Monitor and Control Project Work	2
Manage Vendors	9
Conduct Project Meetings and Updates	11
Tracking/Reporting	10
Update the Project Budget	12
Update the Project Timeline	13

Foundation Topics Section	Questions
Manage Conflict	3, 4
Coordinate a Phase-Gate Review	5
Implement Organizational Change Management	6, 7, 8

CAUTION The goal of self-assessment is to gauge your mastery of the topics in this chapter. If you do not know the answer to a question or are only partially sure of the answer, you should mark that question as wrong for the purposes of the self-assessment. Giving yourself credit for an answer you correctly guess skews your self-assessment results and might provide you with a false sense of security.

1. During which project phase are project deliverables created?
   a. Executing
   b. Planning
   c. Initiating
   d. Discovery

2. Which of the following occurs or is created during the Executing phase?
   a. Requirements
   b. Schedule
   c. Quality assurance
   d. Budget

3. Which conflict-resolution technique involves emphasizing areas of agreement rather than differences?
   a. Smoothing
   b. Forcing
   c. Compromising
   d. Confronting

4. Which conflict-resolution technique should you use as a last resort to resolve a long-lasting conflict?
   a. Compromising
   b. Confronting
   c. Avoiding
   d. Forcing

5. During a project, the project managers from the different phases meet with the project sponsor to decide whether the project will proceed. What is this process called?
   a. Gate review
   b. Milestone
   c. Audit
   d. Change control process

6. Your company has decided to purchase a competitor to obtain its intellectual property and business contacts. Which type of organizational change is this?
   a. Business acquisition
   b. Business split
   c. Internal reorganization
   d. Outsourcing

7. While you are managing a project, your company announces that the sales and marketing departments will be merged into a single department. Which type of organizational change is this example?
   a. Business merger
   b. Relocation
   c. Business process change
   d. Internal reorganization

8. While you are managing a project, your company decides that all purchases more than $25,000 must go through a formal approval process that involves three members of upper management. Your project plans to make multiple purchases over this amount. Which type of organizational change is this example?
   a. Outsourcing
   b. Business split
   c. Business process change
   d. Business merger

9. Which of the following is considered part of managing vendors during project execution?
   a. Risk reporting
   b. Phase-gate review

c. Gap analysis

d. Rules of engagement

10. Which report is best provided to individuals or groups that are not part of the project team or project stakeholders?

a. Risk report

b. External status report

c. Overall progress report

d. Gap analysis

11. Which of the following should be used to document the meeting types and frequencies?

a. Communication management plan

b. Procurement management plan

c. Schedule management plan

d. Project schedule

12. How should the project budget be updated?

a. Based on the expected costs as the work is completed

b. Based on the actual costs accrued as the work is completed

c. Based on the expected costs as the work is estimated

d. Based on the actual costs as the work is estimated

13. How should the project schedule be updated?

a. Based on the estimates documented in project planning

b. Based on the budget documented in project planning

c. Based on the actual time it takes to complete the project work

d. Based on the expected time it takes to complete project work

Foundation Topics

Execute Tasks According to the Project Management Plan

The ***Executing phase*** involves the actual project work that is mostly completed by the project team. The work that is completed produces the project deliverables, which are the unique work packages defined in the WBS. The project manager generally oversees and monitors the work to ensure it is progressing as expected. The project manager may have to implement measures to control the project.

Technically, the tasks are broken down in the WBS and then given a timeline in the schedule. In adaptive projects, the project team may need to refer to the backlog. The tasks identified in either the WBS or the backlog are completed during the Executing phase.

NOTE The project WBS and backlog are discussed in detail in Chapter 5, "Schedule Development and Management."

As tasks are completed, the project manager should update the project schedule with the actual time required for the tasks and the project budget with the actual costs related to the task. The project manager needs to carefully monitor task durations, especially tasks on the critical path or tasks that take longer than originally estimated. The project manager needs to carefully monitor task cost and notate any effects on the budget.

Monitoring and controlling activities are performed during the Executing phase to ensure that deliverables fit within the parameters defined during the Planning phase.

Monitor and Control Project Work

As project work executes, the project manager also tracks, reviews, and organizes the project's progress, identifies areas where changes are required, and initiates the approved changes. The key purpose of monitoring and controlling activities is to measure and analyze project performance at regular intervals to identify variances from the project management plan.

In the Executing phase, the project manager monitors and controls the project's work, scope, schedule, budget, quality, communication, risks, and procurements. This phase involves the following project documentation and activities:

- Issues log
- Performance measuring and reporting

- Quality assurance/governance
- Change control
- Budget

NOTE The CompTIA objectives for the Project+ exam do not specifically mention monitoring and controlling project work. Monitoring and controlling run parallel to the Executing phase. Monitoring and controlling do still occur; however, many of the monitoring and controlling actions are considered part of project execution. Monitoring and controlling all aspects of a project are still key parts of the project manager's job.

Manage Vendors

Project managers must manage vendors and keep track of the status of all procurements. Managing vendors includes enforcing ***vendor rules of engagement***, monitoring performance, and approving deliverables. We covered much of this in depth in Chapter 8, "Project Procurement and Vendor Selection."

Enforce Vendor Rules of Engagement

Rules of engagement define expectations around how the project team and the vendor interact at all times during the project: how much information is shared, when it is shared, and how it is shared. They also define situations that would require immediate communication (such as a delay in procurement due to raw material shortages).

Project managers should ensure that both the project team members and vendor representatives understand the rules of engagement and the communication requirements set forth in the communication management plan.

Monitor Performance

Project managers should ensure they regularly monitor vendor performance and the progress of procurements. Having a regular meeting with the vendor to check in is often the best solution. However, emergencies or issues may arise at any moment. Vendors should have guidelines for communicating emergencies or issues in a timely manner. Risks that could occur as part of procurement management should be carefully monitored as well so that mitigations can be initiated if needed.

Approve Deliverables

Once procurements are delivered, the project manager will need to formally accept them, provided that the documented quality standards are met. The project team assesses the procurements for conformity to the procurement contracts and metrics set forth. This needs to occur in a timely manner in case rework or changes to the procurements need to occur.

Once procurement deliverables are approved, the project manager or assigned team member needs to approve procurement payments as set forth in the procurement contract and procurement management plan. Timely payment ensures that late payment penalties are avoided. In contrast, the project manager should consult the contract if procurements are late. Sometimes contracts have penalties for late delivery.

Conduct Project Meetings and Updates

As project work is completed, project managers must conduct regular meetings and provide updates to project stakeholders and the project sponsor. We covered much of this in depth in Chapter 7, "Communication and Meeting Management."

The project team should refer to the communication plan that was created during project planning to ensure that project meetings and updates are carried out as documented.

Tracking/Reporting

As project work is being completed, the project manager must track and report on project progress. We have discussed in previous chapters some of the tracking and reporting that is done. For the Executing phase, a project manager needs to understand team touch points, risk reporting, external status reporting, overall progress reporting, gap analysis, and ad hoc reporting.

Team Touch Points

Team touch points are the points during the project where the project manager has full team meetings and one-on-one meetings with each team member. Team meetings allow the entire team to discuss the project. One-on-one meetings allow the project manager to ask the team members' viewpoints regarding overall project performance feedback and discuss personal goals. Both types of meetings are important to ensure both project and team success.

Risk Reporting

The project manager or responsible team member should provide regular updates on any new risks that have been identified, any risks that have occurred and their responses, and any risk indicators. Risk management is covered in Chapter 4, "Risk and Issue Management."

Risk reporting documentation includes the risk register and risk reports. The risk register is a list of all risks documented during project planning. A risk report is produced on a regular basis to provide stakeholders with an update on project risks. Both of these documents are covered in more detail in Chapter 13, "Project Management Tools."

External Status Reporting

External status reports are those that are shared with individuals outside the project team and stakeholders. These reports should be brief and provide only high-level status, not status on individual components or activities. If the project involves new innovation or intellectual property, the external status reports may be even more vague to protect the organization.

Too much information often results in questions and confusion because the audience may not understand all the components or terminology of the project. The communication management plan should provide guidance on the information that should be included in these reports and the individuals or groups that should receive these reports.

Overall Progress Reporting

Overall progress reporting is generally provided to stakeholders who have an understanding of the project. This report should contain more details than the external status reports but should not go too far for the same reasons given for external status reports.

In some organizations, the progress reports are customized based on the audience. For example, one version of the progress report may stress schedule and costs more, while another version stresses the project risks. Again, project managers need to decide the format of any reports. If a project management office (PMO) exists, it will often supply templates, but the templates may need to be revised based on project needs.

As with external status reports, the communication management plan should provide guidance to the project team and project manager on the structure and frequency of these reports, as well as who should receive them.

Gap Analysis

Gap analysis was explained as it relates to team management in Chapter 2, "Team and Resource Management." A ***gap analysis*** compares actual results or performance with desired results or performance. Project managers would use a gap analysis to analyze the project budget, schedule, quality, and scope.

If the project is over budget based on the gap analysis, adjustments may need to be made to bring costs down, including sourcing cheaper procurements, utilizing lower-rate personnel more than higher-rate personnel, and removing some requirements from the project scope.

If the schedule is behind based on the gap analysis, adjustments may need to be made to speed up the project, including bringing on more team members or removing some requirements from the project scope.

If the quality of the deliverables is less than expected based on the gap analysis, the project manager may need to work with team members to improve deliverable quality. This could include providing team members with training and incorporating peer reviews of all project work prior to release.

If the scope of the project is more than can be handled in the time allotted or if the documented scope is not achievable, the project manager may need to meet with stakeholders and the project sponsor to discuss the options, including changing the project requirements or increasing the project schedule to give more time for development.

A gap analysis allows a project manager to make decisions about the project schedule, budget, quality, and scope while consulting with the project team, stakeholders, and sponsor.

Ad Hoc Reporting

Ad hoc reporting involves reports created on an as-needed basis, usually the result of a request by a stakeholder or the sponsor. Ad hoc reports should be kept to a minimum. However, if the project manager and stakeholders see value in a certain ad hoc report, the project manager should assess whether the report should be added to the communication management plan as a regular report.

Assessing the value provided by the ad hoc report should be performed prior to creating the report. Also, the time that will be expended to create the report should factor into whether it should be provided.

Update the Project Budget

The project budget is updated and managed based on the actual costs accrued as the work is completed. Actual costs should always be compared to the baseline budget, which is the original approved budget. Management and contingency reserves should also be analyzed to document how much of each remains. Updating the project budget on a regular basis will help ensure that the budget reconciliation process carried out at project closing is easier and faster.

As one of the main project constraints, the project budget should be regularly analyzed to determine any discrepancies from the baseline. The quicker the project manager denotes deviations from the baseline, the quicker actions can be taken to correct or mitigate future budget deviations. More information on the project budget can be found in Chapter 10, "Planning Phase Activities."

Update the Project Timeline

The project schedule, also referred to as the project timeline, is updated and managed based on the actual time it takes to complete project work. The updated project schedule should always be compared to the baseline schedule, which is the original approved schedule. Management and contingency reserves should also be analyzed to document how much of each remains. In addition, the critical path must be carefully monitored, as any change in it will affect the overall project deadline.

As one of the main project constraints, the project schedule should be regularly analyzed to determine any discrepancies from the baseline. As with the project budget, the quicker the project manager denotes deviations from the baseline, the quicker actions can be taken to correct or mitigate future schedule deviations. More information on the project schedule can be found in Chapter 5.

Manage Conflict

Conflict in a project is not a matter of *if* it will happen but rather *when* it will happen. Common sources of conflict include resource scarcity, scheduling issues, and work style. When conflicts occur, the project manager is responsible for working with team members and stakeholders to resolve the issue, regardless of its source.

All team members (as well as stakeholders) should have access to the communication plan and use it to guide formal and informal communication. However, communication issues are inevitable in any project. Poor communication can lead to differences in expectations, decreased productivity, or scope creep.

Because the project manager is ultimately responsible for project communication, it is important to understand the following common communication issues and ways of handling them. Truly effective leadership fosters a culture of mutual respect and embraces, not avoids, diverse viewpoints among the team.

- **Failure to focus or listen:** Remind project team members to practice active listening during collaboration, and to focus on the speaker during meetings. Use team exercises to help team members with listening issues.

Group techniques, such as those used by focus groups, may help keep the entire team engaged.

- **Geographical issues:** Ensure that remote team members are provided with regular synchronous communication (such as video conferencing and phone calls) that enables them to build rapport with coworkers.
- **Attitude and ego:** Strong personalities may monopolize meeting time or try to dictate project policies. The project manager should step in to help the team come to a mutual understanding through negotiation as well as ensure that quieter team members are not overruled or disregarded. Sidelined team members should provide input, even if that means actively soliciting their feedback.
- **Authority or hierarchy issues:** Team members may be reluctant to express issues in a group setting, particularly if the group includes individuals with authority. The project manager should set up private channels so that the team member can express any issues confidentially. No team members should feel belittled for their point of view.
- **Poorly written communication:** Make sure that all communication is clear and concise. Formal written communication should be reviewed by someone other than its author to check for errors.
- **Gender bias:** All team members should feel equally respected, regardless of gender, and understand the relevant HR policies for avoiding and/or reporting problems.
- **Inadequate knowledge:** Make sure that all individuals involved in the project understand all the jargon, acronyms, and other language used by the team. It may be helpful to keep a dictionary of terms. Experienced team members could mentor new members and quietly define jargon through a side channel during meetings.
- **Relationships:** Cliques, inside groups, or even friendships within the team may cause division or result in ***groupthink***—groups making decisions in a way that discourages individual creativity or responsibility.

If unchecked, communication issues can escalate into outright conflict. Conflict-resolution techniques include smoothing, forcing, compromising, confronting, avoiding, and negotiating. The following sections discuss these techniques in detail.

Smoothing

Smoothing, also known as ***accommodating***, emphasizes areas of agreement rather than differences. With this technique, the project manager helps team members to accommodate the concerns of other people. Smoothing may be appropriate in the following circumstances:

- When temporary relief from the conflict or buying time is important
- When the issue is more important to one person than to another
- When one of the parties is wrong
- When continued conflict would be detrimental to the project

In some cases, the project manager may choose smoothing in order to protect interests that are more important, while giving up on some interests that are less important. Smoothing gives team members an opportunity to reassess the situation from a different angle.

Use smoothing only when needed; it should not be the go-to solution for all conflict. Parties in the conflict may try to take advantage of smoothing, and some team members may not like the use of smoothing for conflict resolution. In addition, smoothing may have a negative effect on the team's confidence in the project manager's ability to respond to aggressive conflict situations. Finally, smoothing makes it more difficult to transition to a future ***win-win*** solution, in which the chosen solution is the one that best satisfies the concerns of both parties.

Forcing

Forcing, also known as ***directing*** or ***competing***, pursues one viewpoint despite the existence of other viewpoints on the team. It often involves resisting another team member's actions. Forcing may be appropriate in the following circumstances:

- When less-forceful methods do not work or are ineffective
- When the team is receiving pressure to pursue a particular viewpoint that the project manager feels is wrong
- When a quick resolution is required and using force is justified
- As a last resort to resolve a long-lasting conflict

Project managers sometimes use forcing to provide a quick resolution to a conflict. Forcing increases respect when firm resistance is a response to aggression or hostility.

Forcing may negatively affect the project manager's relationship with the opponent. In addition, it may cause the opponent to react in the same manner. With this method, the strong points of the other side's position are ignored. Taking this approach requires a lot of energy.

Compromising

With ***compromising***, also known as ***reconciling***, the team searches for a solution that will bring satisfaction to all parties by partially resolving the conflict. Compromising may be appropriate in the following circumstances:

- When goals are only moderately important and not worth the use of other approaches
- To reach temporary resolution on complex issues
- To reach expedient solutions on important issues
- When the involved parties do not have a high level of mutual trust
- When collaboration or forcing do not work

Compromising is faster than other conflict-resolution techniques and may be practical when time is a factor. It can provide a temporary solution until a win-win solution can be found. Compromising lowers tension levels and stress in conflict situations.

In a ***lose-lose situation***, the compromise does not satisfy either party. Unfortunately, compromising does not contribute to building trust and may require monitoring to ensure that agreements made during the compromise are met.

Collaboration/Negotiation

Collaboration brings two viewpoints together to discuss and reach a solution. Collaboration is considered more of a win-win situation than negotiation. Collaboration requires trust and shared goals.

Organizations are moving toward using collaboration rather than negotiation, as collaboration creates value for both involved parties. To truly collaborate, we must move away from controlling or competitive mindsets and toward open access to data and free exchange of information regardless of the individuals' roles in the organization or project.

Collaboration is not forming strategic alliances or partnerships. While alliances and partnerships can lead to collaboration, true collaboration takes partnering to the next level.

Negotiating brings two viewpoints together to discuss issues and reach a solution. Negotiation skills include setting goals and limits, controlling emotions, listening, verbal communication, and understanding when to close the negotiation. However, usually negotiation is more of a win-lose situation, or at least an "I win bigger than you win" scenario. Negotiation can often involve suspicion (or at least lack of trust) and separate agendas.

Project managers use two categories of negotiation:

- **Competitive negotiation:** Concerned with getting the best deal, competitive negotiation is mostly used in contractual negotiations with third parties. Avoid this type of negotiation if possible.
- **Collaborative negotiation:** Seeks a win-win situation, as with confronting. Collaborative negotiation works to build relationships while minimizing conflict. (This is very close to collaboration.)

Negotiation is helpful when the project manager does not have full project authority, such as when the organization has a functional or matrix structure.

Negotiation includes planning, discussing issues, proposing solutions, bargaining for trade-offs, agreeing to a solution, and reviewing the resolution. But watch for these issues with negotiation:

- Failing to prepare properly
- Making an unreasonable offer
- Neglecting to take time-outs in protracted negotiations
- Rushing negotiations
- Failing to walk away
- Failing to remain calm

Project managers may need training in negotiation skills. They must be able to spell out the guidelines to any team members involved in the negotiations.

Again, collaboration should be preferred over negotiation, as it is often easier to reach an agreement with a collaborative mindset.

Avoiding

Avoiding, also known as ***withdrawing***, postpones the issue until the project manager can be better prepared or other parties can resolve the issue. This technique often involves sidestepping the issue. Avoiding may be appropriate in the following circumstances:

- When the issue is trivial
- When dealing with the issue directly is impractical because time is limited
- When more information is needed to make a decision
- When it is not the right time or place to address the issue

- When unreasonable effort would be required to resolve the issue
- When the discussion could lead to hostility
- When another party needs to be involved

Avoiding is often used to postpone the decision until more favorable circumstances allow for pushing back from the opposing viewpoint. When the conflict is short-term, withdrawing is a low-stress approach. It gives the team time to focus on more important issues, and it allows the team to collect information before taking action.

Avoiding an issue may weaken relationships with the project team or any parties that expect immediate action. Avoiding also requires skill and experience to prevent negative effects in the project manager's position.

Confronting

With ***confronting***, also known as ***problem-solving***, the team uses multiple viewpoints to lead to consensus. With this method, the team attempts to work together to find a win-win solution to the problem in hand. The goal of this approach is to find a mutually beneficial result. Confronting may be appropriate in the following circumstances:

- When consensus and commitment are important
- When in a collaborative environment
- When multiple stakeholders' interests need to be addressed
- When a high level of trust is present
- When a long-term relationship is important
- When animosity is involved
- When the team needs to share responsibility

Confronting usually leads to solving the actual problem while reinforcing mutual trust and respect. It also builds a foundation to help bring about effective collaboration in the future. Project managers who use this technique are often seen as good negotiators. This method of conflict resolution usually results in less stress than with most of the other methods.

When confronting a conflict, all parties must be committed to finding a mutually acceptable solution; therefore, this method of conflict resolution requires more effort and time than other methods. Confronting is not practical if time is crucial, because a win-win solution may not be evident. If trust within the team is ever damaged, this method cannot be used until trust is reestablished.

Coordinate a Phase-Gate Review

To understand gate reviews, project managers must first understand the ***phase-gate model***, also known as ***phase-gate process*** or ***stage-gate process***. Most projects consist of a single pass through all of the project life-cycle processes. In a phase-gate project, an initiative or project is divided into stages or phases, separated by gates. Each gate completes that phase of the project life cycle and then undergoes review before the project moves on to the next phase.

EXAMPLE: A large, multistory construction project uses a phase-gate process to subdivide processes into individual gates to ensure project management success. Each separate facet is its own project that runs through the phases, with gate reviews occurring as each portion is finished. The site preparation is one project gate, the concrete work is another project gate, the steel work is another project gate, and so on. In this manner, the overall project is more manageable, with each project manager being responsible for only their individual gate.

In projects with a phase-gate design, individual gates have relationships similar to the task relationships discussed earlier. ***Gate reviews***, also referred to as ***phase-gate reviews*** or ***stage-gate reviews***, are completed as detailed on the project schedule to clear the project to continue. At a gate review, the project managers and project sponsor meet to determine whether to continue the project. Gate quality-control checks are also performed at this time. Project sponsors make go/kill decisions based on criteria defined during the Planning phase of each gate.

The project manager is responsible for ensuring that the appropriate entities are aware of the gate review and participate in gate review meetings as necessary. In most projects, gate reviews are the sole responsibility of the project sponsor, with project managers participating to provide project details should questions arise. Once a project gate review is complete, the project manager must ensure that the gate review is documented and communicated with the appropriate project entities, usually the project stakeholders and project managers of the other gates.

Implement Organizational Change Management

Organizational change is any change within the organization but outside the project. Such organizational changes can positively or negatively affect the project. Project managers should understand the different organizational changes that can occur, the impact these changes can have on a project, and the responses or actions that should be taken if the organizational change occurs.

Organizational change can be caused by internal or external sources. Any organizational change will involve adapting or assimilating the project to fit into the new organizational state.

Organizational Changes

Just as projects change, organizations also change. The hierarchy can change, altering the reporting structure of the business. Other organizational changes that can affect projects include business mergers/acquisitions or demergers/splits, business process changes, internal reorganization, relocation, and outsourcing.

The following sections discuss these specific types of organizational changes and how they might affect a project. For every type of organizational change, the project manager must fully analyze the change to determine its potential effects on all aspects of the project, including scope, schedule, budget, resources, and so on. If other project team members or stakeholders might be affected, the project manager needs to consult them to gain their input on the change. Each of the following sections notes any differences in how that specific type of organizational change is handled.

Business Merger/Acquisition and Demerger/Split

Business mergers combine two organizations into one entity. Typically, one of the businesses purchases the other as a ***business acquisition***, or the two businesses join forces due to shared interests or to deepen market penetration. If the merger occurs through acquisition, the purchaser usually makes all the decisions on how the merger will occur and which assets will be retained after the merger is complete. Often an overlap of departments and job types means that departments may merge and personnel may be terminated or transferred because job role duplication is not necessary.

A business merger or acquisition could affect a project in several ways:

- New stakeholders and team members may be identified.
- The acquired company may have technologies or expertise that could affect the project's budget and schedule in positive ways.
- Similar projects may have already been undertaken by the other company.
- Other resources (such as necessary supplies, equipment, or other assets) may be shared with the project.
- Business mergers or acquisitions usually have positive effects on the project.

A ***business demerger*** splits a business into separate entities. In this situation, management must determine how the split will affect the disposition of assets, including personnel. Shared resources, especially hardware assets, may be allocated to one of the new organizations. The other new organization then may need to replace or purchase assets to ensure that business processes can continue.

A business demerger or split could affect the project in multiple ways:

- Stakeholders and team members may be split off from the company retaining the project.
- Technologies or expertise needed by the project may no longer be owned by the company retaining the project.
- Needed resources may be split off from the company retaining the project.
- The budgetary resources needed for the project may be gone.
- Business demergers or splits usually have negative effects on the project.

No matter which type of corporate restructuring occurs, the project manager will need to analyze the effects of the restructure on all aspects of the project, including project scope, budget, schedule, resources, stakeholders, and communication. Editing the project documentation, particularly the budget and schedule, may take a bit of effort to ensure that the project can continue as originally planned.

Business Process Change

A business process change is usually implemented when an organization wants to improve performance, reduce costs, and/or increase profitability. Process changes may have dramatic results, but gauging the degree of change requires before-and-after performance measurements. Before implementing the process change, the organization should take baseline performance measurements of the process, which then can be compared to the performance measurements achieved after the change is implemented.

When any type of business process change affects a project, the project manager will need to analyze the effects of the change on all aspects of the project.

EXAMPLE: A company adopts new accounts payable procedures to pay invoices for goods in a more timely manner. Because this new process will affect several projects, the project manager for each project will need to document the change in the project's procurement management plan and any other affected areas of the project. Making this update will help to ensure that the project team members follow the appropriate procedures for accounts payable.

Internal Reorganization

An internal reorganization is an overhaul of a company's internal structure and may involve some or all of the company's departments. Companies reorganize to improve efficiency, cut costs, reposition the business, and/or deal with corporate changes such as mergers and acquisitions.

EXAMPLE: An organization has a team of IT technicians at each office location. The company decides to go to a shared-services model in which most IT services are handled by a single team at a central location. For most day-to-day operations, this model may be sufficient, but complex issues may result in a delay in recovery or resolution. The project manager will need to analyze the effects of this internal reorganization on the project. If the project has a high priority and will have IT requests outside the norm, it may be necessary to have an IT technician on location as a project team member. This organizational change would definitely affect project costs but would also ensure that any issues can be handled quickly.

Relocation

When all or part of a company relocates from one place or facility to another, all of the business assets must be moved from the original location to the new one. For IT assets, the systems must be brought back online and necessary services restored as quickly as possible. Some business assets will have a lower priority than others in the restoration process. The project manager will need to analyze the effects of the relocation on all aspects of the project.

EXAMPLE: An organization is moving its entire operation across town to a new facility. The actual moving of the assets can take place after normal business hours, but not all assets will be operational the next morning. The project manager will need to identify the assets that are vital to the project and ensure that those assets are restored to full operation as quickly as possible.

Outsourcing

When business processes are contracted to entities outside the organization, this *outsourcing* may provide cost benefits. However, outsourcing can adversely affect schedules because the contracted workers are not under the direct control of the organization. Some sources provide work for multiple organizations, which may result in delays.

The project manager will need to analyze the effects of outsourcing on all aspects of the project, including project scope, budget, schedule, resources, stakeholders, and communication. The primary constraints affected by outsourcing are usually the project schedule and budget.

EXAMPLE: A music production company has a project to launch a new music application. The coding work for the project is outsourced to freelance software developers. The project manager will need to stay in constant communication with the contract developers to ensure they stay on task and on schedule. The project manager may decide to pad the schedule to allow for missed deadlines.

Impacts and Responses

As organizational changes occur, the project manager should assess the change and its impact on the project. Once the impact of the change is understood, the project manager may need to come up with a response to the change to ensure project success.

Project managers have a variety of actions that may need to happen, including training, ensuring adoption of change and project responses, reinforcing the adoption over time, communicating with team members and stakeholders regarding the change, documenting the change and its effects on the project, and possibly even adopting new knowledge bases and processes.

Training

Organizational change may lead to the need for personnel training. No matter the source of organizational change, personnel will need training that covers how the organizational change affects personnel and how day-to-day duties may change. Also, some changes could affect compliance, privacy, and security. As a result, the project team may need to be trained in how any new compliance, privacy, or security issues will affect the project.

Ensure Adoption

When organizational change occurs, it is important that the project team adopts any process change that may be required. For example, if a new law is enacted that affects the project, the project will likely need adjustments to ensure compliance with the new law. It is the project manager's responsibility to ensure implementation of any project changes as a result of the new law. This may include informing the project team as well as initially checking work as it is completed to ensure compliance.

Reinforce Adoption over Time

Once the project manager ensures adoption, the project team will carry on with the project tasks. However, over time, the team members may forget about the organizational change and its effects on the project. The project manager should periodically remind team members and ensure that the project remains on track based on the organizational change.

Communication

Communication is considered one of the most important skills for a project manager. When any type of organizational change occurs, the project manager's responsibility is to communicate with the project team and stakeholders about the organizational change. Equally as important is explaining how the change will affect the project and any adjustments that will need to be made due to the change. It is always better to be proactive about organizational changes, meaning informing the team and stakeholders prior to them asking questions. While the project manager may not initially have all the answers, at least the project manager is maintaining an open line of communication whereby team members and stakeholders can freely ask questions.

Documentation

Organizational change may result in new project documentation or revisions to existing project documentation. The project manager should work with the project team to ensure documentation is created or edited that addresses the organization change's effects on the project. Version control of existing documentation should be implemented so that team members work with the latest version. In addition, once documentation is created or edited, the project team should receive communication regarding the new or edited documentation, including a request that it be read.

New Knowledge Bases

Some organizational changes may result in new knowledge bases. An example of this could be when two organizations merge or form a partnership. In this scenario, the project team may need access to the other organization's project management and other knowledge bases. This is especially true if one of the organizations is affected by laws and regulations with which the project team is not familiar.

The project manager should assess the new knowledge bases prior to giving the project team access. This assessment should include determining which areas of the knowledge base the project team may need to access. While the project manager may need to give the team total access to the new knowledge base, it can become easy for the team members to be overwhelmed. By assessing the knowledge base first, the project manager can guide the team to the areas that affect the current project.

New Processes

Organizational changes may result in new or changed processes. Once the processes are documented, the project manager must ensure that the project complies with the new processes. An example of this would be a new approval process for expenditures. Project procurements would need review. The procurement management plan would need to be revised based on the new expenditure approval process. Often already approved procurements would be unaffected by the new process, but any future procurements that have not been approved would need to be completed based on the new process. Tied into this, the project manager would need to update the documentation, communicate the change to the project team, and ensure adoption of the new process, as mentioned in earlier sections.

Exam Preparation Tasks

As mentioned in the section "How to Use This Book" in the Introduction, you have a few choices for exam preparation: the exercises here, Chapter 17, "Final Preparation," and the exam simulation questions in the Pearson Test Prep Software Online.

Review All Key Topics

Review the most important topics in this chapter, noted with the Key Topics icon in the outer margin of the page. Table 11-2 lists each reference of these key topics and the page number on which each is found.

Table 11-2 Key Topics for Chapter 11

Key Topic Element	Description	Page Number
Paragraph	Vendor rules of engagement	326
Paragraph	Team touch points	327
Paragraph	External status reporting	328
Paragraph	Ad hoc reporting	329
Paragraph	Smoothing	331
Paragraph	Forcing	332
Paragraph	Compromise	333
Paragraph	Collaboration	333
Paragraph	Negotiation	333
Paragraph	Avoiding	334
Paragraph	Confronting	335
Paragraph	Phase-gate model	336
Paragraph	Gate reviews	336
Section	Organizational changes	337
Paragraphs	Impacts and responses to change	340

Define Key Terms

Define the following key terms from this chapter and check your answers in the glossary:

Executing phase, vendor rules of engagement, rules of engagement, team touch points, external status reports, overall progress reporting, gap analysis, ad hoc reporting, groupthink, smoothing, accommodating, win-win, forcing, directing, competing, compromising, reconciling, lose-lose situation, collaboration, negotiating, avoiding, withdrawing, confronting, problem-solving, phase-gate model, phase-gate process, stage-gate process, gate review, phase-gate reviews, stage-gate reviews, business mergers, business acquisition, business demerger

Review Questions

The answers to these questions appear in Appendix A. For more practice with sample exam questions, use the Pearson Test Prep practice test software online.

1. Which of the following occurs during the Executing phase of a project?
   a. Creating the project management plan
   b. Developing the project charter and identifying stakeholders
   c. Estimating costs and defining scope
   d. Performing quality assurance

2. The project team you are managing comes to you with an issue. After hearing both sides of the issue, you realize that one side is clearly wrong. Continued discussion of the issue could be detrimental to the project. Which conflict-resolution technique should you use?
   a. Forcing
   b. Smoothing
   c. Compromising
   d. Confronting

3. Recently the project team you are managing experienced conflict over a project issue. Unfortunately, the resolution of the issue resulted in a lose-lose situation. Which type of conflict resolution did you most likely use?
   a. Smoothing
   b. Forcing
   c. Compromising
   d. Confronting

4. Which of the following describes a gate review?
   a. A significant event that is part of the project schedule but does not actually have a duration
   b. A meeting held to determine whether a project will continue

c. The process of verifying compliance with the project guidelines and validating the performance of the project

d. An event in a project that could lead to a disruption in the project

5. Which of the following is an example of internal reorganization?

   a. A software development company decides to use third parties to complete some unfulfilled development projects.

   b. Management decides to move a branch office from one city to another.

   c. A company splits the sales and marketing personnel into two different teams, each reporting to a different supervisor.

   d. Management decides to sell an application the company owns that is no longer profitable.

6. A manager within your company has requested information on the project you are managing. The manager is not part of the project team, nor is he listed as a stakeholder. Which report should you provide him?

   a. Team touch point

   b. Risk report

   c. External status report

   d. Overall progress report

7. You are concerned that the project projections are not accurate. You need to compare actual results and performance with projections. Which of the following should you do?

   a. Create an ad hoc report.

   b. Update the project budget and timeline.

   c. Perform a gap analysis.

   d. Complete a gate review.

8. What should you do prior to paying a vendor for a procurement?

   a. Perform a gap analysis.

   b. Complete an external status report.

   c. Implement a gate review.

   d. Review and approve the procurement deliverable.

9. You are concerned that a new critical path has emerged based on project deviations from the plan. What should you do *first* to determine if this has occurred?
   a. Update the project timeline.
   b. Update the project budget.
   c. Implement a gate review.
   d. Perform a gap analysis.

10. Of the given responses to organizational change, which should be the first focus of a project manager to ensure team members and stakeholders are aware of the change, even if its implications on the project are not fully understood?
    a. Implement training.
    b. Communicate with the team and stakeholders about the change.
    c. Adopt the change within the project.
    d. Document how the change affects the project.

This chapter covers the following topics:

- **Project Evaluation:** Includes involving the project team and stakeholders in the project evaluation process
- **Deliverable Validation:** Discusses deliverable validation throughout the project and how it provides input for the project closure report
- **Contract Closure:** Describes contract closure that can occur throughout the project
- **Access Removal:** Covers ensuring that physical and digital access removal for team members and stakeholders has occurred
- **Resource Release:** Explains that both team members and other physical resources must be released
- **Project Closure Meeting:** Includes project team members, stakeholders, and sponsor
- **Project Closeout Report:** Documents the project outcomes, lessons learned, and other aspects of the project
- **Stakeholder Feedback Collection:** Explains the importance of and the means whereby stakeholder feedback is collected
- **Documentation Archival:** Describes why documentation should be archived
- **Budget Reconciliation:** Covers the process of reconciling the project budget
- **Rewards and Celebration:** Explains the importance of celebrating the project end and rewarding individuals whose efforts were especially important
- **Project Sign-Off:** Discusses formal project sign-off

CHAPTER 12

Closing Phase Activities

The Closing phase completes all project activities. During this phase, the project manager verifies that the project's defined processes are complete. The key purpose of this phase is to close the project formally. Projects are closed when all the work is complete, but they can also be closed prematurely because of project cancellation or critical situations.

In the Closing phase, the project manager closes the project and all procurements that are part of the project. This phase involves the following project activities:

- Project evaluation
- Deliverable validation
- Contract closure
- Access removal
- Resource release
- Project closure meeting
- Project closeout report
- Stakeholder feedback collection
- Documentation archival
- Budget reconciliation
- Rewards and celebration
- Project sign-off

The following sections briefly describe these activities.

This chapter covers the following objective for the CompTIA Project+ exam:

2.5 Explain the importance of activities performed during the Closing phase.

"Do I Know This Already?" Quiz

The "Do I Know This Already?" quiz allows you to assess whether you should read this entire chapter thoroughly or jump to the "Exam Preparation Tasks" section. If you are in doubt about your answers to these questions or your own assessment of your knowledge of the topics, read the entire chapter. Table 12-1 lists the major headings in this chapter and their corresponding "Do I Know This Already?" quiz questions. You can find the answers in Appendix A, "Answers to the 'Do I Know This Already?' Questions and Review Quizzes."

Table 12-1 "Do I Know This Already?" Section-to-Question Mapping

Foundation Topics Section	Questions
Project Evaluation	1
Deliverable Validation	2
Contract Closure	6
Access Removal	5
Resource Release	7
Project Closure Meeting	3
Project Closeout Report	8
Stakeholder Feedback Collection	9
Documentation Archival	10
Budget Reconciliation	11
Rewards and Celebration	12
Project Sign-Off	4

CAUTION The goal of self-assessment is to gauge your mastery of the topics in this chapter. If you do not know the answer to a question or are only partially sure of the answer, you should mark that question as wrong for the purposes of the self-assessment. Giving yourself credit for an answer you correctly guess skews your self-assessment results and might provide you with a false sense of security.

1. Which process within project closure is all about soliciting opinions from project team members and stakeholders?
   a. Deliverable validation
   b. Project evaluation
   c. Budget reconciliation
   d. Document archival

2. Which aspect of project closure likely only involves the project team members and project manager?
   a. Deliverable validation
   b. Project evaluation
   c. Rewards and celebration
   d. Project sign-off

3. Who is most likely responsible for documenting the agenda for the project closure meeting?
   a. Project team members
   b. Project sponsor
   c. Project manager
   d. Project stakeholders

4. Which of the following is *least* likely to take place prior to project closure?
   a. Rewards and celebration
   b. Contract closure
   c. Stakeholder feedback collection
   d. Project sign-off

5. Which aspect of project closure will ensure that assets are properly secured?
   a. Access removal
   b. Budget reconciliation
   c. Documentation archival
   d. Contract closure

6. A procurement needed for your project has been delivered, and payment has been approved. Which project closure process should you implement?
   a. Access removal
   b. Budget reconciliation
   c. Documentation archival
   d. Contract closure

7. Several Windows servers were allocated to your project for the team to use for code development, while others were dedicated to code testing. While the team is still performing testing, all code development activities are complete. You need to ensure that the code development servers are made available for other projects. Which project closure process should you implement?
   a. Access removal
   b. Resource release
   c. Documentation archival
   d. Deliverable validation

8. What is produced from the project closure meeting?
   a. Access removal
   b. Documentation archival
   c. Project closure report
   d. Project sign-off

9. Which closure output is created from meetings, questionnaires, and surveys?
   a. Stakeholder feedback collection
   b. Budget reconciliation
   c. Project closure report
   d. Project sign-off

10. Why is document archival important?
    a. To ensure deliverables meet the stated objectives
    b. To ensure that documents are maintained until they are no longer needed
    c. To document procurement vendor performance
    d. To gain formal approval of project closure

11. During which project closure process are management and contingency reserve usage fully documented?

    a. Document archival

    b. Project closure report

    c. Budget reconciliation

    d. Project sign-off

12. During which project closure process is team member effort recognized?

    a. Project evaluation

    b. Project closure meeting

    c. Budget reconciliation

    d. Rewards and celebration

Foundation Topics

Project Evaluation

The project manager, project sponsor, and key stakeholders evaluate the project and its results. The deliverables should have been evaluated as they were produced, but the ***project evaluation*** ensures that the deliverables provide the needed results. Often project evaluation with stakeholders involves completion of questionnaires and surveys to obtain opinions that are anonymous. The project manager should ensure that the questions include solicitation of both positive and negative information about the project. For any negative feedback given, individuals should be required to provide details about the issue.

EXAMPLE: Suppose stakeholders must provide project feedback where project qualities are ranked on a numbered scale. Automation should be used so that quality scores that are below a certain level require the individual to provide more feedback. This feedback can become part of the project's lessons learned and closeout report.

Deliverable Validation

As deliverables are completed throughout the project, deliverables are examined to ensure they provide the functionality documented in the project or sprint plan. However, at project closure, deliverables should be validated again to ensure they are within the project scope, meet project requirements, and work together for the documented project result. During ***deliverable validation***, any outstanding stakeholder requirements that were not met for whatever reason should be documented and included as part of the closeout report. Often this documentation will then serve as a future guide for improvements or future releases.

All aspects of the project must be validated, including coding deliverables and documentation. It is important to assess deliverables as soon as they are completed to verify that they meet the requirements and do not need rework.

EXAMPLE: A software development project is completed. As part of this project, documentation was created to go along with the software. However, the documentation tasks were not given the priority as the project progressed. While the documents were completed, a technical review of the documents was not always completed. It is discovered that the naming conventions and formatting within the documents do not match. Much rework of the software documentation is required. To prevent the delay of the release of the software, multiple technical writers and editors had to be brought in to complete the documentation. If the documents had been validated at delivery, this issue would have been discovered sooner and likely without the need for more resources or time.

Contract Closure

The project manager must close all project procurement contracts; this is called ***contract closure***. Documenting the vendor's performance and any issues is important to ensure that future project procurements will have this data to analyze. Procurements must be delivered and approved. Once payment has been authorized and completed, the procurement can be closed. This process should be carried out for each procurement as the procurement is completed and based on the contract terms. In many projects, procurements are often closed earlier than the actual project completes.

EXAMPLE: Suppose you are managing a project that includes three procurements—two from one vendor and one from another. According to the three separate procurement contracts, each procurement will be delivered at a different time in the project but much earlier than the project end date. As each procurement is completed, the project manager and team members should examine the procurement to ensure that it meets all the conditions and terms set forth in the contract. Once this validation occurs, and provided no rework is needed, the project manager should authorize payment for the procurement and then close the contract.

Access Removal

As part of any project, team members and stakeholders may be granted both physical and digital access as needed. This may include facility, device, and file access. The project manager should ensure that access that is no longer needed is revoked. ***Access removal*** is particularly important if contractors or stakeholders are external to the organization that sponsored or completed the project.

When considering digital access, project managers should be careful about deletion of user accounts. In many systems, user accounts may become owners of digital assets, particularly those that the users created. User account deletion can result in orphaned objects, such as files, that no one else can access.

EXAMPLE: A project includes multiple in-house team members and contractors. All team members, including contractors, are given the ability to create and edit documents in the project's shared folder. The resource management plan states that when each contractor exits the project, the contractor's user account should be disabled, not deleted. This ensures that any documents or other resources created by the contractor do not become orphaned (and possibly inaccessible by other team members). The default owner of a file or folder is the user who created the resources. The project manager should have full control of the project's shared folder, including the ability to take ownership of files and folders.

Resource Release

During the Closing phase, project managers should formally *release* all resources in use (***resource release***). For personnel, this should include completing an evaluation of the project team member's performance. For equipment, services, supplies, and funds needed to complete the project, the project manager must formally release these assets back to the project sponsor or the owner.

EXAMPLE: A project includes dedicated team members and shared team members. The shared team members have project tasks to complete but must also complete daily tasks as part of their regular jobs. The project also has dedicated access to resources in a lab environment for development and testing purposes. The resource management plan should define the steps that the project manager should complete to release a shared team member from the project, including documenting the team member's accomplishments. This ensures that the shared team member's manager knows when the team member is fully released back to their regular duties. The resource management plan should also define the process whereby the lab resources are reserved for the project and then released once the resources are no longer needed.

Project Closure Meeting

The ***project closure meeting***, also called the ***closeout meeting***, must be held as soon as possible after the sprint, phase, or project is complete to ensure that project information is captured and recorded while the knowledge is still fresh. During this meeting, the attendees should review the project artifacts, especially the risk and issues logs, and decide what the organization can learn from the results. The closure meeting should answer and document questions like these:

- What were the major project successes?
- What were the major challenges?
- What was learned about scheduling, budgeting, risk management, and other aspects of the project?
- Were the right people included in the project team? If not, who could have made the project more successful?
- Were stakeholders and the project sponsor satisfied with the project results?
- Have all contracts and documents been finalized and formally closed, if applicable?

The closure meeting may include the project manager, project team, project sponsor, and project stakeholders. Its primary purpose is to document information that should be included in the closeout report.

EXAMPLE: When a software development project completes, the project manager is responsible for all project closure steps. As part of this process, the project manager should schedule a closure meeting and invite the project team members, major stakeholders, and sponsor. In this meeting, the invitees should discuss project successes and challenges, lessons learned, and other aspects of the project. The project manager should ensure that the closure meeting minutes are documented and stored as part of the project documentation.

Project Closeout Report

The product of the closure meeting is the ***project closeout report***, which includes a "lessons learned" section that is made available to future projects, managers, and teams. This document records any knowledge gained during the project and shows how project issues and events were addressed. ***Lessons learned*** are documented solely to improve future project performance.

NOTE In some cases, confidential information will need to be included in the "lessons learned" document. Any document that includes confidential information should have a defined access control list (ACL) to ensure that only authorized personnel can read that document. If someone needs access and does not have the appropriate permissions, a redacted version of the "lessons learned" document should be provided.

The closure report records the final project sign-off from the sponsor, assesses success, and initiates follow-up activities. It documents best practices for future projects, assigns items to be addressed (issues, future initiatives, future projects, and so on), provides final stakeholder communication, includes a performance analysis, summarizes the project budget, and ensures operational transition.

While the project closeout report is created by the project manager, usually the project manager creates a "draft" version to use during the project closure meeting. The final edition of the project closure report is not completed until after the project closure meeting is over. The project closure report is not considered final until the project sponsor provides formal sign-off.

Stakeholder Feedback Collection

As mentioned earlier in the "Project Evaluation" section, stakeholder feedback should be collected. It can be solicited in a variety of ways, including meetings, questionnaires, and surveys. However, keep in mind that questionnaires and surveys are often better mechanisms for soliciting an individual's true opinion.

Keep in mind that stakeholder feedback should be solicited throughout the project. Feedback can often help the project team make small project corrections throughout the project life cycle rather than discovering at project's end that stakeholders have issues. However, depending on stakeholder analysis, some stakeholders' expectations will affect the project more than other stakeholders' expectations.

Project closure feedback should focus on the successes, challenges, and lessons learned.

Documentation Archival

Project managers must archive all project documents to ensure they are maintained until they are no longer needed. Laws and regulations may govern how long and in what form records must be retained. Project managers should follow set procedures to ensure that the documents are stored in a location and format from which they can be retrieved. This documentation can be used as a baseline for future projects and can help new project managers and team members with future project initiation and planning. In addition, this documentation may have legal or regulatory requirements for retention. If there are legal or regulatory requirements, document archival should be retained for the maximum required by the law/regulation. For example, if a federal law requires that documents be retained for 3 years but a state law requires retention for 5 years, then the organization should ensure that the longer duration is used.

If a centralized project management office (PMO) exists, the project manager should consult with the archival policies that may be established by the PMO.

EXAMPLE: During a project, the project manager has created all the formal project documents, including the project contracts, budget, schedule, project management plan, stakeholder feedback, and meeting minutes. When the project closes, the project manager finalizes all the documentation and then stores it all in the designated project archival folder on the organization's file server. As part of the archival process, the project manager also sets the minimum archival period as deemed by industry regulations.

Budget Reconciliation

Budget reconciliation is the process of reviewing transactions and documentation and resolving any discrepancies that are discovered. It is important that both the transactions and the documentation that supports those transactions are reviewed. The documentation can be in the form of receipts, invoices, purchase orders, time cards, bank statements, and credit card statements. This reconciliation can be completed as transactions are made, on a regular basis, or at the end of the project. However, holding all budget reconciliation to the project's end is not recommended, as it can be a very daunting task.

As part of this reconciliation, a project manager should examine the usage of both management and contingency reserves and ensure that documentation exists to support the usage of the reserves. Proper budget reconciliation also ensures that any leftover funds are returned to the project sponsor.

Rewards and Celebration

Project managers should ensure that the project team and stakeholders take time to celebrate the project closure. While it may not be possible for all team members and stakeholders to participate in a formal celebration meeting, the project manager should still ensure that communication is distributed that celebrates the project closure, recognizes the efforts of the team, and rewards those individuals whose efforts were especially important.

Project managers should make sure that personnel files are updated to include reviews regarding individual performance. Most companies provide an annual review process, but without documenting performance at the project's end, a team member's contribution to the project may not be fully remembered later when the annual review occurs.

Project Sign-Off

The ***project sign-off*** provides a formal method for validating project completion according to the project management plan. The sign-off is usually completed by the project manager and signed by the project sponsor.

While not specifically mentioned as part of project closure, the project manager must also understand operational handoff. Operational handoff is documented during project planning as part of the transition or release plan for an IT project. To close an IT-based project, product, or phase, the completed product or the completed deliverables for the release must be validated against quality requirements, successfully migrated to the live environment, and accepted by the client or sponsor. At this stage, the project team should follow the transition/release plan to train the new product's operators and ensure that control is successfully transferred to the client. Until this operational handoff occurs, the project's results are the responsibility of the project team.

Exam Preparation Tasks

As mentioned in the section "How to Use This Book" in the Introduction, you have a couple of choices for exam preparation: the exercises here, Chapter 17, "Final Preparation," and the exam simulation questions in the Pearson Test Prep Software Online.

Review All Key Topics

Review the most important topics in this chapter, noted with the Key Topics icon in the outer margin of the page. Table 12-2 lists each reference of these key topics and the page number on which each is found.

Table 12-2 Key Topics for Chapter 12

Key Topic Element	Description	Page Number
Paragraph	Describes project evaluation	352
Paragraph	Explains deliverable validation	352
Paragraph	Discusses contract closure	353
Paragraph	Describes the project closure meeting	354
Paragraph	Explains project closeout report	355
Paragraph	Discusses budget reconciliation	356

Define Key Terms

Define the following key terms from this chapter and check your answers in the glossary:

project evaluation, deliverable validation, contract closure, access removal, resource release, project closure meeting, closeout meeting, project closeout report, lessons learned, budget reconciliation, and project sign-off

Review Questions

The answers to these questions appear in Appendix A. For more practice with sample exam questions, use the Pearson Test Prep practice test software online.

1. You are documenting the lessons learned for a project that researched a new product line for your company. You release the project resources and obtain project sign-off from the project sponsor. Which project phase are you completing?
   a. Initiating
   b. Planning
   c. Closing
   d. Executing

2. Which of the following is *least* likely to provide data to use in the closeout report?
   a. Project evaluation
   b. Deliverable validation
   c. Stakeholder feedback collection
   d. Access removal

3. Throughout the project, vendors complete and deliver project procurements. Which aspect of project closure is this likely to affect?
   a. Project evaluation
   b. Resource release
   c. Contract closure
   d. Documentation archival

4. You are documenting the usage of management and contingency reserves. Which aspect of project closure are you completing?
   a. Budget reconciliation
   b. Documentation archival
   c. Stakeholder feedback
   d. Resource release

5. During project closure, you ask a systems administrator to provide an audit report of accounts that were used by your project team to access the system. You have asked the systems administrator to provide the last login date for each team member's account. The team consisted of both internal employees and outside contractors. Which process within project closure are you likely completing?
   a. Project evaluation
   b. Access removal
   c. Documentation archival
   d. Rewards and celebration

6. Which of the following project closure activities is likely to be revised based on the closure meeting?
   a. Budget reconciliation
   b. Contract closure
   c. Documentation archival
   d. Project closeout report

7. Which of the following is *least* likely to be part of the rewards and celebration activity during project closure?
   a. A team member obtained new skills during the project.
   b. A team member completed a training course during the project.
   c. A team member was given a raise during the project.
   d. A team member successfully passed a certification during the project.

8. Which of the following is likely the most effective way of collecting stakeholder feedback?
   a. Questionnaires and surveys
   b. Interviews and meetings
   c. Interviews and questionnaires
   d. Meetings and surveys

9. Which of the following is *least* likely to have an effect on project documentation archival?

   a. Project manager

   b. Project team members

   c. Project management office

   d. Project sponsor

10. You are managing a data center remodel project. During the project, several skilled laborers who are employees of the sponsoring organization are used to help with the facilities redesign. You have moved to the phase where the new networking and storage equipment and computers are being installed. Which activity will ensure that the laborers can return to their regular job tasks?

    a. Access removal

    b. Contract closure

    c. Budget reconciliation

    d. Resource release

This chapter covers the following topics:

- **Tracking Charts and Diagrams:** Gantt charts, milestone charts, burnup and burndown charts, project network diagrams, PERT charts, process diagrams, and project organizational charts
- **Project Management Tools:** Risk register, issue log, defect log, change control log/change log, and requirements traceability matrix; project dashboards, project status reports, and risk reports; version control tools, time-tracking tools, and task board
- **Scheduling and Ticketing/Case Management Tools:** Project management scheduling tools (in the cloud, on-premises, and locally installed) and ticketing/case management systems
- **Communication Tools:** Email, messaging, telephone, meetings/face-to-face communication, video and remote conferencing, and enterprise social media; meeting tools, including surveys/polling, calendaring tools, print media, and conferencing platforms
- **Collaboration Tools:** Real-time multi-author editing software, file sharing platforms, workflow and e-signature platforms, whiteboards, wikis, and vendor knowledge bases
- **Documentation and Office Production Tools:** Word processing, spreadsheets, presentations, and charting/diagramming software

CHAPTER 13

Project Management Tools

This chapter covers some of the most important tools in the project management process. While most have already been mentioned in this book, this chapter delves into the details of how they are constructed and how they serve the work of project management. Each type of tool described in this chapter fulfills a specific need within the project, such as predicting scheduling conflicts, analyzing task performance, or graphically depicting quality issues. After the project closes, the artifacts become valuable data repositories to guide future planning.

The project manager should fully research features and select the best available tools for the job, though some projects will be limited to tools already selected by their organization or PMO.

> **NOTE** Do not expect to be tested on specific name-brand tools. These objectives test your understanding of the purposes of these tools and when you would select them.

This chapter covers the following objectives for the CompTIA Project+ exam:

3.1 Given a scenario, use the appropriate tools throughout the project life cycle.

3.2 Compare and contrast various project management productivity tools.

"Do I Know This Already?" Quiz

The "Do I Know This Already?" quiz allows you to assess whether you should read this entire chapter thoroughly or jump to the "Exam Preparation Tasks" section. If you are in doubt about your answers to these questions or your own assessment of your knowledge of the topics, read the entire chapter. Table 13-1 lists the major headings in this chapter and their corresponding "Do I Know This Already?" quiz questions. You can find the answers in Appendix A, "Answers to the 'Do I Know This Already?' Questions and Review Quizzes."

Table 13-1 "Do I Know This Already?" Section-to-Question Mapping

Foundation Topics Section	Questions
Tracking Charts and Diagrams	1–4
Project Management Tools	5–7
Scheduling and Ticketing/Case Management Tools	8–9
Communication Tools	10
Collaboration Tools	11
Documentation and Office Production Tools	12

CAUTION The goal of self-assessment is to gauge your mastery of the topics in this chapter. If you do not know the answer to a question or are only partially sure of the answer, you should mark that question as wrong for the purposes of the self-assessment. Giving yourself credit for an answer you correctly guess skews your self-assessment results and might provide you with a false sense of security.

1. You are using values of most optimistic, most pessimistic, and most realistic to estimate project task durations and are putting the results in a project network diagram. What are you creating?
   a. Velocity chart
   b. Gantt chart
   c. PERT chart
   d. Forward pass

2. Which document should the project manager use to determine the reporting structure for project team members?
   a. Precedence network diagram
   b. RACI matrix
   c. Organizational chart
   d. Project charter
   e. Requirements traceability matrix

3. During a project status meeting with senior management, the project manager shows a chart that displays project time on the x-axis (horizontal) and budget on the y-axis (vertical). There are two trend lines that run from the upper-left

corner down to the lower-right corner of the chart. What is the purpose of the chart?

a. To show the budget expended to date against the planned value
b. To show the remaining time allocated to the sprint
c. To show the story point velocity against the budget baseline
d. To show the budget baseline against the schedule baseline

4. Which statement best describes the purpose of Gantt charts, PNDs, and PERT charts?

a. To graphically depict the relationships between project deliverables
b. To graphically depict the variance between the schedule baseline and actual work
c. To graphically depict the variance between the planned scope and actual scope
d. To graphically depict the sequence of tasks in a schedule

5. Which document would *best* convey the overall level of risk in a given project?

a. Risk report
b. Project charter
c. Risk management plan
d. Risk register

6. A stakeholder thinks that the project is over budget, but the project manager does not have time to prepare a current budget report. Which project tool is *most* likely to help the stakeholder?

a. Dashboard
b. Latest status report
c. Budget baseline
d. Project charter

7. Which project document lists problems that occur during project execution that are *not* on the risk register?

a. Status report
b. Issue log
c. Action items
d. Defect log

8. Which project tool is used mainly to track project activities, their durations, and the personnel assigned to them?
    a. Spreadsheet applications
    b. Ticketing software
    c. Case management system
    d. Project scheduling software

9. What *best* describes the purpose of a case management system?
    a. To ensure source code in a repository does not branch
    b. To consolidate bug reports for further action
    c. To maintain version control for project management plan documents
    d. To ensure projects in a program are uniformly managed

10. Which tool would be most suitable for obtaining real-time opinions from team members and avoiding consensus-driven opinion-making during a meeting?
    a. Anonymous polling via a live video conference platform
    b. Emailed surveys sent after a status report meeting
    c. One-to-one text messaging on mobile phones
    d. Writing responses in a real-time multi-authoring document

11. Which characteristic of a wiki is both an advantage and a disadvantage in a team environment?
    a. Wikis are less expensive than other content management systems.
    b. Wikis do not require expertise in web content development.
    c. Wikis can be edited by anyone on the team.
    d. Wikis capture organizational knowledge.

12. Which tool would be the *most* useful when preparing for a product demonstration before a live audience?
    a. Diagramming software
    b. Presentation software
    c. An online task board
    d. The project dashboard

Foundation Topics

Tracking Charts and Diagrams

By their very nature, projects create large amounts of raw data that must be analyzed to reveal trends before it can be useful to stakeholders. Charts and diagrams can put the data into a format that is more easily understood, especially when shared in meetings with low-information or high-priority stakeholders. A chart can be used both to analyze data and to display the results of an analysis.

Gantt Chart

A ***Gantt chart*** is a sophisticated bar chart that displays a project's scheduled activities or tasks over time, often including the activity's dependencies and relationships. Gantt charts are one of the main tools used for project scheduling and can also depict the project schedule baseline. The left side of the chart lists the activities, and the top or bottom of the chart shows the time scale. The length and position of the bars within the grid depict each activity's start date, duration, and end date (see Figure 13-1). A Gantt chart can display all of the following schedule characteristics:

- Project activities
- Activity start and end dates
- Activity durations
- Activity overlap
- Project start and end dates
- Dependencies between activities (not shown on the sample chart but frequently included in real charts)

Gantt charts may be modified to include information about the resources allocated to the activity, add milestones as zero-duration tasks, and mark critical activities. Gantt charts are developed during project planning and are heavily referred to during the Execution and Closing phases. They include all project-related tasks, not just team activities, but can be modified to display only the activities in a certain phase or period of time.

Task	2022							2023				
	Jun	Jul	Aug	Sept	Oct	Nov	Dec	Jan	Feb	Mar	Apr	May
1. Find Sponsor												
2. Analyze Collected Data												
3. Summer Report												
4. Database Design												
5. ER Model												
6. Coding Applications												
7. Progress Report												
8. Implementation of Database												
9. Testing and Evaluation												
10. Final Report												
11. Poster												
12. Oral Presentation												
13. Project Demonstration												

Figure 13-1 Example of a Gantt Chart

Milestone Chart

A ***milestone chart*** is more complex than a ***project roadmap*** but simpler than a Gantt. It shows significant events in the project's life cycle in relation to the timeline. This chart is included in an early form in the project charter and the kickoff meeting, revised as the schedule is planned, and revised again as schedules change. While it can be depicted in a Gantt-style bar chart, it is most commonly shown as a linear chart (see Figure 13-2) and generated from the schedule data using project management software. Milestones may also be grouped by their dependency on one another and then color-coded or given a certain shape to show that relationship. For example, if features within an application are being developed separately, but each feature has several milestones, you could give each feature its own color. A milestone chart is best suited for reporting progress in status meetings and for publishing to project dashboards.

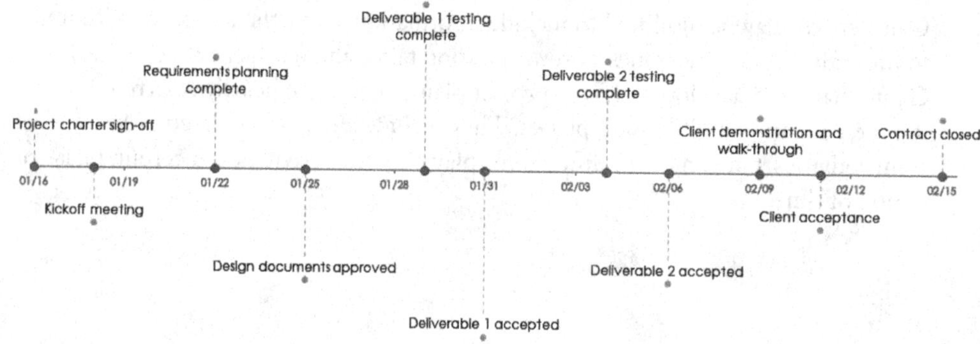

Figure 13-2 Example of a Milestone Chart

Budget Burndown Charts

Burnup and burndown charts (covered in the next chapter) are primarily used as Agile tools for tracking activity progress in a sprint. However, the burndown format is also useful for cost reporting. A ***budget burndown chart*** shows time on the x-axis (horizontal) and budget on the y-axis, with the budget as a line that starts at the upper left (no time elapsed, maximum budget) and slants down to the right to terminate at zero (no dollars or days remaining). A second line shows the actual money spent to date.

The burndown report in Figure 13-3 has a budget of $300,000 allocated across 1 year. The actual expenditures line terminates at the start of the 8th month, indicating that the project has just finished its 7th month of work. This chart tells you the following:

- At the beginning of the 4th month, expenditures were under budget (the project had spent less than the planned value to date).
- At the end of 7 months, expenditures were over budget (the project had spent more than the planned value to date).

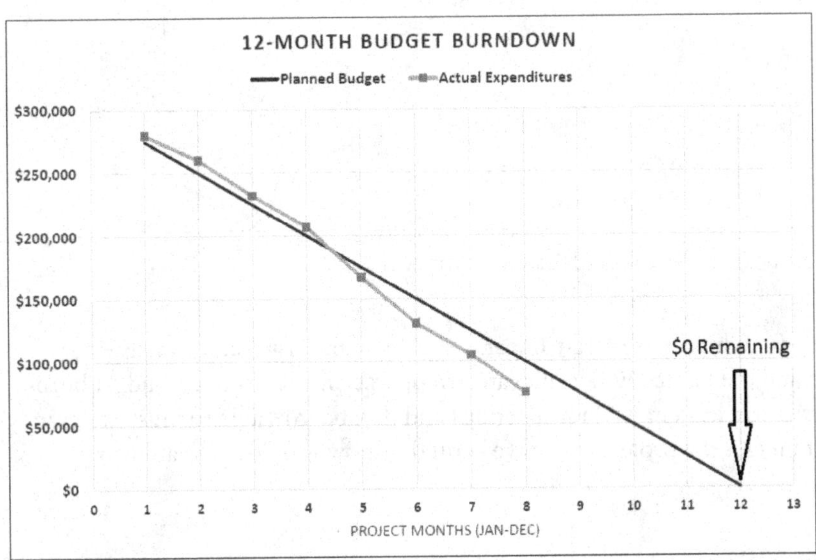

Figure 13-3 Example of a Budget Burndown Chart

When reading a budget burndown report, remember these two key visual relationships:

- If the actual expenditures line is *above* the planned value line, then the project has spent *less* budget than allocated to date, and the ***burn rate*** is less than 1.

- If the actual expenditures line is *below* the planned value line, then the project has spent *more* budget than allocated to date, and the burn rate is greater than 1.

Figure 13-4 shows the same chart with an additional trend line (the dashed line) based on actual expenditures. *If* the project continued to spend money at the same rate, it would run out of funds in the middle of the 10th month, and the project would end the year approximately $50,000 over budget.

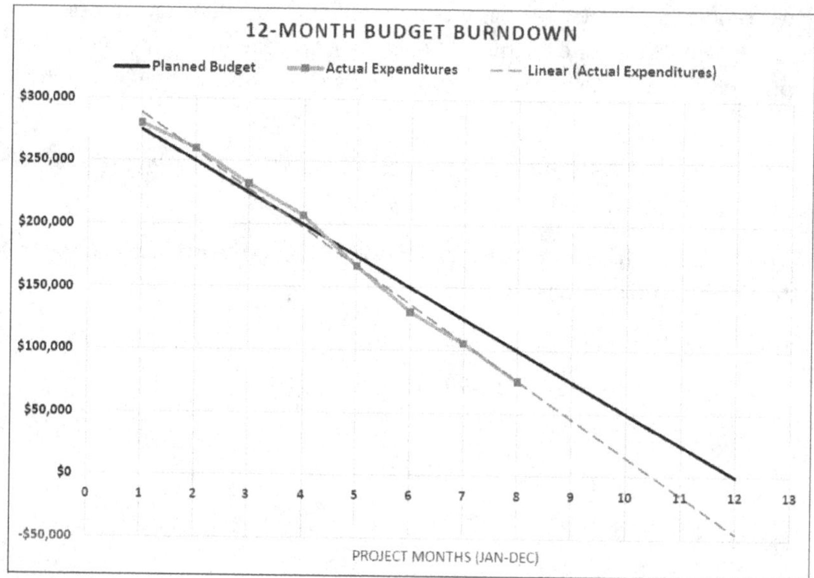

Figure 13-4 Example of a Progressed Budget Burndown Chart

In real life, expenditures are rarely linear. There may be large early expenses for equipment and then a steady rate allocated to operations. However, a budget burndown chart is an excellent tool for meetings and dashboards, able to illustrate exactly how far off budget the project may have drifted or how well its costs are being managed.

Project Network Diagram

A project network diagram (PND) refers to any schedule-tracking tool that shows activities over time and their relationships in a format that resembles a flowchart so that all tasks can be seen in relation to one another. It serves as a basis for determining the critical path (the project path with the longest duration), the activity early start/finish dates (using a forward pass), the activity late start/finish dates (using a backward pass), and activity precedence relationships. Both PERT charts and critical path diagrams are project network diagrams. (Refer to Figures 5-2 and 5-4 to see critical path diagrams.)

Another way to depict project network diagrams is by using a ***precedence diagram method (PDM)***. Figure 13-5 shows a simple PDM diagram with task relationships shown. The diagram shows that task B cannot start until both tasks A and E have started and that task I must start before tasks G and J can start, among other precedence relationships.

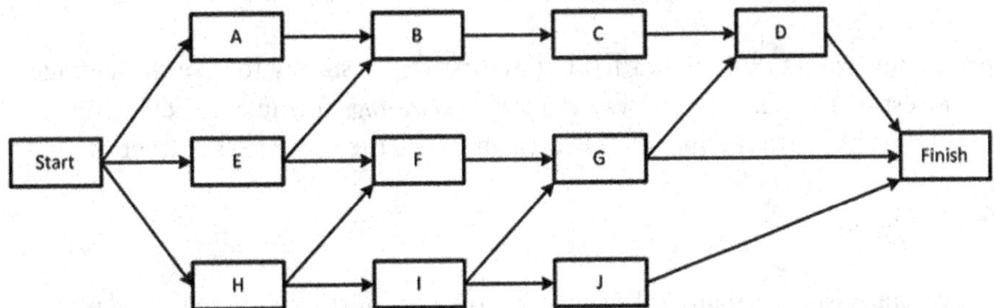

Figure 13-5 Example of a Simple Precedence Diagram Method (PDM) Diagram

While a network diagram initially only shows activities and relationships, it is developed throughout schedule planning to include task durations, early and late start and finish dates, and the other components mentioned earlier. It is primarily a project team tool, as it is usually a bit too complicated for stakeholders. (You may also see these referred to as activity-on-node or AON diagrams.) Figure 13-6 shows a finished PND with a high level of detail regarding task durations, including early and late start and finish estimates.

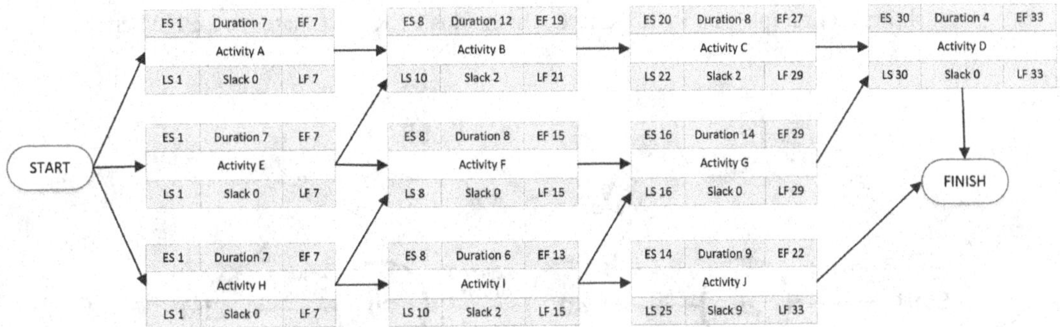

Figure 13-6 Example of a Detailed Project Network Diagram Showing Activity Estimates

Program Evaluation Review Technique (PERT) Chart

A ***Program Evaluation Review Technique (PERT)*** chart is a PDM that identifies activities, durations, and dependencies between the activities and then uses a

technique known as the *three-point estimate* to calculate the task durations. A three-point estimate is used when there is no historical task data available and is one of the more accurate methods available. Using expert judgement, the project manager gathers three estimates of the time it will take to complete an activity:

- **Best case**: Most optimistic estimate (O), the shortest time frame
- **Worst case**: Most pessimistic estimate (P), the longest time frame
- **Most realistic**: Most likely estimate (L), the probable time frame

There are a few ways to calculate PERT. The first way is simply to take the average of all three estimates. The second way is a *weighted average* formula, which assigns four times the weight to the most likely estimate as to the other two estimates:

$$O + P + (4 \times L) / 6$$

If the most optimistic estimate is 4 days, the most pessimistic estimate is 12 days, and the most likely estimate is 8 days, the PERT value would also be 8 days:

$$4 + 12 + (4 \times 8) / 6 = 8$$

PERT charts are represented by lines and nodes. The biggest difference between PERT and PDM is that PERT uses the three-point estimate. In traditional PERT diagramming, the activities are arrows and the nodes are milestone events. (You may also see these referred to as activity-on-arrow or AOA diagrams.) Recent standards have merged the PERT three-point averaging technique with PDM because PDM is more widely used. However, the PERT technique gives more accurate estimates. Figure 13-7 shows an example of a PERT chart, which adds PERT estimates to a PDM chart.

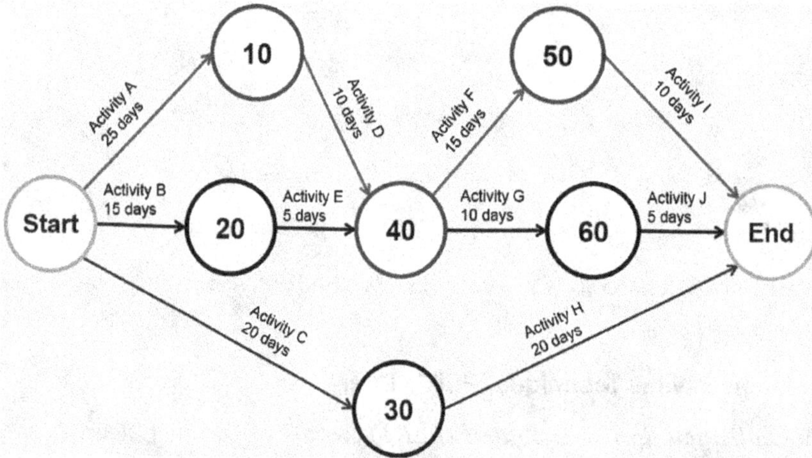

Figure 13-7 Example of a PERT Chart

Process Diagram

A ***process diagram*** or ***flowchart*** is a sequential breakdown of the steps required to complete a business process, displayed in relation to each other. It includes the sequence of actions, inputs, and outputs for each step, decision points, personnel involved, and time required. Process diagrams should be created for any procedure that is part of the project or necessary for its completion, particularly business, fulfillment, and manufacturing processes. Completed process diagrams, as shown in Figure 13-8, can be analyzed to find potential improvements or to understand why a process is vital to the project. These diagrams can also be used to demonstrate to team members, clients, and stakeholders how a process is conducted.

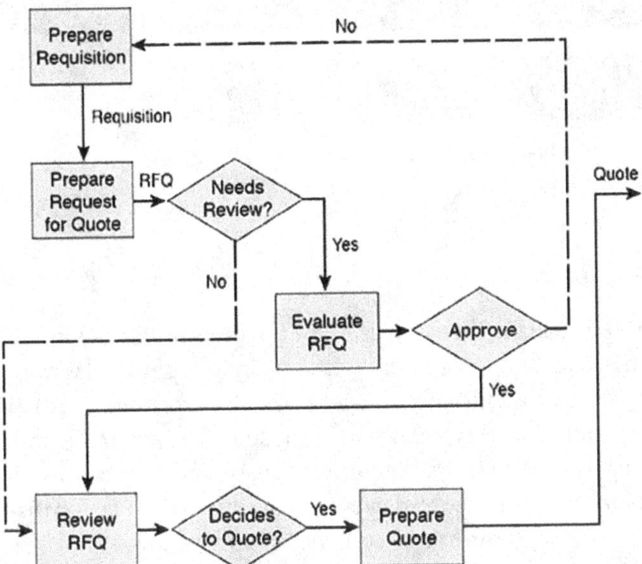

Figure 13-8 Example of a Procurement Process Diagram

Project Organizational Chart

A ***project organizational chart*** is a diagram that shows the structure and hierarchy of the project team, including extended and core team members, and the stakeholders within the organization: the sponsor, the steering committee, and senior management. The chart clarifies authority and removes ambiguity from project work. In some cases, you may also need to document the overall organizational chart, particularly if the project is sharing team members with functional department heads. It is a good practice to include titles in an organizational chart. In addition to Figure 13-9, you should refer to Figures 2-1 through 2-5 in Chapter 2, "Team and Resource Management," to see other examples of organizational charts.

Project Organization Chart

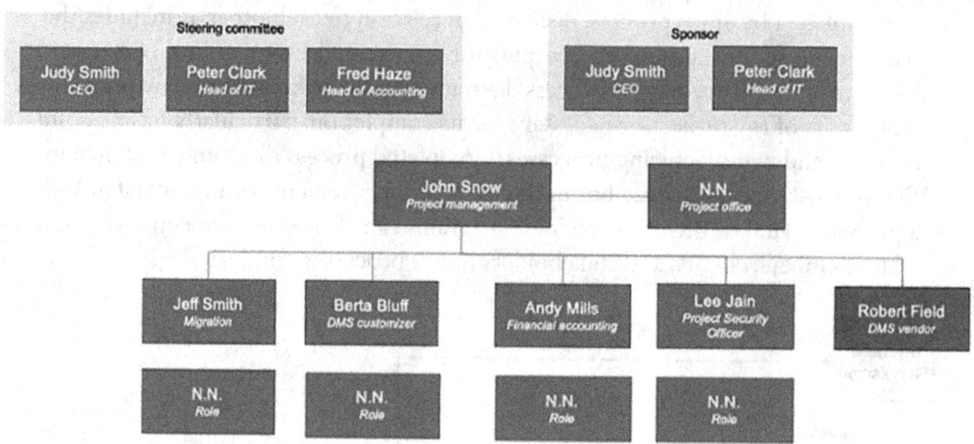

Figure 13-9 Example of a Project Organizational Chart

Project Management Tools

Logs and registers are vital to project management. All of the tools in this section are primarily used during the Executing phase, though some may begin in Planning. In particular, the issue log, change log, and risk register track all events that could affect the project's triple constraints of cost, scope, and schedule. The ***defect log*** and the ***requirements traceability matrix*** manage the project's scope and quality. Logs and registers show both resolved and unresolved events, ensuring that no factor that could impact the project slips through the cracks and goes unaddressed.

NOTE Risk registers, change logs, issue logs, and defect logs are all structured similarly. The following exhibits show detailed excerpts from a risk log as well as higher-level overviews of the other three logs.

Risk Register

The ***risk register*** template is part of the risk management plan. The actual risk register is created during project planning and should contain basic risk notes, risk assessment information, and risk response details. Each risk in the register has a unique risk ID for that project. New risks should be added to the risk register as they are discovered. Old risks should not be deleted, even if they are no longer judged as risks or if they become issues.

Figures 13-10a, 13-10b, and 13-10c show three sections of a sample risk register. (In practice, these sections would be contiguous columns on a spreadsheet, but here they are separated for readability.)

1. BASIC RISK INFORMATION				
Risk Number	**Risk Description / Risk Event Statement**	**Responsible**	**Date Reported Day-Month-Year**	**Last Update Day-Month-Year**
Provide a unique identifier for risk.	A risk event statement states (i) what might happen in the future and (ii) its possible impact on the project. "Weather" is not a risk event statement. "Bad weather may delay the project" is a risk event statement.	Name or title of team member responsible for risk.	Enter the date the risk was first reported.	Enter the date the risk (not the entire log) was updated.
Example R1	Concrete prices may increase, causing the project to go over budget.	Materials Acquisition Manager	1-Dec-2023	12-Jan-2024

Figure 13-10a Risk Register Template: Basic Risk Information

2. RISK ASSESSMENT INFORMATION					
Risk Number	**Impact H / M / L**	**Impact Description**	**Probability H / M / L**	**Timeline N / M / F**	**Status of Response N / P / PE / EE**
	Enter here **H** (High); **M** (Medium); or **L** (Low) according to impact definitions.	List the specific impact the risk could have on the project schedule, budget, scope, and quality. Other impacts can also be listed.	Enter here **H** (High); **M** (Medium); or **L** (Low) according to probability definitions.	Enter here **N** (Near-term); **M** (Medium-term); or **F** (Far-term) according to timeline definitions.	Enter here **N** (No plan); **P** (Planned but not enacted); **PE** (Plan enacted but effectiveness not yet known); or **EE** (Plan enacted and effective).
R1	M	The cost of the concrete could be as much as 50% more expensive than budgeted, resulting in an overall cost overrun of 15% on the budget.	H	M	PE

Figure 13-10b Risk Register Template: Risk Assessment Information

3. RISK RESPONSE INFORMATION			
Risk Number	Completed Actions	Planned Future Actions	Risk Status Open / Closed / Moved to Issue
	List, by date, all actions taken to respond to the risk. This does not include assessing the risk.	List, by date, what will be done in the future to respond to the risk.	State here if the risk is **Open** (still might happen and still has to be managed); **Closed** (has passed or has been mitigated successfully); or **Moved to Issue** (risk has happened).
R1	10-Jan-2024: Asked concrete supplier to guarantee a price; request denied.	12-Jan-2024: Investigating cost of purchasing materials now and storing them until needed.	Open

Figure 13-10c Risk Register Template: Risk Response Information

Basic risk notes in the risk register should include the following:

- **Risk number**: A unique identifier for the risk
- **Risk description**: What event might happen to affect the project
- **Impact description**: Which specific aspect(s) of the project would be affected, such as budget or scope
- **Responsibility**: Who is responsible for handling the risk
- **Status**: Current status, such as *open* (still could happen), *closed* (has passed or been successfully mitigated), or *moved to issue* (risk has occurred)

Risk assessment information in the risk register could also cover the following:

- **Date reported**: When the risk was originally reported (leave blank if the risk has not occurred).
- **Last update**: When the risk information was last updated (as during a risk review).

- **Impact level**: How much effect the risk could have, as determined by the risk assessment.
- **Probability**: The assessed likelihood that the risk will occur.
- **Timeline**: When the risk could occur (usually given in broad terms like *near term*, *medium term*, and *long term*).
- **Status of response**: Whether plans have been made for responding to the risk.

Other risk response details could include completed actions (such as actions taken to avoid or mitigate the risk) or planned future actions intended to address the risk.

Issue Log

As discussed in Chapter 4, "Risk and Issue Management," issues are uncontrolled events that occur during project execution, such as a power outage, and must be resolved for work to move forward. Issues may have occurred from known, logged risks or from unknown risks. Regardless of origin, the ***issue log*** or issue register tracks all problems or events that currently affect project work and require a response.

Like changes, risks, defects, and requirements, issues should be fully tracked via a numbering system with a unique issue ID assigned to each entry. The issue log should also track the issue's priority, its impact, the issue type, its owner, the target resolution date, and the status (open/active or closed). If the issue arose from a realized risk, the corresponding risk ID could be added to the issue's entry in the log; you could also amend the risk register to note where a risk materialized as an issue. Issue logs from old projects can be analyzed to help identify risks for a current project, because issues often arise as unanticipated risks that were not recorded during project planning.

Remember that risks may become issues, but not all issues start as risks. Issues that might occur again can be judged as risks and retroactively added to the risk register if the project manager thinks that a plan for them should be formalized. Figure 13-11 shows a sample issue log.

ID	Name	Comments	Type	Priority	Status	Responsible	Opening date	Closing date
I-1	RAM shortage at supplier	Supplier does not have enough RAM for all the desktops needing upgrades. Follow up: 11/3 - Urged Thomas (Supplier Manager) to get more RAM. 11/28 - Thomas confirmed the arrival of RAM.	Procurement	2	Closed	Thomas from supplier "Electronix" Tel. 111-222-3333	10/28	12/15
I-2	Employee shortage in IT department	The IT department has been having trouble retaining technicians. There might not be enough technicians to handle the upgrade workload. Next step: 1) Request all IT personnel, no matter their level, to help, or 2) contract with a local computer repair store to provide the labor	Risk	1	Open	John, IT department head	11/28	
I-3	Locked offices in Accounting department	Offices in the Accounting department were locked and therefore inaccessible Follow up: 12/21 Contacted Judy, department head - waiting to hear back 12/23 Office will reopen 12/27 regular office, upgrades scheduled for then	Time	3	Open	Judy	12/20	

Figure 13-11 Example of an Issue Log

Change Log

Chapter 3, "Change Control Process Throughout the Project Life Cycle," describes the change control log (or change log) and its general layout. As with risks, defects, and issues, all changes should have a unique ID and an owner (who is either the requestor or the person responsible for implementing the change). The change log is continually updated throughout project execution as changes are implemented. Activity in the change log is shared in status reports and status meetings. You can refer to Figure 3-2 for an example of a change log.

Requirements Traceability Matrix

Requirements that are approved during scope planning or solution design are classified into categories and documented in the ***requirements traceability matrix (RTM)***. The purpose of the RTM is to ensure requirements are correctly incorporated into the product or have a documented reason for being rejected. A standard RTM is a table or document that follows each requirement through the project life cycle and maps it to project objectives and/or the work breakdown structure (WBS). For IT projects, it may map to a component in the architectural design. All functional or nonfunctional requirements will be given a unique ID and linked to a business requirement. (If there is no matching business requirement, then a functional requirement has no basis for inclusion in the project.)

A requirement is not considered complete until it has been tested. The RTM should include testing specifications and test results and should be traceable both backwards and forwards, from the end artifact or test to the requirement that prompted it and vice versa. If defects are found during testing, they should be added to the RTM along with their unique defect ID(s) from the defect log. If the requirements have legal or regulatory implications, the RTM should be maintained after the project closes for auditing purposes. Figure 13-12 shows a sample RTM generated from a template.

Requirements Traceability Matrix									
Project Name:									
Project Description:									
Project Manager:									
ID	**Functional Requirements Description**	**Business Requirements Description**	**Functional Requirements ID**	**Current Status**	**Architectural /Design Document:**	**Department Impacted**	**Test Scenario ID**	**Test Case ID**	**Defect ID**	**Tracking Comments**
001										
002										

Figure 13-12 Example of a Requirements Traceability Matrix Template

Defect Log

A *defect* is a flawed project component or deliverable that fails to meet requirements for performance, quality, or functionality. The term is most often used in IT projects, where a defect can be a bug that affects behavior, a missing functional requirement, or some other malfunction. All defects should be tracked in the defect log and assigned a unique ID. If the defect was uncovered during a test scenario, the defect ID should be added to the RTM, and both the test scenario or test case ID and the requirement ID should be added to the defect log. The ***defect log*** should include the results of the failed test, the conditions that caused it to occur and how to reproduce it, and the current status (such as open, fixed, or in progress). Defects, like risks and issues, are assigned owners. The defect log should list the defect owner and the steps taken to rectify the defect in the current deliverable and prevent the defect in future deliverables.

In software development projects, defects are assessed based on their impact to the deployed code or application or by the priority of the requirement. Ranking defects by their impact and priority is usually done with qualitative measurements, such as high, low, urgent, and critical. Lower-priority or low-impact defects are likely to go into the backlog rather than being addressed in the current sprint. The defect log should always be available to project team members.

Project Dashboard

A type of graphical report called a ***project dashboard*** dynamically displays important project status information, usually including key performance indicators, project metrics, current progress, and related issues. It gives stakeholders and team members a quick look at the overall project without overwhelming the audience. Project management software or standalone dashboard applications allow the project manager to customize the information available on the dashboard. For example, the project manager may decide to create one dashboard with summary data for stakeholders and a separate dashboard for project team members with more detailed information. Views can be filtered based on the stakeholder's need to access information, such as cost and budget expenditures. Here are some common dashboard formats:

- **Burndown dashboard:** Shows how many activities are completed and what is left to be done
- **Cost overview dashboard:** Displays the current cost status of the project, usually including planned costs, remaining costs, actual costs, cumulative costs, baseline costs, and percentage of completion
- **Project overview dashboard:** Reports project phase, percentage of activities completed, milestones, and past due activities
- **Sprint dashboard:** A team-focused dashboard that shows sprint-related metrics such as velocity, task status, story points, highest priority defects, and total worked hours
- **Work overview dashboard:** Includes a work burndown for the project and the work statistics for all top-level tasks to help determine the percentage of completion and remaining work

Popular project management applications with dashboard functionality include Microsoft Project, Asana, Basecamp, Mavenlink, and Smartsheet. A quick search online for "project overview dashboard images" will present plenty of ideas for constructing useful dashboards for your project and help you identify their general formats and purpose at a glance.

Project Status Report

A ***project status report*** provides the latest information on project activities, issues, changes, and risks. It is a summary document sent to the project sponsor and any stakeholders who need aggregated information. These reports are also distributed and discussed in status meetings. Status reports ensure that stakeholders who do not attend the status meeting still understand the project's current status. They can also be shared with external clients and stakeholders. The latest status report should be incorporated into the project dashboard, and charts from the dashboard may be part of the written status report.

Status reports should be tailored for internal and external audiences. An internal status report should include high-level information about changes that were approved and implemented since the last status report, newly realized or resolved risks, a high-level view of opened or closed issues, milestones reached, budget performance, and schedule performance. A client-facing or customer-facing status report would summarize project progress, milestones achieved, budget spent or remaining, and artifacts delivered. Internal status reports give stakeholders the insight needed to prioritize the project's next steps, while external status reports should share the progress gained to date from the time and budget spent.

Risk Report

A ***risk report*** summarizes individual project risk information and describes the overall level of risk exposure in the project. Unlike a risk register, a risk report provides a narrative analysis of project risks and helps guide decision-making among stakeholders. It would include a list of all project risks ranked by their priority, the types and categories of risk represented, observable trends, and forecasted risk status. The report would also list the risks with the highest risk scores along with high-level recommendations for handling the most threatening or most opportunistic risks. If risks have been realized, the report should summarize the realized risks, the response taken, and the risk's impact to the scope, timeline, and budget. The risk report is continually revised during project execution and distributed according to the communication plan.

Version Control Tools

Document ***version control*** tracks and labels project documents across different stages of distribution, revision, and archiving, with changes noted by author and date. Version control can be handled with a simple spreadsheet and a policy, or with a commercial- or enterprise-level document and records management system. These tools provide a central repository and features to enable finer control over document flow, such as rollbacks and file check-in/check-out systems. Regardless of the tool chosen to handle documents, the project manager should establish three tenets for document versioning:

- File naming conventions that keep filenames consistent and predictable.
- Document versioning conventions, such as V0.0.1, V1, V1.0.2, and V2.0, that indicate when the file was last modified and whether it was a major or minor revision.
- A central method of tracking the author, date, and revision number of each released version.

Major project documents should be clearly labeled with the date and version, such as the circulated draft or the approved final. Only the latest version of project documents should be in circulation, but the record management plan might dictate that drafts and prior versions be retained for reference.

In software development, version control systems manage source code so that multiple developers can make changes to the application without overwriting each other or causing the source version to fork. Two common tools are Microsoft Azure DevOps Server and Git. Both systems have check-in/check-out versioning, use hashing to compare file integrity, allow changes to be selectively rolled back, and support a variety of third-party tools for the automated building and deployment of common applications. Version control in the context of continuous integration/continuous delivery (CI/CD) and code repositories is covered in Chapter 16, "Foundational IT Concepts and Operational Change Control for IT Project Management."

Time-Tracking Tools

Time-tracking tools differ from project scheduling software in that they allow a project manager to track time spent by the project team on different project activities, and they allow team members to log their time spent on individual tasks. Whereas a Gantt chart might designate 3 days for task A, a time-tracking tool can log that the team member actually worked 4 hours on Monday, 6 hours on Tuesday, and 2.5 hours on Wednesday to finish the task. Keeping logs of actual (instead of estimated) time spent in activities makes future estimates more accurate, and it can also reveal where a team member would benefit from training or support. Contract and part-time employees may need their overall hours tracked to accurately calculate base pay and overtime, so time-tracking also assists with payroll and budget activity.

Most project management software includes time-tracking capabilities of some kind, but standalone tools also exist. Time can be tracked by installing a browser plug-in that logs time spent using a specific application or with a counter that the team member clicks on or off as they move from task to task. Hours worked can be aggregated from RFID card swipes at secured doors or badge entry logs.

Task Board

A ***task board*** represents current project work in a visual flow, much like a Kanban board. Task boards can be part of an online project tool like a dashboard, or they can be an actual physical whiteboard with notecards or sticky notes for each individual task. As tasks on the board are begun, handled, and completed, they are moved from activity zone to activity zone, commonly referred to as lanes or swimlanes. Lanes represent common processes, such as "Testing," "In Development," and "For Defect Repair." The task cards (whether physical or virtual) are labeled with the responsible team member's name. Task boards are a common scrum tool used to visually organize the tasks to perform in the current sprint. (Both Kanban boards and scrum were covered in Chapter 1, "Project Characteristics, Methodologies, and Frameworks.")

Scheduling and Ticketing/Case Management Tools

Having just the right tool can make the project manager's job much easier. Modern project scheduling software (both programs and apps) supports "what-if" scenarios, tracks project efficiency, and analyzes schedules by using customizable Gantt charts and other tools. Ticketing and case management tools centralize defect reporting and tracking and request handling. The project manager needs to consider whether to include the ability to run on multiple operating systems and the option to work in the cloud or via local installation.

Project Management Scheduling Tools

Project scheduling software allows the project manager to enter the raw data for project tasks, project resources, and task durations, displaying the results in multiple common formats as needed. Most project scheduling software also includes the ability to create custom charts and reports. The ability to quickly create, update, and share these charts means everyone stays on the same page when it comes to tasks, dependencies, responsibilities, and deadlines.

The selection of software tools is often influenced by their price as much as their usability. For example, Microsoft Project is a popular choice, but it can be expensive; Microsoft Project Pro for Office 365 is offered as a per-user license, which can be cheaper than the full Project software suite if you only require a few licenses. Other commercial options include Asana, Zoho Projects, FastTrack Schedule, Monday.com, and Workfront.

Cloud-Based Solutions

Venders such as Microsoft offer monthly cloud-based solution payment plans as well as on-premises standard, professional, and server-based solutions. A cloud-based solution allows for easy access to the application from any device with an Internet connection and a web browser. Cloud-based solutions are usually purchased with a monthly or annual subscription or licensed per user. Access and storage fees are usually their only expenditures. However, long-term use might end up costing more than an up-front purchase for on-premises or local installation.

On-Premises Solutions

An on-premises solution is installed by the organization on an organization's assets and can only be accessed from the organization's hardware; this can include the internal network or intranet. If an on-premises solution is provided through the organization's network, users will have to be inside the facility to connect to it. If they are remote, they must use a virtual private network (VPN) connection to reach the internal network from their location. The organization must buy or license the solution and either purchase or maintain the hardware (including database storage) that runs it.

Local Installation

A local installation means that a full copy of the software or application is installed on your organization's own hardware, such as a laptop computer. You would need to install the software on all devices that will be used to access the files. If that is not possible, you must upload all the files you create to a central location on the network, because they would not be continually saved to cloud storage. Local installation allows for a large degree of control at the local level, but staff will need to be responsible for maintenance, backups, and updates.

Some cloud-based applications, such as Office 365, can provide locally installed versions of the software that run on the client's hardware without needing to access a network. This provides nonstop use of the applications in areas with no connectivity, but the user will need to periodically connect to the Internet (usually every 30 days) to sync with the service provider and keep the license active.

Ticketing/Case Management Systems

A ***ticketing system*** or ***case management system*** is built to separate incoming tickets into clear, customizable categories or buckets, which can be organized by priority, team, source, or user. IT departments often use a ticketing system to track user requests for help or service or to log incoming bug/defect reports from users. They can also be used internally to manage project team issues. Most of these systems provide features that allow the incoming tickets to be scanned for keywords that can then be matched to a user or group responsible for that service, application, or device. The ticketing system logs all communication about the ticket; tickets can be flagged or assigned to specific users for follow-up and then archived. Any help desk system is a ticketing system, such as Zendesk or HubSpot.

Communication Tools

While all of the following communication tools will (and should!) seem familiar to any project manager, it's important to understand the best use and limitation of each type of tool so that communication is smoothed, not impeded. As discussed in prior chapters, you may have to choose different tools according to your stakeholders' needs and comfort levels.

Email

Email is probably the most common means of communicating about a project, whether formally or informally. Using digital signatures can provide integrity (message cannot be changed), authentication (the sender and receiver are verified), and nonrepudiation (the message came from the verified sender). It is the easiest way to transmit documents quickly outside your organization, as for e-signatures or bidding. Because it creates a record, it is best for routine project communications that do not need to be synchronous and for sharing project information with a large or external audience. Email is not hindered by boundaries; it can be received from any compatible device and sent to any recipient.

Messaging

Messaging refers to asynchronous text-based messages that are exchanged over cellular services or through an application platform (whether installed on a mobile device or a PC). Messaging is best for casual communications or for communications that have more urgency: think sending alerts about bad weather to team members or asking a coworker a question about a file. All messaging has the advantage of multitasking: you can message while driving (if using hands-free technology) or while in a meeting, have several messaging conversations at once, and access messages from almost any device, at any time, and in any location. As with all asynchronous communication, misunderstanding is common because tone and body language cannot be transmitted. Also, too-frequent messaging can annoy the recipient or interrupt important tasks.

While *instant messaging* and *text messaging* are terms often used synonymously, they actually describe two different technologies. Instant messaging uses computer or mobile applications managed by a provider, such as Google or Microsoft. Text messaging is textual "conversations" conducted on mobile devices via the cell phone provider's communication bandwidth.

Short Messaging Service (SMS)

SMS is a cellular technology that allows phones to send and receive texts to mobile phone numbers (unless you are using special software that sends it through the Internet). SMS messages can be received by any phone hardware, most tablets, and some computer applications. Cellular SMS can send images or hyperlinks, but it cannot exchange files. To compose a group SMS message, you will have to enter each phone number individually. Projects would generally use SMS only for short one-way communication or time-sensitive coordination (such as finding team members at a conference). It is also a staple in disaster communication because it does not rely on Internet connectivity.

Because it is mainly used on mobile phones, the only way to compose an SMS message is by typing on the phone keyboard or using voice dictation. When used without caution, autocorrect and text-to-voice features can produce hilarious (or insulting) communication errors. Other drawbacks are receiving messages out of order and hitting character limits. Project managers should explain the rules of texting within the team. While SMS is great for quick questions, typing a long response on a mobile device's keypad can be annoying for some users. If a message requires more than a sentence in reply, email may be a better choice.

Chat

Chat refers to instant messaging or computer applications that send and receive text messages. Most chat apps can be installed on any device, but all participants are limited to using the same chat platform, such as Internet Relay Chat (IRC), Slack, or Google Chat. Chat applications are more robust than SMS services. For example, Slack is primarily a chat messaging platform, but it functions more as a lightweight all-purpose platform for collaboration by adding document exchange, push notification, and ad hoc video conferencing to its group and individual chat features. Chat tends to be informal and can mimic synchronous communication if both participants are active, facilitating easy project communication. It allows team members to communicate while working on their tasks, but it can be distracting if not regulated.

Telephone

Telephone combines the immediacy of voice communication with the ability to talk to people all over the world from any location. Telephony services have evolved from hardwired copper landlines with switchboard capability to Voice over IP (VoIP) and cellular/mobile transmission, but all three have advantages and drawbacks to their use. Copper landlines cannot lose power, so they still work during power outages and many large-scale weather events, but the handsets are not mobile. VoIP mimics a traditional landline that transmits over the Internet, not physical cables, so it will stop providing service if the Internet connection is lost. VoIP telephony adds the ability to manage voice mails, outgoing calls, contacts, and call logs from a software interface. Cellular phones are widely distributed and also transmit without Internet, but they represent a huge security risk if lost or stolen. Phone calls are still the best choice when you cannot hold a face-to-face discussion and text messages are not efficient for the message.

Enterprise Social Media

Social media sites such as Facebook and LinkedIn are used today for both personal and business needs. Organizations can create private groups that include only team members and stakeholders, using these groups to communicate and distribute appropriate material.

The features of social media applications are continually evolving and require careful organizational policies for acceptable use. Social media should be handled with great caution. It is often easier to disallow posting to social media outlets than to ensure that team members understand and follow the organization's social media guidelines. Some projects may need to employ public relations personnel to ensure that the appropriate message is published to social media. Involving PR professionals reduces the likelihood of confidential or sensitive information being released inadvertently. It may be necessary to have employees (except for marketing personnel) sign an NDA to prohibit them from posting information about any active projects on social media sites.

Video

Physical meetings are best for co-located team members, but virtual meetings are the option of choice for remote or distributed teams. A virtual meeting is conducted using technology, such as video conferencing software and webcams, that allows personnel from different geographical areas to attend. The communication plan should provide guidelines on when to hold virtual versus in-person meetings and which platforms are to be used.

Keep in mind that even virtual meetings may not be possible if team members are in remote locations or do not have the technology to support a virtual method. If team members are traveling off site or if they are setting up a home office for the first time, it is the organization's responsibility to provide cameras, microphones, video-enabled hardware, and other tools. Joining from a mobile phone handset makes it impossible to see any shared presentation and should be a connection of last resort. If using an Internet connection, video conferencing requires more bandwidth than voice conferencing, but video conferencing provides the added benefit of being able to see other attendees and read their body language.

Meetings/Face-to-Face Communication

Whether in formal scheduled meetings or impromptu meetings, face-to-face communication is the most effective method for making project decisions and for addressing (or detecting) interpersonal issues. Kickoff meetings, change control board meetings, and closure meetings are usually conducted face to face. Some shareholders may also prefer to receive certain important communications, such as project status updates, face to face. Project managers often prefer face-to-face communication.

Meeting Tools

Meeting tools remove administrative headaches and make meetings more full-featured and productive by providing more ways for the audience to interact, especially remote audiences. CompTIA's objectives list specific categories of these tools.

Real-Time Surveys/Polling

Real-time surveys/polling should be used in meetings when a project manager needs to get opinions on a matter and protect against group think. While a group discussion may be the best way to *get* the ideas, deciding on *which* idea is best requires that you get everyone's honest opinion. Depending on the size of the project team and the relationships between the team members, you need to use a tool that provides anonymity. Real-time surveys/polling also provides immediate tabulation of votes, meaning a ranking of the ideas is provided quickly so that the team can focus on a few most promising ideas rather than all of them.

Calendaring Tools

Calendaring tools provide a means whereby a project team can schedule meetings and time using a particular resource. For meetings, calendaring tools allow team members to check availability of other meeting attendees to schedule the meeting time so that a quorum can attend. Calendars can be color-coded and configured to send automated reminders of upcoming events. Physical resource calendaring is also a good idea, particularly if the physical resource can be used by multiple projects or departments within an organization. Physical resources can be assigned their own calendar account in most email applications, such as Outlook.

Print Media

Most projects result in a plethora of documentation, often distributed in printed form and stored in a central location to provide easy access for team members and stakeholders. Project managers should retain a list of printed media that pertains to the project, noting who owns the master files or should receive copies. Recording this information will help ensure that all interested parties receive documentation when it becomes available and that documentation is not lost if a team member suddenly leaves a project.

Conferencing Platforms

Because virtual teams are becoming more commonplace, your chosen conferencing platform has to support audio, video, file exchange, presentations, and sometimes collaborative tools. Most conferencing platforms provide features that allow you to hold video calls and share a device screen. You can often also chat with members, ask poll questions, take screenshots, record the session, and even provide closed captioning on the meeting in real time. You should research the different options and decide which to use based on the organizational and project needs. If you frequently share confidential or sensitive data, you may need a platform that allows you to block recordings, share redacted screens, and keep people from sharing screens if certain information is visible. Conferencing platforms are used to host webinars and large-scale presentations.

Collaboration Tools

Poorly chosen ***collaboration tools*** can be clunky, hard to install or interact with, or lack features that actually help the team. It is always best to gather actual user feedback during project execution and tailor guidance to specific project activities or deliverables. For example, documents requiring version control might not be best for real-time multi-authoring editing. On the whole, though, the tools in this section are so well-suited to project work that they have rightly become ubiquitous.

Real-Time, Multi-Authoring Editing Software

Real-time, multi-authoring editing software is a cloud-based tool that allows multiple users to access a file and simultaneously edit it without needing to download or check out the file first. Edits are synchronized across all the users' devices as they appear, usually in an Internet browser. Examples include Microsoft Office on the Web and Google Docs. Edits can be done in succession, or they can happen in an active session that includes a chat function. One downside of real-time authoring is that people can overwrite each other's changes or make contradictory editorial decisions. It can be hard to discern who wrote a particular passage without rolling back the file version or implementing some kind of change-tracking system. For this reason, these documents are better suited to brainstorming, informal documentation, and collaborative drafts. Because the files are shared in the cloud, users can tag other team members inside the document and trigger email alerts when an action is required.

File Sharing Platforms

File sharing platforms allow users to upload files for other users to download and collaborate on. Many organizations today rely on the use of cloud or document sharing applications to distribute documents to multiple recipients and to centrally store project files. Project managers need to choose the best solution that provides the features needed by the project. Team members and stakeholders should be granted appropriate access to each document; some people may need full read-and-write permissions, and others may have only read permission. You should also weigh the security concerns of using a third-party cloud-based platform to share files. Microsoft OneDrive, Google Drive, and Dropbox are common file sharing systems.

Whiteboards

Collaborative ***whiteboard*** software provides a shared, singular design space where users can simultaneously make edits and share content from their respective devices. It supports virtual and co-located teams, and it's useful for drafting process flows and solution diagrams. As the name implies, it resembles a physical whiteboard; it might provide a single blank canvas or have several template tools to fast-track common uses, such as one-click diagram templates and virtual Kanban cards. Conference platforms such as Microsoft Teams and GoToMeetings have whiteboard add-ons, while Ziteboard and Miro add virtual whiteboards to existing platforms like Slack and Zoom. Finished whiteboard files can be saved and may need to be retained as project records.

Virtual whiteboards can have clunky interfaces and be slower than physical writing or drawing. People can be unfamiliar with their tools or capabilities, and they are limited by the device or monitor's screen size. The old-fashioned wall-mounted whiteboard is still a classic project management and programming tool.

Workflow and E-Signature Platforms

Processes that have traditionally relied on in-person interaction are now implementing workflow and e-signature platforms to digitize processes that previously required physical contact, such as signing legal documents and contracts. E-signatures are secure and legally binding. Unlike physical forms, electronic documents can have e-signature fields with rules that prevent a document from being finalized until it is signed and initialized, ensuring that no signature fields are overlooked. E-signed documents can be opened on any compatible device and transmitted by email or upload. In some states, electronic signatures can be notarized. The only risk to e-signatures is the same risk inherent with all online document exchange. You should verify with your organization's record management plan to determine which electronically signed documents should be retained as printouts. Adobe Acrobat Sign and DocuSign eSignature both provide e-signature workflows.

Wikis and Knowledge Bases

A ***wiki*** is a type of website that is used to manage collaborative content. The wiki users determine the structure of the site and are able to edit the content on demand without going through a formal editing or upload process and without having to program website content. Wikis are particularly useful for projects requiring lots of documentation that will be accessed and edited by team members in multiple locations and time zones. For project management, using a wiki offers several advantages:

- Anyone can edit the content.
- Posting information on wiki pages is easy and tracked by author.
- Wiki pages can be linked to related data.
- Launching and maintaining a wiki is often less expensive than other options.

However, wikis also have disadvantages:

- Anyone can edit the content.
- Published sites may be open to spam and malware.
- Wiki structures can quickly become disorganized.

You may have noticed that the first advantage and disadvantage are the same: the ease of editing increases the likelihood of conflicting changes among multiple users. Larger organizations may need to create style guides specifying product trademarks and service marks as well as direct what can and cannot be published and/or changed in project documents. They may also want to separate collaborative wiki pages from strict knowledge base articles, which are authoritative, internally developed resources intended to remain static unless they are revised in a formal process.

A ***vendor knowledge base*** provides authorized information about project tools. Vendors such as Cisco, Microsoft, and Apple have extensive knowledge bases that are searchable by the public, though some content is reserved for subscribers or product owners. Knowledge bases are particularly helpful when the team is not familiar with a tool needed for project work. You can link essential or frequently accessed vendor knowledge base articles into your internal wiki or knowledge base.

Documentation and Office Production Tools

Like collaboration tools, office production tools are longtime project workhorses. Modern office applications have evolved from standalone, locally installed software applications to distributed apps that incorporate cloud storage, document sharing, version control, author tagging, document-level read or write protection, and other sophisticated features.

Word Processing

Word processing is such a fundamental part of project work that it is hard to list all of the tools that provide this feature. Simple freeware text editors such as Notepad++ are frequently used for coding because they produce formatting-free files that can be imported anywhere and converted to common formats like XML. Microsoft Office and LibreOffice all provide robust features for desktop publishing and creating documents with fields, images, charts, tables, and embedded functions such as document locking and macros. Teams that do not need to produce lengthy reports or elaborately formatted documents may meet their needs with Google Docs or other web-based platforms.

Spreadsheets

Both spreadsheet programs and all-in-one project management software can be used to create tools like the ones discussed in this chapter and Chapter 14, "Quality and Performance Charts." Popular spreadsheet applications such as Microsoft Excel include charting capabilities and can convert data into project-specific displays. All-in-one solutions also have these tools built in, and they typically allow you to export your data to and from common spreadsheet formats so that the data can be used across multiple tools.

When using a spreadsheet program, the project manager will need to enter the project data and apply spreadsheet functions to convert the data to a bar chart, Pareto chart, run chart, or any other chart template. It is possible to create a functional Gantt chart with a spreadsheet application, but to do so is time-consuming and unnecessary for all but the simplest schedules.

Presentation

Presentation software allows you to create a slideshow to support a speech or lecture by stringing together text, images, and audio/video. Commonly used platforms for this purpose include Microsoft PowerPoint and Google Slides. Presentations can be shared in physical meetings or used in video conferencing and webinars.

Charting/Diagramming

As with spreadsheets, a number of commercial software applications can make creating process diagrams easier. Microsoft Visio and other such applications vary in complexity, cost, and features. The project manager or the PMO should find the product that best suits the organization's needs. Some applications provide highly specialized templates and pre-built units for specific diagrams, including network diagrams, data flow diagrams, decision trees, flowcharts, business management, and construction management.

Exam Preparation Tasks

As mentioned in the section "How to Use This Book" in the Introduction, you have a few choices for exam preparation: the exercises here, Chapter 17, "Final Preparation," and the exam simulation questions included in the Pearson Test Prep Software Online.

Review All Key Topics

Review the most important topics in this chapter, noted with the Key Topics icon in the outer margin of the page. Table 13-2 lists each reference of these key topics and the page number on which each is found.

Table 13-2 Key Topics for Chapter 13

Key Topic Element	Description	Page Number
Paragraph	Discussion of Gantt charts	367
Figure 13-1	Example of a Gantt Chart	368
Paragraph	Discussion of milestone charts	368
Figure 13-2	Example of a Milestone Chart	368
Paragraph	Discussion of budget burndown charts	369
Figure 13-3 and Figure 13-4	Examples of Budget Burndown Charts	369
Section	Discussion of project network diagrams	370
Figure 13-6	Example of a Detailed Project Network Diagram	371
Paragraph	Discussion of Program Evaluation Review Technique (PERT) charts	371
Figure 13-7	Example of a PERT Chart	372

Key Topic Element	Description	Page Number
Paragraph	Discussion of project organizational charts	373
Figure 13-9	Example of a Project Organizational Chart	374
Section	Discussion of the purpose of a risk register	374
Figure 13-10	Example of a risk register	375
Section	Discussion of the purpose of an issue log	377
Figure 13-11	Example of an Issue Log	378
Section	Discussion of the purpose of a change log	378
Section	Discussion of a requirements traceability matrix	378
Paragraph	Defines defect log	379
Section	Discussion of a project dashboard and a list of dashboard formats	380
Paragraph	Summarizes the purpose of a risk report	381
Paragraph	Discusses version control tools	381
Paragraph	Discussion of time-tracking tools	382
Paragraph	Defines the purpose of a task board	383
Section	Discussion of scheduling and ticketing/case management tools	383
Section	Covers important meeting tools	388
Section	Details various collaboration tools	389
Section	Discussion of documentation and office production tools	392

Define Key Terms

Define the following key terms from this chapter and check your answers in the glossary:

Gantt chart, milestone chart, project roadmap, budget burndown chart, burn rate, precedence diagram method (PDM), Program Evaluation Review Technique (PERT), process diagram, flowchart, project organizational chart, defect log, requirements traceability matrix, risk register, issue log, requirements traceability matrix (RTM), defect, defect log, project dashboard, project status report, risk report, version control, time-tracking tools, task board, project scheduling software, ticketing system, case management system, calendaring tools, collaboration tools, whiteboard, wiki, vendor knowledge base

Review Questions

The answers to these questions appear in Appendix A. For more practice with sample exam questions, use the Pearson Test Prep practice test software online.

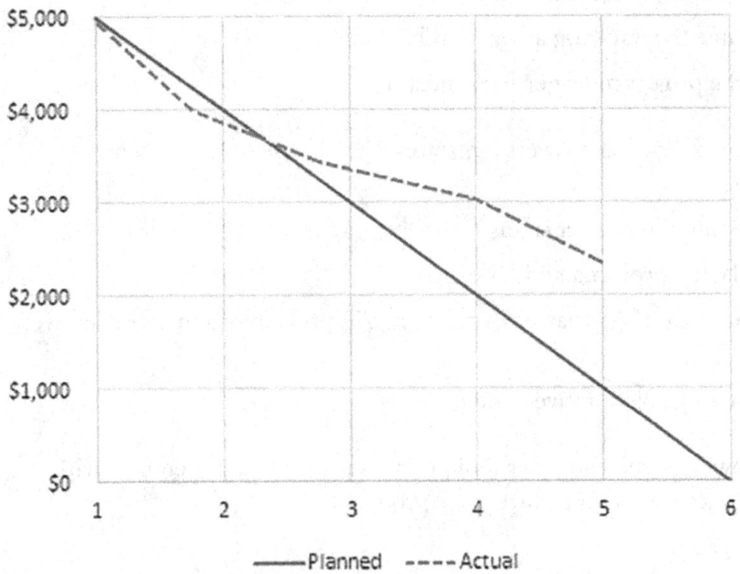

Figure 13-13 Planned Versus Actual Chart

1. The chart shown in Figure 13-13 indicates a project that is likely to be ____________________.
   a. under budget at 6 months
   b. over budget at 6 months
   c. at budget in 12 months
   d. The answer cannot be determined from the chart.

2. A project manager works with the marketing and public relations departments to develop a series of press releases for a current project. These releases should be published regularly throughout the project to update customers and other interested parties on the progress of the project. Which communication method is best for this purpose?
   a. Instant messaging
   b. Social media
   c. Corporate website
   d. Quarterly webinar

3. A key stakeholder has been on vacation for a week. When she returns, she needs to get caught up on the project and its progress. What is the quickest way to do this?
   a. Examine the dashboard and status reports.
   b. Examine the project schedule.
   c. Examine the issue log and action items.
   d. Ask the project manager for a meeting.

4. Which of the following answers *best* states the purpose of the project dashboard?
   a. Providing the project status
   b. Displaying project activities over time
   c. Showing trends, variations, or declines/improvements in a project over time
   d. Managing collaborative content

5. Which knowledge management tool provides project team members with answers to questions about third-party products?
   a. Wiki pages
   b. Vendor knowledge base
   c. Intranet site
   d. Collaboration tool
   e. Dashboard

6. Which of the following tools would require unique ID numbers to be assigned to each entry? (Choose all that apply.)
   a. Issue log
   b. RTM matrix
   c. Change log
   d. RACI matrix

7. All of the following tools or charts would be used to show relationships and sequences between tasks, *except* for a:
   a. Gantt chart
   b. Calendaring tool
   c. PERT chart
   d. PND

8. You are presenting a budget burndown chart in a status meeting, and a stakeholder asks you to explain the lines. If the line representing the actual cost terminates below the line representing the planned value, what should you tell the stakeholder?
   a. That the project needs more funds allocated to the budget
   b. That the project is expending funds at the planned rate
   c. That the project's expenditures are less than the planned value to date
   d. That the project's expenditures have exceeded the planned value to date

9. Your team is spread across two countries but needs to brainstorm to work out the potential components of a new code module. Which tool should you direct the team to use?
   a. A file sharing platform
   b. A real-time, multi-authoring platform
   c. A virtual whiteboard
   d. A video calling platform

10. A project team member has several questions about how sales of the final product will occur, including how shipping decisions are made. Which document should the team member consult?
    a. Process diagram
    b. Histogram
    c. RTM
    d. Project organizational chart

This chapter covers the following topics:

- **Histogram:** A column chart or bar graph that represents the frequency of data points over a continuous range and is used to find quality gaps
- **Pareto Chart:** A line-and-column chart with descending bars of frequency and an ascending line of percentage that is used to set priorities for quality control
- **Run Chart:** A graph plotted to show the same data point's frequency across a time sequence that is used in quality management to show trends, variations, or declines/improvements over time
- **Scatter Diagram:** A diagram used to show the presence or absence of correlation between two variables, such as traffic speed and number of accidents
- **Fishbone/Ishikawa Diagram:** A cause-and-effect diagram used to brainstorm the potential causes of a problem and rank all contributing factors
- **Control Chart:** A graphical display of data points plotted over a time sequence that is compared with preestablished control limits to monitor quality
- **Burnup/Burndown Charts:** Combined linear progression charts that can show both work completed and work remaining for the same sprint or iteration
- **Velocity Chart:** A chart that visually represents an Agile project's status and rate of completion by displaying completed story points per iteration, usually as a bar graph
- **Decision Tree:** A flowchart-style graph that plots each factor influencing a decision and the possible outcomes of taking each available action.

Quality and Performance Charts

Projects by their very nature create large amounts of raw data that must be analyzed to reveal trends before it can be useful. Charts can put the data into a format more easily understood by stakeholders. Displaying project information graphically can also demonstrate trends in the project's status that help decision-makers identify issues and their causes.

While many types of charts are used in projects, CompTIA has identified specific quality and/or performance charts that Project+ candidates need to understand: histograms, Pareto charts, run charts, scatter diagrams, fishbone or Ishikawa diagrams, control charts, burnup and burndown charts, velocity charts, and decision trees.

In addition to recognizing these common types of charts from their shape and format, exam candidates should be able to interpret the chart's findings in relation to quality and performance as well as to pinpoint potential causes of quality issues from the data contained in a sample chart.

This chapter covers the following objectives for the CompTIA Project+ exam:

3.3 Given a scenario, analyze quality and performance charts to inform project decisions.

NOTE For purposes of this chapter, the terms *chart*, *diagram*, and *graph* are generally synonymous.

"Do I Know This Already?" Quiz

The "Do I Know This Already?" quiz allows you to assess whether you should read this entire chapter thoroughly or jump to the "Exam Preparation Tasks" section. If you are in doubt about your answers to these questions or your own assessment of your knowledge of the topics, read the entire chapter. Table 14-1 lists the major headings in this chapter and their corresponding "Do I Know This Already?" quiz questions. You can find the answers in Appendix A, "Answers to the 'Do I Know This Already?' Questions and Review Quizzes."

Table 14-1 "Do I Know This Already?" Section-to-Question Mapping

Foundation Topics Section	Questions
Histogram	1
Pareto Chart	2
Run Chart	3
Scatter Diagram	4
Fishbone/Ishikawa Diagram	5
Control Chart	6
Burnup/Burndown Charts	7–8
Velocity Chart	9
Decision Tree	10

CAUTION The goal of self-assessment is to gauge your mastery of the topics in this chapter. If you do not know the answer to a question or are only partially sure of the answer, you should mark that question as wrong for the purposes of the self-assessment. Giving yourself credit for an answer you correctly guess skews your self-assessment results and might provide you with a false sense of security.

1. What is the purpose of a histogram?
   a. Setting priorities for risk management
   b. Categorizing the potential causes of a problem to identify root causes
   c. Depicting the approximate distribution of statistical data in a bar chart
   d. Depicting the steps in a business process in sequential order
2. Which project tool helps the project manager identify the largest single source of problems in a project?
   a. Decision tree analysis
   b. Fishbone diagram
   c. Scatter chart
   d. Pareto chart

3. How are data points ordered when calculating a run chart?
   a. In chronological order
   b. By magnitude
   c. By velocity
   d. By priority

4. Which project chart is used to find a correlation between two variables?
   a. Run chart
   b. Scatter diagram
   c. Pareto chart
   d. Gantt chart

5. A project team member is conducting some research on the project you are managing. When the research is complete, the project team member gives you an Ishikawa diagram. What is the diagram's function?
   a. Brainstorming steps in a process flow
   b. Finding correlation between related data sets
   c. Showing the outcome of interrelated decisions
   d. Categorizing the potential causes of a problem

6. Which chart or graph plots the result of a process over time against an upper and lower acceptable threshold and a desirable mean?
   a. Histogram
   b. Control chart
   c. Run chart
   d. Burnup chart

7. Which elements are found in both a burnup chart and a burndown chart? (Choose two.)
   a. Planned work completed
   b. Story point average
   c. Actual velocity
   d. Actual work completed
   e. Planned velocity

8. In which direction does the activity line travel in a burnup report when the chart is read from left to right and from the start to the finish of the sprint?
   a. Upward from the bottom-left corner
   b. Downward from the upper-left corner
   c. Straight across from left to right at 50% of tasks completed
   d. Straight across from left to right at the average velocity of tasks completed

9. What does a velocity chart display?
   a. The average rate at which actual cost exceeds planned value
   b. The average rate at which backlog items are added to sprints
   c. The average number of stories or story points completed per iteration
   d. The average number of story points assigned per user story

10. You have just completed a decision tree analysis. Which outcome should you choose based on the results?
    a. The one with the fewest errors above the acceptable threshold
    b. The one with the fastest velocity
    c. The one with the shortest critical path
    d. The one with the highest revenue

Foundation Topics

Histogram

A ***histogram*** is a specialized type of bar graph. A standard bar graph depicts data by presenting different categories in separate bars, such as comparing the number of people who work outside the home against the number of people who commute to work by car. By contrast, the bars of a histogram represent continuous data for a specific range, such as the number of commuting drivers on the road during each hour of a 12-hour period. The data within the range is measured in terms of frequencies and intervals, with the frequency data on the y-axis (vertical axis). The histogram's primary purpose is to graphically depict the approximate distribution of statistical data. It makes it easy to see the frequency distribution (such as the two highest bars on the chart representing the most drivers on the road at 7:00 a.m. and 5:00 p.m.).

In project management, histograms are often used to show the frequency of causes of quality problems, in order to determine and understand preventive or corrective actions. However, histograms can also show other project data, such as the distribution of resources based on job title, resource usage by time block, or the usage of equipment. They can even be used to represent data gathered for a project, such as statistical population or income data that could be used as input to the project.

Figure 14-1 shows an example of a histogram that represents the number and types of reasons order fulfillment was missed by a warehouse.

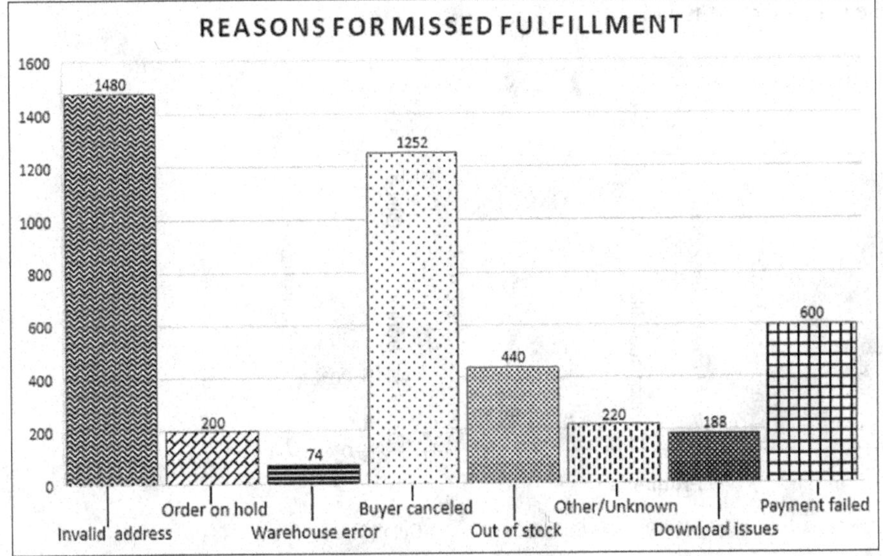

Figure 14-1 Example of a Histogram

Pareto Chart

A ***Pareto chart*** helps project managers set priorities for quality control and is most often used in conjunction with fishbone diagrams. Project managers can find out the relative importance of or causes behind a project's problems as part of quality management. The theory behind a Pareto chart is the "80/20 rule," which suggests that most of the problems in a project (80%) are caused by the same few factors (20%). The project manager can eliminate the largest number of issues by identifying which root cause to address first.

A Pareto chart combines a vertical bar chart with a line graph, showing importance or other values graphed from highest to lowest. The project manager uses a list of the project's problems as the base of the bar chart. The most common problem should be listed on the left side, and the least common problem on the right. Each parameter's importance is measured by several factors, such as frequency, time, and cost. Data points that represent the cumulative total percentage are plotted on the line graph.

Many Pareto charts include a cutoff cumulative percentage (such as 80%, although any value can be chosen). Any bar that rises above the cutoff value shows the highest cumulative percentage of problems, which indicates the cause to prioritize. Data falling below the cutoff line indicates lower-priority root causes.

Figure 14-2 shows an example of a Pareto chart. In this example, the project team should prioritize fixing the download issues ("Unable to download") first and then provide an improved user manual or vendor knowledge base ("Cannot find file") second. Addressing all of the other causes put together will have less impact than fixing the single largest issue.

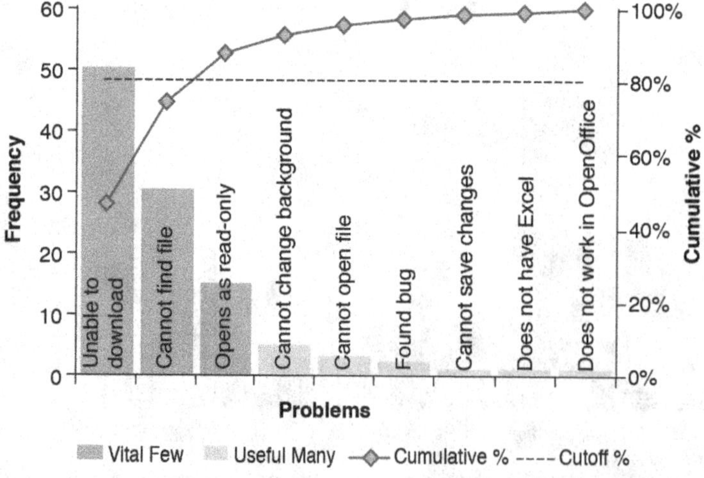

Figure 14-2 Example of a Pareto Chart

Run Chart

Like a Pareto chart, a ***run chart*** is used in quality management. Run charts show trends, variations, or declines/improvements in a project over time, using a line graph with time on the x-axis and data to measure on the y-axis (see Figure 14-3). A center line represents the mean or average data. Project managers can use run charts to analyze the following data trends:

- Too many runs above or below the center line
- Too many points continuously increasing or decreasing
- Too many points on the same side of the center line
- Too many points alternating up or down

For example, you need to document the number of coding errors detected weekly throughout an application development project. Team members work in teams to develop code, and then the teams review each other's code. They report the number of coding errors to you, and you document the total count in a run chart, with the goal of reducing the number of coding errors as the project progresses.

Run charts help both to detect issues in quality and to measure the success of a solution. Comparing the results of a run chart before and after implementing a solution to the problem can measure its impact.

EXAMPLE: Figure 14-3 tracks the yearly student enrollment in STEM programs at a college campus over 11 years. The run chart shows that enrollment trended above the period's average from 2018–2023. The college administration could use this information to gauge the success of its recruitment measures, such as the STEM scholarship program that was launched in 2017.

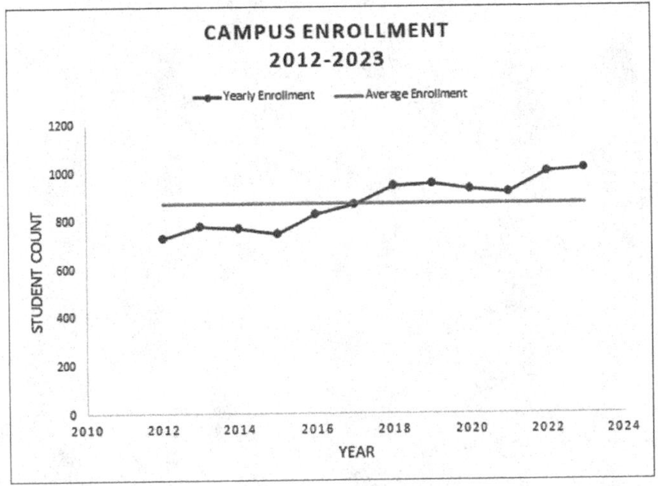

Figure 14-3 Example of a Run Chart

Scatter Diagram

A ***scatter diagram***, also known as a ***scatter chart***, ***scatter plot***, or ***correlation chart***, is used to find the correlation between two variables, such as traffic speed and number of accidents. The first variable is independent, and the second variable is dependent on the first variable. The diagrams show how the dependent variable is affected by changes to the independent variable:

- **No correlation between the variables**: No pattern to the dots (see Figure 14-4)
- **Moderate correlation between the variables**: Moderately aligned dots (see Figure 14-5)
- **Strong correlation between the variables**: Tightly aligned dots (see Figure 14-6)

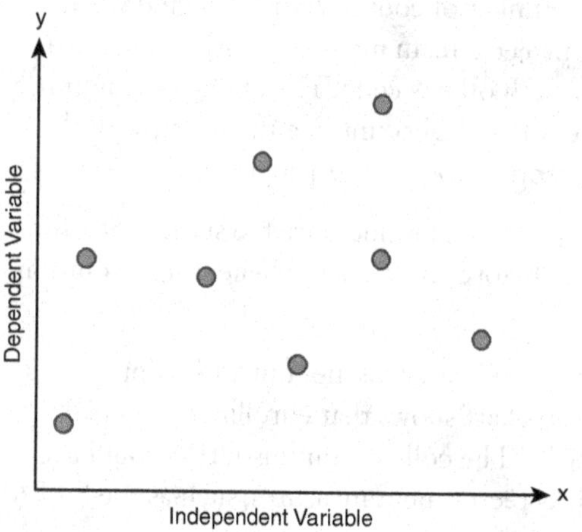

Figure 14-4 Scatter Diagram with No Correlation Between the Variables

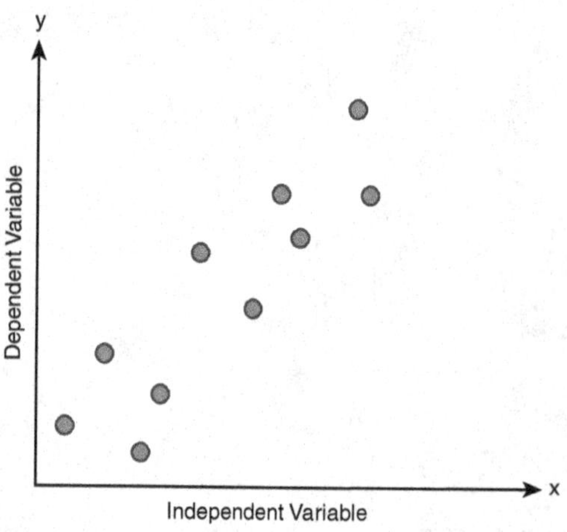

Figure 14-5 Scatter Diagram with Moderate Correlation Between the Variables

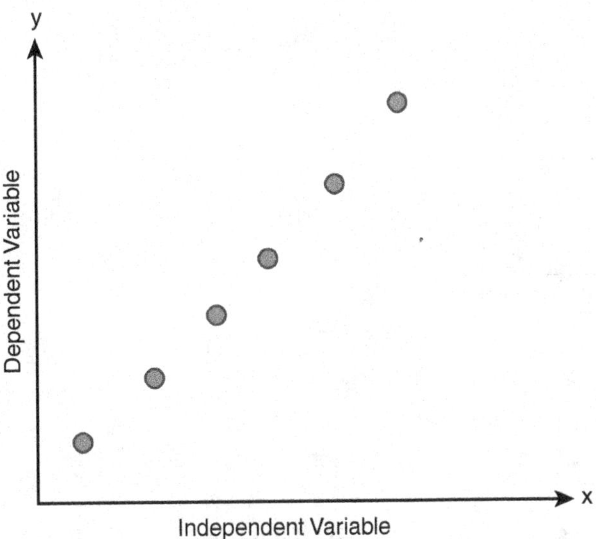

Figure 14-6 Scatter Diagram with Strong Correlation Between the Variables

To interpret the scatter chart correctly, the project manager needs to understand outliers, which are data points that fall outside the pattern of the majority of the points, and the trend line. The ***trend line*** of a scatter chart is the line along which most of the points lie (if one exists). If dots are scattered above and below the trend line, there is a moderate correlation between the two variables. If dots lie right on the trend line, there is a strong correlation between the two variables.

The final step of interpreting a scatter chart is observing whether the trend line slants up to the right or down from the left:

- If the trend line goes from bottom left to top right, the correlation is *positive*, which means that as one variable increases, the other variable increases as well.
- If the trend line goes from top left to bottom right, the correlation is *negative*, which means that as one variable increases, the other variable decreases (or vice versa).

The scatter chart in Figure 14-7 shows a positive (slanting up to the right) correlation between the number of visitors and the average daily temperature at a beach. If the chart were re-created to show the average number of visitors to a ski resort increasing as the temperature was decreasing, it would display a negative (descending) correlation.

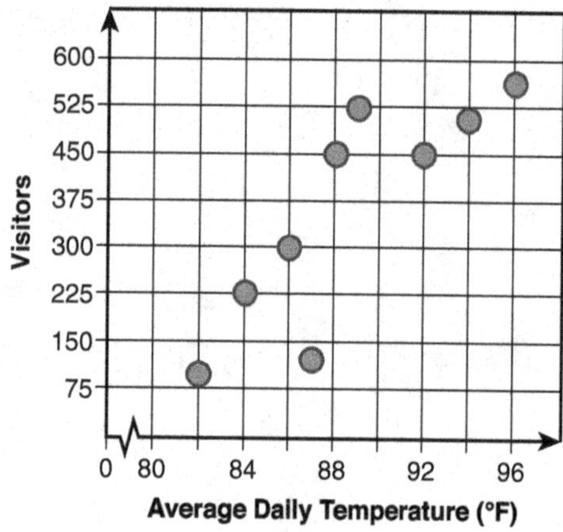

Figure 14-7 Example of a Scatter Chart with Positive Correlation

The main risk of using a scatter chart is incorrectly interpreting strongly correlated data points as showing true cause and effect. If data variables are not well selected, they could show a false cause-and-effect relationship, when in fact both data variables are being affected by a third variable not on the chart.

EXAMPLE: Instead of "Visitors" on the y-axis, Figure 14-7 could show the same correlation trend between the rise in average daily temperature and increasing numbers of people stung by jellyfish. Obviously, hot temperatures do not cause jellyfish to attack out of the blue; the missing factor is that rising temperatures correlate with more visits to the beach, which in turn correlate with increased exposure to jellyfish.

Fishbone/Ishikawa Diagram

A ***fishbone diagram***, also referred to as a ***cause-and-effect diagram*** or ***Ishikawa diagram***, is used to brainstorm the potential causes of a problem to help the project team identify and rank all contributing factors. To create the diagram, a problem statement is formulated and placed in the fish's "head," usually an oval or square at the right of the diagram. The next step is brainstorming the potential causes or factors influencing the problem and grouping them into categories. The categories are placed above and below the "spine" along the arrows. Next, the team should identify the factors that contribute to each cause and group the factors around each cause arrow. As the diagram develops, the most influential causes and factors should be moved closest to the problem statement (toward the "head" and center line) and the less influential ones moved further away (toward the "tail").

The fishbone diagram in Figure 14-8 shows reasons why product quality does not match quality standards. Raw materials and equipment are the two main causes, while delivery delays of materials and poor maintenance of equipment are the strongest contributing factors. To generate fixes, the team should ask why each cause exists ("Why are deliveries late? Why is maintenance not done?").

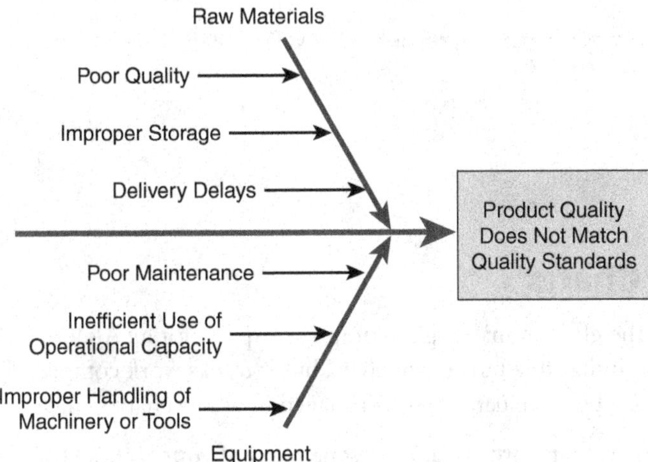

Figure 14-8 Example of a Fishbone Diagram

Fishbone diagrams are usually hand-drawn during project team meetings, but they can be created using tools like SmartDraw, EdrawMax, RCAXPress Fishbone Diagram Builder, XMind, and Nevron.

Control Chart

A ***control chart*** is a graphical display of data over time—usually the performance of a process. The data is compared against preestablished control limits to monitor quality. The chart has a center line that assists in detecting a trend of plotted values toward either of the control limits: the upper control limit (UCL) or the lower control limit (LCL). The area between the UCL and LCL defines the acceptable range of variation for the data or the process. These limits can be adjusted as processes are monitored and improved. For example, an old control limit may have been exceeded when 10 out of every 1000 units produced were defective. Now that you have upgraded the manufacturing process, the limit can be exceeded when only 2 out of every 1000 units are unsellable.

Figure 14-9 shows a control chart with a single data point exceeding the upper control limit. The out-of-control data point represents an unusual variation in a process or measurement. All out-of-control data that falls above or below the control limit should be analyzed to find and address the cause of the anomaly, whether positive or negative.

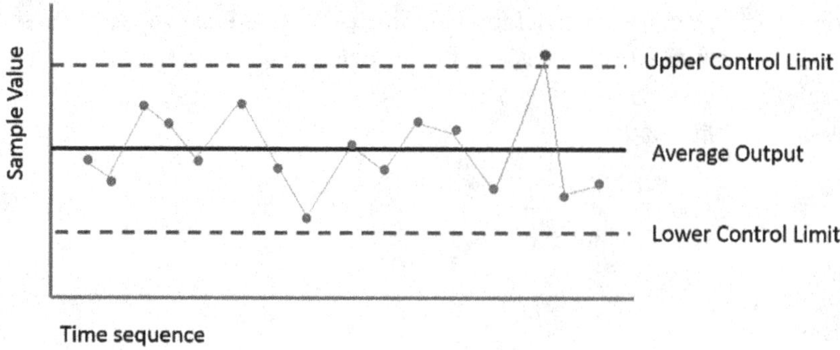

Figure 14-9 Example of a Control Chart

Burnup/Burndown Charts

A ***burndown chart*** tracks the effort remaining to complete a sprint for an Agile project. A ***burnup chart*** is similar to a burndown chart, but it tracks work completed and the total project scope. The same data can be displayed in either chart.

Burnup charts and burndown charts are visual representations of your team's progress over time, showing planned work completed against actual work completed (or budget spent). A combination burnup/burndown chart can show both work completed and work remaining for the same sprint or iteration. Figure 14-10 shows a burndown chart where the project team still has work remaining past the estimated completion date of 2/14.

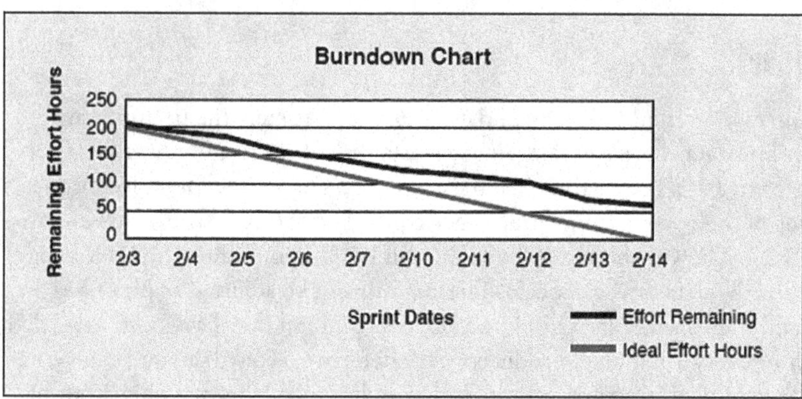

Figure 14-10 Example of a Burndown Chart

Burnup and burndown charts can be rendered as line charts or as bar charts, or as a combination of the two. The lines trend down from the upper-left corner to the bottom-right corner in burndown charts, and lines trend from the bottom-left corner to the upper-right corner in burnup charts.

The total work line in a burnup chart should remain horizontal (flat) as long as the scope remains the same. If work is subtracted or (more likely) added, the total work line will change. Figure 14-11 shows a burnup chart where the total story points jumped from 1500 to 1700 in the tenth sprint.

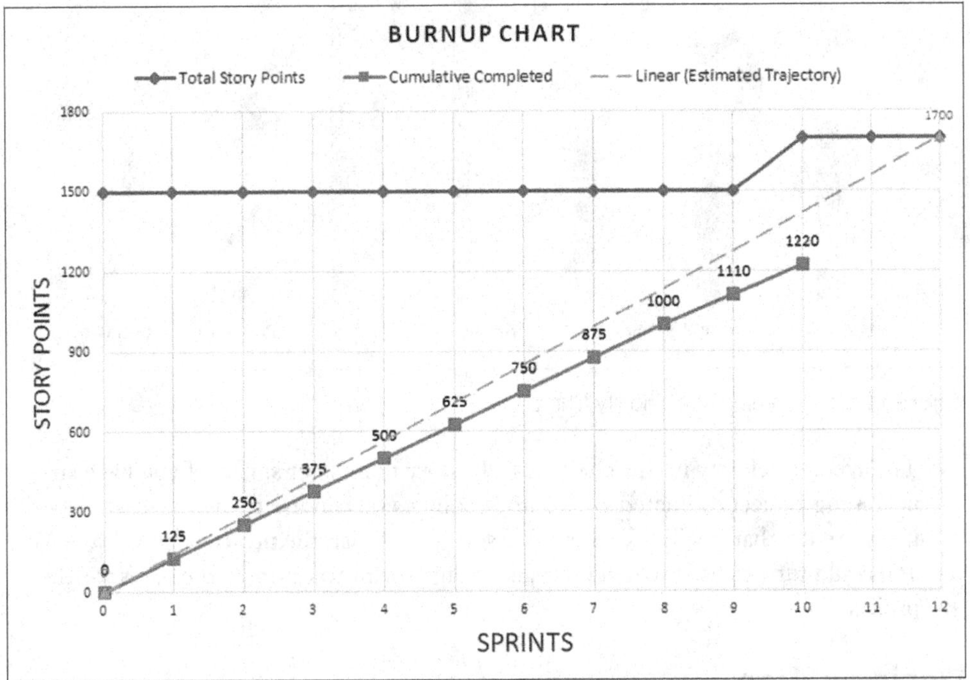

Figure 14-11 Example of a Burnup Chart

Velocity Chart

A ***velocity chart*** is both a visual representation of an Agile project's status and a measure of how much work your team can accomplish in future sprints. To calculate ***velocity***, you must add up story points from all the sprints and then calculate the average. You need to have completed at least two or three sprints prior to creating a velocity chart. The results indicate how many story points or how much work your team is likely to accomplish in an average sprint, which helps in capacity planning. With the help of the chart, you can determine how much work is left, how much work you have accomplished, and how long it will take to complete the project. A velocity chart can also be used to assess the team's performance over time and determine if they are becoming more or less efficient.

Figure 14-12 shows a velocity chart that compares committed hours to completed hours. (As a reminder, story points are subjective units used to measure the amount of work required in a user story.)

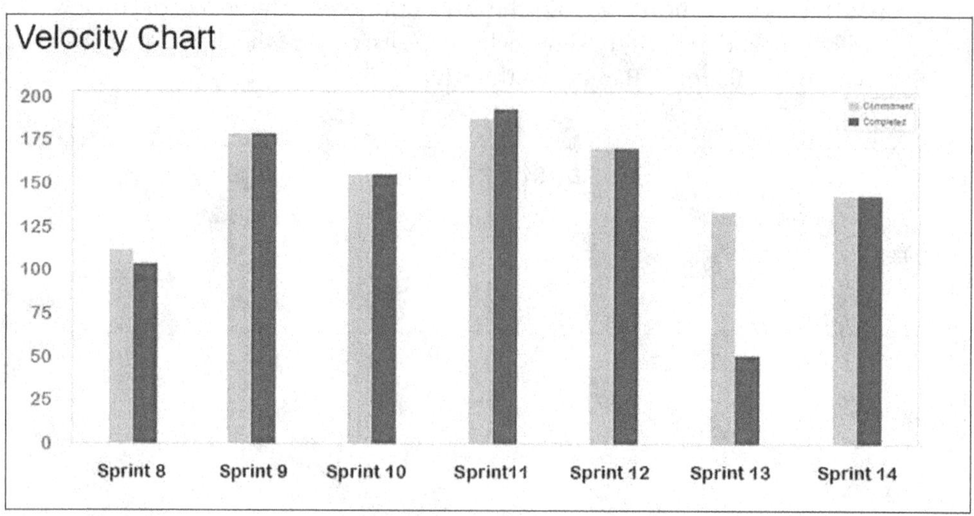

Figure 14-12 Example of a Velocity Chart

The average velocity in this chart was 140 story points per sprint. If you have an upcoming project estimated at 700 story points, you can use the team's past velocity to predict that it will take them five sprints to finish the project (700 / 140 = 5). You could further use the length of an average sprint to estimate the dates for the project.

Decision Tree

Decision tree analysis allows project managers to set out the available options when making a decision and then plot the possible outcomes of those decisions. Paths are shown through branches in the decision tree. Each event branch has a this-or-that decision, with a gain or loss from an outcome associated with each decision. It uses expected monetary value (EMV) by calculating the costs associated with the different paths so that the optimal path can be selected. To find the EMV of each decision, you would add the expected value of each outcome and deduct the costs associated with the decision or multiply it by its percentage of likelihood. Figure 14-13 shows an example of a decision tree analysis that assesses the risk of two different contractors on a project that penalizes any day over the schedule estimate.

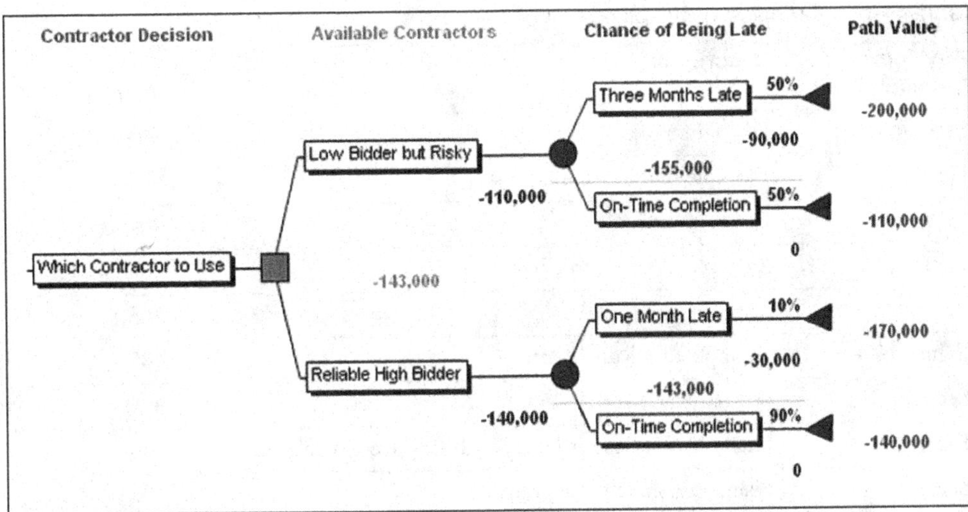

Figure 14-13 Example of a Decision Tree

The decision tree sets out the possible outcomes for each decision, along with the EMV. In this example, the high-bid contractor has a 90% chance of completing the work on time for $140,000, while the low-bid contractor has a 50% chance of completing the work late for $200,000. The high-bid contractor is therefore the better financial risk. Decision trees seek to find the path with the highest net gain (or lowest loss), which might not be the most obvious or plausible-seeming path before the decision tree analysis is made. However, they become less certain and rely more on estimates as more branches are added to the tree.

Exam Preparation Tasks

As mentioned in the section "How to Use This Book" in the Introduction, you have a few choices for exam preparation: the exercises here, Chapter 17, "Final Preparation," and the exam simulation questions included in the online Pearson Test Prep Software Online.

Review All Key Topics

Review the most important topics in this chapter, noted with the Key Topics icon in the outer margin of the page. Table 14-2 lists each reference of these key topics and the page number on which each is found.

Table 14-2 Key Topics for Chapter 14

Key Topic Element	Description	Page Number
Section	Histogram	403
Figure 14-1	Example of a Histogram	403
Section	Pareto chart	404
Figure 14-2	Example of a Pareto Chart	404
Section	Run chart	405
Figure 14-3	Example of a Run Chart	405
Section	Scatter diagram	406
Figure 14-7	Example of a Scatter Chart with Positive Correlation	408
Section	Fishbone/Ishikawa diagram	408
Figure 14-8	Example of a Fishbone Diagram	409
Section	Control chart	409
Figure 14-9	Example of a Control Chart	410
Section	Burnup/Burndown charts	410
Figure 14-10	Example of a Burndown Chart	410
Figure 14-11	Example of a Burnup Chart	411
Section	Velocity chart	411
Figure 14-12	Example of a Velocity Chart	412
Section	Decision tree	412
Figure 14-13	Example of a Decision Tree	413

Define Key Terms

Define the following key terms from this chapter and check your answers in the glossary:

histogram, Pareto chart, run chart, scatter diagram, scatter chart, scatter plot, correlation chart, trend line, fishbone diagram, cause-and-effect diagram, Ishikawa diagram, control chart, burndown chart, burnup chart, velocity chart, velocity, decision tree

Review Questions

The answers to these questions appear in Appendix A. For more practice with sample exam questions, use the Pearson Test Prep practice test software online.

1. Which project constraint is addressed when you analyze Pareto charts, fishbone diagrams, and control charts?
   a. Scope
   b. Quality
   c. Cost
   d. Schedule

2. While managing a project, the project manager gives a histogram to a team member. Which of the following options *best* describes the purpose of this document?
   a. Identifying potential causes of problems
   b. Showing trends
   c. Graphically depicting the frequency distribution of a process data set
   d. Displaying activities or tasks over time, including the activity's dependencies and relationships

3. Which of the following tools could depict the most frequent sources of quality issues? (Choose two.)
   a. Run charts
   b. Histograms
   c. Scatter diagrams
   d. Control charts
   e. Pareto charts

4. You have decided to create a Pareto chart for the project you are managing. What is the purpose of this chart?
   a. Showing the causes of problems, ranked by occurrence
   b. Showing trends in quality
   c. Showing correlation between two variables
   d. Showing relationships between project activities

5. A project team has created the chart shown in Figure 14-14. What type of chart is this team using?

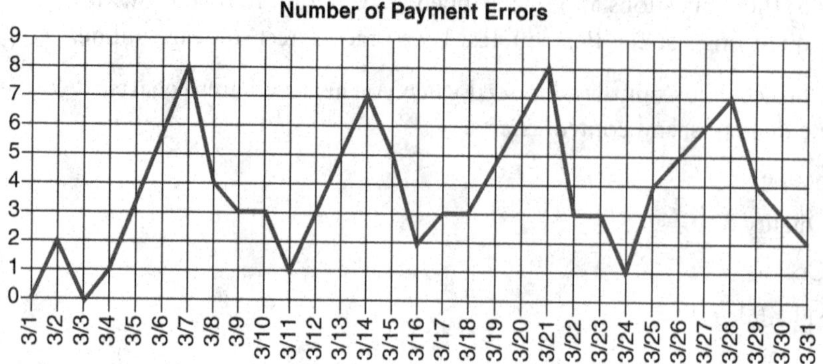

Figure 14-14 Chart Showing Payment Errors

a. Root cause analysis

b. Pareto chart

c. Run chart

d. Scatter chart

6. When data points are tightly grouped together on a scatter diagram, you would say they are what?

a. Negatively correlated

b. Strongly correlated

c. Positively correlated

d. Falsely correlated

e. Weakly correlated

7. When would there be a change in the line depicting the amount of work to be completed on a burnup chart?

a. When the sprint is 50% complete

b. When the sprint is 100% complete

c. When the scope changes

d. When additional requirements are added to the backlog

8. What is the main risk of using a scatter chart when assessing quality issues?
   a. Finding no correlation between two variables
   b. Finding false correlation between two variables
   c. Finding negative correlation between two variables
   d. Finding weak correlation between two variables
   e. Finding positive correlation between two variables

9. You are examining the fishbone diagram shown in Figure 14-15.

   What can you determine from this breakdown?
   a. The problem definition is the length of wait times for Help Desk support
   b. The root cause of the issue is found in the Processes category group
   c. The diagram investigates seven categories of root causes
   d. The Technology group is the least important part of the diagram

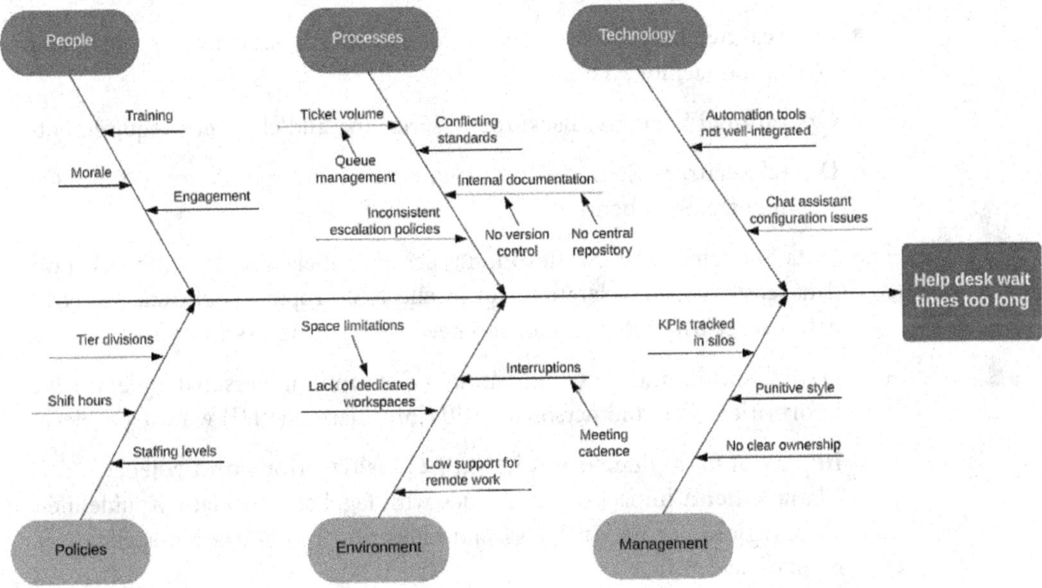

Figure 14-15 Acme Corporation's Help Desk

10. How many decisions should you expect to generate with a decision tree?
    a. None; it is for displaying possible options only.
    b. None; it is for displaying steps in a process only.
    c. One.
    d. The answer depends on the decision tree.

This chapter covers the following topics:

- **Environmental, Social, and Governance (ESG) Factors:** The project's impact on the local and global environment and on the company's brand, values, vision, and mission statement; the impact of applicable regulations and standards on the project
- **Corporate IT Security Policies and Restrictions:** Logical, operational, and technical policies to regulate data handling and network security as well as restrictions governing the use of brand collateral
- **Physical Security:** Considerations for securing mobile devices, removable media, and facility access
- **Operational Security:** Background screening and clearance requirements
- **Digital Security:** Resource access and permissions, remote access restrictions, and multifactor authentication
- **Data Security:** Data classification types and labels, classification based on data sensitivity, considerations for intellectual property and trade secrets, national security information, and need-to-know access
- **Data Confidentiality:** Considerations for handling personally identifiable information (PII) and personal health information (PHI) within a project
- **Impact of Compliance and Privacy Considerations on Project Management:** Impact of compliance with legal and regulatory guidelines, local, regional, or national laws, and industry- or organization-specific regulations

CHAPTER 15

Environmental, Social, and Governance (ESG) Factors and Compliance, Data Security, and Privacy Considerations

Environmental, social, and governance (ESG) factors measure an organization's commitment to sustainable practices and positive social impact as well as shareholder returns. A project that is misaligned with the organization's ESG stance or its corporate values and mission statement can negatively affect its brand. These nonfinancial factors can pose a significant risk to the organization if they are not considered during the Discovery phase.

Project managers must always ensure their project complies with applicable regulations, laws, and industry standards, some of the most important of which govern data privacy. Failing to safeguard sensitive data, especially personal health records (PHI) and personally identifiable information (PII), carries regulatory and financial risk. These types of data should have sufficient security controls applied before initiating project work.

Labels are used to classify data records and impose standards for how the data should be viewed, stored, used, and disposed of. Each label carries a set of access controls that match the data record's need for protection from disclosure. Data handling is also affected by whether the data is intellectual property or classified as relevant to national security.

Corporate IT security policies govern how information assets and equipment are protected in the organization by technical, managerial, and physical means. Common methods of ensuring security in the organization are by implementing physical, operational, digital, and data security controls. These controls range from securing facility access to adding multifactor authentication, managing mobile devices, conducting background screenings, meeting security clearance requirements, restricting remote access, and off-boarding former employees to remove prior access.

This chapter covers the following objectives for the CompTIA Project+ exam:

4.1 Summarize basic environmental, social, and governance (ESG) factors related to project management activities.

4.2 Explain relevant information security concepts impacting project management concepts.

4.3 Explain relevant compliance and privacy considerations impacting project management.

"Do I Know This Already?" Quiz

The "Do I Know This Already?" quiz allows you to assess whether you should read this entire chapter thoroughly or jump to the "Exam Preparation Tasks" section. If you are in doubt about your answers to these questions or your own assessment of your knowledge of the topics, read the entire chapter. Table 15-1 lists the major headings in this chapter and their corresponding "Do I Know This Already?" quiz questions. You can find the answers in Appendix A, "Answers to the 'Do I Know This Already?' Questions and Review Quizzes."

Table 15-1 "Do I Know This Already?" Section-to-Question Mapping

Foundation Topics Section	Questions
Environmental, Social, and Governance (ESG) Factors	1–2
Corporate IT Security Policies and Restrictions	3
Physical Security	4
Operational Security	5
Digital Security	6
Data Security	7–9
Data Confidentiality	10
Impact of Compliance and Privacy Considerations on Project Management	11

CAUTION The goal of self-assessment is to gauge your mastery of the topics in this chapter. If you do not know the answer to a question or are only partially sure of the answer, you should mark that question as wrong for the purposes of the self-assessment. Giving yourself credit for an answer you correctly guess skews your self-assessment results and might provide you with a false sense of security.

1. Which of the following would be an ESG factor to consider in a construction project?
   a. Underestimating the cost of materials
   b. Producing wastewater runoff
   c. Hiring a subcontractor that does low-quality work
   d. A high risk of flooding at the building site

2. During project planning, you identify a risk of quality defects that could cause unacceptable safety issues in the finished product. Which ESG factor are you applying to this situation?
   a. Impact on the environment
   b. Company mission statement, vision, and values
   c. Project's impact to brand value
   d. Applicable regulations and standards

3. Your newly acquired project team members must sign an agreement that they will not visit online auction sites while connected to the company network unless they are using a personal mobile device. Which type of IT security policy did they review?
   a. BYOD policy
   b. Security awareness policy
   c. COPE policy
   d. Acceptable use policy

4. Which of the following is *not* a precaution you should take when issuing company-owned mobile devices to team members?
   a. Enable remote locking and remote wiping.
   b. Disable GPS services to avoid tracking.
   c. Enroll the devices in a mobile device management application.
   d. Disable the use of third-party applications.

5. Which of the following is used by the United States government, and other countries, to denote how much access a person should be granted to classified national security information?
   a. Data classification
   b. PII

c. Clearance

d. PHI

6. When team members log in to the network locally, they must provide a username and password. When they log in to the network remotely, they must provide a username, password, and one-time code. Which two statements are true regarding your organization's security? (Choose two.)

   a. The local network login uses single-factor authentication.

   b. The local network login uses two-factor authentication.

   c. The remote network login uses three-factor authentication.

   d. The remote network login uses two-factor authentication.

   e. The remote network login uses single-factor authentication.

7. Which statement does *not* describe the purpose of data classification in an organization?

   a. To comply with clearance requirements

   b. To prevent the negative impact from its exposure

   c. To determine the appropriate security controls to apply

   d. To avoid legal fines

8. Which of these labels would not be a common data classification for private enterprise?

   a. Internal

   b. Restricted

   c. Sensitive

   d. Secret

9. If an organization did not protect the confidentiality of this asset type, it would no longer be legally considered ________________.

   a. a patent

   b. a trade secret

   c. a copyright

   d. intellectual property

   e. proprietary

10. You have been asked to identify all PII data in your project's databases. Which information in the databases is considered to be PII? (Choose all that apply.)

    a. Gender

    b. Fingerprints

    c. Social security number

    d. Date of birth

    e. Full name

11. Which of the following regulations or laws applies to all entities that store, process, and/or transmit data that identifies EU citizens in the course of commercial activity?

    a. PIPEDA

    b. CCPA

    c. HITECH

    d. GDPR

Foundation Topics

Environmental, Social, and Governance (ESG) Factors

A project does not execute in a void, and its return on investment (ROI) is not its sole measure of success. The impact of projects can reach beyond the client, stakeholders, and end users to affect the environment in which they are built and the culture in which they operate. If not considered in advance, these impacts can pose risks to the organization's brand or its bottom line. A project (or an organization) that focuses solely on a project's returns can overlook its social impact or its effect on the local ecosphere. Unsustainable development can be defined as pursuing short-term returns without regard for their potential long-term systemic harm. As organizations increasingly commit to sustainable growth principles, they have adopted ***environmental, social, and governance (ESG)*** guidelines to drive initiatives in line with this commitment. The three ESG factors are as follows:

- **Environmental factors**: How the organization or project affects the physical world
- **Social factors**: How the company develops relationships and upholds human rights
- **Governance factors**: How the company operates, including its policies, transparency, and structure

Table 15-2 gives real-life examples of ESG factors.

Table 15-2 ESG Factors That Impact the Organization

ESG Factor	Negative	Positive
Environmental	Produces greenhouse emissions	Uses renewable fuels
	Displaces landscape features	Recycles waste material
	Causes runoff or flooding	Improves local water quality
	Increases landfill waste	Sequesters carbon
Social	Frequent workplace accidents	Labor rights support
	Lack of employee benefits	Strong data privacy protections
	Discrimination against communities	Occupational safety controls
	Social media controversies	Ethical product sourcing

ESG Factor	Negative	Positive
Governance	Low financial transparency Frequent regulatory fines Tax avoidance Anti-competitive practices	Financially transparent operations Diverse representation in management Ethical investment standards Risk oversight and compliance audits

ESG factors equate to good corporate citizenship and a focus on expanding a project's benefits beyond stakeholders to the environment in which the project operates. The adoption of ESG principles can be voluntary or regulatory. Large-scale projects, such as projects that build airports, power plants, or landfills, may require a written plan for ESG compliance before the project is funded. ESG compliance in the early stages of project discovery may avoid expensive and reputation-destroying incidents like major oil spills, unethical product development, serious data breaches, and financial mismanagement that destroys employee pensions.

Project Impact to the Local and Global Environment

Organizations should analyze a project's impact on the local and ***global environment*** during project discovery and initiation. It is always best to anticipate any issues that could arise *before* the project actually starts. Construction projects are perfect examples of projects that can greatly impact the local and global environment. Many large corporations recognize this issue and may seek other ways to offset these effects. The global and local environment correlate strongly to the environmental factor of ESG.

EXAMPLE: A large online marketplace purchases electric vehicles for its delivery fleets and develops padded paper-cell envelopes to reduce its use of nonrecyclable poly bubble mailers.

Awareness of Applicable Regulations and Standards

Laws, regulations, and standards can vary from country to country, state to state, and by industry. Project managers should ensure that applicable regulations and standards for the particular jurisdiction and industry are researched to determine their impact on the project. Building construction codes, municipal zoning laws, federal transportation safety rules, and securities and trade regulations are all common project constraints. The following are some of the major laws, regulations, or standards that may apply to projects in specific industries:

- **PCI DSS (Payment Card Industry Data Security Standard)**: Applies to all entities that store, process, and/or transmit credit cardholder data.
- **HIPAA (Health Insurance Portability and Accountability Act)**: Applies to entities that store, process, and/or transmit healthcare data for U.S. citizens.
- **SOX (Sarbanes-Oxley)**: Applies to all publicly traded companies in the U.S. and is mainly concerned with corporate accounting practices.
- **Gramm-Leach-Bliley Act (GLBA) of 1999**: Applies data privacy to financial institutions and protects their customers from having their information shared with third parties.

The main difference between standards and laws/regulations is that standards are established by private sector bodies, such as the International Standards Organization (ISO), Underwriters Laboratory (UL), and American National Standards Institute (ANSI). Laws and regulations are set by government bodies. Voluntary standards apply to nearly every type of consumer product, especially children's and babies' products and home chemicals, and are being developed for emerging technologies like Internet of Things (IoT)-connected products and artificial intelligence. Standards are meant to maximize the safety and reliability of consumer products. Following applicable standards ensures a higher-quality product and provides liability protection for manufacturers in the case of consumer complaints.

The best way to maintain awareness of applicable regulations and standards is to build compliance assessments into project work and to consult with internal or external legal counsel. Compliance specifications that map project requirements to laws or standards can be added to the requirements traceability matrix (RTM).

Awareness of Company Vision, Mission Statements, and Values

> **NOTE** Use of the term "master" is ONLY in association with the official terminology used in industry specifications and standards, and in no way diminishes Pearson's commitment to promoting diversity, equity, and inclusion, and challenging, countering and/or combating bias and stereotyping in the global population of the learners we serve.

Project managers should remain aware of the company's published vision statement, mission, and corporate values to ensure that any projects adhere to all of these standards. In cases where two companies are working together to complete a project (as when one company is the sponsor and the other is actually completing the project, or when a master service agreement is in place), the project will need to take the vision statement, mission, and corporate values of both organizations into account.

Vision, mission, and values correlate strongly to the social and governance factors of ESG. Social factors include how your company interacts with its employees, its consumers, and society at large, such as by providing diversity, equity, and inclusion training (DEI) or by supporting workers' rights and humane workplace policies. Governance factors include decision-making and corporate cultures, transparency, accountability, inclusivity, compliance, and stakeholder relations.

Project Impact to Company Brand Value

A company's brand is its distinctive persona. Branding goes beyond slogans and trademarks to associate intangible traits with the company, like innovation, trustworthiness, safety, disruption, and credibility. While the enterprise can try to influence these traits with its public vision, mission, and values statements, branding is heavily shaped by public perception. Corporate behavior at odds with a company's image can seriously damage its reputation. For that reason, a well-chosen or ill-timed project can substantially influence the company's brand value.

EXAMPLE: A furniture brand that promotes itself as "sustainable and environmentally friendly" launches a project to build a showroom with low-energy light fixtures, rainwater harvesting, and electric vehicle charging stations. The chosen site already has an award-winning eco-friendly building. Instead of reusing the existing building, the furniture brand demolishes it and rebuilds from the ground up, producing substantial construction waste and causing regional backlash.

No project that would produce an outcome that is significantly misaligned with the company's brand or its value/mission statement should be approved unless the project is part of a strategic rebranding. A project can be justified on the basis that it is likely to generate positive publicity and improve the company's and/or the brand's reputation; this is considered an intangible ROI. Projects can address an unpopular aspect of the company's operations or build community goodwill to offset negative feedback.

Corporate IT Security Policies and Restrictions

All organizations should have an information security policy or IT security policy. Like a project management plan, it provides governance, guidelines, and roles to help manage how security is implemented in the organization. These policies are owned by senior management and define common security requirements for all personnel, systems, data, and equipment connected to the corporate network. They also define access and usage restrictions, training, and security awareness guidelines.

Digital, physical, operational, and data security are implemented in the enterprise with *access controls*. Broadly speaking, there are four categories of access controls:

- **Technical** controls restrict access using hardware, software, or firmware components. These controls include passwords, encryption, data loss prevention technologies, firewalls, IP address restrictions, network architecture, and multifactor authentication.
- **Managerial** or **management** controls are based on oversight and risk management. These controls are implemented with policies and plans and guide behaviors and actions to align with the organization's security goals.
- **Operational** controls create safety through personnel behaviors. These controls include policies, procedures, best practices, training, and testing, and are enforced by supervision and repercussions for noncompliance. They are sometimes called administrative controls.
- **Physical** controls restrict physical access to an object or physically restrict insecure objects. These controls include door locks, CCTV, guards, perimeter security, work area separation, line-of-sight safeguards, phone privacy booths, physical media handling, secure disposal, and secured cabling.

One common control is an acceptable use policy (AUP), which documents the constraints that employees and contractors must agree to before using company technology or accessing the company network. Noncompliance may result in disciplinary action and removal of access. An AUP is a managerial control since it attempts to guide, constrain, or manage user behavior to comply with security practices. A password policy combines two categories of access control: the policy that requires users to create passwords that follow best security practices is a managerial control, but it is enacted with technical controls that will reject a user's credentials if the password is not strong or complex. The corporate information security policy is itself a managerial control that guides the organization's implementation of physical, technical, operational, and other managerial controls.

Project managers should ensure that all project team members know and adhere to the organization's security policies. One company may allow the use of personal mobile devices on the company network or to access internal resources, known as a bring-your-own-device (BYOD) policy. Another company may only allow the use of company-issued devices to access any internal resource, called a company owned/personally enabled (COPE) policy. Any contractors who join a project team may need security awareness training to ensure they understand the IT security policies of the organization(s) responsible for the project.

Branding Restrictions

While not actually part of IT security policies, many companies have ***branding restrictions***. Organizations often establish brand guidelines. These guidelines are clearly defined rules and standards that spell out how the organization wants the brand represented to the world. They establish what the company is, what it does, and what it stands for. Project team members need to understand the guidelines under which they should operate as it relates to branding. Public-facing project documents, websites, press releases, or social media posts may be required to use certain fonts, font sizes, RGB color palettes, and templates provided by the marketing department to match the project organization's established brand. Branding restrictions usually mean that logos cannot be resized or sampled to a different resolution from the approved guidelines. They also set forth guidelines regarding the use of copyright, trademark, and registered symbols.

EXAMPLE: Your company is partnering with a well-known university to develop a line of instructional materials that will be co-branded by both organizations. According to the university's branding restrictions, the project's collateral cannot rotate or distort the university's logo, alter the logo, or combine its logo with your company's logo to create a new logo. You also cannot use any part of the university's domain name in an online project resource without a contract addendum.

Physical Security

Physical security is often overlooked in the rush to install technical controls, but basic security precautions like storing project files and tools in locked cabinets and securing access to project areas with smart cards or badge-only entry should be fundamental operations. CompTIA calls out access control for removable media, mobile devices, and facilities as areas of focus.

Mobile Device Considerations

Mobile devices, including tablets and cellular phones, can be easily misplaced or stolen. Some organizations may choose to restrict users to company-issued devices rather than allowing enterprise data to be accessed from or stored on personal phones. That said, the sweeping integration of business apps with cloud-based tools and mobile platforms means that nearly every personal phone is a potential workstation. You should follow basic precautions for the physical safety of mobile devices:

- Require a PIN or some other login mechanism with each use of the device after a certain idle period (no more than 10 minutes of inactivity).
- Implement GPS and other location services for device tracking.

- Never leave company-issued devices unattended and store them in secured areas or locked drawers when not in use.
- Use a Faraday cage, which is an enclosure used to block electromagnetic fields, to hold mobile devices in secured rooms or when dealing with project data that requires a security clearance.
- Immediately report any missing or stolen device.
- Reset mobile devices to factory defaults before disposing of them or transferring ownership.

You should also ensure technical controls are deployed on all mobile devices. The easiest way to do so is to enroll the devices in a mobile device management (MDM) application, which is a centralized policy repository that will automatically control the permissions and access granted to mobile devices with one-click revocation or unenrollment on the administrator's part. Other important technical controls for mobile devices are enabling remote wipe, remote lock, and find-my-device features, backing up data continually to the cloud, avoiding insecure public Wi-Fi, and limiting or blocking the installation of third-party software or unapproved software.

Removable Media Considerations

Removable media such as USB flash drives, plug-in external hard drives, and SD image cards is easily misplaced or stolen. Even a mobile phone can become removable media if it is connected to the computer with a USB or Lightning cable. The following are some physical security measures that should be taken for removable external media:

- Always keep approved removable media in a secure location when not being used, such as a locked desk drawer.
- Encrypt all data on removable media (a technical control).
- Erase project data from removable media once it is no longer needed, when disposing of the media, or when transferring ownership.

Because removable media is easy to hide and easy to install, it is also a frequent tool of the insider attack. USB flash drives can be used to install malware on computers, infect local networks, or copy confidential or sensitive internal files. If these threats are a consideration, project managers should work with the organization's IT department to add technical controls that will log USB connections and block data from being uploaded to or downloaded from any removable media to a computer or mobile device.

Facility Access

Facility access should be granted only to authorized personnel. Even public areas may need a certain level of security, and you should provide security awareness training to personnel who require secure facility access. The following are some physical security measures that should be taken for facilities:

- Layer the defense approach by incorporating perimeter security, exterior door security, interior door security, and locked cabinets and safes.
- Implement systems to prevent, deter, and detect intrusion.
- Implement visitor procedures, including signing in on a visitors log and personnel escort.
- Provide internal physical security to highly secure areas, such as wiring closets and data centers.

Besides fences and locks, here are some of the common physical controls used to secure facility access:

- **Turnstiles**: A type of gate that allows movement in a single direction at a time and prevents tailgating.
- **Access control vestibules**: A set of double doors that can be entered one at a time, usually monitored by a security guard. Also called a mantrap.
- **Bollards**: A concrete post that prevents vehicles from driving into restricted areas.

Operational Security

Operational security, or OPSEC, is a process that organizations deploy to prevent sensitive information from getting into the wrong hands. Even the most secure organizations have hired trusted individuals who later exfiltrated (stole) data or information. Operational controls are a series of best practices designed to impede all but the most determined attacker. Operational controls are implemented with policies (which are a type of managerial control).

Two key operational security practices are background screening and the granting of security clearance; these practices ensure that untrustworthy individuals are never given the ability to access secured project data. Another operational security practice is routine security awareness training for all employees and project team members who handle network resources.

Finally, an offboarding policy is an operational control that systematically removes a previous employee or contractor's access to internal systems and devices once their job role has ended. Offboarding decreases the threat of a malicious insider attack or espionage. Project-specific offboarding tasks should be recorded in the resource management plan, but the overall corporate IT security policy will contain the complete offboarding procedure.

Background Screening

Background screening, also called a *background check*, is a process for validating a job applicant or employee's identity, employment history, criminal record, financial health, and educational experience. Its purpose is to detect any issues in a person's background that are red flags to employment. A background screening should verify any claim made on the applicant's application or resume regarding their skills and experience. Credit history may also be part of the screening, particularly if the individual will have access to financial transactions. If you hire a professional third party to provide the background screening, you will have to notify the applicant of the screening based on the rules in the Fair Credit Reporting Act (FCRA).

Clearance Requirements

Clearance is used by the United States government, and other countries, to denote how much access a person should be granted to classified national security information. A security clearance is a status granted to individuals after a thorough background check that allows them to access classified information (state or organizational secrets) or to enter restricted areas in secured government facilities. Clearance requirements document the requirements to give personnel access to classified assets, including data, that match the clearance level (such as Confidential or Secret). To understand how clearance intersects with data classification, see "National Security Information" later in this chapter.

Digital Security

Digital security means employing technical controls to protect data and any digital asset, including personal identities. Keep in mind that any digital asset that is provided for a project will also need to be revoked once the project ends, particularly if temporary or contract personnel are used.

Resource Access and Permissions

Resource access and permissions involve creating user accounts and giving those accounts the appropriate permissions to digital resources. Organizational security access policies and procedures should be followed. Follow the principle of least privilege by granting users only the access they need to complete their job duties.

Some users may not need any access to some digital assets, while other users may need to view them and others to edit them. Be careful when granting full control of digital assets to users, as this gives them the ability to modify and delete files and data. Make sure you enable logging and auditing if team members are given access to sensitive or proprietary data.

Remote Access Restrictions

Remote access restrictions involve providing access to digital assets for remote users. With cloud deployments being so commonplace today, this isn't the issue it was once. When network resources are kept on the premises, remote team members may need to be given virtual private network (VPN) access to log in to access digital assets. Again, those permissions are important, so project managers should only grant the minimum necessary permission. Some organizations will even go so far as to lock down the times of remote access and the devices from which a user can remotely access digital assets.

Multifactor Authentication

Multifactor authentication is a technical control that will verify the identity of a user against their claimed identity when logging in to a system or application. There are three primary authentication factors used in single-factor and multifactor authentication (knowledge, ownership, and characteristic) and two additional lesser-used factors (location and performance):

- **Knowledge factor**: This is something you know, such as password, PIN, or username.
- **Ownership factor**: This is something you have, such as a smart card or a device with an authentication app.
- **Characteristic factor**: This is something you are and includes biometrics, fingerprints, facial recognition, and iris prints.
- **Location factor**: This is somewhere you are, determined by using a trusted device's MAC address or the GPS location of the device/phone used to log in.
- **Performance factor**: This is something you do, determined by using typing cadence or gait analysis.

Multifactor authentication requires the use of two or more separate factors in the same authentication session, not two or more varieties of the same factor. The classic username/password combination is single-factor authentication because it only includes the knowledge factor.

Data Security

Data security is a series of operational practices and physical, managerial, and technical controls that protect digital information from unauthorized access, corruption, or theft throughout its entire life cycle.

Data security and privacy governance overlap. In general, security is the technical oversight of information that includes ensuring its confidentiality. Privacy governance is the oversight of principles that safeguard the user's identity and dictate how personal information is used, collected, stored, disclosed, and managed.

Data Classification

In information technology terms, a data asset is classified when an organization categorizes it by the level of protection it requires, from unguarded (public) to most guarded. There are two primary reasons to classify data: to assess the negative impact from its exposure, and to determine the appropriate security controls that should be applied. Classification guidelines are defined in the organization's information security policy and applied to associated policies, like the records management plan.

Data's ***sensitivity*** measures how much impact the data's unauthorized exposure would have. Data ***classification*** is the process of determining how sensitive a data record is, which in turn dictates its access control strategy. Organizations can classify data with labels like Internal, Confidential, and Restricted, and they can restrict access to the data by job role or immediate need to know.

To understand how (and whether) data should be classified, it should first be assessed to determine its criticality, or value to the organization, and its *sensitivity*, or inherent need for protection and special handling. Data classification is meant to answer these questions:

- How valuable is the data to the organization?
- What harm would occur if it were exposed, altered, corrupted, or lost?
- Who should be allowed to access the data?
- How should the data be used, stored, and retained?
- Which laws and regulations apply to the data's governance?

Classification guidelines for private industry and associated data controls are documented in the organization's Information & Data Classification Policy, which can be a subset of the organization's overall IT policy. This policy should clearly define roles, such as ***data owner***, ***data subject***, and ***data user***, as well as answer all of these questions:

- **When** is data classified? (This is typically done upon the collection or creation of the data record.)
- **Who** classifies the data? (This is typically the *data owner*.)
- **How** is classified data maintained?
- **What** defines the terms under which data is collected, used, stored, and disposed of?

Finally, some standard roles are defined for data that are common industry terms:

- **Data subject**: The living individual whose data is collected
- **Data user**: The organization's employee who interacts with some or all of the data record while performing a business function
- **Data owner**: The individual responsible for accurately labeling and securing data records when they enter the organization

Classification of Information Based on Sensitivity of the Data

Private industry and businesses do not have a single standard for classifying data. Common labels used to evaluate data by its sensitivity are Public, Private/Restricted, Internal or For Internal Use, Sensitive, and Confidential. Common labels used to evaluate data by its criticality are Proprietary and Critical. The greater the impact of the data's exposure, the higher the sensitivity and the higher the classification label.

- ***Public data***: Public data has no restrictions. Public data can be stored and discarded without security precautions.
- ***Internal or for internal use data***: Data classified as Internal is meant for use within the organization and should not be disclosed without managerial permission, but is not sensitive and will not cause regulatory impact if it is exposed.
- ***Confidential data***: This is the only common category between commercial and military classification systems. Confidential information requires authorization for each access and is available to those employees in the organization whose work relates to the subject.
- ***Sensitive/restricted data***: Sensitive or Restricted information requires special protection from unauthorized modification or deletion according to regulations and laws, such as PHI, PII, and credit card data. It would harm the organization if exposed.

- ***Private/restricted data***: Private or Restricted information would cause severe financial or reputational harm to the organization if exposed, and should be protected with the strongest access controls, but is not a legally recognized category of "sensitive" data.

> **NOTE** Some organizations may choose to label sensitive and private data in a single category of "Restricted." Any data labeled Sensitive, Restricted, or Private should have the highest security controls applied.

Table 15-3 shows examples of each data type and some associated controls.

Table 15-3 Common Business Data Classifications and Example Controls/Safeguards

Data Classification	Impact of Disclosure	Access Protections	Example of Data	Example of Control/ Safeguard
Public	None	Not protected from disclosure; may be legally protected from unauthorized use	Press releases, software user manuals, job postings, copyrighted works, patents	Internally approve before release; file a patent or copyright.
Internal/ For Internal Use	Low	Protected by policies and managerial controls, including AUPs	Internal procedures and policies, status reports, internal contact lists	Restrict file downloads from the company intranet.
Confidential	Medium	Protected by operational, physical, digital, and managerial controls, including NDAs	Internal audits, financial analysis documents, performance reviews, proprietary assets	Limit access to authorized users/job roles; use password protection.
Sensitive/ Restricted	High	Protected by operational, physical, digital, and managerial controls, NDAs, and applicable laws/regulations	SSNs, PHI, credit card information, internal financial account numbers	Maintain in a secured database and encrypt during transmission; restrict access by job role and need-to-know.

Data Classification	Impact of Disclosure	Access Protections	Example of Data	Example of Control/ Safeguard
Private/ Restricted	High	Protected by operational, physical, digital, and managerial controls (including need-to-know), NDAs, and applicable laws/ regulations	Trade secrets, computer password repositories, administrative credentials	Store in rooms secured with biometric locks; restrict access to need-to-know.

Intellectual Property and Trade Secrets

Intellectual property (IP) is a unique, internally generated creative asset owned by the organization that is legally protected from being infringed upon or copied by competitors. Inventions, advances in technology, formulas, business processes, source code, music, movies, books, logos, and graphics can all be intellectual property. In the United States, there are four legal categories of intellectual property:

- **Copyright**: Applies to an artistic, literary, visual, or other creative work that exists in tangible form (including digital formats)
- **Trademarks**: Applies to logos, graphics, words, phrases, or designs that uniquely identify an organization's goods or service in the marketplace
- **Patents**: Applies to mechanical processes, designs, chemical formulas, and other inventions that are new, unique, and have application in industry
- **Trade secrets**: Applies to proprietary intellectual property that must be protected from disclosure to maintain its value to the owner

When a trademark, patent, or copyright is registered with the government, the owner can legally prevent others from using the same asset or a clearly derivative asset for profit without permission. These assets are publicly exposed, but not in the public domain, because their for-profit use is exclusively reserved for the organization that holds the rights. However, patents and copyrights eventually expire and release the asset for public use.

Trade secrets are a special class of intellectual property. To register a trade secret, an organization must prove that it is not known to anyone but its owner(s), is actively protected from disclosure by internal controls, and would have economic value to outsiders if it were exposed or stolen, such as the master recipe of a famous beverage. A trade secret never becomes public domain. If it is stolen and used by a competitor, the owner can sue or pursue criminal charges.

Employees and business partners with access to a trade secret sign a non-disclosure agreement (NDA) and are granted access on a need-to-know basis. If project developers must work with code that is protected as a trade secret, the project manager should have confidentiality policies that govern all documents produced by the team, have a clearly established social media policy, have team members provide verbal and written acknowledgement of compliance with these policies, and maintain adequate electronic and physical security of the project's code repository. Note that the parts of an application that are exposed to users (like GUIs) cannot be considered trade secrets, although they can be patented and/or copyrighted.

Proprietary Data

Proprietary data is any unique, internally generated asset owned by the organization. It may cause a competitive disadvantage if the data were copied or exposed, but is not legally protected. Employees and business partners with access to this type of information must typically sign a blanket non-disclosure agreement (NDA). Proprietary data would usually be given a data classification of Internal or Confidential, depending on its sensitivity, and would include assets like sales leads, internal contacts at vendor organizations, paid market analyses of competitors, internal marketing strategies, and internal project processes.

National Security Information

Private sector data classification labels can vary, but government data classification labels do not. In the United States, information that pertains to national security is classified based on the impact from its improper disclosure. From highest (most impact) to lowest, the primary data classifications are as follows:

- **Top Secret**: Unauthorized disclosure could cause the utmost damage to national security, such as the blueprints for nuclear weapons or the keys to encrypted communication channels used by the military.
- **Secret**: Unauthorized disclosure could cause serious, lasting harm to national security, such as military defense plans, troop movements, and information that would damage diplomatic relations with other nations.
- **Confidential**: Unauthorized disclosure would cause harm to national security if it were disclosed, such as military procedural manuals, shipping manifests for raw materials used to manufacture weapons, and government-held trade secrets related to security.

Additional access controls apply within these classifications, including security clearance status and classified information NDAs. Classified information is accessed on a need-to-know basis by personnel whose duties directly relate to the subject. Some categories of classified information add physical security controls to role-based controls, such as restricting document access to a secured room.

Another category, called controlled unclassified information (CUI), is sensitive information that does not affect national security but is protected because it contains the personal or health data of government employees, law enforcement records, taxpayer information, securities filings, trade secrets, or other protected categories of sensitive government-held data.

If a project handles information related to national security, all team members (including the project manager) who can access that information will be required to have the appropriate level of security clearance. Classified digital data should be labeled at the highest level of classification used in the project's information system. Classified physical documents should be stored according to federal requirements. The person who holds the security clearance is responsible for securing the classified data and ensuring its safety.

Access on a Need-to-Know Basis

Need-to-know access is a granular access control that goes beyond the job role to the specific task or activity requiring the data. Implementing need-to-know means that team members are only given access to the data they need to perform a job function. The access lasts for the duration of the time that it takes to perform that function and is then revoked. Furthermore, the access could be limited to only the type of access needed, such as read-only versus full edit permission. Depending on the sensitivity of the data, a person could have a standing need-to-know if their job required the access for ongoing operations.

It is possible to apply data masking to protect sensitive records from routine project operations. Data masking is a technique that displays only the non-sensitive portions of a data record to users and then "masks" sensitive values with invalid or redacted characters (such as displaying only the last four digits of a credit card number or SSN). Masking allows users to run queries and perform operations on the records while letting the organization comply with privacy and confidentiality policies. The data will still appear in its expected format, but privatized.

Data Confidentiality

Data confidentiality means preventing the disclosure of data to unauthorized entities. This includes data when it is in storage (data at rest), in transmission (data in motion), and in use (data in use). Encryption is the best way to protect digital data at rest and in transmission.

There is always the risk that a single data breach can cascade to affect multiple organizations that own, use, or are liable for the affected data records. Your organization is exposed to multi-party risk when you contract with a vendor that will transfer, store, and/or use your sensitive data outside of your network, such as a third-party payment processor. Any business agreement with a contractor or vendor should include explicit terms for handling shared data, including its storage or destruction if you sever the business relationship, and should have penalties for noncompliance. Project managers should remember that a business agreement does not transfer liability. You, as the data owner, are always responsible for performing your own security audit or hiring external auditors to ensure the vendor's compliance with laws governing the protection of your sensitive data when it is handled or stored by a third party.

Sensitive Data Types

Sensitive data includes special classes of data that are protected by laws and regulations that govern how it should be handled and assign penalties for non-compliance. The two main categories of sensitive data that can affect project work are personally identifiable information (PII) and personal health information (PHI).

An impermissible use or disclosure of PII or PHI is defined as a data breach. All organizations should have a data breach response plan that takes into account the scope and scale of each breach. The plan would be enacted by the data breach team. Organizations that handle PHI and PII should also have an internal escalation process whereby any employee who discovers a data incident can notify the correct team members. They may also require an external escalation process to determine when to involve law enforcement, regulatory bodies, the news media, or third parties.

Personally Identifiable Information

Personally identifiable information (PII) includes information collected from living *data subjects* that can be used to uniquely identify that individual. Common examples of PII are names, addresses, and telephone numbers. However, not all PII has the same impact from disclosure. It is permissible for government agencies to disclose real estate records and voter records that link names with address. Companies may disclose the full names of their employees, along with their business contact information, as a condition of employment. For the purposes of this chapter, assume PII to be identifiable information about living data subjects that is held by private organizations for the purposes of commercial activity.

PII data fields include first and last name, address, date of birth, phone number, mother's maiden name, federal and state identification numbers, financial account numbers, GPS location data, and IP address. PII does not include easily anonymized factors, such as gender, ZIP code, or area code.

There are two circumstances when PII would be considered more sensitive: when it is identified as a sensitive standalone data element and when it is linkable. The special categories of PII that are sensitive standalone data elements include the following:

- **Federal**: Social security number, passport number, and taxpayer identification number
- **State**: Driver's license number or state ID number

Any of these data fields could be used as a single factor to uniquely identify an individual. Because they are government-issued data fields, they could also be used to harm or impersonate a data subject or commit fraud in their name. This category of data should always have the highest classification and the strongest access controls applied.

Linkable or linked data refers to PII elements that are not sensitive when taken alone, but are stored in such a way that they could be easily associated together to identify a living data subject and would harm the individual if it were exposed. Sensitive data includes sexual orientation, health status, immigration status, bankruptcy filings, online browsing history, geolocation data and history, and financial account information. The element of impact and harm should be taken into account when calculating the sensitivity of a PII data element.

While there is no single federal law in the United States that protects all PII, there are multiple overlapping laws at the state and federal levels that will apply depending on the data subject's locale. Some states have additional laws regarding data protection and may assess local penalties separately from the federal penalties. In addition, data privacy laws protect special populations (such as children and minors).

NOTE National Institute of Standards and Technology Special Publication 800-122, "Guide to Protecting the Confidentiality of Personally Identifiable Information (PII)," defines U.S. government standards for identifying, classifying, storing, and handling PII and is available for free online. While it is only mandatory for federal agencies, it provides a solid framework for understanding PII. Project managers who handle PII records should be familiar with this resource and its standards.

Personal Health Information

Personal health information (PHI), also called protected health information and electronic personal health information (ePHI), is another highly sensitive and highly regulated category of data. HIPAA regulates the collection, use, storage, and disposal of PHI in the United States. This includes any data held by a covered entity that positively identifies a living individual and associates them with health data, including diagnoses, prescriptions, visits to a provider, and provider billing statements. Covered entities are healthcare providers, health billing agencies, insurance providers, and third parties who manage health data on behalf of covered providers. Employee PHI is also protected by HIPAA when it is collected and held by an employer; employers are not allowed to tell anyone in the project team about a team member's medical diagnosis without their permission, even though the organization is not a covered provider.

Examples of PHI data include the following:

- Pharmacy visits and prescription records
- Billing statements from healthcare providers
- Diagnosis codes and medical test results
- Medical record numbers and health plan beneficiary numbers
- Photographs, images, lab results, and X-rays
- DNA and biometric identifiers

Organizations must follow the HIPAA Breach Notification Rule when unsecured health information is compromised. In the case of a significant breach, organizations can be required to adopt a corrective action plan to bring their data handling in line with HIPAA requirements, and they can be audited to prove compliance.

PHI does not include anonymized data. Doctors may share patient medical records or case histories if the record does not reveal any identifiable detail about the patient. Reporting on health outcomes for women aged 30–35, for patients in a particular city, or for a patient diagnosed with a specific disease, for example, will not expose PHI as long as the data cannot be traced back to the subject.

Impact of Compliance and Privacy Considerations on Project Management

Regulatory issues were touched on in Chapter 3, "Change Control Process Throughout the Project Life Cycle," as project constraints that can significantly affect the project's scope and requirements. When you begin a new project, you may need to perform a Privacy Impact Assessment (PIA) or a Data Privacy Impact Assessment (DPIA) to assess whether your project will require special data controls for protected categories of information.

Data privacy laws cover specific populations of users (such as children under 13), specific types of data (health and personally identifiable data), and users in specific locations (such as California and the European Union). Data privacy laws are also subject to change. As a project manager, you must be aware of how your project may collect user data and know which regulations apply to it now while monitoring the environment for changes that will apply in the future.

Legal and Regulatory Impacts

In addition to federal and international law, many industries must comply with laws, standards, policies, and regulations that govern project-specific activities. The penalty for violations can range from fines to loss of licensure to legal action, both civil and criminal. For example, a construction project must comply with building codes; if it does not, it risks being shut down or made to perform expensive, time-consuming rework. A law or regulation is an immutable risk boundary. If a project manager discovers that a project's activities or outcomes violate a law or fail to comply with applicable regulations, the risk must be avoided completely and/or the project closed.

When factoring in legal and regulatory impacts, project managers should plan for compliance with the strictest applicable law or regulation. Often you will encounter laws and regulations that are stricter than others. To protect the organization, it is better to provide more security than less because many of the laws and regulations in place have penalty provisions that often involve heavy fines. When asked to choose between two conflicting standards, choose to follow the stricter one.

One method for reducing your exposure to the legal and regulatory risk of data collection is data *minimization*. Minimization is not a specific technology; it is the practice of collecting only the personal data that is directly required to perform a function and discarding it when the function is complete. The data subject must explicitly agree to the use, and if the data must be shared with another party, only the least sensitive elements should be made available. Data minimization is one of the GDPR data handling principles and is also a required practice for U.S. federal agencies that handle sensitive data. Even when data minimization is not required by law, practicing it has three benefits for any organization: it reduces the amount of sensitive data being stored and processed, it reduces your potential exposure in a breach, and it reduces data storage costs. When reviewing a project plan, the project manager should work with team members to ensure no extraneous data fields are planned.

EXAMPLE: A grocery store customer loyalty application should be designed to gather customer names and addresses, assign a loyalty ID number, and link the ID to the shopping history. The app should not collect or store birth dates, SSNs, or payment account information. There is no business need for that data, and if the application's database were breached or stolen, the penalties for exposing highly sensitive data would be far more severe than for exposing directory information and a non-government ID number.

Country-, State-, and Province-Specific Privacy Regulations

Project managers should familiarize themselves with country-, state-, and province-specific privacy regulations to ensure that data confidentiality measures comply with regulations. If your project employs international team members or if your product will be released in markets outside of the U.S., you should be aware of the specific country's regulations that apply to the consumer base, even if you are not located in that country. Three major privacy regulations are PIPEDA, GDPR, and CCPA:

- **Canada's *PIPEDA (Personal Information Protection and Electronic Documents Act)***: Applies to private-sector organizations in Canada that collect, use, or disclose personal information in the course of a commercial activity.
- ***GDPR (General Data Protection Regulation)***: Applies to all entities that store, process, and/or transmit data that identifies European Union (EU) citizens or citizens in the European Economic Area (EEA) in the course of a commercial activity.
- **California's *CCPA (California Consumer Privacy Act)***: Applies to all entities that collect the personal data of California residents in the course of a commercial activity.

It is important to remember that the enforcement of these regulations is not based on the local jurisdiction of the organization. It is based on the citizenship or residency of the individuals whose data is collected by a company, or on the location where a consumer transaction occurs. So if a U.S. company stores the data of EU citizens, the company should base its privacy policies and restrictions on GDPR regulations. This applies even if the data is stored within the United States or if the data subject (the individual citizen whose data is collected) does not reside in the EEA. If your project will work with data collected from EEA citizens, you would need to perform a Data Privacy Impact Assessment (DPIA) to ensure data fields are in compliance. If your project collects data from a certain volume of California state residents, it must comply with CCPA. If your project may collect data from California state residents in the future, you should build a forward-facing design that can accommodate that requirement in a later release.

Industry- or Organization-Specific Compliance Concerns

Project managers should also have an awareness of industry- or organization-specific compliance concerns impacting a project. You should consult with the sponsoring organization to get specifics on which compliance concerns should be part of any project:

- **HITECH (Health Information Technology for Economic and Clinical Health Act)**: Applies to organizations that store, transmit, or process electronic health records (EHR) for U.S. citizens.

- **FAR (Federal Acquisition Regulation)**: Applies to organizations that are pursuing, executing, and performing contracts with the U.S. government.
- **Children's Online Privacy Protection Act (COPPA)**: Governs the collection of information about or belonging to minors.

A major example of an industry-specific regulation is the Payment Card Industry Data Security Standard (PCI DSS), which governs the use of credit card payments. Cardholder data (also called payment card data) refers to the unique information associated with a credit card and its owner, including the account number, expiration date, PIN, CVC2/CVV2 code, and billing address. Any entity that processes credit card payments or retains cardholder information in a database must prove its compliance with PCI DSS standards on an annual or quarterly basis. Among other requirements, it dictates that highly sensitive elements (like the PIN and CVC2) are never stored in any form. Some additional state laws regulate how credit card data may be stored or transmitted.

Exam Preparation Tasks

As mentioned in the section "How to Use This Book" in the Introduction, you have a few choices for exam preparation: the exercises here, Chapter 17, "Final Preparation," and the exam simulation questions included with the online Pearson Test Prep Software.

Review All Key Topics

Review the most important topics in this chapter, noted with the Key Topics icon in the outer margin of the page. Table 15-4 lists each reference of these key topics and the page number on which each is found.

Table 15-4 Key Topics for Chapter 15

Key Topic Element	Description	Page Number
Section	Overview of environmental, social, and governance (ESG) factors	424
Table 15-2	ESG Factors That Impact the Organization	424
Section	Explains a project's impact to the local and global environment	425
Section	Explains awareness of applicable regulations and standards	425

Key Topic Element	Description	Page Number
Section	Explains awareness of company vision, mission statements, and values	426
Section; example	Explains project impact to company brand value	427
Section	Covers corporate IT security policies and restrictions	427
Section	Discusses branding restrictions	429
Section	Discusses physical security, including mobile device considerations, removable media considerations, and facility access	429
Paragraph	Explains operational security, including background screening and clearance requirements	431
Section	Explains digital security, including resource access and permissions, remote access restrictions, and multifactor authentication	432
List	List of authentication factors	433
Paragraph	Describes data security	434
Paragraph	Explains data classification	434
Section	Discusses classification of information based on sensitivity of the data	435
Table 15-3	Common Business Data Classifications and Example Controls/Safeguards	436
Section	Overview of intellectual property and trade secrets	437
List	List of National Security Information data classifications	438
Section	Overview of need-to-know access	439
Paragraph	Covers data confidentiality	439
Paragraph	Describes sensitive data types	440
Section	Discusses personally identifiable information (PII)	440
Section	Discusses personal health information (PHI)	441
Paragraph	Explains legal and regulatory impacts of compliance	443
List	Lists important privacy regulations (PIPEDA, GDPR, and CCPA)	444
Section	Covers industry- or organization-specific compliance concerns	444

Define Key Terms

Define the following key terms from this chapter and check your answers in the glossary:

environmental, social, and governance (ESG), global environment, branding restrictions, operational security, background screening, clearance, digital security, resource access and permissions, remote access restrictions, multifactor authentication, data security, sensitivity, classification, data user, data owner, public data, internal or for internal use data, confidential data, sensitive/restricted data, private/restricted data, intellectual property (IP), trade secrets, proprietary data, national security information, need-to-know, data confidentiality, personally identifiable information (PII), data subjects, personal health information (PHI), PIPEDA (Personal Information Protection and Electronic Documents Act), GDPR (General Data Protection Regulation), CCPA (California Consumer Privacy Act)

Review Questions

The answers to these questions appear in Appendix A. For more practice with sample exam questions, use the Pearson Test Prep practice test software online.

1. Your project must comply with federal data privacy controls. The team manages two databases that contain different fields of low-impact PII. The first database contains full names and street addresses, and the second database contains IP addresses and geographical indicators. Which characteristic of PII data would make this a security risk?
   a. None; there is no security risk from low-impact PII.
   b. The data is collected.
   c. The data is unmasked.
   d. The data is linkable.

2. Which data collection technique will reduce project risk when collecting personally identifiable information to use in project work?
   a. Minimization
   b. Optimization
   c. Classification
   d. Retention

3. A major plastics producer begins an initiative to develop a biodegradable diaper. Although the resulting product is advertised as eco-friendly, independent tests prove that it takes 500 years to decompose. Which statement probably describes this project's outcome?

   a. It will impact the company's brand.

   b. It is out of alignment with the corporate mission statement.

   c. It is in alignment with the corporate mission statement.

   d. It will have no impact on the company's brand.

4. A business case with an estimated positive ROI was rejected by the project selection committee after review. Which factor was most likely the reason for the rejection?

   a. The project would require contractors to go through background screening.

   b. The project would require compliance with HIPAA regulations.

   c. The project's result would require an independent audit before it could be released.

   d. The project requires the purchase of carbon offsets.

5. Which of the following are examples of digital security control? (Choose all that apply.)

   a. Security awareness and training

   b. Encryption

   c. Multifactor authentication

   d. USB device restrictions

   e. Closed-circuit cameras

6. Which of the following would an organization *not* do after discovering a breach of 25,000 PHI records?

   a. Repair the issue that led to the breach and keep silent to prevent further attacks.

   b. Adopt a corrective action plan.

   c. Execute a breach response plan.

   d. Escalate externally to regulatory bodies.

7. Your market research project is based in the U.S. Under which circumstances would your project need to comply with GDPR regulations? (Choose all that apply.)
   a. If your project does business with a vendor located in the UK.
   b. If your project collects PII from UK citizens living the UK.
   c. If your project collects PII from U.S. citizens living in the U.S.
   d. If your project collects PII from UK citizens living the U.S.
   e. None; a U.S.-based organization does not have to comply with GDPR.

8. You are managing a project to develop a new medical device. As project manager, you must prove that the device will effectively meet its intended requirements. Which project artifact would assist with auditing when the device is submitted for regulatory approval?
   a. RACI matrix
   b. RTM
   c. Control chart
   d. Defect log

9. What should be employed in addition to physical controls to secure mobile devices in your enterprise? (Choose the best answer.)
   a. Remote access restrictions
   b. Technical controls
   c. Managerial controls
   d. Branding restrictions

10. You have learned that a longstanding team member will be leaving the company at the end of the week. An employee from another department will fill in while you search for a replacement. Which operational security practice will you *most* likely perform this week?
   a. Checking security clearance requirements for the new team member
   b. Implementing security awareness training
   c. Performing a background check on the new team member
   d. Following an offboarding policy

This chapter covers the following topics:

- **Infrastructure:** Covers concepts relevant to IT project management, including computing services, multitiered architecture, networking and connectivity, storage, data warehouses, and documentation
- **Cloud Models:** Explains the features of cloud delivery and cloud deployment models (PaaS, SaaS, IaaS, and XaaS)
- **Software:** Discusses commercial products for enterprise resource planning (ERP), customer relationship management (CRM), databases, electronic document and records management systems (EDRMS), content management systems (CMS), and financial systems
- **IT Infrastructure Change Control:** Examines downtime/maintenance windows schedules, customer notifications, rollback plans, and validation checks
- **Software Change Control:** Covers requirements definition, risk assessment, testing, approval, customer notification, and release
- **Cloud Versus On-Premises Change Control:** Explains change control in the cloud versus on-premises
- **Continuous Integration/Continuous Deployment (CI/CD) Processes:** Discusses continuous integration and continuous deployment
- **Tiered Architecture for Software Development:** Covers tiered architecture, development environment, testing environment, staging environment, and production environment

CHAPTER 16

Foundational IT Concepts and Operational Change Control for IT Project Management

Project managers and the project teams need to understand certain foundational IT concepts, including IT, cloud model, software, and IT infrastructure concepts. Project managers should ensure that the team is provided with training that includes basic IT foundation terminology. In addition, the team needs to understand the organization's usage and meaning of these IT terms and to which assets these terms may apply.

Operational change control may also affect a project. As such, the project team needs to understand an organization's operational change control for the IT infrastructure, software, cloud versus on-premises, continuous integration/continuous deployment (CI/CD), and tiered architecture.

This chapter covers the following objectives for the CompTIA Project+ exam:

4.4 Summarize basic IT concepts relevant to IT project management.

4.5 Explain operational change-control processes during an IT project.

"Do I Know This Already?" Quiz

The "Do I Know This Already?" quiz allows you to assess whether you should read this entire chapter thoroughly or jump to the "Exam Preparation Tasks" section. If you are in doubt about your answers to these questions or your own assessment of your knowledge of the topics, read the entire chapter. Table 16-1 lists the major headings in this chapter and their corresponding "Do I Know This Already?" quiz questions. You can find the answers in Appendix A, "Answers to the 'Do I Know This Already?' Questions and Review Quizzes."

Table 16-1 "Do I Know This Already?" Section-to-Question Mapping

Foundation Topics Section	Questions
Cloud Models	1
Infrastructure	2
Software	3
IT Infrastructure Change Control	4
Software Change Control	5
Continuous Integration/Continuous Deployment (CI/CD) Process	6
Tiered Architecture in Software Development	7

CAUTION The goal of self-assessment is to gauge your mastery of the topics in this chapter. If you do not know the answer to a question or are only partially sure of the answer, you should mark that question as wrong for the purposes of the self-assessment. Giving yourself credit for an answer you correctly guess skews your self-assessment results and might provide you with a false sense of security.

1. Which cloud service model is a pay-as-you-go subscription in which the customer has the sole responsibility for patching the operating systems on their virtual machines?
   a. SaaS
   b. PaaS
   c. IaaS
   d. XaaS

2. You have requested that archived data from your organization's databases be made available for analysis for a current project. Which infrastructure component will you use to analyze the data to make decisions?
   a. Data warehouse
   b. Networking and connectivity
   c. Documentation
   d. Storage

3. Which organizational software is most likely to include customer relations and sales, supply chain, finance, and human resources management?
   a. CRM
   b. ERP

c. EDRMS

d. CMS

4. The IT department rolls out several urgent security patches that a software provider has provided. After the patches have been rolled out, what is the process called that verifies the software still works as expected?

   a. Maintenance window

   b. Customer notification

   c. Rollback plan

   d. Validation check

5. Which software change control step will include a means whereby the change can be rolled back?

   a. Risk assessment

   b. Testing

   c. Requirements definition

   d. Release

6. Which of the following is *not* part of the CI portion of the CI/CD process?

   a. Auto scripts

   b. Version control

   c. Package

   d. Compile

7. Which of the following tiers is usually a replica of the live environment?

   a. Testing

   b. Staging

   c. Production

   d. Development

Foundation Topics

Infrastructure

When it comes to basic IT concepts, project managers should ensure that the project team understands the organizational IT infrastructure on which the project will rely. Infrastructure resources include computing services, multitiered architecture, networking and connectivity, storage, data warehouse, and documentation.

Computing Services

The term ***computing services*** refers to all technology used to transmit, store, process, or analyze data or information. It includes software, service provider services, hosted computing services, information technology and telecommunication hardware, and other equipment. Data or information can be physical or digital. Computing services includes on-premises solutions, remote solutions, and cloud solutions.

At a minimum, projects will rely on computing services for data or information retrieval and storage. However, many IT projects will require access to much more, depending on the project's end result. Any changes to computing services during a project can impact the project. Project managers should maintain open lines of communication to central IT staff and ensure that the IT department understands the project's needs when it comes to computing services.

Any planned service downtime, whether that downtime is for updates, device replacement, or upgrades, needs to be carefully documented in the project schedule. For example, planning an important project data analysis task to run during a database maintenance window could impact the project.

Multitiered Architecture

The term ***multitiered architecture*** refers to any architecture in which multiple tiers are used to logically separate processes, improving performance and security. In a three-tiered model, the presentation, the application processing (sometimes called logic), and the data management are logically separate processes. With a multitiered architecture, the systems split the tasks and often the data across multiple resources, thereby providing scalability, manageability, flexibility, and improved security. While each tier introduced increases the level of complexity in the architecture design, the multiple tiers also generally provide better performance because of all the systems that can participate in the process.

Project managers need to understand the underlying structure of the architecture used as part of the project and ensure that the IT staff understands the project needs as they relate to the deployed architecture.

Networking and Connectivity

Networking and *connectivity* refer to the hardware and software that allow communication between users, devices, apps, and the Internet. Because communication is key to efficient project management, project managers should ensure that the project team has appropriate connectivity regardless of a team member's physical location. While working from an organization's facility may mean that this is not a concern (unless, of course, the network goes down), some team members may need to work from locations with less-than-stellar connectivity.

Project managers should research the connectivity needs of the project and communicate these with organizational IT staff. In addition, the project manager may need to make special requests to aid team members, particularly if remote connectivity is needed.

Storage

Storage typically includes all devices, servers, and network elements that provide data storage. The storage components intersect with the rest of the overall infrastructure. All projects produce documents, including project plans, artifacts, reports, charts, and schedules. The project manager will need to communicate with the IT staff exactly what the project's storage needs are.

The project team must understand where their work should be stored and accessed. In most cases, a data share can be configured for project usage. Then, project team members can be given the appropriate access. Project managers may also need to explicitly state the data backup policy for the project to ensure that files kept on the team member's device are not lost.

Data Warehouse

A ***data warehouse*** is a collection of data sources that allows the organization to use the data therein to guide the organization in making decisions. The stored data can be from multiple sources. It supports business intelligence (BI) activities, especially analytics, and is often considered part of the storage infrastructure.

Projects may need to access data stored in the data warehouse to help make project decisions. Because the data stored can be vast, the project manager may need to work with database personnel to schedule analytics and report generation. Project managers should ensure that project needs are communicated with the appropriate personnel so that timely data retrieval can occur.

Documentation

Documentation is a broad term used to refer to any documents that support the IT infrastructure or a component in the infrastructure. It includes schematics, specifications, configuration designs, and licenses. Actual documentation written to provide instructional material to application or operating system users also falls into this category—think application or operating system help files.

The project team may require access to documentation. Project managers should ensure that any needed documentation can be located. Team members will need to be given copies of the documentation or granted access to digital copies of the documentation.

EXAMPLE: For a new project, the project manager requests that the team be given appropriate access to the file servers (part of computing services and storage) on which project documentation will be stored. In addition, the code developers on the team will need access to the tiered application development environment (part of multitiered architecture). The team must be granted both on-premises and remote connectivity to these resources (part of networking and connectivity). As part of the research involved during project planning, the project manager and a few other team members will need to run reports on data stored in the data warehouse. Finally, the team will be using at least one application with which some may be unfamiliar, so the project manager must request access to the application documentation. From this scenario, you can easily see how all of these IT components are vital to project success.

Cloud Models

In a traditional on-premises infrastructure, all hardware and software components must be sourced, deployed, and maintained by in-house personnel. *Cloud computing* is a way for organizations to use a broad range of applications, networking, virtual machines, development environments, or storage that is maintained by a service provider and delivered over the Internet. If you have ever used Apple's iCloud, Google Drive, or Microsoft OneDrive, you have used cloud computing.

Cloud computing is an on-demand self-service model that provides rapid elasticity and scalability. *Rapid elasticity* means that resources can be quickly added or released to handle surges in demand, while *scalability* means that infrastructure components can be easily added or removed. Another cloud concept is *multitenancy*, which means that several customers are hosted in separate cloud architectures that use the same pool of physical hardware. Finally, most cloud services (except for SaaS) are *metered*, meaning that the customer can track their usage costs per unit consumed.

Given the wide range of offerings currently available, it is often more affordable to outsource IT infrastructure to cloud service providers (CSPs). Cloud costs can be pay-as-you-go models or flat subscriptions, and they can provide a single application or an entire virtual server farm for your custom configuration. How those cloud services are delivered, and the extent of the customer's control over their components, depends on which *cloud service model* is chosen. There are three main service models, plus a catchall definition for niche or newly developing models: IaaS, PaaS, SaaS, and XaaS. Each of these services meets a different set of business standards and requirements. However, no matter which deployment model is being used, the customer organization is *always* responsible for governance, risk, and compliance (GRC), data security, and internal access controls.

Infrastructure as a Service

Infrastructure as a Service (IaaS) is a model where the cloud provider maintains the networking, computing, and storage components and makes them available on a per-use or subscription basis. The customer installs and maintains their own operating systems, middleware, and applications, including virtual machines and servers. The service host maintains the physical data center and secures access to the customer's cloud, while the customer secures access within their cloud with the appropriate firewalls and encryption. IaaS is an affordable alternative to purchasing and maintaining an on-premises physical infrastructure, especially as it can be scaled up or down as needed with low overhead and no maintenance costs. Amazon Elastic Compute Cloud (Amazon EC2), Microsoft Azure, and Google Cloud are all IaaS solutions.

Platform as a Service

Platform as a Service (PaaS) is a complete cloud environment for developing and deploying web applications. It provides access to operating systems, middleware, and runtime in a complete virtualized infrastructure with servers, storage, and networking components that are maintained by the provider. The customer manages the code, services, data, and applications that they build, while the service provider handles hardware and OS maintenance. PaaS also provides built-in software components to make code writing faster; rather than having to buy a license for every operating system, the customer can choose from the cloud provider's library of software. AWS Elastic Beanstalk, Heroku, IBM Cloud Foundry, Google App Engine, and Red Hat OpenShift are examples of PaaS.

Software as a Service

Software as a Service (SaaS) delivers an application to end users over the Internet, typically by subscription or user license. SaaS requires the least effort on the customer's part to maintain because the vendor secures the application, runs it on its own infrastructure, and handles all updates and patches. The customer is only responsible for provisioning users and managing access to their stored data. Most SaaS applications will support any device (for example, laptops and smartphones) that can connect to the service. Zoom, HubSpot, Microsoft 365, Google Workspace, and Dropbox are well-known examples of SaaS.

Anything as a Service

As cloud services have evolved, providers have developed solutions that are more specific in scope than the main three. These solutions are collectively referred to as ***Anything as a Service (XaaS)***. Here are some common types of XaaS:

- **Storage as a Service (StaaS):** Provides storage systems for backups, data, and applications in the cloud
- **Database as a Service (DBaaS):** Provides a cloud-based database for organizations
- **Security as a Service (SECaaS):** Provides security services that are managed by a third party and delivered through a cloud-based model
- **Identity as a Service (IDaaS):** Provides identity and access management (IAM) tools that are managed by a third party and integrated into the client's federated or single sign-on (SSO) environment
- **Desktop as a Service (DaaS):** Provides virtualized applications and desktop services for a workforce to access on any device through a web browser

Because XaaS solutions are cloud-based, they will be unavailable for use if the Internet goes down. Organizations should ensure their SLA guarantees that cloud-based services are provided in a timely and reliable manner.

Public, Private, Community, and Hybrid Clouds

Whereas the cloud service model describes features, the cloud deployment model describes how the cloud environment is made accessible:

- A ***public cloud*** is a commercial service available to anyone who signs up. Its physical components are fully owned and maintained by the service provider.

- A ***private cloud*** is used only by one organization or its federated partners. Its applications and services are delivered only to its internal clients through a locally available gateway. The physical infrastructure may be maintained on-premises, offsite, or by a third party.
- A ***community cloud*** is owned and operated by a group of organizations with a shared audience and requirements (such as a group of universities).
- A ***hybrid cloud*** combines elements of two or more cloud infrastructures (such as public and private) that are linked through a shared technical interface. One example would be an organization that keeps sensitive data on a private cloud but uses a public-facing cloud for most business functions. Another example, called ***cloudbursting***, is when an organization runs out of computing resources in the internal data center and bursts the extra workload to external third-party cloud services.

Software

Project team members will need to use software to aid in the project tasks to which they have been assigned. The project manager needs to understand the software that an organization uses and ensure that the team is given access, as appropriate. Software types that may be used include enterprise resource planning (ERP), customer relationship management (CRM), databases, electronic document and records management (EDRM) systems, content management systems (CMSs), and financial systems.

Enterprise Resource Planning

Enterprise resource planning (ERP) systems allow an organization to manage and integrate business activities by collecting shared data from multiple sources. ERP provides system integration, automation, real-time operations, and tracking and visibility. Examples are Oracle ERP Cloud, Unit4 ERP, FinancialForce ERP, NetSuite, and Acumatica Cloud ERP.

Most ERP deployments include the components shown in Figure 16-1.

Projects usually produce results that will integrate into the business. For this reason, the project manager should be familiar with the organization's ERP software and understand where the project's results fit into the current ERP structure. Understanding where the project fits into the overall organizational structure can help ensure that the project's scope is well defined and scope creep is controlled.

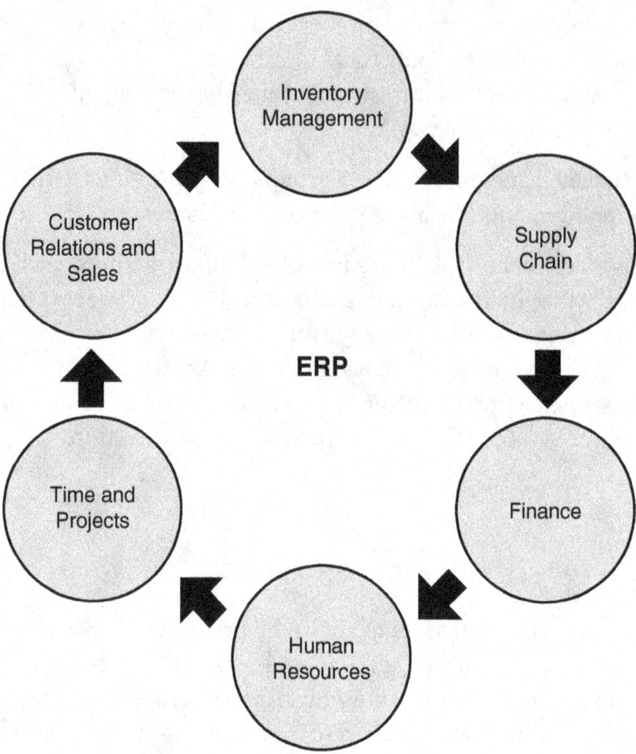

Figure 16-1 ERP Model

> **NOTE** Scope creep was fully covered in Chapter 3, "Change Control Process Throughout the Project Life Cycle."

Customer Relationship Management

Customer relationship management (CRM) solutions provide a process and group of systems that are used to manage all client relations. Marketing designs campaigns, generates leads, and maintains the database. Sales assigns, qualifies, and converts leads and tracks opportunities. Orders delivers products and produces invoices. Support manages cases, provides services, develops knowledge bases, and conducts training. This is all part of the Customer Relations and Sales node in the ERP sample. Examples include Monday.com, Salesforce CRM, Zendesk CRM, HubSpot CRM, and Oracle NetSuite.

Most CRM deployments include the components shown in Figure 16-2.

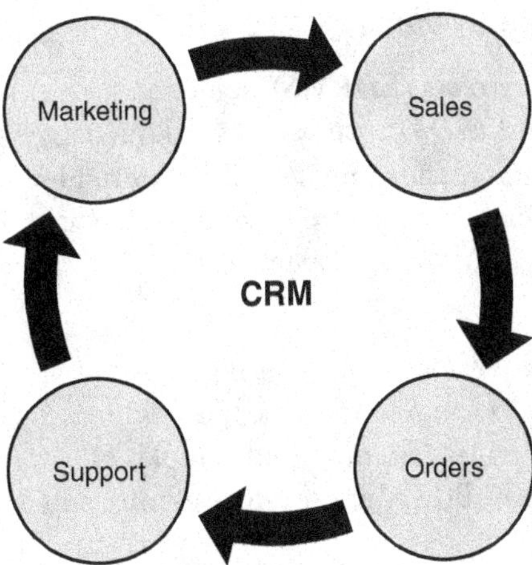

Figure 16-2 CRM Model

Depending on the project type, the project manager may need to communicate with marketing and sales so that they understand the project's result and how they will market and sell it. This is especially true regarding software development projects that produce a new application for other businesses or consumers. Making sure marketing and sales understand the project's scope will ensure that those teams are accurate in their communication with customers regarding the project's result.

Databases

Databases describe a server or group of servers used to store and manage current organizational data, including inventory data, order data, personnel data, and financial data. Data warehouses are related to databases in that data warehouses store data. However, data warehouses hold all archived, not current, data. As data is no longer needed in the current database store, it may be moved to the data warehouse. This ensures that the data can still be accessed and queried.

The stored data is usually viewed and edited via user applications. A data warehouse may be used to centralize the collection of related organizational databases into one location for analysis. Examples are Microsoft SQL Server, MySQL, FileMaker Pro, Oracle Database, and dBASE.

The project manager and team members may need the data stored in the databases or data warehouse. Anyone accessing the data should be given the minimal permission to complete their job. It is particularly important to not give users the ability to edit data if they do not need that ability. Most projects will only need the ability to view or export most data. This will depend on the project type. The project manager is responsible for documenting the data access needs of the project team and ensuring that the principle of least privilege is enforced.

Electronic Document and Record Management Systems

Electronic document and record management systems (EDRMS), sometimes referred to as ***electronic documents management (EDM)***, are systems that manage an organization's paper and electronic documents so they can be easily retrieved in the event of a compliance audit or subpoena. These systems are used to track documents and records. They often include version automation, document checkin/checkout, and archival notification.

The term originally referred to electronic or paper documents, but the meaning has broadened to include email, images, internal-facing documents (like company memos), and external documents (like marketing or sales content). Examples of EDRMS systems include Google Drive, Dropbox, Box, Microsoft SharePoint, and Microsoft OneDrive.

Project managers should ensure that the team members understand the organization's document management policies, especially those that apply to the project.

Content Management Systems

Content management systems (CMSs) provide a nontechnical solution for producing digital content, such as web content. The actual encoding of the data is handled by the CMS, while the user is provided with an easy-to-handle graphical user interface (GUI) with fields to insert the content to be produced. Examples are WordPress, Joomla, Drupal, Magento, Squarespace, Wix, and Ghost.

The project may need its own online space, like a wiki or blog, to help the team and stakeholders communicate. The project manager should designate the team members who will be able to post to the CMS and should give all others read access only. In addition, steps will likely need to be taken to ensure that the information in the CMS is not shared publicly. Team members and stakeholders may need to sign a non-disclosure agreement (NDA) for CMS content, depending on the nature of the project.

Financial Systems

Financial systems manage the accounting and other financial aspects of an organization. Examples include Intuit QuickBooks and Oracle NetSuite Accounting. The project manager will need to be familiar with the financial system so that procurement invoices are properly entered and payment is authorized. The financial system may also be used to pay contractors.

IT Infrastructure Change Control

Project managers and team members need to be aware that the IT infrastructure is not a static entity. The infrastructure includes many devices, computers, systems, applications, and technologies, all of which must be maintained and updated. Most organizations have IT infrastructure change control policies that need to be understood by the entire project team, as infrastructure changes can mean downtime that affects the project.

Project managers should be familiar with the four main IT infrastructure change control components: downtime/maintenance windows schedules, customer notifications, rollback plans, and validation checks.

Downtime/Maintenance Windows Schedules

Any projects that may be affected by IT infrastructure downtime or maintenance should have the downtime or maintenance windows carefully documented so that planned outages have minimal effect on daily operations. In most cases, downtime or maintenance is scheduled based on periods of lower demand.

The project schedule should include any planned IT outages or maintenance windows, especially if those outages affect resources to which the project team needs access. Important project tasks, especially those on the critical path, should be scheduled so that outages will minimally affect them. In addition, the project manager should monitor planned outages to ensure that the outages do not take longer than originally planned. If outages take longer, project tasks may need to be adjusted accordingly.

Customer Notifications

The project manager should be notified if additional downtime or maintenance is required. These IT customer notifications are vital to ensuring that the project is kept on schedule. IT personnel should work closely with the project manager so that, if possible, emergency downtime or maintenance is scheduled at a time that is better for the project. However, this is not always possible. At minimum, the IT department should notify the project manager and project team if downtime needs to occur and give the project team time to save their work.

Rollback Plans

A ***rollback plan*** allows the IT infrastructure or any component being updated to return to its previous state. Updates sometimes cause unexpected and unwelcome results. This is when the rollback plan is very important.

Validation Checks

Validation is a process whereby confirmation of the accuracy of an object occurs. Any time IT infrastructure updates occur, it is important to perform a validation check to ensure that all components are operational. If issues are discovered during the validation check, the IT department should use the rollback plan to return the system, device, or application to its previous state.

Software Change Control

When software is changed, developers need to carefully plan the changes so that current features in the software are not negatively affected by the change. Software change control must follow a defined process:

- Requirements definition
- Risk assessment
- Testing
- Approval
- Customer notifications
- Release

Requirements Definition

Any time a software or application change is requested, it is important to fully define the requirements. The change request should document the component or feature changing and the reason for the change. The change request should follow the change control process and only be implemented once the formal change approval body has approved the change.

Risk Assessment

All software changes should be assessed for risks. Both a qualitative and quantitative risk analysis should be performed. All risks should be documented as part of the change request so that the approving body is aware of the risks should the change be implemented.

Testing

Software changes must be tested prior to deployment in the live environment. Two types of testing are used: automated and manual. In automated testing, tests are executed automatically via test automation frameworks, along with other tools and software. In manual testing, a programmer performs the tests. Both types of testing should be used.

Approval

This involves getting formal approval from the change control board or approving entity. At this point, the change could be denied or given approval for a later iteration or project.

Customer Notifications

Once the change has been tested, customers should be notified of when the change will be deployed. The notification should include information on any downtime that may occur and details on the software features that may be affected by the change.

Release

This is the actual deployment of the change. After the change is released, developers will need to monitor the software for unexpected issues. End users will need a way to report any issues they encounter. As part of the change release, developers should document a rollback plan if major issues are discovered with the change.

Cloud Versus On-Premises Change Control

On-premises changes and cloud changes are managed differently. In an on-premises or on-site deployment, only internal personnel need to be involved in the change control. This is the easiest change deployment.

With each step up the cloud model ladder, more and more resources are the responsibility of cloud service provider (CSP) staff. No matter where the change must occur, it will be necessary to carefully coordinate the deployment of the changes, depending on the cloud model used and the component being affected.

Continuous Integration/Continuous Deployment (CI/CD) Process

Modern models of software development like DevOps mean that developer teams continually develop and publish updates to the product. The source code and its related content files are retained in a shared container known as a *repository*, or *repo*. Repositories provide version control so that changes made by one developer are not wiped out by changes submitted by another developer and so that the definitive source code does not fork or branch in an unplanned way.

Version control systems and repositories, such as Git and Microsoft's Team Foundation Server, manage those changes across the development team and all process stages. They also support tools that provide continuous integration/continuous deployment (CI/CD). CI/CD automates the process of testing and deploying code as follows:

- ***Continuous integration (CI)***: The tools automate standard unit and integration testing so that they validate new components immediately after builds. The test environment is then provisioned based on configuration profiles, where further system and acceptance testing occurs using staging parameters. This is the build pipeline.
- ***Continuous deployment (CD)* and delivery**: After each component passes testing in the staging environment, configuration files and scripts are used to move that component into production, where the working component is integrated with the rest of the application and goes live. This can be done automatically or performed as a manual process at scheduled intervals. This is the release pipeline.

The CI/CD process is shown in Figure 16-3.

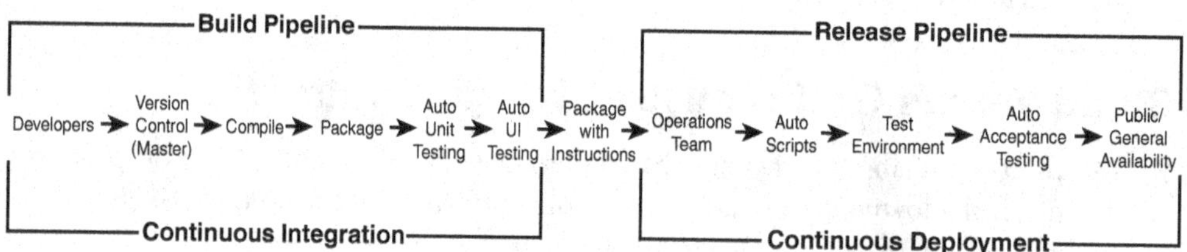

Figure 16-3 CI/CD Process

Tiered Architecture in Software Development

When software changes are approved, changes should be deployed through the software development tiers to ensure proper testing prior to deployment. Most tiered environments are logically divided into three systems, which can be combined on the same physical system or kept separate, plus a production environment.

Having staged tiers reduces risk to customers and to source code. In a ***tiered architecture***, you isolate each tier and deploy changes through the tiers in a controlled manner. Then, if an issue arises with the change in an earlier tier, the change can be revised prior to the change's deployment in the production environment.

Development Environment

In most application development and deployment models, the development environment exists in its own tier that only the project team, developers, and key stakeholders will be able to access. Often the code in this tier exists in a variety of locations—from the developer's local computer to a central code repository. Multiple development environments can exist concurrently.

The development (commonly referred to as DEV) environment contains base source code and other content files, such as data or configurations, that are updated by developers on a regular basis. It also includes any temporary compilations created for basic error checking. Normally, each developer has their own copy of the source code on a local workstation, which is then synchronized with a central server. Once it is error free, the code moves to quality assurance/quality control (QA/QC).

Testing or Quality Assurance/Quality Control Environment

The testing or QA/QC environment contains source code and other content files that are ready for automated or manual functionality testing. Typically, these tests are binary pass/fail decisions. If the code is rejected, it is returned to the responsible developer. If the code is accepted, it is built and integrated into the larger solution and deployed to staging.

Beta/Staging Environment

The beta or staging environment is a close replica of the live environment in which the application will be deployed. This is the system where performance testing and customer acceptance occurs. Because this environment is isolated, any issues discovered at this point do not affect day-to-day operations. If the application meets the performance criteria and customer satisfaction, it is then deployed to production.

Production Environment

The final tier is the production environment. The production environment is where users access the final code after all of the updates and testing. Of all the environments, this one is the most important. Once you are in production, any bugs or errors that remain will be found by a user—and you can only hope bugs are minor.

Production is known as the higher environment because it is available to the intended end users. There may be a series of releases, such as ALPHA or BETA, before the application gains full adoption, but if it is in production, it is running actively within the business. New features and patches will be introduced in DEV and then moved back up the process again until these changes are widely available.

Exam Preparation Tasks

As mentioned in the section "How to Use This Book" in the Introduction, you have a few choices for exam preparation: the exercises here, Chapter 17, "Final Preparation," and the exam simulation questions in the Pearson Test Prep Software online.

Review All Key Topics

Review the most important topics in this chapter, noted with the Key Topics icon in the outer margin of the page. Table 16-2 lists each reference of these key topics and the page number on which each is found.

Table 16-2 Key Topics for Chapter 16

Key Topic Element	Description	Page Number
Paragraph	Explains computing services	454
Paragraph	Explains multitiered architecture	454
Paragraph	Describes network and connectivity	455
Paragraph	Explains data warehouse	455
Paragraph	Describes IaaS	457
Paragraph	Describes PaaS	457
Paragraph	Describes SaaS	458
Paragraph	Describes XaaS	458
Figure 16-1	ERP Model	460
Figure 16-2	CRM Model	461
Paragraph	IT infrastructure change control	462
Figure 16-3	CI/CD Process	466

Define Key Terms

Define the following key terms from this chapter and check your answers in the glossary:

computing services, multitiered architecture, data warehouse, Infrastructure as a Service (IaaS), PLatform as a Service (Paas), Software as a Service (Saas), Anything as a Service (XaaS), public cloud, provate cloud, community cloud, hybrid cloud, cloudbursting, enterprise resource planning (ERP), electronic document and record management systems (EDRMS), electronic documents management (EDM), content management systems (CMSs), rollback plan, validation, continuous integration (CI), continuous deployment (CD), tiered architecture

Review Questions

The answers to these questions appear in Appendix A. For more practice with sample exam questions, use the Pearson Test Prep practice test software online.

1. Your organization uses an SaaS application to manage your HR functions. The application provides internal controls to restrict unauthorized access to sensitive records. Which aspect(s) of security would be the responsibility of the customer and not the service provider? (Choose all that apply.)

   a. Access to data records from within the application

   b. Access to valid user credentials

   c. Access to the data being transmitted over the Internet

   d. Access to the server that stores the data records

2. You have been hired to manage a project for a healthcare organization. The organization has strict rules in place regarding all documents involving patient data. You have requested that your project team be granted access to the organizational system that manages all physical and electronic documents. Which of the following is most likely involved in this scenario?

   a. ERP

   b. CRM

   c. EDRMS

   d. Database

3. What is the first step in the software change control process?

   a. Risk assessment

   b. Approval

   c. Testing

   d. Requirements definition

4. The software development project you are managing follows a CI/CD process. As part of this process, the team is being given training on the CI/CD process. Which of the following is part of the CI portion??

   a. Version control

   b. Operations team

   c. Acceptance testing

   d. Release pipeline

5. In a tiered architecture for software development, where is the base source code that is updated located?

   a. Testing environment

   b. Development environment

   c. Staging environment

   d. Production environment

This chapter covers the following topics:

- **Testing your readiness for the Project+ exam:** How to take advantage of this book's special features in your final preparation for the exam.

CHAPTER 17

Final Preparation

Congratulations! You have completed 16 chapters of this book, covering the knowledge and skills required to pass the CompTIA Project+ PK0-005 exam. Although these chapters supply the detailed information you will need to know for the exam, most people need more preparation than just reading the text. This chapter suggests additional ways to get ready for the exam.

TIP Before going through the final preparations in this chapter, and again before taking the Project+ exam, download and carefully review the latest exam objectives from CompTIA. The information in the objectives is subject to change without notice.

Take Advantage of the Tools in This Book

This book's special features are designed to help you self-test your understanding of the content on the Project+ exam. Perhaps you used some of these features as you worked your way through each individual chapter. Now you can combine them to see if you are really ready for the exam or if you need more study in some areas.

Retake the "Do I Know This Already?" Quizzes

Use the multiple-choice "Do I Know This Already?" quiz in every chapter to assess whether you actually grasp the topics tested by the quizzes. Check your answers against those in Appendix A, "Answers to the 'Do I Know This Already?' Quizzes and Review Questions." If your answer to a question was wrong, reread the relevant topic in the chapter.

Work Through the "Exam Preparation Tasks" Sections

If you have not yet worked through the "Exam Preparation Tasks" section in every chapter (or even if you have), use the features in that section to make sure you are thoroughly conversant with the content that is likely to be on the Project+ exam:

- **Review All Key Topics:** The Key Topics table guides you to the most important information in the chapter. If your understanding of a topic is limited or vague, jump to the specified page number in the table, find the Key Topic icon in the margin, and start reviewing.
- **Define Key Terms:** The most important terminology in the chapter is listed in this section. Define each term and then compare your definitions against those in the glossary. If your definition was incorrect or incomplete, find that term in the chapter and refresh your memory.
- **Review Questions:** Use the multiple-choice questions in each chapter to test your understanding of the chapter content. Check Appendix A for the answers, along with explanations that can help solidify the details you need to grasp.

Complete the Memory Tables Appendices

Appendix C, "Memory Tables," is available as a file on the companion website for this book. (To access the website, follow the instructions in the "Companion Website" section of the Introduction to this book.) Open the Appendix C file on the website, print the entire appendix, and complete the tables. Check your results against the completed tables in Appendix D, "Memory Tables Answers." If you are unsure of some of the answers or your answers were wrong, go to the relevant section in the chapter and refresh your memory. You will need to know the terms, formulas, and definitions in the memory tables to pass the Project+ exam.

Review the Examples

Even if you know all the facts in this book, you will not pass the Project+ exam unless you can analyze scenario-based questions and select the answer that best fits the conditions described. Before you take the practice tests or the live exam, page through this book one last time, scanning for **EXAMPLE** (all caps and boldfaced) in the text. These memorable project examples are designed to help you understand how the subject under discussion is related to handling real-life situations.

Practice with Pearson Test Prep

This book includes access to the Pearson Test Prep practice test software, which provides two exam-realistic test banks available only with this book. Following the instructions in the "Using the Pearson Test Prep Practice Test Software" section of the Introduction, use the practice tests developed with this book to verify your readiness for the Project+ exam.

Ready, Set, Test!

This book was developed with the intention not just to present information you will need to pass the Project+ certification exam, but to help you understand the relevant details and learn how to apply them in project management. The authors and editors of this book wish you every success!

APPENDIX A

Answers to the "Do I Know This Already?" Questions and Review Quizzes

Answers to the "Do I Know This Already?" Questions

Chapter 1

1. Correct Answer: B. Explanation: A project is temporary, not permanent. A project has a defined start and finish, is unique, and has a stated reason or purpose.
2. Correct Answer: A. Explanation: An organization's portfolio consists of all the projects, programs, and operations it manages in order to reach its strategic objectives.
3. Correct Answer: D. Explanation: Agile projects are adaptive, allowing a project to meet changing conditions.
4. Correct Answer: C. Explanation: The iterative quality of an Agile project allows each incomplete area to be refined until the result is satisfactory.
5. Correct Answer: B. Explanation: User stories are used in Agile planning to help with requirements gathering.
6. Correct Answer: B. Explanation: Continuous feedback is required for an Agile project to succeed.
7. Correct Answer: D. Explanation: "What went wrong during this sprint?" is not answered in the daily scrum meeting. All of the other questions are answered in the daily meeting.
8. Correct Answer: B. Explanation: Agile teams are self-organized and self-directed.
9. Correct Answer: A. Explanation: The Software Development Life Cycle (SDLC) is a predictive model. All of the other options are adaptive models.
10. Correct Answer: B. Explanation: The Operations team is responsible for the Release, Deploy, Operate, and Monitor steps of the DevOps model.

Chapter 2

1. Correct Answer: B. Explanation: Hybrid is not a project team structure. CompTIA defines the project team structures as matrix, functional, and projectized.
2. Correct Answer: A. Explanation: In a projectized team structure, resources report to the project manager.
3. Correct Answer: A. Explanation: The retirement of a team member during a critical stage of project work should be classified as a risk and recorded in the risk register.
4. Correct Answer: B. Explanation: A team member with a unique skill set who is assigned to a high-priority project would be a critical resource.
5. Correct Answers: A, B, C, D. Explanation: All of the listed documents would help a project manager find and analyze a resource gap in skill sets, availability, or equipment.
6. Correct Answer: C. Explanation: Storming is the phase in the team life cycle when the team starts making decisions about the project.
7. Correct Answer: B. Explanation: The product owner manages and prioritizes the backlog. This role sets the vision for the product.
8. Correct Answer: A. Explanation: The sponsor gives the final approval for a project.
9. Correct Answer: B. Explanation: The project manager does not create the project deliverables; the project team creates the deliverables. The project manager manages the team, creates the budget, and creates the schedule.
10. Correct Answer: C. Explanation: The project stakeholders provide project requirements.
11. Correct Answer: C. Explanation: The project management office (PMO) is not concerned with estimating costs. The PMO sets project management standards and provides templates and tools.

Chapter 3

1. Correct Answer: D. Explanation: This is an example of a change request because the new feature was formally approved by the project sponsor.
2. Correct Answer: C. Explanation: Change control is a monitoring and controlling activity that takes place in the Executing phase.
3. Correct Answers: C, E. Explanation: According to CompTIA, the project manager should formally communicate with stakeholders after the change is

approved or denied and after the change has been both implemented *and* verified as successful.

4. Correct Answer: D. Explanation: After you create or receive a change request, your first step is to identify the change and document the request.
5. Correct Answer: C. Explanation: The change control board (CCB) is most likely to be the approval authority for a change request, although they can be overruled by the project sponsor in rare cases.
6. Correct Answer: B. Explanation: The purpose of a regression plan is to ensure the change can be rolled back to restore the project to a prior state.
7. Correct Answer: A. Explanation: Because the project sponsor requested ten additional server racks, which negatively affected the budget and schedule, this is an example of scope creep. Scope creep occurs when the scope changes without adjusting other project constraints in response.
8. Correct Answer: D. Explanation: A customer requesting rework of a deliverable during a sprint would cause scope creep because the resources would have to fit more effort than was estimated into the given timebox.
9. Correct Answer: C. Explanation: Because this request will affect major project constraints, such as schedule, resources, tasks, budget, and processes, it is a project change. Because the product has the same requirements as before, the MVP's scope is unaffected.
10. Correct Answer: A. Explanation: The triple constraint is scope, time, and cost.

Chapter 4

1. Correct Answer: C. Explanation: A negative risk response was followed if you had anticipated a problem and made plans to mitigate its impact.
2. Correct Answer: C. Explanation: A negative risk is a threat. A vulnerability is one negative risk, but not the generic term for all threats. Unknown risks may be positive or negative. Any risk becomes an issue after it materializes. An opportunity is a positive risk.
3. Correct Answer: B. Explanation: Using infrastructure that has reached its end of life and fallen out of support only generates project threats. The other three general risk scenarios are associated with both positive and negative risks.
4. Correct Answer: C. Explanation: Risk prioritization is the process of identifying the risks that pose the greatest threat or present the greatest opportunity for the project and then ranking them in order of impact. Prioritization is a qualitative measure. The other three actions are quantitative.

5. Correct Answer: D. Explanation: Quantitative risk analysis analyzes the statistical probability of a risk's occurrence. Qualitative analysis assigns a risk score based on the risk's projected likelihood and impact. Once the scores are assigned, the risks can be prioritized.
6. Correct Answer: A. Explanation: A triggering condition must occur before the project should enact its fallback plan or contingency plan. Without the trigger, there is nothing to react to. Many issues can be handled without a fallback plan.
7. Correct Answer: F. Explanation: The risk is mitigated by implementing a redundant network backbone. While access to the network could still fail for other reasons, the primary cause of this problem has been addressed and the risk's likelihood has been reduced.
8. Correct Answer: A. Explanation: Risk acceptance is a strategy for both positive and negative risks. Negative risks are transferred or avoided, while positive risks are shared. Only positive risks are enhanced or exploited.
9. Correct Answer: B. Explanation: In any project methodology, the risk owner is the individual who monitors the project environment for signs of the risk, including risk triggers. The other roles should remain aware of general project risks.
10. Correct Answer: C. Explanation: You are closing an issue. When issues are closed, you or the issue owner will continue to monitor the project environment for its effects, remove workarounds, update the issue log, and document the outcomes for lessons learned.
11. Correct Answer: A. Explanation: A workaround is a temporary solution that keeps project work moving forward while an issue that impeded it is resolved. If it was ineffective, it would not be a workaround. A workaround is not necessarily expensive, though it may be less convenient or more expensive than the typical process. While some workarounds are risky, all are temporary.

Chapter 5

1. Correct Answer: A. Explanation: A dependency occurs if task B relies on the completion of task A and should start after task A is complete.
2. Correct Answer: B. Explanation: The critical path is the sequence of tasks comprising the project path that takes the longest amount of time.
3. Correct Answer: C. Explanation: The method for determining the late start (LS) and late finish (LF) of project tasks is to start with the last task(s) and perform a backward pass through all the tasks.

4. Correct Answer: B. Explanation: The work breakdown structure (WBS) is used to determine project tasks.
5. Correct Answer: B. Explanation: A predecessor task must be completed prior to starting the next task.
6. Correct Answer: A. Explanation: Milestones are significant events in a project.
7. Correct Answer: C. Explanation: The critical path is used to calculate each task's early start (ES), early finish (EF), late start (LS), and late finish (LF).
8. Correct Answer: D. Explanation: The team does not estimate the tasks during sprint planning. In sprint planning, the team uses burndown charts to gather requirements, decides on the sprint duration, and selects the target backlog that will be addressed during the sprint.
9. Correct Answer: A. Explanation: Project milestones should be noted on the project schedule to ensure that proper communication occurs.
10. Correct Answer: D. Explanation: When a task cannot start until its predecessor task finishes, it is a finish-to-start (FS) relationship.

Chapter 6

1. Correct answer: D. Explanation: Quality gates provide acceptance criteria to ensure that the project tasks are completing deliverables within the quality control guidelines established during project planning.
2. Correct answer: C. Explanation: The scrum master should document and prioritize actions and lessons learned prior to starting the next sprint.
3. Correct answer: B. Explanation: A scrum retrospective should be held after every sprint.
4. Correct answer: D. Explanation: A project audit is the result of verifying compliance with project requirements.
5. Correct answer: A. Explanation: Cost control involves monitoring the project's costs and managing changes to the cost baseline.
6. Correct answer: C. Explanation: The formula for calculating PV is (planned % complete) × budget.
7. Correct answer: D. Explanation: The AC + ETC formula calculates EAC using ETC.
8. Correct answer: D. Explanation: A TCPI greater than 1 indicates that the project is under budget.
9. Correct answer: D. Explanation: Earned value (EV) is used to show the value a project has earned from the money spent to date.

10. Correct answer: C. Explanation: Stress testing determines the point at which the application or device falters.
11. Correct answer: A. Explanation: Verification measures the quality of the project's deliverables against the requirements baseline and the quality benchmarks established during initiation and planning.
12. Correct answer: B. Explanation: Post-implementation support can be provided by an internal source after an internal application development project to ensure that the application remains operational and includes a patching process.
13. Correct answer: C. Explanation: A service level agreement (SLA) is between a service provider and customer and includes service metrics that the provider should meet.

Chapter 7

1. Correct Answer: D. Explanation: The most effective method is face-to-face communication, which allows the participants to respond in real time, read nonverbal cues, and rapidly tailor the message as it is delivered.
2. Correct Answer: A. Explanation: You should hold separate face-to-face meetings with each of the team members. Separate meetings will give each team member a chance to speak freely. Also, verbal communication is the quickest way to exchange information, and meeting face-to-face will provide context through tone of voice, body language, and facial expressions. Simply observing them will be ineffective.
3. Correct Answers: B, C, D. Explanation: Developing the communication platforms or modalities for project work includes configuring them for external access with approved contractors, securing and documenting shared social media credentials, and tailoring the platform to meet project needs. The project manager is developing the platforms, not procuring them.
4. Correct Answer: B. Explanation: Geographical factors and cultural differences are the two most likely communication issues the team will need to address.
5. Correct Answer: D. Explanation: The time zone factor is the challenge. A geographical challenge would affect travel (such as seasonal weather) or overall availability (such as a local holiday). A technological challenge would affect the communication medium. No culture should be expected to attend a meeting at night.
6. Correct Answer: A. Explanation: You should consult with the project sponsor to verify that the stakeholder needs the information. This approach ensures that the original evaluation denying the stakeholder access to this information is valid.

7. Correct Answers: A, B. Explanation: The team member should timebox the requests and stop when the time is up, even if she does not have an answer. The escalation plan outlines when and how to pass communications on to a higher authority in the project. Escalating the question to someone who already knows the answers or has time to research them will free the team member to complete her project tasks.
8. Correct Answer: B. Explanation: The meeting minutes are produced during the meeting by the scribe. The agenda is prepared prior to the meeting, although the scribe can update the agenda to reflect the actual topics covered. The scribe does not produce status reports. Documents can be electronic or printed.
9. Correct Answer: A. Explanation: A timebox allocates a fixed period of time (such as 10 minutes) to each line item in a meeting agenda, ensuring speakers do not run too long and that every topic is addressed.
10. Correct Answer: D. Explanation: The daily stand-up is an informative meeting, as are status meetings, presentations, and demonstrations. Recurring is not a meeting type.
11. Correct Answer: D. Explanation: A demonstration educates the participants about a product or process. While it may have a Q&A session at the end, its purpose is to teach, not to gather new requirements. Collaborative meetings like focus groups and JAD sessions are explicitly designed to gather requirements, and brainstorming can be used to imagine possible requirements and features for a new product.

Chapter 8

1. Correct Answers: A, C, D. Explanation: You would not issue a purchase order until after the vendor contract was established with the procurement terms. The other steps would happen before contracting with a vendor.
2. Correct Answer: B. Explanation: A pay-as-you-go (PAYG) service accumulates costs at a specified rate only as the service is being used. It is important that someone on the project team monitors PAYG consumption for cloud services and shuts down idle workloads to avoid wasting funds on unused resources.
3. Correct Answer: D. Explanation: A request for information (RFI) should be issued if the purchaser is unsure of the specifications of a procurement.
4. Correct Answer: A. Explanation: A request for quote (RFQ) solicits price quotations from prospective sellers of common products or services.
5. Correct Answers: C, E. Explanation: A request for proposal (RFP) or a request for bid (RFB) would be given to prospective sellers to obtain price quotes or bids.

6. Correct Answer: D. Explanation: Prequalifying a vendor means to pre-screen them against a set of required criteria and then maintain them in a database of vendors who will be shortlisted for proposals and fast-tracked for new contracts or purchase orders. Qualifications are client-defined standards that vendors must meet or characteristics they must have that prove their fitness to be awarded a contract. Until qualifications are assessed, the vendor is not shortlisted.
7. Correct Answer: C. Explanation: Demonstrations may be needed to fully assess the capabilities of the vendor or of the procurement. A product demo is one of the most accurate ways to evaluate proposed software or hardware solutions.
8. Correct Answer: B. Explanation: A competitive analysis is used to perform market research and to compare the products and services offered by similar vendors, including their prices.
9. Correct Answer: A. Explanation: A fixed-price contract establishes a lump sum to be paid for the work performed. Whereas a firm fixed-price (FFP) contract sets the payment in stone after the contract is signed, this type can be modified slightly with a fixed-price incentive fee (FPIF) or fixed-price with economic price adjustment (FP-EPA) contract.
10. Correct Answer: D. Explanation: A non-disclosure agreement (NDA) should be used to ensure that vendors and contractors do not share details of the project.

Chapter 9

1. Correct Answer: C. Explanation: All monitoring and controlling activities, including controlling project costs, take place during project execution, or the Executing phase.
2. Correct Answer: D. Explanation: Any tangible document, output, product, or template used in project work is referred to as an artifact, including electronic documents stored locally or in the cloud. This could include (but is by no means limited to) lessons learned, document templates from the PMO, and deliverables.
3. Correct Answer: A. Explanation: The project's potential financial gain, or return on investment, is first calculated during the Discovery phase. While project work has not technically begun, CompTIA considers it the first phase of the project life cycle.
4. Correct Answer: B. Explanation: You should use return on investment (ROI) calculations to estimate the total dollar return that the project sponsor will receive for the project.

5. Correct Answers: A, D. Explanation: Operational expenses (OpEx) are recurring purchases or purchases that have a useful life of 1 year or less, like surcharges to video conferencing platforms, rent, salaries, and utilities. Purchased phone handsets and server hardware are examples of capital expenses (CapEx).
6. Correct Answer: C. Explanation: The document is a responsibility assignment matrix (RAM), also referred to as a RACI chart.
7. Correct Answer: B. Explanation: The authority for all project work is the project charter, which is developed during the Initiating phase and signed by the project's sponsor.
8. Correct Answer: A. Explanation: The process of identifying stakeholders will produce the stakeholder register. This key document is used later to develop the stakeholder engagement plan (or stakeholder management plan), the RAM, the communication plan, and other stakeholder-centric project documentation.
9. Correct Answer: E. Explanation: The architect, meaning the solution architect or software architect, is the SME with the most knowledge of this area and has the highest level of input into the solution's technical design.
10. Correct Answer: C. Explanation: You should hold a second kickoff meeting to make sure they understand their project duties. Kickoff meetings should be synchronous communications with as many members as possible joining live so that they can meet and ask questions. It is fine for a project to have more than one kickoff as the team is acquired or as the project enters a new iteration or phase.

Chapter 10

1. Correct Answer: D. Explanation: Before moving on to activities that involve establishing a project schedule, setting goals and targets, and allocating resources to the project, a project manager must define the project scope. The milestones, budget, and WBS depend on having a scope defined.
2. Correct Answer: B. Explanation: The detailed scope statement includes a project scope description, acceptance criteria, description of key deliverables, exclusions, estimated budget, preliminary schedule, constraints, and assumptions.
3. Correct Answer: D. Explanation: The requirements traceability matrix (RTM) is not part of the scope baseline. The scope baseline includes the scope statement, the WBS, and WBS dictionary.
4. Correct Answers: A, B, D. Explanation: While developing the schedule, the project manager determines start and end dates for the activities, allocates resources across the project duration, and estimates the total time to complete the project. Milestones are placed on the schedule, but they are determined

during project initiation and refined as the scope is refined in the Planning phase.

5. Correct Answer: A. Explanation: The purpose of a preliminary procurement needs assessment is to identify where the organization lacks the resources needed to meet the project's requirements. The purpose is not to inventory available resources, though a current inventory will help identify gaps. Gap analysis is the next step to take after the assessment, not the purpose of it. Understanding the requirements is necessary for assessing procurement needs, and not the other way around.

6. Correct Answer: C. Explanation: The stakeholder's preference to receive status reports as text messages should be included in the communication plan. It may also be noted in the stakeholder engagement plan. The schedule does not record stakeholder preferences. The resource management plan includes scheduled dates of availability for resources, including materials. The stakeholder register includes contact information, but contact preferences are best placed in the communication plan, where they can be referred to when communications are sent out.

7. Correct Answer: D. Explanation: A reserve analysis is performed so that funds will be held back to pay for cost uncertainties, including risk events, issues, and changes.

8. Correct Answer: A. Explanation: The schedule for testing would be part of the schedule, not the quality assurance plan. However, the quality assurance plan would note if there was a required cadence or timing for testing, such as "three weeks after the concrete has cured at a minimum temperature of 50 degrees Fahrenheit."

9. Correct Answer: B. Explanation: The risk identification process that occurs during initial risk assessment creates the first version of the risk register. Risks cannot be reviewed, reported, or have responses planned until they are identified. Risk planning refers to the process by which risks will be identified, assigned weight and probability, tracked, responded to, and reported.

10. Correct Answer: D. Explanation: The first step in risk management is to establish the risk management plan, which includes guidelines on how risks will be identified, analyzed, reported, controlled, and closed.

11. Correct Answer: C. Explanation: Project management plans do not use a resource baseline. The cost, schedule, and scope baselines are established during planning and become the performance measurement baseline against which the project is measured.

12. Correct Answer: B. Explanation: The minimally viable product is established as a usable prototype that will gather early feedback from customers and improve the product in later iterations.
13. Correct Answer: C. Explanation: The process for training the customer's staff to operate the released project or product is contained in the transition plan or release plan. A planned transition is needed to successfully close a software project or a project that provides an operation or service.

Chapter 11

1. Correct Answer: A. Explanation: Project deliverables are created during project execution.
2. Correct Answer: C. Explanation: The project manager directs quality assurance during the monitoring and controlling activities in the Executing phase of a project.
3. Correct Answer: A. Explanation: Smoothing involves emphasizing areas of agreement rather than differences.
4. Correct Answer: D. Explanation: Forcing should be used as a last resort to resolve a long-lasting conflict.
5. Correct Answer: A. Explanation: A gate review is when the project sponsor decides whether a project will proceed based on the completion of previous phases.
6. Correct Answer: A. Explanation: A business acquisition occurs when a company purchases a competitor.
7. Correct Answer: D. Explanation: An internal reorganization occurs when a company merges departments.
8. Correct Answer: C. Explanation: A business process change occurs when a formal approval process is revised.
9. Correct Answer: D. Explanation: Rules of engagement are part of managing vendors during project execution.
10. Correct Answer: B. Explanation: An external status report is best provided to individuals or groups that are not part of the project team or project stakeholders.
11. Correct Answer: A. Explanation: The communication management plan should be used to document the meeting types and frequencies.

12. Correct Answer: B. Explanation: The project budget should be updated based on the actual costs accrued as the work is completed.
13. Correct Answer: C. Explanation: The project schedule should be updated based on the actual time that it takes to complete project work.

Chapter 12

1. Correct Answer: B. Explanation: Project evaluation within project closure is all about soliciting opinions from project team members and stakeholders.
2. Correct Answer: A. Explanation: Deliverable validation likely only involves the project team members and project manager.
3. Correct Answer: C. Explanation: The project manager is most likely responsible for documenting the agenda for the project closure meeting.
4. Correct Answer: D. Explanation: Project sign-off is *least* likely to take place prior to project closure. All of the other events can take place throughout the project, although it is important to make sure that they occur during closure as well.
5. Correct Answer: A. Explanation: Access removal will ensure that assets are properly secured.
6. Correct Answer: D. Explanation: You should implement contract closure for a procurement that has been delivered and for which payment has been approved.
7. Correct Answer: B. Explanation: You should implement the resource release process to ensure that the code development servers are made available for other projects.
8. Correct Answer: C. Explanation: The project closure report is produced from the project closure meeting.
9. Correct Answer: A. Explanation: The stakeholder feedback collection is created from meetings, questionnaires, and surveys.
10. Correct Answer: B. Explanation: Document archival is important to ensure that documents are maintained until they are no longer needed.
11. Correct Answer: C. Explanation: During budget reconciliation, management and contingency reserve usage is fully documented.
12. Correct Answer: D. Explanation: During rewards and celebration, the efforts of the team members are recognized.

Chapter 13

1. Correct Answer: C. Explanation: You are using three-point estimates to create a Program Evaluation Review Technique (PERT) chart, which shows tasks and their estimated durations in a network connected by arrows indicating the order of precedence. Gantt charts are bar charts, not diagrams. A forward pass is performed over a critical path diagram to estimate early start and finish dates. Velocity charts show the average amount of work a scrum team completes during a sprint.
2. Correct Answer: C. Explanation: The organizational chart should be used to determine the reporting structure for project team members.
3. Correct Answer: A. Explanation: This is a budget burndown chart, which shows the budget expended to date against the planned value over the length of the project, sprint, or iteration.
4. Correct Answer: D. Explanation: Gantt charts, precedence network diagrams, and PERT charts are all tools used in project schedule management. While they have other uses, they can all display the sequence of tasks in all or part of a schedule.
5. Correct Answer: A. Explanation: A risk report describes the project's overall risk exposure. The risk register lists all known risks and gives details about all known risks. The risk management plan does not include specific risks. The risk report is continually updated, while the charter is not. The project charter contains an estimate of high-level risks.
6. Correct Answer: A. Explanation: The project dashboard will provide the fastest access to updated project status information and key performance indicators (KPIs), such as the cost performance index (CPI) and cost variance (CV).
7. Correct Answer: B. Explanation: The issue log lists problems that occur during project work that were not captured on the risk register.
8. Correct Answer: D. Explanation: Project scheduling software mainly tracks project activities, their durations, and the personnel assigned to them.
9. Correct Answer: B. Explanation: The best description of a case management system, or ticketing system, is to track and consolidate all help desk tickets about bug reports, client requests, and end-user complaints.
10. Correct Answer: A. Explanation: Many video conference platforms offer a polling feature that can be anonymized. A meeting poll would provide real-time opinions. Emailed surveys would be answered after a time delay and may not provide the team member's unfiltered opinion. Text messaging would disrupt a meeting. Anything written in a multi-authored document would be visible to other team members and could influence their thoughts.

11. Correct Answer: C. Explanation: The fact that anyone can edit the content is both an advantage and a disadvantage. Content may become disorganized or thread in too many directions, and "finished" documentation may be later edited to remove useful data.

12. Correct Answer: B. Explanation: Presentation tools that create visual slideshows would be best suited to an informative meeting used to demonstrate a product. A project dashboard and a task board would show project-level information, not product information. Diagramming software is used in brainstorming meetings, not informative meetings.

Chapter 14

1. Correct Answer: C. Explanation: A histogram depicts the approximate distribution of statistical data.

2. Correct Answer: D. Explanation: A Pareto chart helps the project manager identify the largest single source of problems in a project. This type of chart ranks project defects or sources of problems in order, typically by highest frequency or greatest cost to the business.

3. Correct Answer: A. Explanation: Data points in a run chart represent a sequence in chronological order, preferably over a minimum of 20–25 days.

4. Correct Answer: B. Explanation: A scatter diagram or scatter chart is used to find a correlation between two variables.

5. Correct Answer: D. Explanation: An Ishikawa diagram or fishbone diagram categorizes the potential causes of a problem to help the project team identify root causes.

6. Correct Answer: B. Explanation: A control chart graphically displays data over time against established control limits: the upper control limit (UCL) and the lower control limit (LCL).

7. Correct Answers: A, D. Explanation: Both burndown and burnup charts contain a planned work completed line and an actual work completed line.

8. Correct Answer: A. Explanation: The line representing activity in a burnup chart begins in the bottom-left corner of the chart and slants upward to the right across the sprint's duration to end at 100% (all tasks completed).

9. Correct Answer: C. Explanation: Velocity charts display the average number of stories or story points completed per iteration. Past velocity is used to predict future sprint effort.

10. Correct Answer: D. Explanation: A decision tree analysis attempts to find a decision path that will lead to the highest revenue or lowest cost.

Chapter 15

1. Correct Answer: B. Explanation: A construction project would need a plan to manage its wastewater runoff to avoid silting or contaminating local streams, incurring environmental fines, and giving the organization a bad reputation as a polluter.
2. Correct Answer: D. Explanation: You are bringing awareness of applicable regulations and standards to the project. A wide variety of regulations protect the market from unsafe quality, including consumer safety standards and building codes.
3. Correct Answer: D. Explanation: This is an example of an acceptable use policy, which dictates how company-owned IT resources may be used. A BYOD policy sets terms around how corporate data and private data can coexist on a user-owned mobile phone or device, but this scenario governs the use of the company's network. A COPE policy issues corporate-owned mobile devices to users in lieu of personal devices. A security awareness policy trains employees to avoid common cyber threats.
4. Correct Answer: B. Explanation: You would not typically disable GPS services on a mobile device; instead, you would enable them to ensure the device could be located if it were stolen or to verify a team member's location for multifactor authentication.
5. Answer: C. Security clearance is used by the U.S. government, and other countries, to denote how much access a person should be granted to classified national security information.
6. Correct Answers: A, D. Explanation: The local network uses single-factor authentication (something you know). The remote network uses two-factor authentication (something you know and something you have). Usernames and passwords are both knowledge factors. One-time codes are generated by an authenticator app or provided by some other token-based system that you possess.
7. Correct Answer: A. Explanation: Data is not classified to comply with clearance requirements. Clearance refers to a U.S. government approval for an individual to access information classified as important to national security. The other options are all factors behind data classification.
8. Correct Answer: D. Explanation: Secret is one of three U.S. government data classifications for national security information, along with Confidential and Top Secret. Private enterprise uses the Confidential label, along with Sensitive, Restricted, and Internal (or For Internal Use).

9. Correct Answer: B. Explanation: To register a trade secret with the government, organizations must prove that the asset is maintained in secrecy and that its use is protected by confidentiality policies, non-disclosure policies, and restricted internal access. Trade secrets are intellectual property, as are patents and copyrights, but patented and copyrighted material can be shared without affecting their protections. Proprietary data is not a legal classification.
10. Correct Answers: B, C, D, E. Explanation: Gender is not considered to be PII because it is information about an individual that is considered easy to determine without knowing anything personal about the individual. The other factors are all PII.
11. Correct Answer: D. Explanation: The EU's General Data Protection Regulation (GDPR) applies to all entities that store, process, and/or transmit data that identifies European Union (EU) citizens or citizens in the European Economic Area (EEA) in the course of a commercial activity.

Chapter 16

1. Correct Answer: C. Explanation: With the IaaS model, the vendor provides and maintains the physical servers and firewalls, while the customer installs and maintains their own software (including operating systems) on their virtual machines.
2. Correct Answer: A. Explanation: The data warehouse will be used to analyze the archived data from the organization's databases to make decisions for a current project.
3. Correct Answer: B. Explanation: Enterprise resource planning (ERP) software is most likely to include customer relations, supply chain, finance, and human resources management.
4. Correct Answer: D. Explanation: The process that verifies the software still works as expected is called a validation check.
5. Correct Answer: D. Explanation: The release step of software change control will include a means whereby the change can be rolled back.
6. Correct Answer: A. Explanation: Auto scripts are part of the CD portion of the CI/CD process, not the CI portion.
7. Correct Answer: B. Explanation: Staging is usually a replica of the live, or production, environment.

Answers to the Review Quizzes

Chapter 1

1. Correct Answer: C. Explanation: Installing the latest operating system and application updates is *not* a project. It is part of day-to-day operations and will be repeated each time updates are ready to be deployed.
2. Correct Answer: D. Explanation: It is not true that all of the projects listed are part of the project portfolio. The antivirus and antimalware updates are not a project. They are normal day-to-day operations and will be repeated each time updates are ready to be deployed.
3. Correct Answer: B. Explanation: Agile allows the project direction to be modified easily based on the organization's needs.
4. Correct Answer: A. Explanation: With each iteration of an Agile project, the product is improved.
5. Correct Answer: C. Explanation: When you are creating user stories, you are gathering the requirements for an Agile project.
6. Correct Answer: C. Explanation: During a daily scrum meeting, all team members should give updates regarding sprint tasks.
7. Correct Answer: B. Explanation: In the SDLC, the Gather Requirements step is completed after initiating the project. The steps to the SDLC are:
    1. Plan/Initiate Project
    2. Gather Requirements
    3. Design
    4. Develop
    5. Test/Validate
    6. Release/Maintain
    7. Certify/Accredit
    8. Change Management and Configuration Management/Replacement
8. Correct Answer: A. Explanation: The second phase of PRINCE2 is "Direct the project." The phases of PRINCE2 are as follows:
    1. Start the project.
    2. Direct the project.
    3. Initiate the project.
    4. Control a stage.
    5. Manage product delivery.

6. Manage stage boundaries.
7. Close the project.

9. Correct Answer: D. Explanation: The final phase of DevOps is the Monitor phase. The phases of DevOps are as follows:
   1. Plan
   2. Code
   3. Build
   4. Test
   5. Release
   6. Deploy
   7. Operate
   8. Monitor
10. Correct Answer: C. Explanation: The Waterfall approach is likely to work best with a project that is heavily influenced by regulations and industry standards.

Chapter 2

1. Correct Answer: C. Explanation: The trust-building stages of a project team are forming, storming, norming, performing, and adjourning.
2. Correct Answers: A, B, C, D. Explanation: All of the listed options are disadvantages of using virtual teams.
3. Correct Answer: C. Explanation: You should obtain approval of the project charter and preliminary budget from the project sponsor.
4. Correct Answer: C. Explanation: A functional organization gives department or organizational unit managers the most authority and gives project managers the least authority.
5. Correct Answer: D. Explanation: You will fill the project manager role.
6. Correct Answer: A. Explanation: The project team is not responsible for creating the project schedule. That is the job of the project manager (or project scheduler, if applicable).
7. Correct Answers: A, B, C, D. Explanation: All of the listed options can be project stakeholders.
8. Correct Answer: D. Explanation: In an Agile project, constant feedback from the stakeholders is used to refine the project requirements.

9. Correct Answer: C. Explanation: Project management does not recognize a category of asset called tangible. Capital, human, and physical assets are used for project work.
10. Correct Answer: D. Explanation: In response to a planned retirement, you have followed a succession plan.

Chapter 3

1. Correct Answer: B, D. Explanation: Releasing a deliverable earlier than planned affects multiple critical factors, including resources, budget, and schedule. A request to replace materials with a less expensive variety should be analyzed to ensure it does not affect the quality of project deliverables. A late delivery from a vendor is an issue (if not anticipated) or a risk (if anticipated). A team member being ahead of schedule does not alter any other project success factor, such as quality or scope.
2. Correct Answer: B. Explanation: The first step in the formal change control process is to create a change request using the approved form that will be entered in the change control log. The first step could also be to receive a change request from another party.
3. Correct Answer: D. Explanation: After implementing the approved change and validating its implementation, the final step is to communicate the change deployment to the relevant team members and stakeholders according to the communication plan.
4. Correct Answer: B. Explanation: The authority for approving changes will be recorded in the change management plan, along with templates for the change request form and the change log.
5. Correct Answer: B. Explanation: The provision for on-site training is a requirement, not a constraint. It must be delivered 3 weeks before project closure, but no constraint affects the closure date. The other options describe a time constraint, a cost constraint, and a scope constraint.
6. Correct Answer: A. Explanation: This is an example of a change request.
7. Correct Answer: B. Explanation: This is an example of scope creep because the change occurred without the other constraints being adjusted to accommodate its requirements. Constraint reprioritization shifts the emphasis from one primary constraint (such as cost) to another (such as schedule) in a controlled way and compensates for the shift by reducing or increasing other project characteristics. There is no competing project. A change request would result in adjustments to other project constraints.

8. Correct Answer: A. Explanation: A change might affect the project's scope, schedule, budget, quality, resources, risks, communication, procurements, and/or stakeholders. Both the project manager and skilled team members who work in the area possibly affected by the change should perform the impact assessment. The assessment should also document the estimated outcome of *not* making the change.
9. Correct Answer: C. Explanation: The change control board (CCB) is a cross-functional group that represents each business process. The CCB makes the decision to accept or reject a change during its monthly meeting. In theory, the only role that can overrule the CCB's decision is the project sponsor.
10. Correct Answer: B. Explanation: Until you evaluate the impact of the change, you cannot know how it will affect overall project risk; however, it is always possible for changes to reduce existing risk. Approving a change does not automatically increase project risk. An increased or reduced budget could increase or decrease the funds available for risk response, and changes to requirements can generate entirely new project risk.

Chapter 4

1. Correct Answers: A, B. Explanation: A business merger or acquisition is likely to involve merging disparate corporate technologies and altering workflow processes. Digital transformation occurs when workflows are altered by adopting new technologies. The other three scenarios do not necessarily trigger changes in technology or workflows.
2. Correct Answer: C. Explanation: Purchasing insurance from a third party is the most common way to transfer risk impact, so risk transference occurred. Only negative risks are transferred. The flooding has not occurred, so it is not an issue that actively affects the project, has no root cause, and cannot trigger a workaround or contingency plan. Management reserves may be required to treat risks that were not discovered until after the project budget was set.
3. Correct Answer: A. Explanation: You should perform risk review to ensure that all project risks are identified. The main benefit of risk review is identifying new risks using structured questionnaires. Only identified risks can be quantified or prioritized. A risk report will only include recognized risks.
4. Correct Answer: C. Explanation: Risk sharing divides a positive risk between the two companies.
5. Correct Answer: A. Explanation: Because it has not yet occurred, the loss of the venue is still a risk and should be documented in the risk register so it can be assigned a risk owner and a response. If the venue is canceled before a

contingency or solution is found, it will become an issue. An action item does not have the same level of urgency as a risk response.

6. Correct Answer: B. Explanation: Using expert judgment and reviewing historical data to assess the impact and likelihood of a risk is qualitative risk analysis. Risk prioritization can only occur after impact and likelihood are assessed. Using a mathematical model to simulate the outcome of a risk is quantitative risk analysis.

7. Correct Answer: D. Explanation: The project manager exploited the opportunity to reduce production costs by adding the new process to the project's scope. This action changed the project's parameters to ensure that the organization would benefit from the opportunity.

8. Correct Answer: A. Explanation: Risks, not issues, are analyzed for probability; if an issue has already occurred, its probability is 100%. Issues should be assigned priority scores to help scale the appropriate response. Once an issue is closed, any workarounds should be removed and prior processes restored. The root cause should be analyzed and all issue information should be recorded in the issues log.

9. Correct Answer: D. Explanation: Risks and issues that cause changes to the project should go through formal change control so their impact can be analyzed and other project constraints adjusted. Risk avoidance can change a project parameter, including aspects of the scope. Issue response is usually reactive to a trigger. Only risks are documented during project planning; issues arise during execution and may or may not come from recognized risks.

10. Correct Answer: B. Explanation: An escalation point describes the project conditions that would trigger the need to communicate an issue to a designated contact. Scenario analysis is a forward-looking risk analysis technique, while root cause analysis is a backward-looking risk analysis technique. The scenario describes a communication trigger, not analysis. Contingency plans describe a sequence of actions to take in response to an issue that affects project work.

Chapter 5

1. Correct Answer: A. Explanation: Project time management includes sequencing activities.

2. Correct Answer: B. Explanation: The possible paths for this project are A–E–H–I–L–M, A–E–H–J–L–M, B–H–I–L–M, B–H–J–L–M, C–F–H–I–L–M, C–F–H–J–L–M, and D–G–K–L–M. The critical path is A–E–H–J–L–M, which has a value of 27. A–E–H–I–L–M has a value of 26. B–H–I–L–M has a value of 16. B–H–J–L–M has a value of 15. C–F–H–I–L–M has a value of 17. C–F–H–J–L–M has a value of 18. D–G–K–L–M has a value of 14.

3. Correct Answer: D. Explanation: Task E's predecessor is task A, which has an early finish (EF) of 10. Task E's early start (ES) is the same day as task A's EF (10). Therefore, the ES of task E is 10.
4. Correct Answer: A. Explanation: Task E's predecessor is task A, which has an EF of 10. Task E's early start (ES) is the same day as the EF of task A (10). To determine task E's EF, add task E's duration (3) to its ES value (10). Task E's EF is 13.
5. Correct Answer: B. Explanation: An event on the project calendar that has no duration is most likely a milestone.
6. Correct Answer: D. Explanation: Float for a task is the difference between the late start (LS) and early start (ES) values for the task.
7. Correct Answer: C. Explanation: Use the late start (LS) and early start (ES) values of a task to determine float or slack.
8. Correct Answer: B. Explanation: A forward pass determines ES and EF for all project tasks.
9. Correct Answer: C. Explanation: Resource leveling might increase the critical path.
10. Correct Answer: D. Explanation: The schedule baseline will help you determine if tasks are slipping and will affect the final completion.
11. Correct Answers: A, B, C. Explanation: The team members, product owner, and scrum master must attend the sprint planning meeting.

Chapter 6

1. Correct Answer: A. Explanation: Governance gates are included in project schedules to ensure that required approvals are obtained.
2. Correct Answer: D. Explanation: You should hold a scrum retrospective prior to starting the next sprint.
3. Correct Answer: D. Explanation: You should perform a project audit to determine whether the project is complying with project requirements and quality metrics.
4. Correct Answer: D. Explanation: Planned value (PV) = (planned % complete) × budget. Therefore,

   PV = 40% × $1,000,000 = $400,000.
5. Correct Answer: C. Explanation: Actual cost (AC) is the actual money spent to date on a project. Therefore, AC = $600,000.

6. Correct Answer: B. Explanation: Earned value (EV) = (% of completed work) × budget. Therefore,

   EV = 40% × $1,000,000 = $400,000.

7. Correct Answer: B. Explanation: Schedule variance (SV) = EV – PV. EV = 40% × $1,000,000 = $400,000.

   PV = 60% × $1,000,000 = $600,000. Therefore, SV = $400,000 – $600,000 = –$200,000.

8. Correct Answer: D. Explanation: Cost variance (CV) = EV – AC. EV = 40% × $1,000,000 = $400,000.

   AC = $600,000. Therefore, CV = $400,000 – $600,000 = –$200,000.

9. Correct Answer: D. Explanation: Schedule performance index (SPI) = EV / PV. EV = 40% × $1,000,000 = $400,000, and PV = 60% × $1,000,000 = $600,000. Therefore, SPI = $400,000 / $600,000 = .67.

10. Correct Answer: C. Explanation: Cost performance index (CPI) = EV / AC. EV = 40% × $1,000,000 = $400,000. AC = $600,000. Therefore, CPI = $400,000 / $600,000 = .67.

Chapter 7

1. Correct Answer: C. Explanation: The most value is generated by interactions among the participants representing the customer (the target audience).

2. Correct Answer: A. Explanation: They are using synchronous communication. Some synchronous communication is verbal, like hallway meetups, but active chat sessions are written communication that is synchronized.

3. Correct Answer: B. Explanation: Your primary concern for communications on this project is possible language barriers. Cultural differences and geographical factors will not have as large an impact on communication and relationships. Relationship building also relies on overcoming language barriers.

4. Correct Answers: C,D. Explanation: Because agendas are prepared in advance, a scribe could update the agenda to reflect the actual meeting content, ensuring the most accurate document archive. Version control would ensure readers know which version is more accurate. Although you should use a document naming convention, it would not ensure integrity. A VPN connection would be used to ensure security.

5. Correct Answer: D. Explanation: The team member's unreliable Internet access is a technological factor for project communication.

6. Correct Answer: C. Explanation: Intraorganizational differences occur when team communication is influenced by conditions within the organization.

7. Correct Answers: A, C. Explanation: The most important reasons to capture written notes that detail an important project decision are to preserve the integrity of project communication and to facilitate archiving the record.
8. Correct Answer: B. Explanation: A prerecorded message announcing a service outage that plays when a customer calls would be an example of formal, asynchronous, external, pull communication.
9. Correct Answer: B. Explanation: The purpose of a decisive meeting is to come to consensus on an action and then assign the action to a responsible party.
10. Correct Answer: D. Explanation: The purpose of a workshop is to collaborate and let information flow in all directions. An informative meeting, like a presentation, directs the information flow from the presenter to the audience, so it would not be a successful workshop format. Attendees would move around the room if they were placed in breakout groups, as a workshop is likely to do.

Chapter 8

1. Correct Answer: B. Explanation: You should use a request for information (RFI) to obtain details about motorized mechanisms to rotate the stage.
2. Correct Answer: C. Explanation: You should use a request for quote (RFQ) because you know the exact specifications and models for the equipment you need to purchase.
3. Correct Answer: D. Explanation: After receiving and analyzing all the vendors' responses to the request for information (RFI), the next step is to issue a request for proposal (RFP).
4. Correct Answer: B. Explanation: You implemented a fixed-price incentive fee (FPIF) contract at a specified price for the procurement and included a bonus for early delivery.
5. Correct Answer: D. Explanation: A time and materials (T&M) contract will be used for this procurement.
6. Correct Answer: C. Explanation: You should use a cease-and-desist letter to inform the other company of the issue and request (or demand) that they stop infringing your patent. Non-compete clauses and non-disclosure agreements are only enforceable when two parties have an existing mutually binding contract. A letter of intent is a precursor that states a legally binding document will be forthcoming.
7. Correct Answer: B. Explanation: You should use a non-disclosure agreement to ensure that personnel from the third party do not share information regarding the new mobile app.

8. Correct Answer: A. Explanation: You should evaluate their physical capacity, which in this case would mean a walkthrough of their factory to observe the production line. A request for proposal would tell you what the vendor thinks their capacity is but would not provide the evidence to support it. A technical approach also relies on the vendor's own estimate of their abilities.
9. Correct Answer: C. Explanation: You need to provide a statement of work (SOW) that describes the scope of the new project and its requirements, including its specifications, the quantity desired, quality levels, performance data, and the duration and location of project work.
10. Correct Answer: C. Explanation: You should check the warranty to determine whether the equipment is guaranteed to last for the duration of the project.

Chapter 9

1. Correct Answer: A. Explanation: Once the project's sponsor signs off on a charter, the project is formally approved, and it moves from the Initiating phase into the Planning phase.
2. Correct Answer: B. Explanation: A RACI chart or matrix is used to determine a person's level of responsibility for each project activity and whether they are responsible, accountable, consulted, or merely informed about the activity status. There can only be one accountable role for each activity: the buck stops there.
3. Correct Answer: C. Explanation: A kickoff meeting is held to ensure that team members and stakeholders understand the overall project goals and their part in the project. The responsibility assignment matrix matches stakeholders to their area of responsibility, but it is not enough to ensure they also understand the overall project's goals.
4. Correct Answer: A. Explanation: Project A is estimated to have a higher ROI once you equalize the time frames between both projects. If Project B will return 54% in 2 years, then it would (presumably) return 27% in 1 year, during which Project A would have earned 29%. However, additional factors should be weighed before you determine which (if either) project should be initiated.
5. Correct Answers: B, D. Explanation: The requirement for a product to meet standards for data security is a constraint, not an assumption (note the word "must"). Stating that the product will not be developed for the Android OS is an example of scope. The other two statements are project assumptions: that the customer base will be primarily English-speaking and that the team members will have the skills to develop the product.

6. Correct Answer: B. Explanation: If the lead developer does not have the right level of access to sensitive client data, the access requirements were not correctly defined. The records management plan does not manage client records, only internal records. The solution design chooses the technical products that will be used to create project deliverables. Even if the developer knew how to get in touch with the client, access mechanisms still need to be established by those with the authority to do so.
7. Correct Answer: C. Explanation: The only listed factor that could keep a proposal from moving forward is lack of scope. Without a clear scope, it will be difficult to build a business case or correctly estimate the ROI. A negative ROI would not be enough to kill a project that may have other benefits, such as regulatory compliance. A product can be developed before its market or client is known.
8. Correct Answer: C. Explanation: This describes a functional requirement that the solution should provide, because an error message is a tangible output of the application. The fact that the application only recognizes certain shippers is not a constraint or an environment.
9. Correct Answer: B. Explanation: If possible, you would review artifacts from the client's prior project while developing the project charter. The prior project's artifacts, particularly the charter and the final evaluation, will help guide decisions made for the current project.
10. Correct Answers: A, D. Explanation: You would perform a gap analysis and an ROI analysis to help create a persuasive business case. Gap analysis is part of describing the journey from current state (before the project begins) to future state (after benefiting from the project's work). The ROI calculates an estimated return on investment. Together, future improvements and the potential for gain make a clear business case. The scope, requirements, and lessons from prior projects would be analyzed as the project charter is developed.

Chapter 10

1. Correct Answer: D. Explanation: The risk identification process that occurs during initial risk assessment creates the first version of the risk register. Risks cannot be reviewed, analyzed, or quantified until they are identified. Risk planning refers to the process by which risks will be identified, assigned weight and probability, tracked, responded to, and reported.
2. Correct Answers: A, D, E. Explanation: The budget, schedule, detailed scope, and baselines are created during the Planning phase. High-level requirements and high-level risks are captured during the Initiating phase. Deliverables are produced during the Executing phase.

3. Correct Answer: C. Explanation: You would consult the communication plan to determine which stakeholders should receive a particular report. The topics for the next meeting would be recorded in an agenda. The communication plan contains the meeting cadence but not specific dates; the dates would be on the project schedule along with urgent actions.
4. Correct Answers: A, B, C, D. Explanation: All of these components would be part of a transition plan. Deployment describes how the product will be moved into the live environment. Asset transfer describes how necessary components will be moved from development to operations, including intangible assets. A rollback plan will revert the environment to its prior state if the deployment causes issues. A training plan describes how the project team will transfer knowledge to the operations team.
5. Correct Answer: D. Explanation: You should provide just the facts orally because a stakeholder with a dominant personality prefers short, fact-based communications delivered face to face.
6. Correct Answers: B, C. Explanation: The stakeholder register will list project team members, along with an overview of their skills. You could also consult the resource management plan or resource plan. The WBS dictionary contains WBS levels and descriptions of work components. The resource breakdown structure describes how project resources are organized or categorized. The stakeholder engagement plan contains communication strategies, not skills.
7. Correct Answer: C. Explanation: The quality assurance plan serves as the guide to the project team to ensure that the project's result meets the project sponsor's requirements. The scope statement contains acceptance criteria and success criteria, but the project management plan also includes the quality assurance plan, which is used to verify that deliverables meet requirements.
8. Correct Answer: A. Explanation: You are conducting a needs assessment by comparing the project's requirements against existing resources, their skills, and their availability. After identifying gaps, you would perform a gap analysis, which could result in training a team member to fill the missing need or acquiring additional resources. You would not assign resources until you knew they had the skill and availability to perform a task.
9. Correct Answer: C. Explanation: Quality assurance does not manage the project's scope. Quality assurance intersects with risk management, regulatory compliance, and customer relationship management.
10. Correct Answer: D. Explanation: The team mutually agrees to the length after considering the size and the complexity of the project.

Chapter 11

1. Correct Answer: D. Explanation: Performing quality assurance occurs during the Executing phase.
2. Correct Answer: B. Explanation: Because one side of the issue is clearly wrong and continued discussion of the issue could be detrimental to the project, you should use smoothing.
3. Correct Answer: C. Explanation: You most likely used compromising, because you reached a solution that did not satisfy either party.
4. Correct Answer: B. Explanation: A gate review is a meeting held to determine whether the project will continue.
5. Correct Answer: C. Explanation: Splitting the sales and marketing personnel into two separate functional teams is an internal reorganization. The software development company in answer A is outsourcing. The management in answer B is relocating the business. The company in answer D is experiencing a business demerger or split.
6. Correct Answer: C. Explanation: As an individual who is considered external to the project, the manager should be provided with an external status report.
7. Correct Answer: C. Explanation: You should perform a gap analysis to compare actual results and performance with projections.
8. Correct Answer: D. Explanation: You should review and approve the procurement deliverable prior to paying a vendor for the procurement.
9. Correct Answer: A. Explanation: You should first update the project timeline so you can determine if a new critical path has emerged.
10. Correct Answer: B. Explanation: The project manager should communicate with the team and stakeholders about the change, even if the implications on the project are unknown.

Chapter 12

1. Correct Answer: C. Explanation: You are completing the Closing phase when you document the lessons learned, release the project resources, and obtain project sign-off from the project sponsor.
2. Correct Answer: D. Explanation: Access removal is *least* likely to provide data to use in the closeout report.
3. Correct Answer: C. Explanation: When vendors complete and deliver project procurements, it is likely to affect contract closure.
4. Correct Answer: A. Explanation: The usage of management and contingency reserves is part of budget reconciliation.

5. Correct Answer: B. Explanation: You are likely completing the access removal process within project closure. Determining which accounts were used and whether those accounts are still active is the first step of access removal.
6. Correct Answer: D. Explanation: The project closeout report is likely to be revised based on the project closure meeting.
7. Correct Answer: C. Explanation: A team member being given a raise during the project is the *least* likely of the options given to be part of the rewards and celebration activity.
8. Correct Answer: A. Explanation: Questionnaires and surveys are likely the most effective way of collecting stakeholder feedback because they provide anonymity to the person providing the feedback.
9. Correct Answer: B. Explanation: Of the options given, the project team members are least likely to have an effect on project documentation archival.
10. Correct Answer: D. Explanation: Resource release will ensure that the laborers can return to their regular job tasks.

Chapter 13

1. Correct Answer: A. Explanation: This budget burndown chart indicates that the project is expending less than its allocated funds. As of the fifth month, half of the budget is unspent, so it is likely to be substantially under budget at six months.
2. Correct Answer: B. Explanation: Social media would be the best communication method to ensure that customers and other interested parties see the press releases on the project progress. Customers are likely to follow a favored brand on social media apps, which can provide push notifications. While the project manager should publish the press release on the corporate website, it would require the customer to visit the site first. Customers are not likely to be part of an instant message group. Attending a video conference requires a much larger outlay of time than reading a notification on social media.
3. Correct Answer: A. Explanation: To get caught up on the project, the stakeholder should examine the dashboard and status reports.
4. Correct Answer: A. Explanation: The purpose of the project dashboard is to provide the project status.
5. Correct Answer: B. Explanation: A vendor knowledge base provides project team members with answers to questions about third-party products.
6. Correct Answers: A, B, C. Explanation: An issue log, an entry in the requirements traceability matrix, and a change log will all require a unique identifier number be assigned to each issue, change, or requirement for tracking

purposes. A RACI matrix links roles to a task number copied from the WBS, not to an identifier that is uniquely assigned in the matrix.

7. Correct Answer: B. Explanation: Calendaring tools are not used for task dependencies. They are used to coordinate meeting times between attendees and share meeting documents. A precedence network diagram, PERT chart, and Gantt chart could all be used to show task sequences.
8. Correct Answer: D. Explanation: If the line showing budget spent to date is lower than the planned budget line, the project's expenditures to date have exceeded the planned value for that date, and the project may exceed its budget if the same trend continues. However, other variables (such as rate of expenditure) would affect whether the project needs more funds or will exceed its allocated funds.
9. Correct Answer: C. Explanation: You should direct the team to use a virtual whiteboard to collectively brainstorm the components in a shared design space. While the whiteboard application may integrate with a remote meeting platform, there is not necessarily a need for the team members to work synchronously on the design. Real-time multiauthoring platforms mostly provide document and spreadsheet functions, which would be more difficult to use than a whiteboard. File sharing is already incorporated into a whiteboard, and whiteboard files can be saved when complete.
10. Correct Answer: A. Explanation: The team member should consult the process diagram for the sales and shipping processes.

Chapter 14

1. Correct Answer: B. Explanation: Pareto charts, fishbone diagrams, and control charts are all tools used to control the quality of project deliverables.
2. Correct Answer: C. Explanation: A histogram graphically depicts the frequency distribution of a process data set.
3. Correct Answers: B, E. Explanation: Histograms and Pareto charts are both bar charts that can graphically depict the most frequent cause of quality issues.
4. Correct Answer: A. Explanation: The purpose of a Pareto chart is showing the causes of problems, ranked by occurrence.
5. Correct Answer: C. Explanation: Figure 14-14 shows a run chart.
6. Correct Answer: B. Explanation: Data points that are grouped together on a scatter diagram are said to be strongly correlated. Whether the correlation is positive or negative can only be determined by the direction of the trend line (slanting up or slanting down).

7. Correct Answer: C. Explanation: The line depicting the amount of work to be completed remains a straight line across the top of the chart unless the scope changes.
8. Correct Answer: B. Explanation: The main risk of using a scatter chart is incorrectly interpreting strongly correlated data points as showing true cause and effect. If data variables are not well selected, they could show a false cause-and-effect relationship, when in fact both data variables are being affected by a third variable not on the chart.
9. Correct Answer: A. Explanation: The problem definition, problem statement, or issue to be investigated is placed at the "head" of the fishbone diagram in a circle or box. Here the issue is a poor quality product.
10. Correct Answer: C. Explanation: A decision tree should originate with one question and end in one decision that will either earn the most revenue or lose the least money.

Chapter 15

1. Correct Answer: D. Explanation: Even low-impact PII like full name can increase sensitivity if it is easily linkable with additional PII elements that could be taken together to identify a living person. In this case, addresses and IP addresses could be used to positively link full names with online browser habits.
2. Correct Answer: A. Explanation: When possible, organizations should minimize the use, collection, and retention of PII and gather only what is strictly necessary to perform the task requiring the PII. The PII data will be classified after it is collected, while minimization is a strategic decision that should be made before the PII is gathered. Project data fields should be evaluated to ensure they do not capture more PII than is needed. Optimization is a database technique that improves record retrieval. Retention happens after collection.
3. Correct Answer: A. Explanation: The most likely result is that the mismatch between the marketing message and the reality of the product will diminish the company's brand and reputation.
4. Correct Answer: D. Explanation: Requiring the purchase of carbon offsets implies that the project would have an environmental impact that falls under local or national environmental regulations. This kind of purchase would require more extensive cost-benefit analysis to ensure the project met net-zero ESG initiative standards. Background screenings, compliance with HIPAA, and audit requirements are not major project hurdles.

5. Correct Answers: B, C. Explanation: Encryption of data and multifactor authentication are both digital security controls. Any control that restricts access to digital resources or requires specific permissions to access digital resources provides digital security. Security awareness and training is a managerial security control. Restrictions on removable media and use of closed-circuit cameras are physical security controls.
6. Correct Answer: A. Explanation: Obviously, no organization should remain silent after discovering a data breach.
7. Correct Answers: B, D. Explanation: If your project collects or stores PII from European Economic Area (EEA) citizens, including UK citizens, your project needs to comply with GDPR regulations. This law applies regardless of where your organization is located and where the EEA citizens are currently living. Because the law applies to commercial data collection activities, having a single vendor in the EEA is unlikely to trigger a need for compliance. GDPR does not apply to the data of U.S. citizens collected in the U.S.
8. Correct Answer: B. Explanation: The requirements traceability matrix (RTM) tracks the project's design requirements, tests, test results, and issues. The completed RTM proves that requirements are fulfilled, and it validates that all test modules and test scenarios were successfully completed. The defect log will show where the product did not meet quality requirements, but all defects should have been repaired before the device was submitted for approval. The RACI matrix would show who was accountable for the project's requirements, but not whether they were successfully met. A control chart would show upper and lower tolerances for test results on the project's deliverables.
9. Correct Answer: B. Explanation: In addition to implementing physical controls, you should employ technical controls for all mobile devices. The easiest way to do so is to enroll the devices in a mobile device management (MDM) application. Remote access restrictions refer to controlling internal resource access from outside the network. Managerial controls are implemented with best practice policies. Branding restrictions would not apply to mobile phones.
10. Correct Answer: D. Explanation: Offboarding is a procedure for the rapid and secure removal of a former employee or contractor's access to internal company resources, such as files, network shares, login accounts, and RFID badges. Offboarding is usually outlined in the corporate IT security policy and is an operational control. You would not perform a background check on or train an employee of the same organization, and the scenario does not indicate a need for security clearance.

Chapter 16

1. Correct Answers: A, B. Explanation: The customer would be responsible for configuring the application to secure the data records and for granting access to valid users only. The provider would secure the data being transmitted over the Internet and the servers that store the customer's data records.
2. Correct Answer: C. Explanation: An electronic document and record management system (EDRMS) is most likely involved in this scenario, as this system is used to manage an organization's paper and electronic documents so they can be easily retrieved in the event of a compliance audit or subpoena.
3. Correct Answer: D. Explanation: The first step in the software change control process is requirements definition.
4. Correct Answer: A. Explanation: Version control is part of the CI portion of the CI/CD process. All of the other options are part of the CD portion.
5. Correct Answer: B. Explanation: In a tiered architecture for software development, the base source code is located in the development environment.

APPENDIX B

Master Table of Project Management Artifacts, Documents, and Plans

Table B-1 lists each artifact, document, and subsidiary plan used for project management that is covered in this book. Some or all of these components will be included in the overall project management plan.

Table B-1 Master Table of Project Management Artifacts, Documents, and Plans

Artifact, Document, or Plan	Purpose
Backlog	Holds the scope and requirements for Agile projects
Business case	Establishes and justifies a new project in the Discovery phase
Change log	Records all change requests and their disposition, including rejected requests
Change management plan	Manages and tracks all project changes
Communication plan	Manages communication audience, requirements, format, and cadence
Cost baseline	Contains the approved budget for a project, including reserves
Cost management plan	Manages budgeting, estimating, reporting, and expenditure tracking
Defect log	Links bugs or missed requirements with test environments for resolution
High-level scope definition	Sets the preliminary scope in a business case or project charter
Issue log	Records all project issues, their status, their responses, and their outcome
Issue resolution plan	Guides contingency responses and analysis to resolve project issues
Iteration plan	Establishes the scope of work for the current sprint or iteration

Artifact, Document, or Plan	Purpose
Lessons learned register	Holds historical project information useful for project planning
Milestone list	Describes the project's major goalposts
Procurement management plan	Guides standards and processes for acquiring project resources
Procurement plan	Guides procurement of a specific project resource
Project charter	Establishes authority for project work
Project roadmap	Sets high-level overview of the project and key milestones
Quality assurance plan	Establishes how project deliverables are assessed against requirements and acceptance criteria
Records management plan	Guides document retention, security, versioning, and archiving
Requirements documentation	Holds detailed requirements gathered during project planning
Requirements management plan	Establishes how requirements should be gathered, analyzed, and managed
Requirements traceability matrix	Tracks requirements against project deliverables
Resource breakdown structure	Decomposes project work by the types of resources needed for each activity
Resource calendar	Lists dates of availability and scheduled hours for project resources
Resource management plan	Defines how to acquire and manage project resources and team members
Risk management plan	Establishes how project risk will be defined, assessed, managed, and reported
Risk register	Logs all recorded risks, their status, their planned responses, and their disposition
Schedule baseline	Contains the approved schedule for the project
Schedule management plan	Establishes how the schedule will be created, logged, changed, and monitored
Scope baseline	Contains the project's approved scope, WBS, and WBS dictionary
Scope management plan	Manages requirements gathering, scope definition, and changes to scope

Artifact, Document, or Plan	Purpose
Scope statement	Contains the detailed project scope established during the Planning phase
Stakeholder engagement plan	Guides strategic interaction with stakeholders
Stakeholder register	Lists project stakeholders' contact information and key characteristics
Test plan	Establishes how deliverable quality will be verified
Transition/release plan	Establishes operational handoff and user training for project deliverables
WBS dictionary	Defines the work packages in the WBS
Work breakdown structure	Decomposes project requirements into work packages or activities for planning purposes

Glossary

AC See *actual cost.*

acceptance See *risk acceptance.*

access removal An activity within project closure during which both physical and digital access to facilities and assets are revoked.

accommodating See *smoothing.*

action item owner The team member who has ownership of an action item, including follow-up, resolution, or escalation.

action items Activities that are identified during the meeting as tasks that need to be completed or followed up on, generally before the next meeting occurs. Action items should require few resources, require only a few days to resolve, and not should cause delays in the project.

actual cost (AC) The actual expenditures to date on a project.

ad hoc reporting Reports created on an as-needed basis, usually the result of a request by a stakeholder or the sponsor.

adaptive An approach that breaks a project into small components over an undetermined timeline, thereby allowing flexibility throughout the project. Adaptive projects produce an end result that is not very clear at product initiation and can have surprising outcomes.

adjourning The team life-cycle phase in which the team completes the project.

agenda A document published and distributed prior to a meeting that describes the meeting's purpose, schedule, attendees, and topics. Agendas must be retained as records of project communication.

Agile A development model that helps teams respond to unpredictability through incremental, iterative work and feedback. Agile is an adaptive model.

alternatives analysis An analysis method that allows a project team to look at the different alternatives to weigh resource, cost, and duration variables to determine the best approach.

analogous estimating An estimation method that uses historical data from a similar activity or project.

Anything as a Service (XaaS) An umbrella term that describes any specialized computing service that is delivered to the customer over the Internet.

architect Includes network architects, software architects, and security architects who verify the safety and the applicability of the project's technological environment.

archive 1) A location where project documents are stored. 2) An activity completed during the Closing phase of a project. The project manager archives project documentation to ensure that it is maintained until it is no longer needed.

artifact Any tangible document, output, product, or template used in project work or produced by project work. Artifacts can be electronic (such as video files) or physical (such as paper files); they can be outputs of project management (a stakeholder register) or outputs of project work (a prototype).

assumption A factor that you consider to be true for the purpose of project planning and may be formally recorded in an assumptions log for project reference.

asynchronous communication A communication method in which the participants interact with the information being communicated, but not with each other. Asynchronous communication is not time-bound.

audit A process that verifies project deliverables comply with the guidelines set forth in the project management plan, in order to validate the performance of the project.

authentication factor Something you have, something you are, something you know, somewhere you are, or something you do to verify your identity.

avoidance See *risk avoidance*.

avoiding A conflict resolution technique that postpones the issue until the project manager can be better prepared or other parties can resolve the issue. This technique often involves sidestepping the issue.

background screening (background check) A process for validating a job applicant or employee's identity, employment history, criminal record, financial health, and educational experience.

backlog In an Agile project, a backlog is a document derived from the project roadmap that contains any project requirements not being addressed in the current iteration or sprint, but that are intended to become part of the product.

backlog prioritization The process whereby the owner identifies the priority of the tasks on the backlog, including the sequence of those tasks.

backward pass The method used for calculating LS and LF values that start with the last task.

baseline revision The process of revising the schedule or budget because something has changed. However, the original baseline is still retained.

behavioral constraints The behavioral rules for each culture that affect verbal and nonverbal communication. Examples include eye contact, direct discussion versus talking around an issue, and even how close people stand to each other.

brainstorming A collaborative meeting technique that inspires creative, associative, nonlinear thinking from the participants.

branding restrictions Guidelines that control how and for what purpose an organization's brand elements may be used, distributed, reproduced, and shared in digital and physical formats.

budget A document that provides an initial estimate of costs for the project and evolves into an approved estimate of expenditures. The project budget includes a breakdown of costs for individual WBS work packages, procurements, and scheduled activities.

budget reconciliation The project closure activity that includes reviewing transactions and documentation and resolving any discrepancies that are discovered.

buffer utilization The process whereby a project manager decides to use part of the contingency reserve.

build acceptance testing See *smoke testing*.

build verification testing See *smoke testing*.

burn rate The rate at which the project budget is being spent. The burn rate is an inverse of CPI. The formula for computing burn rate is 1 / CPI.

burndown chart (activity) The most common sprint-tracking mechanisms used in Agile development. A burndown chart is a run chart that shows tasks left to perform versus remaining time, or the amount of effort expended versus the time remaining for the current sprint, iteration, or timebox.

burndown chart (budget) A type of chart that shows the actual rate of expenditure versus the planned rate of expenditure for a project, iteration, or sprint budget.

burnup chart A run chart that shows work planned versus work completed, with the planned work trend line starting at 0% at the lower left and ending at 100% at the upper right.

business acquisition A type of business merger wherein one company purchases another.

business analyst The project role that serves as the liaison between the business community and the technical solution providers throughout the project life cycle.

business case A document created during the Discovery phase of a project that creates the rationale for performing project work, establishes the benefits of the project, acts as a basis for project authorization, and is incorporated into the project charter.

business demerger Splits a business into separate entities.

business merger Combines two organizations into one entity. Typically, one of the businesses purchases the other as a business acquisition, or the two businesses join forces due to shared interests or to deepen market penetration.

cadence The regularly scheduled rate at which specific project activities or schedules occur, such as meetings and releases, or the planned length of the standard project timebox, such as sprints.

calendaring tool Software used to coordinate meeting times between attendees and distribute meeting documents in advance.

capital expenses (CapEx) Investments in durable assets that have a useful life measured in years, may appreciate or depreciate, may be sold for a profit or loss, and can incur or offset taxes.

capital resources Nonconsumable assets owned by the company that support the project work.

cause-and-effect diagram See *fishbone diagram*.

CCPA (California Consumer Privacy Act) Applies to all entities that collect the personal data of California residents in the course of a commercial activity.

cease-and-desist letter A letter sent to direct a person or entity to stop doing something immediately (cease) and never do it again (desist). This document usually applies to a particular activity or method of competition.

change control 1. A formal procedure for reviewing all change requests, approving changes, managing the changes, and communicating the changes. 2. A monitoring and controlling activity that takes place during the Executing phase of project work.

change control board (CCB) The group of individuals who are responsible for reviewing every requested project change and approving or rejecting the request.

change control log A comprehensive list of changes requested during the project and their approval status. Also referred to as the *change log*.

change management plan A document created during the Planning phase of a project that defines how project change requests will be managed and implemented, who the approval authorities are, and templates for documentation.

change request A formal proposal to modify any part of the project's critical success factors after project work has begun, such as the scope (requirements), the schedule, the budget, the quality of the deliverables, or the acceptance criteria.

classification (of data) When an entity assigns a protection level and access controls to a data asset.

client statement of work (SOW) A narrative description of a product, service, or result that your project must deliver for the client.

client terms of reference (TOR) A document that defines the tasks and duties you will deliver for the project's client and that highlights the project background and objectives at high level.

close-out meeting See *project closure meeting*.

Closing phase The fifth and final phase of the project life cycle. The Closing phase gains acceptance from the project sponsor, hands off the results of the project or phase, closes contracts, releases resources, and creates lessons learned.

cloudbursting When an organization runs out of computing resources in the internal data center and bursts the extra workload to external third-party cloud services.

CMS See *content management system*.

cognitive constraints The cultural world views that provide a backdrop to which all new information is compared. Examples include religion, literacy level, gender, and economic status.

collaboration A conflict resolution technique that brings two viewpoints together to discuss and reach a solution. Collaboration requires trust and shared goals.

collaboration tools Tools for helping a project team work together. Collaboration tools focus on helping increase efficiency and output within the team, rather than communicating with individuals outside the team.

collaborative meeting A meeting type that has participants work in unison to achieve a specific goal. The purpose is usually to generate value, such as customer feedback, prototypes, new ideas, or a solution to a problem.

communication How project decisions are made and status is provided. Project managers need to document how communication should occur and the cadence of scheduled communications, like meeting schedules and report distribution.

communication management The process of planning, collecting, creating, distributing, storing, retrieving, controlling, and disposing of project information.

communication plan A document created during the Planning phase that describes how, when, and by whom information about the project will be distributed to the project team and stakeholders.

communication platforms/modalities The channels selected by the project team, project manager, or organization to use for exchanging project information. They may be tailored to meet the project needs, such as allowing access to external partners or adding privacy controls.

communication triggers Project events or conditions that must be reported to the appropriate audience after they occur and are recorded in the communication plan.

community cloud A cloud model that is owned and operated by a group of organizations with a shared audience and requirements (such as a group of universities).

competing See *forcing*.

competitive analysis Identifying the competitors who could be vendors for a particular procurement and using research to reveal their strengths and weaknesses.

compromising A conflict resolution technique wherein the team searches for a solution that will bring satisfaction to all parties by partially resolving the conflict.

computing services All technology used to transmit, store, process, or analyze data or information, including software, service provider services, hosted computing services, information technology and telecommunication hardware, and other equipment.

confidential data Requires authorization for each access and is available to those employees in the organization whose work relates to the subject.

confronting A conflict resolution technique wherein the team uses multiple viewpoints to lead to consensus. With this method, the team attempts to work together to find a win-win solution to the problem in hand. The goal of this approach is to find a mutually beneficial result.

constraint Any factor that limits the scope or execution of a project.

constraint reprioritization An event that occurs when a project that is limited by a particular constraint must shift priorities to another constraint.

content management system (CMS) A system that provides a nontechnical solution for producing digital content, such as web content. The actual encoding of the data is handled by the CMS, while the user is provided with an easy-to-handle graphical user interface (GUI) with fields to insert the content to be produced.

contingency plan A planned risk or issue response that describes a sequence of actions to take in response to a specific trigger.

contingency reserve Funds reserved in the budget under the project manager's control to cover known risks, or time reserved in the schedule to accommodate delays.

continuous deployment (CD) The automated installation and configuration of applications following a successful build process.

continuous integration (CI) An environment that continually merges code from multiple authors and storage locations to update a live software solution.

contract The document that spells out the terms and conditions of a legally enforceable transaction between two parties. See also *procurement agreement*.

contract closure An activity during a project wherein a procurement contract is closed once the procurement is delivered and inspected and payment is approved.

control chart A quality assurance chart that plots actual performance of a process over time against established upper and lower control limits. If data points fall above or below the limits, the process is out of control.

core team members Project team members in a strong matrix or projectized organizational structure who perform project work as dedicated resources.

correlation chart See *scatter chart*.

cost baseline The total approved budget for the project, which includes both the expected costs and a contingency reserve. The cost baseline can only change through formal change control.

cost control Monitoring the project's costs and managing changes to the cost baseline.

cost management plan A subsidiary management plan that describes how project costs will be planned, structured, tracked, reported, and controlled.

cost of managing processes An overview of time and resources spent on supervising and managing the project.

cost performance index (CPI) The ratio of earned value to actual cost.

cost plus award fee (CPAF) contract A contract that pays the vendor for all allowed costs and adds an award fee based on performance criteria spelled out in the contract.

cost plus fixed fee (CPFF) contract A contract that pays the vendor for all allowed costs plus a fixed fee, which is a percentage of the estimated costs. The payment does not change unless the project scope changes.

cost plus incentive fee (CPIF) contract A contract that pays the vendor for all allowed costs plus an incentive fee based on the objectives spelled out in the contract.

cost variance (CV) The budget deficit or surplus at any given point in time.

cost-benefit analysis Applying quantitative and qualitative techniques to evaluate whether the proposed cost of a procurement, solution, or risk response exceeds its benefits (for procurements and solutions) or its projected impact (for risks). If the cost is greater than the benefit or the impact, it should be rejected or reevaluated.

cost-plus contract A contract that reimburses the vendor for incurred costs and adds a payment based on the contract type, including cost plus fixed fee (CPFF), cost plus incentive fee (CPIF), and cost plus award fee (CPAF) contracts.

CPAF contract See *cost plus award fee (CPAF) contract.*

CPFF contract See *cost plus fixed fee (CPFF) contract.*

CPI See *cost performance index.*

CPIF contract See *cost plus incentive fee (CPIF) contract.*

critical path The project path that will take the longest amount of time to complete. This critical path also defines the shortest possible duration for a project.

crossed deadline See *overdue project tasks.*

current state Part one of a gap analysis, which defines what is currently happening in the situation to be analyzed.

CV See *cost variance.*

dashboard A graphical report that displays important project status information, usually including key performance indicators, project metrics, current progress, and related issues.

data confidentiality Preventing the disclosure of data to unauthorized entities. This includes data when it is in storage (data at rest), in transmission (data in transit), and in use (data in use).

data owner An organizational role that classifies information assets, ensures the correct security controls exist in the organization, and determines who should have access to each data asset.

data security A series of operational practices and physical, managerial, and technical controls that protect digital information from unauthorized access, corruption, or theft throughout its entire life cycle.

data subject A living individual whose personal data is protected by state, federal, or international regulations regarding data collection, use, and retention.

data user An individual who interacts with data during the normal course of business operations using guidelines set by the organization's data owner.

data warehouse A collection of data sources that allows the organization to use the data therein to guide the organization in making decisions and supports business intelligence (BI) activities, especially analytics.

decision tree A visual method of tracing and comparing all the possible outcomes of multistage decisions, frequently involving estimated monetary values (EMVs).

decisive meeting A meeting type held to direct the project's next steps and then formulate the action to take, including project steering committee meetings, refinement meetings, and task-setting meetings.

decompose The act of breaking the project schedule down into smaller units until individual activities or tasks are identified.

dedicated resources Project resources that are reserved for sole use by that project.

defect A project component or deliverable that fails to meet requirements for performance, quality, or functionality.

defect log A register for tracking and prioritizing flaws in project deliverables that interfere with their performance or that represent failures of function or quality. The defect log is usually tied to the RTM.

deliverable validation An activity during project closure wherein deliverables are examined to ensure they provide the functionality documented in the project or sprint plan.

deliverables The unique work packages defined in the WBS.

demonstrations May be needed to fully assess the capabilities of the vendor or of the procurement. A product demo is one of the most accurate ways to evaluate proposed software or hardware solutions.

dependency When a task that follows the predecessor relies on the completion of the earlier task.

detailed scope statement A document developed during the Planning phase that describes all elements of the project's final scope, including the business need, requirements, activities, exclusions, and methodology, and is entered into the scope baseline after approval. Also called the project scope statement, the project scope, or the detailed scope.

detectability A characteristic of negative risks that describes how likely it is that a risk event would be discovered before it harmed project deliverables (high detectability), versus discovering the harm first and the risk event second (low detectability).

developers/engineers In an IT project, the team members who write the code for an application or deliverable.

DevOps A development approach that includes collaboration, automation, and active monitoring with a focus on speed.

DevSecOps A development approach that is a modification of DevOps and includes collaboration, automation, and active monitoring with a focus on security.

digital security Employing technical controls to protect data and any digital asset, including personal identities.

digital transformation The migration of formerly analog processes to technological solutions, cloud platforms, or entirely new technologies.

directing See *forcing*.

Discovery phase The first phase of the project life cycle. The Discovery phase creates a business case and estimates a proposed project's return on investment.

discretionary dependency See *soft logic dependency*.

EAC See *estimate at completion*.

early finish (EF) The earliest a particular task can finish.

early start (ES) The earliest a particular task can start.

earned value (EV) The percent of the total budget actually spent for work completed at a point in time, also referred to as the value earned from the money spent to date. Formula: Budget of the project × percentage of work that is complete.

earned value management (EVM) A project performance measurement calculation that uses scope, schedule, and resource measurements to assess the project's performance against baselines.

EDRMS See *electronic document and record management system (EDRMS)*.

electronic document and record management system (EDRMS) Systems that manage an organization's paper and electronic documents so they can be easily retrieved in the event of a compliance audit or subpoena. These systems are used to track documents and records and often include version automation, document check-in/checkout, and archival notification.

electronic documents management (EDM) system See *electronic document and record management system (EDRMS)*.

emotional constraints The cultural rules for displaying emotion, such as yelling, crying, deference, and any other exhibition of emotion.

end user The person who will be using the project's results or product on a daily basis.

end-of-life software Applications and operating systems used for project work that are no longer being supported or patched by the vendor, causing a security vulnerability.

enhancement See *risk enhancement*.

enterprise resource planning (ERP) Systems that allow an organization to manage and integrate business activities by collecting shared data from multiple sources, thereby providing system integration, automation, real-time operations, and tracking and visibility.

environmental, social, and governance (ESG) A framework used to assess an organization or a project against various nonfinancial sustainability and ethical factors.

epic A body of work in an Agile project that can be broken down into user stories based on the needs/requests of customers or end users.

escalation path The sequence of individuals who will be contacted to resolve or mitigate an issue, with each escalation being passed to a higher level of decision-making authority.

escalation plan A matrix that provides a predetermined path for redirecting communication issues away from project work for resolution at a higher level.

escalation point A predefined event or scenario that triggers the involvement of the next higher level of management or a technical expert, as described in the escalation plan.

estimate at completion How much money the project will have cost once the new changes are factored into the cost baseline.

estimate to complete (ETC) A value derived from a formula that provides an approximate idea of how much money will be required to complete the remaining balance of project work.

ETC See *estimate to complete.*

EU General Data Protection Regulation (GDPR) A major international regulation, established in 2016 by the European Union, that dictates how all enterprise organizations (regardless of location) must use, store, and dispose of personally identifiable data belonging to European Economic Area (EEA) citizens.

EV See *earned value.*

EVM See *earned value management.*

Executing phase The fourth phase of the project life cycle. The Executing phase expends resources and creates the project's deliverables.

exploitation See *risk exploitation.*

extended team member A temporary team member who is acquired to fill a gap in expertise or manpower, or a team member who belongs to a department or organizational unit and is shared among multiple projects.

external communication Project communication directed outside the project or the organization, such as to customers, vendors, the general public, or other departments.

external dependencies Involve project activities and non-project activities and lie outside the project team's control.

external resources Human or physical resources that are not employed or owned by the organization completing the project work, such as contractors and rental equipment.

external status reports Reports that are shared with individuals outside the project team and stakeholders.

Extreme Programming (XP) An Agile framework that encourages a cross-functional team to sit together in the same space without barriers to communication. It uses pair programming and user stories.

facilitator A meeting role filled by someone who directs but does not participate in meeting activities, keeping participants focused on the agenda.

FFP contract See *firm fixed price (FFP) contract.*

finish-to-finish (FF) The predecessor activity must finish for the successor activity to finish.

finish-to-start (FS) The predecessor activity must finish for the successor activity to start.

firm fixed price (FFP) contract A contract that sets one price for the procurement at the outset and cannot change unless the scope of work changes.

fishbone diagram A cause-and-effect diagram that categorizes the potential causes of a problem in a linear layout to help the project team brainstorm root causes. The effect is written as the problem statement for which the project manager is trying to identify the causes.

fixed-price contract A fixed-price contract establishes a lump sum to be paid for the work performed.

fixed-price incentive fee (FPIF) contract A contract that sets the price for the procurement at the outset but includes a clause that adds financial incentives for the vendor based on certain conditions—usually related to cost, schedule, or technical performance.

fixed-price with economic price adjustment (FP-EPA) contract A contract where the price paid for the procurement is adjusted over a period of time to account for inflation or commodity cost changes. The economic adjustment clause is usually tied to a specific financial index.

float The difference between the LS and ES values for a task. Also referred to as *slack*.

flowchart See *process diagram*.

focus group A collaborative meeting that elicits requirements or feedback on a product from potential end users.

follow-ups Communications sent to update the status of action items or resolve them.

forcing A conflict resolution technique that pursues one viewpoint despite the existence of other viewpoints on the team. It often involves resisting another team member's actions.

formal communication Project communication formatted as reports, minutes, releases, and briefings, frequently based on organizational templates or standards.

forming The team life-cycle phase in which the team meets and learns about how they will work together on the project.

forward pass The method used for calculating ES and EF that starts with the first task and calculates the length of the different project pathways.

FP-EPA contract See *fixed price with economic price adjustment (FP-EPA) contract*.

FPIF contract See *fixed price incentive fee (FPIF) contract*.

framework An approach that is much more flexible and intended to be adapted to fit the problem. Frameworks are more skeletal in nature and act more as guidelines.

functional manager A person who manages project team members in a functional team structure.

functional requirement A mandatory feature of the solution being designed that describes the desired behaviors or functionalities, or tangible things that the solution must do or perform.

functional team member See *extended team member*.

functional team structure Team structure in which each employee reports to a single departmental manager or supervisor.

future state Part two of a gap analysis, which defines the desired or projected outcome of taking action to address the current state.

Gantt chart A chart that displays a project's scheduled activities or tasks over time, often including the activity's dependencies and relationships.

gap analysis A method of comparing actual results or performance with desired results or performance. Project managers can use a gap analysis to analyze the project budget, resources, schedule, quality, or scope.

gate review A type of review that is completed in a phase-gate model project. It is listed on the project schedule. At a gate review, the project managers and project sponsor meet to determine whether to continue the project.

GDPR See *EU General Data Protection Regulation (GDPR)*.

global environment Conditions outside the project's company: regulatory environment, physical environment (the natural world), political environment, and/or fiscal environment.

go-live date The scheduled date the development team deploys the product or deliverable in the client environment.

governance gate A checkpoint within a project that marks acceptance criteria for client sign-off, management approval, or legislative approval. Approval must be gained before the project can proceed.

groupthink A term used for when groups make decisions in a way that discourages individual creativity or responsibility.

hard logic dependency Dependencies that must occur in a certain order based on the project needs. For example, the food for the event must be purchased before it can be prepped for the event.

high-level risks A list included as part of the project charter. High-level risks are uncertain events that may have a positive or negative effect on the project objectives. Risks are assessed more fully after the project is authorized.

high-level scope See *preliminary scope statement.*

histogram A specialized type of bar graph that represents continuous data for a specific range. Graphically depicts the approximate distribution of statistical data.

human resources The team members who perform project work.

hybrid An approach that combines both predictive and adaptive methods within the same project. This approach is often used when certain features or functions can be easily defined during project planning while other features and functions are not fully understood.

hybrid cloud A cloud model that combines elements of two or more cloud infrastructures (such as public and private) that are linked through a shared technical interface.

impact analysis Using qualitative and quantitative techniques to gauge the effect that a given change or risk will have on the project's success factors.

impact assessment Forecasting the effect that a future event, such as a risk or a change to an ongoing project, would have on a project's resources, constraints, and/or execution. Impact can be expressed in qualitative terms (such as high or low) or quantitative terms (such as 2 months, 20%, or 2 million dollars).

increment The features or functions released in an incremental project. Each increment completes the plan/design/build process until the project is complete.

incremental An adaptive method wherein the product team divides the product into fully operational features or functions. Like the iterative method, each feature or function is released separately without waiting on others.

influence Any project event or condition that can affect a project constraint. Influences can be external or internal.

informal communication Unofficial, ad hoc communication between project stakeholders that is not retained in the project records.

informative meeting A meeting designed to share information rather than to collaborate or make decisions, such as a demo, stand-up, or status meeting.

Infrastructure as a Service (IaaS) A cloud service model where the cloud provider maintains the networking, computing, and storage components and makes them available on a per-use or subscription basis.

infrastructure end of life (EOL) Legacy infrastructure end-of-life (EOL) system risks are created by hardware or software that is still used by your organization but no longer supported by the vendor. EOL risks are uniformly negative.

Initiating phase The second phase of the project life cycle. The Initiating phase creates a project charter, obtains authorization to start that project, and kicks off the project.

inspection A process that is similar to an audit, but not as formal, and often just completes a checklist to ensure that deliverables meet certain conditions. Inspections are generally carried out to verify either project governance, compliance, or quality.

intangible outcomes Nonphysical assets such as patents, trademarks, franchises, good will, and copyrights.

intellectual property (IP) A unique, internally generated creative asset owned by the organization that is legally protected from infringement through trademarks, registration, patents, or copyright.

interconnectivity The interrelated nature of risks or systems such that a change or impact in one area alters the probability or impact in another area. Interconnected risks can produce effects that would not be observed from the risk in isolation.

internal communication Communication that takes place within the project, team, program, organization, or group of stakeholders.

internal data Data classified as internal is meant for use within the organization and should not be disclosed without managerial permission, but is not sensitive and will not cause regulatory impact if it is exposed.

internal dependencies Involve project activities and are under the control of the project team. For example, the shopping list cannot be determined until the menu is chosen.

internal resources Human or physical resources that are employed or owned by the organization completing the project work.

intranet site A website that is accessible exclusively within an organization.

Ishikawa diagram See *fishbone diagram.*

issue escalation The process whereby a decision-making process is followed to ensure that project issues are resolved in a timely manner.

issue resolution plan A strategy to mitigate the impact of an issue, find its root cause, minimize or eliminate the chance of its reoccurrence, and monitor all open and closed issues.

issues Problems, gaps, inconsistencies, or conflicts that occur unexpectedly in the life cycle of a project, may or may not have been identified as risks, and block project progress until they are resolved.

issues log A register of the events and conditions that actively affect project work and require a response or resolution.

iteration The features or functions released in an iterative project. When each iteration starts, the scope, approach, and requirements of that iteration are defined, with each iteration adding functionality to the previous iterations.

iteration plan The portion of the backlog that the team commits to delivering in an upcoming iteration or sprint.

iterative An adaptive method wherein the product team builds up the features and functions of the product over time. Each feature or function is usually released separately without waiting on other features or functions.

joint application development (JAB)/joint application review A formal collaborative meeting in which the customer and the project team confer on software product design and review prototypes as they are developed.

Kanban An Agile method that visually manages the project workflow. It places all work into three categories: To Do (Requested), Doing (In Progress), and Done.

Kanban board The visual that lists the three Kanban categories in the columns at the top.

Kanban cards The visual that represents individual activities or tasks and starts off in the far-left column (To Do).

key performance indicator (KPI) A measure that evaluates the success of a project or deliverable in meeting objectives for performance.

key performance parameter (KPP) The U.S. Department of Defense (DoD) term that means the same as KPI.

key result A measure based on the objective that shows how the project manager knows the objective is achieved. Objectives are the *what*, while key results are the *how*.

kickoff meeting A meeting of team members and key stakeholders that is held at the start of a project to formally set expectations, gain a common understanding of fellow team members, and commence work.

KPI See *key performance indicator*.

late finish (LF) The latest a particular task can finish and not negatively affect the project deadline.

late start (LS) The latest a particular task can start and not negatively affect the project deadline.

lessons learned 1. A database or other storage location where lessons learned from all projects are stored. 2. An activity completed during the Closing phase of a project. In the "lessons learned" document, the project manager records any knowledge gained during a project and shows how project issues and events were addressed.

letter of intent (LOI) A document that outlines the plans of an agreement between two or more parties, usually a precursor to a formal contract. In the United States, letter of intent is generally considered synonymous with memorandum of understanding (MOU).

LOI See *letter of intent (LOI)*.

lose-lose situation When a compromise does not satisfy either party. Unfortunately, compromising does not contribute to building trust and may require monitoring to ensure that agreements made during the compromise are met.

maintenance agreement An ongoing service that a vendor will provide to a procurement after you buy it and put it to use, or that your product will provide to the customer after project work is released. Maintenance ensures the product's quality stays at an agreed-upon level.

major cybersecurity event An event that results in unauthorized access to or theft of private data. Common cybersecurity events occur through phishing, supply chain attacks, denial-of-service (DoS) attacks, insider threat attacks, and many others.

management reserves Funds controlled by senior management, not the project manager, that can be allocated to cover project costs from significant, unforeseen risks to complete the project's scope.

mandatory dependency See *hard logic dependency*.

market research Gathering information to find a vendor that offers a niche product or service, to help evaluate a vendor who has submitted a proposal or quote, or to determine which vendor(s) has the largest footprint and strongest reputation in the project's field.

master service agreement (MSA) A broad contract that two parties enter into during a service transaction. It establishes the definitions, terms, and agreements for an ongoing, long-term business relationship, and outlines all future activities to occur between them.

matrix team structure Team structure in which authority is shared between functional managers and project managers, resources are assigned from functional areas to projects, and project manager authority ranges from weak to strong.

meeting agenda A roadmap distributed prior to a meeting that defines the meeting's purpose and lists the topics, action items, activities, and presentations to be covered, the participants, and key roles.

meeting minutes A written record of what was discussed in a meeting, who attended, and what the meeting outcome was, to be distributed after the meeting and retained as a project record.

memorandum of understanding (MOU) Another term for letter of intent (LOI).

methodology An approach that includes steps to be completed. Methodologies explain why the steps are essential and how each step should be accomplished.

milestone A significant project event that indicates when a phase of the project work is complete.

milestone chart A visual mapping of significant events in the project's life cycle in relation to the timeline. This chart is included in an early form in the project charter, revised as the schedule is planned, and revised again as schedules change.

milestone list A list that identifies all project milestones and indicates whether each milestone is mandatory.

minimum viable product (MVP) A release that is complete enough to function according to requirements but does not include all of the planned features.

missed milestones Indicate whether a project is running ahead of schedule, on time, or behind schedule.

MOU See *memorandum of understanding (MOU)*.

multifactor authentication (MFA) A technical control that will use two or more authentication factors to verify the identity of a user against their claimed identity when logging in to a system or application.

multitiered architecture Any architecture in which multiple tiers are used to logically separate processes, providing better performance and security.

mutually binding document A legal agreement between two parties in which one party promises to provide the other party with a product, service, or other consideration in return for payment.

national security information Information deemed by a government as pertinent to national security and subject to protection. In the U.S., that data would be classified as Confidential, Secret, or Top Secret.

NDA See *non-disclosure agreement (NDA)*.

needs assessment An analysis conducted at the start of the Planning phase that contrasts existing resources with the resources required by a project to find gaps that must be filled with procurements, training, or resource reallocation.

need-to-know access A granular access control that goes beyond the job role to the specific task or activity requiring the data.

negotiated resources Personnel the project manager wants on the project team and must negotiate with other managers to obtain.

negotiating A conflict resolution technique that brings two viewpoints together to discuss issues and reach a solution. Usually negotiation is more of a win-lose situation or at least an "I win bigger than you win" scenario. Negotiation can often involve suspicion (or at least lack of trust) and separate agendas.

noise Any interference or barrier that impedes the effective exchange of information, such as simultaneous cross-talk or technical issues with a communication platform.

non-compete clause An agreement that prevents the vendor from pursuing a similar project with the buyer's direct competitors or customers within a specified time period.

non-disclosure agreement (NDA) A type of confidentiality agreement in which the selected vendor and any vendor personnel involved in the procurement agree not to disclose details about the project.

nonfunctional requirement A requirement of the solution design that describes the intangible properties of the finished product, such as its compliance with regulations or portability to other operating systems.

nonverbal communication Contextual cues that enhance oral and visual communication, such as speaking volume, tone of voice, body posture, gestures, and facial expressions.

norming The team life-cycle phase in which the team members begin working together and learn to adjust their work to support the team.

objective States a goal but does not need to be measurable. It simply gives a goal and why the goal is important. Objectives are the what, while key results are the how.

operational expenses (OpEx) Costs for consumables or short-term assets that do not appreciate, depreciate, or require long-term management, such as repairs, services, utilities, salaries, office supplies, and rent.

operational handoff Ensures that all individuals involved with the product know when their responsibilities end or begin. Handoff includes turning over any assets (physical or intangible) required to operate the product according to the asset transfer plan.

operational security (OPSEC) A process that organizations deploy to prevent sensitive information from getting into the wrong hands.

operational team members See *core team members.*

operational training Provides training to the end users, along with product documentation, a list of all assets required to run the product, requirements for operating, patching, and maintaining the product, a maintenance schedule, and a development team contact.

organizational chart A diagram that shows the structure and hierarchy of the project team, including extended and core team members, and the stakeholders within the organization: the sponsor, the steering committee, and senior management.

overdue project tasks Also called crossed deadlines. The number of project activities that are overdue. A calculated percentage of project activities that go past their due date is compared to all completed project activities.

parametric estimating An estimation method that uses an algorithm to calculate duration. Often this algorithm takes into consideration historical data and project parameters.

Pareto chart A vertical bar chart combined with a line graph to show importance or other values graphed from highest to lowest.

pay-as-you-go (PAYG) A service that accumulates costs at a specified rate per unit of value or unit of time so that billing fluctuates with the customer's usage.

performance management The process of comparing raw data gathered from actual project performance against the baselines defined in the project management plan, yielding detailed information about work performance.

performance measurement baseline Composed of the cost baseline, schedule baseline, and scope baseline and used to measure project performance throughout execution.

performance testing A nonfunctional software testing technique that determines how the stability, speed, scalability, and responsiveness of an application holds up under a given workload.

performing The team life-cycle phase in which the team starts working as a unit, with team members depending on each other and working through issues easily.

personal health information (PHI) A highly sensitive and highly regulated category of data that includes the health records, health billing records, and health provider records of an individual.

personally identifiable information (PII) Any information maintained by an organization that could uniquely identify a living individual, such as name, fingerprints, SSNs, birthdate, and genetic data. Handling of PII is governed by local, national, and international regulations.

phase (project) A distinct period in project management in which certain types of activities are completed: Discovery, Initiating, Planning, Executing, and Closing.

phase-gate model A project technique wherein the project is divided into stages or phases, separated by gates.

phase-gate process See *phase-gate model.*

phase-gate review See *gate review.*

physical resources The physical assets, such as equipment, software, hardware, facilities, vehicles, and raw materials required to execute project work and create deliverables.

PIPEDA (Personal Information Protection and Electronic Documents Act) Applies to private-sector organizations in Canada that collect, use, or disclose personal information in the course of a commercial activity.

planned value (PV) The budgeted cost for the work that is currently completed. This is the portion of the project budget planned to be spent at any given point in time.Formula: Budget × percentage of work that should be completed.

Planning phase The third phase of the project life cycle. The Planning phase creates the project management plan and formalizes the scope, schedule, and budget baselines.

Platform as a Service (PaaS) A cloud service model that is often used by application developers because PaaS provides the platform, including the hardware and software tools, for developers to access over the Internet.

portfolio All of the projects, programs, and operations managed by an organization to allow it to reach strategic objectives.

post-implementation support Any support that is provided for both internally released products and those purchased from a vendor. Most vendor post-implementation support is for a defined time period. Thereafter, support from the vendor must be purchased.

precedence diagram method (PDM) A method of showing dependencies between tasks by connecting squares (tasks) with arrows that show the direction(s) in which work must flow between the tasks.

predecessor A task that must be completed prior to starting the next task.

predictive An approach that provides a linear development plan with a known outcome. A structured process is used for producing a pre-determined result within a specific time frame. Predictive projects strive to reduce uncertainty.

preliminary scope statement A high-level version of the project scope that is included in the project charter. See also *project scope* and *detailed scope statement*.

prequalified vendors/sellers A vendor that has already been evaluated for their ability to supply goods or services according to the organization's or the project's requirements.

private cloud A cloud model that is used only by one organization or its federated partners. Its applications and services are delivered only to its internal clients through a locally available gateway. The physical infrastructure may be maintained on-premises, offsite, or by a third party.

private/restricted data Information that would cause financial or reputational harm to the organization, if exposed, and should be protected with the strongest access controls but is not a legally recognized category of "sensitive" data.

probability and impact matrix A grid used to map the likelihood of each risk occurring and its impact on the project if that risk occurs, creating a risk score from lowest impact/probability to highest. The matrix may be used for qualitative or quantitative analysis and is the basis for a risk heat map.

problem-solving See *confronting*.

process diagram A sequential breakdown of the steps required to complete a business process, displayed in relation to each other.

procurement Any product, good, service, or result that needs to be acquired with project funds from a third party to support project work.

procurement agreement Any document that defines the purchase terms of particular goods or services that must be acquired from a third party.

procurement management plan A governance document that describes how goods and services will be procured from outside sources.

procurement needs assessment See *needs assessment*.

procurement plan A plan for acquiring a specific project resource, along with a description of the procurement, a procurement timeline, vendor selection criteria, and the results of the vendor selection process.

product change A request to modify the definition or features of the finished product. Product changes can be added to the backlog for future sprints unless they affect the trajectory of the current project and trigger project changes.

product manager In Waterfall projects, the role that owns the product scope, represents the customer, and advocates for the product but does not directly manage the project.

product owner The role in Agile projects that handles many of the traditional project management tasks, such as prioritizing the order of work, managing the budget, accepting deliverables, and setting release dates. The product owner is the Agile product's key stakeholder, who provides the overall vision for the product.

program A grouping of related projects or activities that are managed in coordination to obtain benefits not available if they were managed individually.

Program Evaluation Review Technique (PERT) chart A precedence diagram that identifies activities and durations, and dependencies between the activities, and then uses a three-point estimate to calculate the task durations.

program manager The role that oversees groups of projects that are linked through a common organizational goal, referred to as a program.

project A temporary endeavor undertaken to create a unique product, service, or result.

project baseline See *performance measurement baseline*.

project change See *change request*.

project charter A document created during the Initiating phase of a project. The project charter authorizes the project and includes its business case, high-level scope, project objectives, success criteria, a milestone list, high-level risks, assumptions, constraints, and preliminary budget.

project closeout report A document that records any knowledge gained during the project and shows how project issues and events were addressed.

project closure meeting A meeting that must be held as soon as possible after the sprint, phase, or project is complete to ensure that project information is captured and recorded while the knowledge is still fresh. During this meeting, the attendees should review the project artifacts, especially the risk and issues logs, and decide what the organization can learn from the results.

project coordinator An optional role that coordinates activities, resources, equipment, and information to support the project manager.

project dashboard A tool that gives stakeholders and team members a quick look at the overall project. The dashboard includes the project's status reports and may include other components such as key performance indicators, project metrics, project progress, and details of other project issues.

project deliverables See *deliverables*.

project evaluation An activity during project closure that ensures that the deliverables and project provided the needed results.

project management office (PMO) An organizational resource that provides project management governance and ensures that resources, methods, tools, and techniques are shared or coordinated across all projects.

project management plan A set of documents that contain a complete description of the project and its activities, its milestones, its anticipated outcome, its resources, the baselines used to measure its performance, and the subsidiary plan documents that describe how each aspect of the project will be executed and governed.

project manager (PM) The individual who is selected to manage the project, lead the project team, and ensure the project's success.

project network diagram (PND) A chart or spreadsheet that visualizes the overall sequence of project activities and events with their relationships, typically as arrows and boxes. Precedence diagrams, PERT charts, and critical path diagrams are all project network diagrams.

project reserves Project funds that are allocated in the Planning stage to mitigate cost and/or schedule risks. Management reserves and contingency reserves are the two types of financial project reserves.

project risk management The formal process of identifying, analyzing, and controlling events that occur during project execution so as to manage their impact to the project's work, scope, budget, schedule, or quality.

project roadmap A high-level overview of a project's intended trajectory that summarizes major activities and their outcomes only. It is used for business analysis, not actual project scheduling.

project scheduler An optional role that develops and maintains the project schedule and works to ensure that resources are available when needed.

project scheduling software Programs and apps that support "what-if" scenarios, track project efficiency, and analyze schedules by using charts and diagrams.

project scope A definition of the project that includes key deliverables, exclusions, timeline, budget, and success factors. See also *detailed scope statement*.

project sign-off A formal method for validating project completion according to the project management plan. The sign-off is usually completed by the project manager and signed by the project sponsor.

project sponsor The individual or organization that must formally authorize the project, provide funding, establish the project charter, complete the business justification for the project, and select or approve the project manager.

project status report A written summary of the latest information on project activities, issues, changes, and risks, distributed via status meetings and the project dashboard.

project steering committee meeting A decisive meeting of high-level project stakeholders and/or senior management that is held regularly to govern project activities and make high-level decisions regarding changes, scope, and budget.

project team The group of individuals who work with the project manager to perform project tasks to ensure the project's completion.

project team members Individuals who have the expertise needed to complete the project and who work together on project activities.

projectized team structure Team structure in which the project manager has full authority, personnel report to the project manager, and resources are allocated to projects on an ad hoc basis.

PRojects IN Controlled Environments (PRINCE2) A predictive, process-based project management methodology that focuses on organization and control over the entire project, thereby ensuring that projects are thoroughly planned before kickoff, with all project stages being very structured.

proprietary data An internally generated asset that is exclusively owned by an organization and which would cause a competitive disadvantage if it were exposed or used in an unauthorized way.

public cloud A commercial service available to anyone who signs up. Its physical components are fully owned and maintained by the service provider.

public data Data that can be stored and discarded without security precautions. It has no restrictions.

pull communication Information retrieved by an audience from the source repository.

purchase order (PO) A document that is issued immediately after a contract is signed, clarifying the details of the purchase. The PO states the financial agreement, terms, method of delivery, delivery date, quantity needed, and so on, and is binding for the purchaser.

push communication Information transmitted by a communicator to an audience.

PV See *planned value.*

qualifications Required characteristics that a vendor must possess before you can send them a request for a quote or proposal or issue a contract.

qualitative risk analysis Performing risk probability and impact assessments to develop a probability and impact matrix, which provides a risk score to guide risk responses.

quality assurance plan A subsidiary project management plan that describes the standards against which the project's outcomes will be verified and validated, both internally and externally, and how the project's quality policies will be implemented. Also called the *quality management plan.*

quality assurance (QA) specialist The project role that checks the implementation of the quality system and conducts quality assurance audits on project deliverables.

quality gate A checklist of acceptance criteria to ensure that project tasks are completing deliverables within the quality control guidelines established during project planning.

quality management The process that ensures quality satisfies the needs of the project.

quality management plan See *quality assurance plan.*

quantitative risk analysis Using a mathematical model to simulate the outcome of a risk, commonly expressed as a currency amount.

RACI matrix See *responsible, accountable, consulted, and informed (RACI) matrix.*

realized risk A risk that has occurred or materialized in the project environment.

rebaseline The process of creating a new schedule or budget because something has changed. Retaining the original baseline is not important.

reconciling See *compromising.*

records management plan A set of policies and procedures governing the creation, use, retention, and disposal of data and documents related to project work.

refinement meeting A decisive meeting type for Agile projects that decomposes the highest priority backlog items into user stories and chooses the ones to include in the next sprint.

regression plan The process whereby an approved project change can be reversed if it causes problems after implementation.

regression testing Testing that takes place after changes are made to the code to ensure the changes have reduced neither functionality nor security.

release plan (adaptive) For adaptive projects, this is a subsidiary management plan that describes the outcomes or features that will be delivered in each iteration, along with a timeline and a plan for training the operations team to use the new product.

release plan (predictive) A synonym for the transition plan.

release retrospective A retrospective that concentrates on the release of a product or service.

remote access restrictions Provide access to digital assets to remote users.

request for bid (RFB) A procurement document in which the buyer invites multiple comparable sellers to submit their best-priced proposal to provide the product/service you are seeking.

request for information (RFI) A procurement document in which the buyer requests that a potential seller provide information related to the product/service or to the seller's capability to provide the product/service. An RFI is used to gather market information and help clarify the scope of the proposed solution.

request for proposal (RFP) A procurement document in which the buyer provides detailed information regarding the project and solicits proposals from prospective sellers of products or services. An RFP is used when the procurement is large or complex and requires in-depth analysis to select the right vendor.

request for quote (RFQ) A procurement document in which the buyer requests price quotations from prospective sellers to meet known requirements for common products or services, such as computers, hourly labor, or building materials. An RFQ is used when price is the main factor and the procurement is readily available.

requirements management plan A document created during the Planning phase of a project that describes how the project requirements will be gathered, analyzed, documented, and managed.

requirements traceability matrix A register of project requirements that is maintained to ensure requirements are either incorporated into the final product or have a documented reason for being rejected.

reserve analysis A method of determining which portion of project funds should be held to cover any cost uncertainty that the project may encounter.

resource access and permissions Involve creating user accounts and giving those accounts the appropriate permissions to digital resources.

resource allocation The process of assigning resources to individual project activities or tasks.

resource breakdown structure A chart that breaks down project work according to the types of resources needed to complete each activity or work package.

resource calendar A document that shows when team members and physical resources are available to be assigned to project activities, along with their skills and/or available quantities.

resource contention An issue that occurs when more than one project in the organization needs the same resource at the same time or on overlapping schedules.

resource leveling The process whereby a project manager adjusts the task's start and finish dates based on resource constraints and might increase the original critical path.

resource life cycle The stages that a physical or human resource goes through while employed for project work by an organization, from acquisition to decommissioning (physical resources) or from hiring to succession (human resources).

resource loading The process whereby a project manager determines the hours of work a resource is available to the project and then utilizes these resources to complete project activities.

resource management The process that ensures that all the supplies needed to complete a project are identified and managed appropriately.

resource management plan Describes how human and physical resources will be structured and managed, including their roles, responsibilities, and reporting relationships.

resource overallocation When a project has too much of a particular resource, resulting in leftover inventory or idle team members.

resource pool Includes the personnel, equipment, services, and supplies that exist in the project environment.

resource release An activity during project closure whereby both team members and physical resources are released.

resource shortage When a project does not have enough of a particular resource to complete an activity or task.

resource smoothing The process whereby a project manager adjusts the activities within their float amounts so that the resource requirements do not exceed the limits of available resources.

resource utilization Measures how the team members' time is used while working on the project.

responsibility assignment matrix (RAM) A project tool that maps all resources to their areas of ownership, oversight, or task assignments using the stakeholder list.

responsible, accountable, consulted, and informed (RACI) matrix A project tool used during the Initiating and Planning phases of a project to analyze the project stakeholder and team member roles and responsibilities in relation to project activities or tasks.

retrospective A meeting type used in Agile projects at the end of each sprint and at the end of the project. Retrospectives foster open communication. See also *scrum retrospective*, *sprint retrospective*, *team retrospective*, and *release retrospective*.

return on investment (ROI) The total dollar/time return the project sponsor will receive for the project. ROI is calculated using one of two formulas:

- (change in operations cost) / (costs of project)
- (change in revenue) / (costs of project)

return on investment (ROI) analysis Financial formulas used to calculate the net profit gained from an expenditure, such as a project or a resource acquisition, expressed as a percentage or as a currency amount.

RFB See *request for bid (RFB)*.

RFI See *request for information (RFI)*.

RFP See *request for proposal (RFP)*.

RFQ See *request for quote (RFQ)*.

risk An event or condition that could occur during project work and would affect the project's objectives or other aspects of the project, such as the project cost, scope, or schedule. The risk's effect could be positive or negative.

risk acceptance A risk strategy for both negative and positive risks. The project team acknowledges the risk but decides not to take any action.

risk activities Planning risk management, identifying risks, performing risk analysis, planning risk responses, and controlling risks. These risk activities occur during the Planning phase and the Executing phase of a project.

risk analysis Derives the key data that will drive response planning and determines the effects of risks on the project objectives so the most effective response can be planned.

risk appetite The amount of uncertainty the organization is willing to take on in hopes of achieving a business objective, such as profit or innovation.

risk avoidance A risk strategy for negative risks whereby the project team eliminates the risk or protects the project from the risk.

risk enhancement A risk strategy for positive risks whereby the project team identifies the key drivers that affect a risk and adjusts them to increase the probability of the risk.

risk exploitation A risk strategy for positive risks whereby the project team ensures that the risk occurs.

risk exposure The estimated monetary value (EMV) of risk, expressed for a single risk or as an aggregate amount for the whole project.

risk identification The process of determining in advance what risks may affect a project and documenting them in the risk management plan.

risk impact The effects that the risk will have on the project's schedule, budget, scope, resources, or quality, typically expressed as a currency amount, period of time, or percentage.

risk management The formal process of identifying, analyzing, and controlling events that occur during project execution so as to manage their impact to the project's work, scope, budget, schedule, or quality.

risk management plan A document that describes all the known risks that may affect a project and the strategies that will be used to handle each risk. Part of the project management plan.

risk matrix See *probability and impact matrix*.

risk mitigation A risk strategy for negative risks whereby the project team reduces the probability that the risk will occur or lessens the projected impact of the risk.

risk owner The stakeholder assigned responsibility for a risk in the risk register based on their expertise in the risk area and their ability to respond effectively to a risk event.

risk planning The project management process that formally creates the risk management plan by ensuring that risks are identified, analyzed, quantified, prioritized, and reviewed, and appropriate responses to each risk are prepared.

risk prioritization Ensuring that risk plans are developed for every identified risk based on its priority.

risk quantification Performing qualitative and quantitative risk analysis to determine the effects of risks on the project objectives.

risk register The document that charts all risks identified during risk planning.

risk report A report that describes the project's overall risk response and risk exposure and summarizes responses to realized risk.

risk response A planned course of action that will enhance opportunities and/or reduce threats to the project when risk events occur.

risk review Periodically investigating risks during project execution to detect any new risks that may have arisen, close risks that no longer apply, and ensure that planned risk strategies are still effective.

risk sharing A risk strategy for positive risks whereby the opportunity is shared with another party so that both may benefit from the project's outcomes.

risk tolerance The amount of risk impact that an organization can withstand before operations are negatively affected.

risk transference A risk strategy for negative risks whereby the risk's potential impact is shifted to or shared with another party.

risk trigger An event or condition that will cause a contingency plan to be implemented.

ROI See *return on investment*.

roll wave planning A method whereby planning for future deliverables occurs when the project is closer to that deliverable being needed. This technique uses detailed planning for closer activities and high-level planning for activities that will be performed in the future.

rollback plan A plan that documents the method whereby a system or application is returned to a previous state. This plan is usually implemented if an update causes issues.

root cause analysis Root causes are conditions or events that set a risk or issue in motion. A root cause analysis looks for the key drivers behind a risk, issue, or impediment.

rules of engagement A documented guide that defines expectations around how the project team and the vendor interact during the project: how much information is shared, when it is shared, and how it is shared. It also defines situations that would require immediate communication (such as a delay in procurement due to raw material shortages).

run chart A chart that shows trends, variations, or declines/improvements in a project over time, using a line graph.

Scaled Agile Framework (SAFe) A framework that implements Agile at the enterprise level and consists of three metaphorical pillars: team, program, and portfolio.

scatter chart A chart that is used to find the correlation or lack of correlation between two variables.

scatter diagram See *scatter chart*.

scatter plot See *scatter chart*.

schedule Shows project activities with their planned start/end dates, durations, dependencies, milestones, and assigned resources.

schedule baseline The approved version of the project schedule created prior to the Executing phase.

schedule management Also referred to as *time management*, this process ensures that project work is completed when it should be. It begins with defining the units of work and creating a work breakdown structure, defining and sequencing the project activities, estimating the activity resources and durations, and then developing the actual schedule.

schedule performance index (SPI) A formula used to indicate how the project is progressing compared to the planned project schedule, also referred to as the ratio of earned value to planned value. Formula: SPI = EV / PV.

schedule variance (SV) A formula used to indicate if the project is ahead of schedule or behind schedule in dollars. Formula: SV = EV – PV.

scope See *project scope*.

scope baseline The project document used as the basis for controlling the scope during the Executing phase. The scope baseline includes the project scope statement, work breakdown structure (WBS), and the WBS dictionary.

scope change In predictive projects, this is an addition to or subtraction from the agreed-upon scope of work for a project or deliverable. In Agile methodologies, it is an addition to or deletion from the features in the product backlog.

scope creep A condition that occurs in a project when the scope of work is changed without adjusting other project constraints, including cost, time, and resources.

scope management plan A subsidiary management plan that describes how the project or phase's scope is defined, developed, monitored, controlled, and verified.

scribe A team member or meeting role that captures the results of more formal meetings in writing, creating documents to be archived with project communications and/or distributed to the team.

scrum A project management framework that emphasizes teamwork, accountability, and iterative progress toward a well-defined goal. The most popular Agile methodology, scrum is both simple and flexible. In the scrum methodology, the scrum master handles any outside distractions or internal complications that could prevent the team from making progress on the project. The scrum master helps translate stakeholder needs into requirements and enforces scrum policies while maintaining the team's focus on project design. The scrum master's goal is to keep the team actively moving forward and on track.

scrum master The role in scrum projects that coordinates the team work. This role works closely with the product owner, taking the instructions and ensuring that activities are completed.

scrum retrospective A meeting held at the end of a sprint wherein the team members and scrum master meet to discuss the sprint that has just concluded and to note any changes that could help make the next sprint more productive. A scrum retrospective is similar to the "lessons learned" meeting in many project management methodologies and is a verification activity.

security clearance A status granted to individuals who pass a federal background check, certifying them as trusted to access national security information or enter restricted areas in secured government facilities.

senior management The higher-level executives of the organization sponsoring or performing the project. They are primarily concerned with how the project affects the parent organization.

sensitive/restricted data Requires special protection from unauthorized modification or deletion according to regulation and law, such as PHI, PII, and credit card data. It would harm the organization if exposed.

sensitivity (data) The degree to which data should be protected from unauthorized access or exposure, where the more sensitive the data, the higher the impact from its unauthorized exposure, and the more protection it requires.

sequencing The process whereby the dependencies and relationships of tasks are determined so that the order of tasks is documented.

service level agreement (SLA) A contract between a service provider and a customer that sets specific metrics the service or product must meet, including quality, availability, and responsibilities. SLAs may be provided by the project organization to support the project's output, or they may be provided by a service that was procured for project work.

shared resources A project resource that may be used by multiple projects or departments at the same time or in an ongoing fashion.

sharing See *risk sharing*.

simulation Also called *Monte Carlo simulation*, this is a quantitative risk analysis method that can use schedule and cost estimates to simulate real-life project results.

situational/scenario analysis A brainstorming technique that asks what-if questions to uncover the positive and/or negative impact or outcomes of a narrative scenario.

SLA See *service level agreement*.

slack See *float*.

smoke testing Also called build verification testing or build acceptance testing, this test checks that the most crucial functions of an application work but does not delve into the finer details.

smoothing A conflict resolution technique that emphasizes areas of agreement rather than differences. With this technique, the project manager helps team members to accommodate the concerns of other people.

soft logic/dependency Dependencies that can be completed in any order in the project. This does not mean that the activities are not completed separately. It just means that they do not need to be in sequential order.

Software as a Service (SaaS) A cloud service model that delivers an application (or software) through the Internet.

Software Development Life Cycle (SDLC) A process framework that provides predictable procedures to identify all requirements with regard to functionality, cost, reliability, and delivery schedule and ensure that each is met in the final solution. As a result, the SDLC is considered to be a predictive model.

solution The set of technologies and technical products that will meet an IT project's requirements and enable it to deliver its planned features. The solution could be one product or many.

solution design The process of choosing the technical product or products needed to develop an IT project's deliverables. The solution architect has the most input into this decision.

SOW See *statement of work (SOW)*.

SPI See *schedule performance index*.

sponsor See *project sponsor*.

sprint The repeated, iterative work cycle around which the scrum method centers. The goal of a sprint is to complete one of the product's requirements in a usable form. Sprints typically start with a sprint planning meeting, cycle through daily scrum meetings, and end with a retrospective meeting.

sprint goal An overarching objective that the scrum teams plan to complete during the sprint.

sprint planning The process that decides the specific work to be handled in the upcoming sprint. It includes themes, epics, user stories, and tasks. The backlog contains all work waiting to be completed.

sprint retrospective A retrospective that occurs at the end of a sprint to assess the team's work processes and brainstorm improvements. This meeting happens throughout the life of a project and often occurs every 2 weeks.

sprint review A meeting held at the end of a sprint wherein accomplishments are noted and stakeholders provide feedback.

stage-gate process See *phase-gate process.*

stage-gate review See *gate review.*

stakeholder Any individual, group, or organization with a vested interest in the success of a project.

stakeholder engagement plan A subsidiary project management plan that strategizes how to interact with project stakeholders, including each stakeholder's engagement level, relationships, and communication requirements. Defines the tools and techniques to engage stakeholders in project decisions and execution.

stakeholder register A document created during the Initiating phase of a project and finished during the Planning phase. The stakeholder register lists all stakeholders, along with their identification information, requirements and expectations, influence on the project, and classification.

stand-up meeting A short informative meeting performed in a daily cadence that allows participants to report the prior day's progress and pain points and to align their daily priorities at a high level. Originally a scrum technique, this meeting type is now widely adopted across many project frameworks.

start-to-finish (SF) The predecessor activity must start for the successor activity to finish.

start-to-start (SS) The predecessor activity must start for the successor activity to start.

statement of work (SOW) A document that gives a detailed description of the procurement item or service to be received from a contract. SOWs can be issued before or after a contract is in place.

status meeting An informative meeting meant to distribute project updates from team members and/or the project manager to stakeholders.

storming The team life-cycle phase in which the team starts making decisions about the project.

story mapping A technique used to discover requirements and generate a full map of the project. With this technique, the team maps out user stories to discover the features that the customer needs. As they write user stories, the team gathers requirements.

story point A measurement point within a user story that is used to estimate the difficulty of implementing a given user story and maintained in the product backlog. This is usually estimated prior to the sprint planning meeting.

stress testing Testing that determines the ability of a computer, network, application, or device to maintain a certain level of effectiveness under unfavorable conditions.

subject matter expert (SME) A stakeholder, team member, or outside consultant who can provide expert feedback on aspects of the project.

subscription A subscription incurs a monthly or annual flat fee regardless of how often the service or product is used in the subscription period (unless it is a usage-tiered subscription).

successor The activity that comes after the activity on which it is dependent.

successor planning Creating a formal plan to capture an outgoing team member's knowledge base and skills and transfer them to other personnel before the team member leaves the organization.

SV See *schedule variance.*

synchronous communication A communication method in which all participants receive and exchange information in the same communication medium in real time.

T&M contract See *time and materials (T&M) contract.*

tangible outcomes Physical assets that can be measured, such as land, vehicles, equipment, machinery, furniture, inventory, and cash.

task Any work item that needs to be completed in a given timeframe. Also referred to as *activity*.

task board A tool that shows active, completed, and pending tasks in a virtual or physical display, like a Kanban board.

task-setting meeting A decisive meeting that chooses which tasks or activities the team will focus on in the next timebox and then assigns the tasks to the appropriate team member.

TCPI See *to-complete performance index.*

team retrospective A retrospective that has a team focus on celebrating, learning, and improving their relationship on a regular basis.

team touch points The points during the project where the project manager has full team meetings and one-on-one meetings with each team member.

technical approach An evaluation that can be performed after a vendor responds to an RFP with a proposed solution. This approach uses predetermined criteria to assess the vendor's ability to meet project requirements, and it assigns a numeric score to the result.

technological factors Barriers to communication caused by the technology used to transmit or receive communication, such as faulty video cameras, erratic Internet connections, or too-small screen sizes.

terms of reference (TOR) A document that often accompanies a complex request for quote (RFQ) and that lays out contract-specific definitions for the objectives, scope of work, activities and tasks, and the expected results/deliverables to be quoted, as well as the responsibilities of the buyer and the bidder if the contract were to be finalized.

test cycles Defined start and end dates for particular tests.

test plan A subsidiary management plan for IT projects that describes how and when the team will test deliverables to verify that they meet requirements, how to log and measure successful outcomes, and how to log and address defects.

testers The project role that conducts both manual and automated tests of software-based project deliverables.

theme An area of focus in Agile projects that helps an Agile team keep track of organizational goals.

three-point estimating An estimation method that uses the most likely (tM), optimistic (tO), and pessimistic (tP) estimates in a formula to calculate the activity duration.

ticketing/case management system IT project management software that separates incoming tickets into clear, customizable categories or buckets that can be organized by priority, team, source, or user.

tiered architecture A software model that usually includes development, testing, staging, and production tiers. Software changes are deployed to each tier prior to reaching the production tier, with the goal of discovering and fixing issues prior to the change being deployed in the production tier.

time and materials (T&M) contract A contract used when a statement of work is not possible. The full value of the contract and quantity of items needed may not be defined, so the contract is considered open-ended. Payment is given based on billable time and all allowed costs. These contracts often include not-to-exceed values, time limits, and unit labor or material rates.

timebox In Agile, setting a fixed period of time (a timebox) in which to complete a task or deliverable. In meetings, a timebox is a maximum time span allotted to an agenda item, a speaker, a presentation, or a meeting.

to-complete performance index (TCPI) A value derived from a formula that gives the required cost performance for the remaining budget.

total estimated costs (TEC) All the estimated costs in the initial project budget.

total project cost All costs specific to a project incurred from project initiation through project closure.

trade secret Sensitive, proprietary data that is unique to an organization, has substantial commercial value, is disclosed only to authorized personnel, and is protected by NDAs and internal security controls.

transference See *risk transference*.

transition/release plan A subsidiary management plan that describes how and when the team will transfer ownership and operation of the released product or project to the client or internal end users, or from development to maintenance. Predictive projects may also call this a release plan.

trend line In a scatter chart, the line along which most of the points lie.

triple constraint The three primary limits on any project: scope, time, and cost. Changes to any one of the three typically affect the other two.

unit testing When each module of code is tested separately.

unit-price contract A contract where the buyer pays a flat fee for a single unit of a procurement, regardless of the number of units completed or purchased.

unknown risk An unforeseen event that has the power to affect the project's constraints or results should it occur, was not uncovered during planning, and does not have a planned response in the risk register (for example, a previously unidentified risk).

user acceptance testing Testing that ensures the end user is satisfied with the functionality of the software.

user story The smallest unit of work in an Agile framework, stated as an end goal expressed from the software user's perspective. User stories are used to determine the sprint requirements.

validation A process that measures how well the end result of the project (or sprint) performs for the customer or the intended audience.

velocity The amount of work an Agile team can handle in a set period of time (typically one sprint).

velocity chart A tool that uses the average effort achieved in prior sprints to estimate when an Agile team will be able to complete a project as well as to assess an Agile team's performance over time.

vendor A third party contracted to provide goods, services, labor, and/or materials for project work. Also referred to as a contractor, supplier, or seller.

vendor knowledge base A database that contains authorized information about a particular vendor's products.

vendor qualification The process of verifying that a vendor meets client-defined standards and/or possesses specific characteristics that prove their fitness to be awarded a contract. Prequalified vendors are maintained on a shortlist and given first consideration for procurements.

vendor rules of engagement See *rules of engagement*.

verification A process that measures the quality of the project's deliverables against the requirements baseline and the quality benchmarks established during initiation and planning.

version control A system for uniquely labeling project assets across different stages of creation, distribution, revision, and archiving, with changes noted by author and date. Both project documents and code require version control, which is typically implemented with software.

warranty A legally binding agreement that the vendor must repair or replace a procurement, or refund the price of a procurement, if it malfunctions within the covered period of service.

warranty period A period of time that a product or resource is guaranteed and supported by a vendor after purchase. Warranties can be extended by paying a fee.

Waterfall A model that breaks the development process into distinct phases. This model is predictive, with the basic process being a sequential series of steps that are followed without going back to earlier steps.

WBS See *work breakdown structure (WBS)*.

WBS dictionary A companion document to the work breakdown structure (WBS). The WBS dictionary provides detailed information about each WBS component, including the identifier, deliverable, description, and scheduling information.

whiteboard A shared blank digital space where multiple people can write, share images or files, and interact with each other in real time.

wiki A type of website that is used to manage collaborative content. The wiki users determine the structure of the site and are able to edit the content.

win-win solution When the chosen solution is the one that best satisfies the concerns of both parties.

withdrawing See *avoiding*.

work breakdown structure (WBS) A hierarchical listing of the activities or work packages that must be completed during the project. This project document subdivides the project's work into manageable components.

work package The smallest unit of work in the WBS.

workarounds Temporary solutions intended to keep some aspect of project work moving forward until the issue affecting it is resolved and the normal or official process can be restored.

workshop A collaborative, facilitated meeting centered around a scheduled activity performed interactively by all attendees, such as a tabletop exercise or strategic planning session.

Index

B

C

D

F

G

H

I

J

K

L

M

P

Q

R

S

U

V

W

X

Y-Z

To receive your 10% off Exam Voucher, register your product at:

www.pearsonitcertification.com/register

and follow the instructions.